AMERICAN
HISTORY
REVISED

200 STARTLING FACTS

That Never Made It into the Textbooks

Seymour Morris Jr.

AMERICAN HISTORY

HISTORY

REVISED

BROADWAY BOOKS

NEW YORK

Copyright © 2010 by Seymour Morris Jr.

All rights reserved.
Published in the United States by Broadway Books, an imprint of the Crown Publishing Group,
a division of Random House, Inc., New York.
www.crownpublishing.com

BROADWAY BOOKS and the Broadway Books colophon are trademarks of Random House, Inc.

Library of Congress Cataloging-in-Publication Data
Morris, Seymour.
   American history revised: 200 startling facts that never made it into the textbooks /
Seymour Morris.—1st ed.
       p. cm.
   Includes bibliographical references.
   1. United States—History—Miscellanea. I. Title.
   E179.M85 2009
   973—dc22

2009023317

ISBN 978-0-307-58760-2

Printed in the United States of America

DESIGN BY ELINA D. NUDELMAN

10 9 8 7 6 5 4 3 2 1

First Edition

CONTENTS

History Through the Skylight

The best illumination comes from above, through the skylight.

—Oliver Wendell Holmes

For most of the past sixteen years I have lived abroad. Living in Romania and Cyprus made me confront the wonderful question posed in 1782 by the Frenchman Hector St. John de Crevecoeur, "What, then, is the American?"

As a foreigner, I encountered considerable skepticism about American foreign policy from European and Middle Eastern businessmen and diplomats. "Oh would some power the gift give us," said the eighteenth-century Scottish poet Robert Burns, "to see ourselves as others see us!" So in my spare time I plunged into hundreds of history books about America's past to help me in political debate and keep the conversation going.

I found that the best way to defuse hostility and single-mindedness was to entertain my audience with little-known stories of history that suggested greater knowledge than theirs, but with humility and a broad perspective. When asked about American militarism, I countered with the many opportunities America had to take over places like Canada and Cuba—and didn't. When people accused America of not being a democracy, I countered that the Founding Fathers never intended it to be (really?). When told that Guantánamo was a violation of the Bill of Rights, I explained that the Bill of Rights was an evolving process. The idea of universal rights was not a legacy of our slaveholding Founding Fathers, but of Afro-Americans and civil rights workers who had battled to correct the injustices of our past, plus the feminists who had paved the way for equal rights for women (an opportunity only late in coming to many of their own countries, by the way).

More often than not, my audience would be flummoxed and not know what to say. They complained America had too much global power; I told them to relax, America has not won a long-lasting military victory since 1945 other than Korea—a stalemate—and possibly Iraq. And look at what happened to a far more powerful empire, England in the early 1900s. We all know what happened to Great Britain . . .

Understanding history, they would tell me, requires seeing many points of view. Excellent idea! When one foreign diplomat argued that the Indians got the raw end of the deal in the sale of Manhattan for twenty-four dollars, I offered the Native American advice to "walk a mile in the other person's shoes." Turn the question around and ask yourself from the buyer's perspective, "How did the Dutch make out on the sale?" Of course nobody knew the answer. When informed that the Dutch invested huge amounts of money in an overseas base and lost it all—raising the obvious parallel of modern-day Iraq where the U.S. is facing insurmountable bills, how my European skeptics immediately agreed with that!

Then there were the hundreds of Romanian young people I met in my part-time capacity as alumni interviewer for high-school students applying to Harvard. I was intrigued at how open and receptive they were to America—in sharp contrast to their American fellow applicants who took so much for granted. It reminded me that my country, which gave me my passport, my education, and my values, is for millions of people . . . a dream. If America is a dream, I must learn more about it. After all, who doesn't want to know more about something so enticing as a dream?

By knowing my history and viewing America with a sense of wonder, I engaged in many delightful debates and dinner-party conversations. Nobody could get angry when I teased them, "Did you know that . . . ?" Touché! It was a clever way to broaden people's perceptions and make them less emotional and judgmental. Whenever I suggested that what's happening in the world today is "not as simple as you think," I would point to "history, supposedly fixed in stone, right?" and then provide examples that proved the opposite, that even history has its massive share of inconsistencies, twists, and turns. I would even go so far as to tease people, "Suppose it never would have happened?" "Impossible!" they would say with utter and complete conviction.

Really? Two weeks before taking office in 1933, Franklin D. Roosevelt was attacked by a madman who sprayed the scene with bullets. Had FDR been assassinated, the next president would have been the mediocre vice president–elect, John Nance Garner. In 1930 Adolf Hitler was sitting in the front passenger seat of a car that collided with a heavy trailer truck. Had the truck braked just one second earlier, Hitler would have been dead. In 1931, while crossing Fifth Avenue in New York, an Englishman used to looking to the right looked the wrong way and was hit by a taxicab—but survived. Had Winston Churchill walked a second faster, he could have been run over. In 1963 the Secret Service in Dallas installed a protective plastic bubble over the president's black Lincoln convertible, but it was such a beautiful day that JFK asked that it be removed so people could see him better.

❧

Much of what history books in school tell us is dry and narrow. Take a look at your child's high-school textbook, and groan! No wonder many kids don't want to study. Dates, battles, presidents, and social trends are all essential building blocks, but not the stuff of day-to-day reality that one can readily relate to. "American history," says the historian and novelist Gore Vidal, "has fallen more and more into the hands of academics" (not to mention textbook publishers and state school boards who insist on including every viewpoint to the point of blandness). One longs for an anecdote, a human-interest story, a startling revelation, an epistle of courage, a killing of the bad guys—a moral lesson (kids know the difference between good guys and bullies). To the ancient Greeks, *istoria* meant a story or a tale as much as history. For centuries before the printed word, the great epics like the *Iliad* or *Beowulf*— even the Bible—were told through stories over the campfire. Said Samuel Johnson (of Johnson and Boswell fame in eighteenth-century England), "Anecdotes are the gleaming toys of history." Asked how to make history interesting to today's schoolchildren, the historian Barbara Tuchman said simply, "Tell stories."

A simple story can speak a thousand words. Years ago, American history came alive to me in twenty seconds. The college professor was giving a lecture about John Adams. Apparently, Adams had a roll-top desk at his Massachusetts farm where he spent much of his time during his term in office. The desk had several cubbyholes, one for each department of government. One was marked WAR, another INDIAN AFFAIRS, another CUSTOMS REVENUE, etc. That, ladies and gentlemen, was how the President of the United States ran the country in those days.

From that moment on, I marveled at our nation's history—not at what it said, but at what it didn't say. Several years later at Harvard Business School—certainly the last place I expected to run into American history—we were told about the early days of IBM. In 1945, founder and chairman Thomas J. Watson was asked the size of the potential world computer market. His prediction?

Just five computers . . .

Even though the story may be apocryphal (it originated from an enemy of Watson), it was not far off the mark. In those days the early computer—the size of a room, with its ungainly wires and bulbs always breaking down—was viewed as an impractical contraption that would be useful only for academia and the military. If you consider that hard to believe, put yourself in the past and ask yourself what you would do with a room-sized box that just clanked and whirred, a machine lacking the "brains" of an operating system like Microsoft's (far off in the future). This exercise—imagining something before it actually exists—is a very difficult effort. Consider the comment of William Lear, inventor of the Lear jet and one of America's great entrepreneurs. In the early 1960s, when he predicted three thousand business jets would be sold by 1970 and the major aircraft companies were predicting only three hundred, Lear said:

> *They don't ask the right questions. The trick is to discern the market—before there is any proof that one exists. If you had said in 1925 that we would build 9 million automobiles by 1965, some statistician would have pointed out that they would fill up every road in the United States and, lined end-to-end, would go across the country eleven times. Surveys are no good. I make surveys in my mind.*

Understanding our past requires imagination, using the talent of a William Lear. In business we try to use this same skill whenever we evaluate a new business deal or try to outsmart the stock market. If predicting the future requires imagination, does not "predicting" the past?

Narrow-mindedness, said William Lear, is the bane of critical thinking. Virtually every history book describing the United States in the 1890s emphasizes "the rise of American power" and the annexation of overseas territories. Viewed in the larger global perspective, however, such a view looks absolutely provincial. Not mentioned and therefore unknown to most Americans today—especially those who swallow the line about America being the only world superpower—America at the turn of the nineteenth century was a minnow compared with Great Britain, an empire that dwarfed anything America has ever achieved (or ever will). The statistics are awesome: England owned an empire covering more than a quarter of the earth's land surface, and ruled the seas with its Royal Navy. Its navy and trading companies (Hudson's Bay, East India, etc.) controlled a third of all world trade. Half the world's ships flew the Union Jack. London was the world's financial hub. The British land possessions encompassed more than 400 million people— 20 percent of the world's population—interlocked by a common language and an undersea cable network of 83,000 miles utilizing the Internet of the day, the telegraph (a British invention). So awesome was Great Britain in 1900 that the South African business magnate Sir Cecil Rhodes (of Rhodes Scholars fame) predicted the day would come when England would recolonize the United States.

When we look at the past, we look at it from the lens of the present—a straight line, if you will. In actual fact, the past was another generation or two far removed, totally different. Take, for example, the hundred-year struggle for women's rights. Look again, carefully. When Alice Paul of the newly formed National Women's Party proposed the Equal Rights Amendment of 1920, prohibiting discrimination in the workplace, she elicited a storm of opposition from, of all people, the League of Women Voters. Women's groups saw the ERA as a threat to their cherished "protective labor laws" that limited excessive hours, required special facilities for women workers, and forbade the employment of women in certain physically demanding occupations. Those in support of the ERA were thousands of men, employers, and members of the political right who actually welcomed the competition of smart women in the marketplace.

❧

We all know Santayana's dictum that those who cannot remember the past are condemned to repeat it, but what is it we are trying to remember? We need to dig beneath the surface to understand what actually happened, and why people did what they did. What happened in "the past" is fixed in stone; what we say about it later is "history." The two are not always the same. What makes history intriguing is discovering these discrepancies—to learn that what we know is not necessarily so, to discover "secrets" we didn't know, and to recognize that what happened almost didn't happen. This is the delightful stuff of cocktail party conversation: Did you know . . . ?

Every day we open the newspaper and read stories about the inability of Congress to reach a decision and pass a bill. So what else is new? During the days of Valley Forge, when Washington's troops were freezing and starving, Congress's reaction to the problem was to give it to a committee. There were only twenty-five active members of Congress, but they managed to create 114 committees in 1777, then another 258 in 1778. General Washington got so fed up handling all the inquiries, he wondered how he would find time to fight the war. Several years later, after the war was over, the Confederation of American States sent the thirteen states a $3-million bill to pay the war debts incurred in fighting the British. A legitimate bill, you say? Well, by 1787 it had collected less than $120,000—4 percent. Congress could no better manage the country's affairs then than it can now.

"The past is a foreign country," a historian once wrote. Perhaps. But the closer one looks, the less foreign it becomes. Even the "godlike" Washington, the founder of our country, the only man to be elected by unanimous vote, had his problems. Was his presidential holiness really the case (the way we view it through "history")? Halfway through his presidential term he made a treaty with the British that made many congressmen so angry they sought to have him impeached. Hard to believe? Well, the leader of this movement was a man who later became president himself, one of our great ones: Andrew Jackson.

A popular buzzword nowadays is "bipartisanship," with many people pleading for better relations and cooperation between the two major parties and between the White House and Congress. Back in the 1830s President Andrew Jackson had such acrimonious relations with Congress, especially with Henry Clay, the Speaker of the House, that when the new Treasury Building was being built, he had it situated right next to the White House so as to block his view of the Capitol. "Now I can't see the Capitol anymore!" he bragged. For this great president, "bipartisanship" meant drawing a line in the sand.

History teaches us facts, but understanding history requires going beyond the facts and learning the full story, especially the human element. Go to the Lincoln Memorial in Washington DC and gaze upward at the solemn face of

Abraham Lincoln. Our greatest president, yes—but also a virtual manic-depressive who hired a gravedigger on two separate occasions to dig up his dead son Willy so he could see him again (a privilege exercised, so far as we know, by no other president). And to have a wife like he did! In 1864 she was telling friends that Mr. Lincoln must win reelection so she could use his $25,000 salary to pay off her $27,000 in clothing bills. When he won, she still went out and splurged on three hundred pairs of gloves and a $2,000 dress for the inauguration. Trivia? Hardly: maybe having such a wife was what brought out Lincoln's innate qualities of sagacity and patience. Said Lincoln to a merchant annoyed at the First Lady: "You ought to stand, for fifteen minutes, what I have stood for fifteen years."

Go down the road to the Jefferson Memorial, and stand in awe of the powerful phrase "Life, Liberty and the Pursuit of Happiness." Except for one thing: Jefferson never wrote it. A major landowner, he wrote "Life, Liberty and Property," and when his fellow members of the Constitutional Convention objected and changed "Property" to "Pursuit of Happiness," Jefferson got so upset he went to all his friends and tried to mount a lobby to get "Property" restored. He failed, and so we glorify him—for sentiments he did not feel. Even today, historians teach children misunderstandings: by "liberty," Jefferson meant not liberty from tyranny, but liberty for property (later immortalized in the Fourteenth Amendment to the Constitution protecting Americans from being deprived of "life, liberty or property without due process of law").

It is fine to read about great people and great deeds, but how can we relate to people at such a high level? They seem to live on another planet. In the late 1940s, Eleanor Roosevelt was the closing speaker at an international conference, and she was asked, "Mrs. Roosevelt, how did you come to be such a great woman?" She responded in a very interesting way:

Because I was married to a great man, and he taught me many things. He was the governor of the State of New York, and he could not travel, but he sent me. I came to see people, to understand people, and I would come back to him and report and say, "Oh, yes, I went to that orphanage and they were beautiful, and they have good meals and all." And he would say, "Eleanor, don't you think that when the wife of the governor appears, the meals are going to be better than usual? The next time you go, don't go to do just what they have planned for you beforehand, find out the poorest neighborhoods, and then ask to go to those neighborhoods. And when you do, look at the clothes hanging on the line and they will tell you something about the people. And look out to see how many people are just sitting around the streets. And what are the men doing? Are they all off at work or are they sitting around wishing for work?"

Concluded Eleanor Roosevelt, "That made a difference." A small difference, but by paying attention to detail and constantly asking questions, are great people made.

We all know about the radiation unleashed by the atomic bombs dropped on Japan. Recently, I was on a business flight from Athens to Cyprus, reading the Olympic Airways in-flight magazine, when I came across this astounding statistic: "The radiation released at Chernobyl . . . is estimated to have been at least 200 times greater than that of Hiroshima and Nagasaki combined."

But don't stop there; keep asking questions like Eleanor Roosevelt did. The country that suffered the greatest radiation, it turned out, was the United States. In top-secret tests hidden from the public, the U.S. Atomic Energy Commission conducted 126 atmospheric tests in Nevada from 1951 to 1962. Those tests released 148 times the radiation of Chernobyl. How much compared with Hiroshima and Nagasaki? Multiply 148 by 200, and the answer is almost 30,000!

Our most creative insights come from questioning what we hear, and exerting the effort to dig deeper and use our imagination to make connections. Said Oliver Wendell Holmes:

> *There are one-story intellects, two-story intellects, and three-story intellects with skylights. All fact collectors, who have no aim beyond their facts, are one-story men. Two-story men compare, reason, generalize, using the labors of fact collectors as well as their own. Three-story men idealize, imagine, predict; their best illumination comes from above, through the skylight.*

What follows is history through the skylight. We let it fall where it may—like it or not, liberal or conservative, friendly or unfriendly, achievement or pure chance. By showing events that are surprising or not widely known, we enlarge our understanding and appreciation of the richness of America's past. Unlike most "revisionist" or "multicultural" histories being written nowadays that focus on injustices, we have no particular preconception other than a fascination and curiosity about what really happened.

❧

Truth and insights rarely come in a neat package wrapped with a ribbon. "It is better to be vaguely right," said John Maynard Keynes, "than precisely wrong." It is better to have judgment and common sense and be able to see the big picture, than to possess detailed minutiae that really are not important (like a lawyer trying to trip up the other side on a technicality). In all of American history, there is probably no better example of this than the ongoing dispute about Pearl Harbor, a controversy that refuses to die. Rather than stirring up the controversy further, let us take a different approach and look at how the world was back then. Everyone knew full well Japan was pounding the war drums; the only question was where and when. When war finally came on an early Sunday morning, it came as a jolt, but it was, in historian John Lukacs's memorable words, "a surprise that was expected." Yet for decades now, academicians bent on proving conspiracy have been poring over every document coming in and out of the White House, trying to find incriminating memos proving FDR secretly knew about the coming attack. They could have saved themselves a whole lot of trouble by asking one fundamental question that cuts through all the fog: Assuming FDR wanted war, why not warn the fleet and make the first battle a victory? Wouldn't that be the logical thing to do? End of discussion.

Or take the other great twentieth-century event that has every conspiracy buff looking under unturned stones: the JFK assassination. Maybe there was a "second shot" from the grassy knoll, maybe there wasn't. Because of the configuration of the surrounding buildings, which created an echo, it was scientifically impossible to say exactly where the gunshot sounds were coming from. But no matter, the more important fact was that "the area was teeming with people." Assassins do not use rifles when there are a lot of people around; they use handguns. Observes one historian, "It is conceivable that a man with a rifle might have escaped notice. However, not only is this most unlikely, but attempting to assassinate from the knoll would be so dangerous that it is hard to believe any assassin with even minimum rationality would have chosen such a spot." Again, end of discussion.

Re-creating history does not require genius; sometimes it takes common sense and an ability to recognize the obvious. Beware of too much history, for often the causes are quite superficial. Ever wonder why so many Irish immigrants to America settled in Boston rather than New York? Very simple:

The boat fare was $6.50 cheaper.

Ever ask yourself why the British drive on the "wrong" side of the road? Back in the early days of the automobile, all cars had the steering wheel on the right. This was because most roads were unpaved, and the driver wanted to make sure he didn't drive off the path into the ditch. Then came along Henry Ford, who moved the steering wheel to the left. He foresaw the day of paved roads and fast cars, when the driver's main concern would be the oncoming traffic. America is a forward-thinking nation.

It is also one with a limited appreciation of history. According to the American Bar Association, nearly half of all Americans cannot identify our three branches of government. Eighty-three percent of Americans never take a course in American history beyond high school (though that may not be such a bad thing, given what they seem to be taught nowadays). Many college students think that Martin Luther King Jr. was advocating an end to slavery in his "I Have a Dream" speech. The state of New Jersey recently issued new history standards that omitted any mention of George Washington, and students at one college in our celebrity-obsessed era rated Bill Clinton a better president than George Washington. Many American citizens don't know what war Ulysses Grant fought in, or why the League of Nations failed, or why espionage was such a critical factor in World War II. Do you think any of them are aware that there was once a book read by a greater number of people than the entire American voting population? (*Common Sense* by Thomas Paine.) Politics was a passionate subject in those pre-TV days: newfound freedoms and liberties were not taken lightly. In the 1854 debates over the Kansas-Nebraska Act expanding slavery into the territories, four years before he debated Lincoln, Stephen A. Douglas said he could have "travelled from Boston to Chicago by the light of the fires kindled to burn him in effigy."

None of us can ever be like the hyperkinetic Theodore Roosevelt—he read a book a day—but we can certainly do better in our understanding of how America came to be. Consider the story of Benjamin Franklin. When the Second Continental Congress declared rebellion against King George III, Benjamin Franklin was sent to Paris to enlist the support of King Louis XVI. It was a difficult assignment, trying to get a king to help a group of anti-royal reactionaries overthrow another king. The French monarch invited Franklin to play a game of chess. Franklin surveyed the various pieces—king, queen, knights—and made his move. It was a move that had never been done before, and has never been done since. But was it effective? Yes, absolutely.

His move? He took the two king pieces off the board. "In America we have no kings," he told his startled host. The two men then played the only kingless game of chess ever played. Months later, the king agreed to support the man whose candor had so impressed him.

The people and events chosen for this book meet two criteria: they are largely unknown, and they make a point worth remembering. By relating them to the present, we experience "the thrill of learning singular things."

Seymour Morris Jr.

History is lived in the main by the unknown and forgotten.
But historians perforce concentrate on the happy few
who leave records, give speeches, make fortunes, hold offices,
win or lose battles and thrones. . . . Then occasionally
voices ring out of the darkness.

—Arthur M. Schlesinger Jr.

Over the past twenty to thirty years, textbook publishers have
become averse to bold historical narratives for fear of
being labeled too liberal, too conservative, too patriotic,
or too sexist and rendering themselves unattractive to buyers
on the textbook market. Instead, they have become
encyclopedias of historical names, places, and timelines. . . .
They are doing away with what is most interesting about history:
perspective, interpretation, historiography, bias,
debate, and controversy.

—Dana Lindaman and Kyle Ward

Americans' lack of passion for history is well known.
History may not quite be bunk, as Henry Ford suggested,
but there's no denying that, as a people, we sustain a passionate
concentration on the present and the future. . . .
Backward is just not a natural direction for Americans
to take—historical ignorance remains a national characteristic.

—Larry McMurtry

ONE

A Razor's Edge: It Almost Never Happened

An interviewer once asked that notable man of letters Gore Vidal, "What would have happened in 1963 had Khrushchev and not Kennedy been assassinated?" Vidal answered, "With history one can never be certain, but I think I can safely say that Aristotle Onassis would not have married Mrs. Khrushchev."

Humor aside, the real point of the story is, don't take history too seriously. There's a lot of history that barely managed to happen. History, said Hugh Trevor-Roper, is what happened "in the context of what could have happened." Like baseball—"a game of inches"—famous people and events can be more circumstantial than historic. Many books will aver that history is made by great men and women performing prodigious feats. Sometimes this is so, but often not. As we all know from our own lives, the prize we won in school, the career we chose, the person we married, the big sale we made—these are frequently a function of our being at a particular place at a certain time and making the right choice at a pivotal fork in the road. "Every true story," says the novelist Siri Hustvedt, "has several possible endings." Ecclesiastes says, "I returned and saw under the sun that the race is not to the swift, nor the battle to the strong, neither bread to the wise nor riches to men of understanding, but time and chance happeneth to them all." (9:11) That's right: timing and chance.

One of the reasons history can be so distant and uninteresting to schoolchildren is that it is fixed in stone. What happened, happened—end of story. There are no possible alternative endings, unless we engage in counterfactual "what if?" exercises. Stimulating though they may be, they tend to be exercises in intellectual gamesmanship: "Interesting, but so what?" More useful is to focus on "the fork in the road": What really happened at that pivotal moment, seconds ticking away? However it turned out, call it luck, coincidence, perseverance, or whatever—much of history was a close call, a razor's edge.

Take our greatest foreign-aid program, the Marshall Plan. When President Harry Truman proposed it in 1948, he knew he had a problem: winning congressional support for a costly new program that would consume 16 percent of the federal budget. An additional problem was that the most powerful man in the Senate was also a strong isolationist: Senator Arthur Vandenberg of Michigan. When Truman's aides did their homework, however, they uncovered a fascinating nugget: for the previous seventeen years Senator Vandenberg had taken his annual vacations abroad, to a different country each time, and had stayed for as long as two months. Clearly this was not your typical provincial congressman. The president met with

the senator and they eventually reached a meeting of the minds, and history was made—all because of a senator's unusual vacations that enlightened him to the needs of other countries.

Consider a different subject etched in black-and-white finality: war. Even here the determining factors can be quite happenstance. The weather, for example. One does not read in history books how important the weather was. In 1776, General George Washington lost the Battle of Long Island and needed desperately to get his army out of the clutches of the superior British forces. The only path of retreat was to cross the East River and escape to Manhattan. But in the meantime the British fleet, parked off the southern end of Manhattan, was trying to sail upriver and block off any chance of escape. The weather intervened. For the better part of a week a fierce rainstorm prevented the British ships from moving. On the chosen day, Washington's rowboats made numerous sorties throughout the night. As dawn approached and the rebels were fearful of being seen by the advancing British army, a pea-soup fog—a "manifestly providential" fog, "an American fog"—descended upon the riverbank, obliterating all vision and enabling the American rebels to conduct their escape. Alas, a woman living near the ferry woke up and sent her servant off to warn the British. The man made his way through the lines to a German officer heading the British patrol, but the German spoke no English and arrested the servant! Had it not been for the incredible triple luck of first a storm and then a fog and finally a non-English-speaking German officer, Washington and half of the American army would have been captured and the American Revolution all but over.

One of Jefferson's crowning achievements as president was the Louisiana Purchase. What is not widely known, however, is that the French territory was offered first to England, who refused it. A further irony: the funding that enabled Jefferson to pull off his coup came from bonds provided by Hamilton's U.S. Bank, which Jefferson had once viewed as unconstitutional. Finally, the money to buy the bonds came mostly from French and Dutch investors, not American, meaning that the U.S. got the land for practically nothing by using other people's money. Jefferson, no financier himself, had pulled off one of the greatest financial deals of all time.

The United States was even luckier in its other mammoth land acquisition, the Treaty of Guadalupe Hidalgo, which ended the Mexican-American War. On January 25, 1848, after nine months of intense negotiations with the defeated Mexicans, Nicholas P. Trist, special envoy for President Polk, got the Mexicans to accept $15 million for California, Nevada, Arizona, New Mexico, Utah, and parts of Colorado and Wyoming. Trist consummated the deal just in time.

The day before—January 24, 1848—gold was discovered in California.

"Hindsight," says the British broadcaster Melvyn Bragg, "is the bane of history."

It is corrupting and distorting and pays no respect to the way life is really lived—forwards, generally blindly, full of accidents, fortunes and misfortunes, patternless and often adrift. Easy with hindsight to say we would beat Napoleon at Waterloo; only by a whisker, according to the honest general who did it. Easy to say we would win the Second World War: ask those who watched the dogfights of the Battle of Britain in Kent in 1940. Easy to say the Berlin Wall was bound to fall. Which influential commentator or body of opinion said so in the 1980s? Hindsight is the easy way to mop up the mess which we call history; it is too often the refuge of the tidy-minded, making neat patterns when the dust has settled. As often as not, when the dust was flying, no one at the time knew what the outcome might be.

"Very nearly everything that happened in history very nearly did not happen," said the renowned mathematician and philosopher Alfred North Whitehead. Here are some other histories that almost never made the history books.

A Statement of Allegiance, Not of Rebellion

➤ **1776** Might war have been avoided? Most likely not, but the way it started was the result of boneheaded miscalculations.

In an effort to appease the American colonists who were smuggling in Dutch tea rather than pay the stiff duty on British tea, the British came up with what they thought was a noble plan. Under the new Tea Act of 1773, they would cut the twenty-shillings-per-pound duty in half.

The plan backfired: instead of appreciating the ten-shilling savings, the colonists reacted to the ten-shilling duty and instigated the Boston Tea Party. It was a classic case of glass half full or half empty: one side seeing it one way, one side seeing it the other way.

How could the British get it so wrong? By being out of touch with their subjects. Ever since 1760 the British Parliament had been conducting much debate about how to handle the colonies, with arguments and ideas being tossed to and fro. But never once during this period did a British minister or member of Parliament bother to go to America and investigate what was going on. Had the British exercised some basic hands-on management, this breakdown in diplomacy might not have occurred.

As late as 1776, England was still "the mother country." On January 1, during the siege of Boston, George Washington raised a new flag visible to many of the British soldiers on the other side. It was the first flag in America. It had thirteen red and white stripes, signifying the union of the thirteen colonies, and in the upper left corner was the Union Jack, representing the British Empire. "The flag," says the historian Thomas Fleming, "affirmed America's determination to resist Britain's authoritarian pretenses—and at the same time somehow to maintain an allegiance to the ideal of a united British empire." Called the Grand Union flag, it was more a statement of allegiance than of rebellion. A British intelligence agent in Philadelphia described the flag as "English colors but more striped." The commanding general of the British army, William Howe, agreed: the flag was a signal of the colonies' respect for British authority.

America's first flag, January 1, 1776: English colors, but more striped

Unfortunately, the king didn't see it that way. Proving the axiom that people invariably see only what they want to see, King

George III saw the flag as exactly the opposite: an act of rebellion. How dare the colonies put the Union Jack in a small corner! When the Continental Congress sent an emissary with an "Olive Branch Petition" expressing loyalty to the Crown and requesting a possible reconciliation, the king refused to consider it.

Had he interpreted Washington's gesture correctly, he might have had a New World partner for decades longer. Washington continued to be conciliatory: when he crossed the Delaware in his famous Christmas victory a year later, the flag he took was the Grand Union flag (not the Stars and Stripes we see in every painting). Rebels though they were, the colonists still thought of themselves as subjects of the king.

Six months later, in mid-1777, the colonists finally changed their flag to the Stars and Stripes. After further fighting and neither side getting anywhere, the British in early 1778 changed tack and offered the colonists a sweeping program of concessions so radical that it left Parliament "stunned and unbelieving." Under the Conciliatory Propositions, the tea duty and other punitive acts would be repealed entirely, all taxation by Parliament would cease, Congress would be granted full recognition as a constitutional body, and membership in the House of Commons would be offered.

No question, this was quite an offer. Problem was, it was too little, too late. The colonists had upped their demands, and now wanted complete independence and removal of all troops and warships. Continued

negotiations might have been fruitful except for one basic fact: having taken on France as an ally, America could not have cut a deal with Britain even if it had wanted to.

But old sentiments don't die easily. In the American Centennial celebration of 1876, the flag flying above Independence Hall in Philadelphia was not the flag showing the thirteen colonies, but the Grand Union Flag showing the Union Jack.

Crucial Messages That Never Reached Their Destinations

➤**1776** On three occasions, the simple failure to deliver a message shaped the destiny of America. No great immutable forces of history here, just plain blind luck.

When George Washington decided to launch his daring crossing of the Delaware on Christmas Day 1776, he was down to his final out—and he knew it. "I fear the game will be pretty well up," he confessed to his brother in despair. After eight months of fighting, he had lost almost all his battles, and the enlistment period of more than half his army was due to expire at the end of the year, leaving him with no resources to carry on the struggle. His crossing of the Delaware, as we all know, was a stroke of genius that breathed new hope into the revolutionary cause.

On the night of the Delaware crossing, however, things did not get off to a good start. A contingent of nervous American troops shot five Hessians, waking up the

Hessian guard. When the contingent caught up with Washington, Washington did not mince his words: "You, sir, may have ruined all my plans by putting them on their guard." Fortunately, when the Hessians found the bodies of their dead comrades, Johann Rall, the Hessian colonel in charge of the British forces, dismissed it as the work of some local farmers. Then when he returned to his Trenton tavern, he neglected to leave an outpost to guard the river; advised to mount patrols all along the river, he said no, it could wait until the morning. For the rest of the night, he and his officers played cards and got drunk. Around midnight he received a visit from a loyalist farmer. Refused access because the colonel was busy playing cards, the farmer scribbled an urgent note to Rall alerting him that the Americans were about to cross the Delaware. Rall got the note, but never bothered to read it. He put it in his pocket and continued with his card game. Three hours later, drunk and asleep, he got a rude surprise. George Washington's army had crossed the Delaware and was about to attack.

❧

The year: 1862 The Civil War was beginning to look very bleak for the North. General Grant had just barely escaped defeat at the bloody Battle of Shiloh, where both armies lost more men than the total casualties in the American Revolution, the War of 1812, and the Mexican War put

together. Robert E. Lee had taken command of the Confederate Armies of Northern Virginia and shown everyone why he was the most esteemed general in the nation, the man Lincoln had once tried to hire. In less than thirty days, Lee had beaten two Union armies, one under George McClellan and the other under John Pope, and proceeded all the way up to the outskirts of Washington, D.C. Lee was on a roll. On the offensive for the first time in the war, he prepared to take on the North at Antietam and then march into Washington. Panic set in at the Northern capital, and citizens began to pack their bags. Who was going to stop the invincible Lee now?

Fate intervened. Two Union soldiers, resting at a site where the Confederates had camped several days earlier, discovered a copy of Lee's Special Orders #191 wrapped around three cigars, obviously lost by a careless Southern courier. In full detail, these orders presented a picture of Lee's attack plan, allowing General McClellan to anticipate Lee's moves. The advantage of the attacker—surprise—shifted from Lee to McClellan.

The odds against this incredible piece of luck? At least a million to one.

Several days later there occurred the three-day Battle of Antietam, the bloodiest of the war. McClellan, knowing what Lee was going to do, reorganized his forces and slugged it out with Lee, neither side able to win. His momentum blunted, Lee was forced to withdraw. Never again would he mount a sustained offensive or come close to Washington, D.C.

What if the cigars had not been lost? The historian James McPherson outlines what might have happened if the cautious McClellan had had to cope with a massive Confederate army, whereabouts unknown. The Battle of Antietam would not have occurred. Instead, Lee, undetected by the Union, would have moved north into Pennsylvania to reprovision his army and settle in at Gettysburg. This time the result would not have been a draw, but a rout of the Army of the Potomac.

The hypothetical repercussions would have been swift. In the Northern congressional elections, the Democrats were in control of the House of Representatives and voters expressed their desire for immediate peace, even if it meant giving the Confederates their independence. Britain and France, lurking in the wings for a sign of Confederate victory, immediately came forth and offered to mediate an end to the war. The British, eager to avenge their humiliation in the American Revolution, rejoiced at the prospect of a large land grab. Recognizing the sorry state of the Union Army, the will of the voters, and the prospect of European meddling, the North gave in and the United States ceased to exist as "one nation, indivisible." The peace candidate, George McClellan, went on to win the 1864 presidential election. It didn't happen, of course, only because the cigars fell into the wrong hands.

⁂

Finally, there is World War II. Overconfidence breeds in people an inability to act on what they hear. In 1940 hardly anyone in America was concerned about a Japanese attack; most eyes were fixed on Europe. Said *Fortune* magazine in its August issue that year, "War with Japan is the only war for which the U.S. is prepared." What *Fortune* really meant was that America was protected on the west side by a very large ocean.

Sitting in front of the radar screen on a Sunday morning in Pearl Harbor, Lieutenant Joseph McDonald had a job to do: make sure the "Japs" weren't coming. Up since 5:00 a.m. the previous day, McDonald stayed beyond his 6:00 a.m. departure so his colleagues (against regulations) could go get some breakfast. Exhausted and barely still awake at 7:20 a.m., waiting for his colleagues to come back from breakfast, he got a call from an outlying radar base at Opana reporting a large contingent of planes headed toward Pearl Harbor. He rushed into the next room and found Lt. Kermit Tyler, on his second day of training in his new post. It was nothing to worry about, Tyler told him.

Upon calling back the Opana radar station to verify the situation, McDonald now heard emergency warnings: "Hey, Mac, there is a heck of a big flight of planes coming in and the whole scope is covered!" McDonald ran back to the other room, only to find the inexperienced lieutenant cavalierly dismissing "the attacking planes" as a fleet of U.S. B-17 bombers expected to arrive that morning from the West Coast. Asked if he shouldn't relay the frantic message to the admirals in charge of the base, the lieutenant told him, "Don't worry about it."

Unsure what to do and hesitant to "pull rank," McDonald obeyed orders. Forty-five minutes later, the Japanese planes bombed Pearl Harbor.

It is remarkable how military analysts to this day gloss over the facts. Pontificates one historian for the U.S. government's website about Pearl Harbor, "The use of radar was not fully incorporated into an integrated air defense system. While the technology of radar functioned as intended and detected the incoming planes, there was no way to accurately assess this information and communicate this knowledge to those in command."

So, in other words, no one is to blame. This, of course, is complete nonsense. The Opana warning was crystal clear. For an equally clear assessment of what happened, we should listen not to government historians writing public-relations fluff, but to military officers risking their lives on the ground at the time. Testified one such officer, Corporal George Mooney: "I finally talked to him [Lieutenant Tyler] and told him to immediately call someone with authority and pass the word that we have picked up over 150 blips on our radar screen and get some action right away. He gave me a bunch of BS. As far as he was concerned, there was no action needed at this time. He had at least one and a half hours of time [to warn Pearl], but he chose to do nothing. The rest is history."

Actually, history wasn't finished yet. Within twenty-four hours another saga occurred thousands of miles away, this one a message that *was* delivered—only to be ignored. In the Philippines there was a large American base headed by General Douglas MacArthur. MacArthur had been told all about Pearl Harbor and ordered to go on full alert, yet he did nothing. He kept all his planes on the ground. The result was a total wipe-out, capture by the Japanese, and the infamous march to Bataan in which almost 30 percent of the American prisoners died.*

In all this there is a lesson to be learned: even with a vital message in their hands, people frequently do nothing. Says historian Ronald Spector about the twofold Pacific debacle of December 7–8, 1941: "The mere presence of accurate information among a mass of inaccurate or misleading information is no guarantee that the accurate information will be recognized or acted upon."

---

* The only reason MacArthur didn't get court-martialed like the Pearl Harbor navy commanders was that FDR was so desperate to tell the American public some good news that he twisted the story around and praised MacArthur for gallantry and awarded him the Medal of Honor in 1942. It remains, to this day, the greatest government cover-up of all.

Watching the Whales

➤**1781** Observing nature can be a good way to discover new knowledge and technology. In the colonial days, the country that knew how to sail across the Atlantic the fastest would have a significant commercial and military advantage.

The observers were the whalers of Nantucket. Following the migration of whales, they became curious about the course and speed of the currents of the Gulf Stream. By dropping thermometers at regular intervals and measuring the speed of surface bubbles and noting changes in the color of the water, they were able to map the Gulf Stream. This knowledge enabled American sea captains to save days against their British counterparts by crossing over the Gulf Stream instead of sailing against it. Benjamin Franklin heard about this discovery from his cousin, a Nantucket whaling captain, and utilized it for his mail ships when he was postmaster general. In 1776 he tested it himself by taking an ocean voyage and dropping his thermometer two to four times a day from early morning to late night. His report on the Gulf Stream, kept secret until after the Revolutionary War, was shared with American and French sea captains.

In early 1781, the Americans and the British were getting ready for the showdown and anticipated end of their long war. Washington pinned his hopes on the arrival of French reinforcements from the Caribbean. Waiting in the Caribbean, to knock out the arriving French fleet of Admiral Henri de Grasse, was commanding British admiral Sir George Rodney. Also waiting in the nearby Leeward Islands was Rodney's junior admiral, Alexander Hood. On March 21, British spies in France prepared an intelligence report to Rodney informing him of de Grasse's departure the following day: fleet size 173, headed by the world's biggest warship, destination Leeward Islands. Rodney should immediately get together with Hood and prepare to annihilate the oncoming Henri de Grasse.

The report was put on a fast mail cutter headed for the Caribbean. But by the time Rodney got the report, it was too late. Delivered by British sea captains who did not know the currents of the Gulf Stream, the report reached Rodney a week after de Grasse had arrived in the Leeward Islands and fought Admiral Hood into submission.

That a huge French armada could outrace a British mail cutter across the Atlantic was not only remarkable, it was pivotal. Had Rodney been able to get together with Hood to stop de Grasse, the battle at Yorktown would not have occurred and the British would have won the war. Yankee ingenuity and inventiveness—and whales—played a key role in saving America.

Still, all was not lost for the British. In fact, they still had the advantage. Come fall of 1781, after a year of marching through the south "like an English knife through colonial butter," the British army under General Cornwallis arrived at Yorktown for the pivotal showdown. It was a time, says British historian Robert Harvey, when "the Americans' own view was that they had probably lost the war." Even Washington was despondent: "We are at the end of our tether." Cornwallis had slightly more troops than the rebels, but he also had to contend with a huge contingent of 11,000 French troops that had just arrived, thanks to de Grasse and the Yankee observation of whales. Finding himself outnumbered 16,800 to 7,200, Cornwallis urgently awaited the return of the powerful British navy, due to arrive on October 5 after completing repairs in New York.

Inexplicably, the British shipyard took its merry time. Observed one English staff officer, "If the Navy are not a little more active they will not get a sight of the Capes of Virginia before the end of this month, and then it will be a little too late. They do not seem to be hearty in this business."

Pleas by Cornwallis went unanswered. Informed by the commanding British general that the British fleet would be ready in another two weeks, Cornwallis responded it would be too late.

On October 16 the ships finally were ready. They took another three days to load up with supplies and ammunition, then another five days to reach the Chesapeake on October 24, only to learn that they had come too late. Cornwallis, lacking naval reinforcements, had surrendered his entire army on October 18, six days earlier.

Three Financiers Who Put Their Entire Wealth on the Line to Save the U.S. Government from Bankruptcy

➤**1782** Three times the U.S. government has teetered on bankruptcy/insolvency: 1782, 1813, and 1895. The government didn't have the cash flow to meet its bills the following week, and it had nowhere to turn for credit. On all three occasions, it was rescued at the eleventh hour by a patriotic financier. The three patriots were Haym Salomon, Stephen Girard, and J. Pierpont Morgan.

When the colonists rebelled against England, King George was confident of victory not because he had more soldiers, but because he had more money. "My one true ally," he said, "is the rebels' money—or their lack of it." He was absolutely right, but occasionally in extraordinary times one single man can make a difference. Such a man was Haym Salomon. Arriving in the early 1770s from Poland, Salomon established himself as a brilliant financier and personal friend of George Washington. Captured and sentenced to death by the British in 1776, Salomon used his mastery of eight languages to persuade his Hessian jailer to let him escape to the American side. During the Revolution, he went to Paris and, passing himself off as a French diplomat, raised $3.5 million for America from major merchant banking houses. He negotiated additional subsidies from the governments of France, Holland, and Spain, all based on his personal credit. He also acted as paymaster-general of the French military forces in America and, when funds ran out, advanced his own money to keep the soldiers on duty.

In 1781, Congress established the Office of Finance to save the United States from fiscal ruin. The new nation had a fundamental problem, an inherent contradiction that threatened its very philosophical basis for being: taxation. "The congressmen feel they can't tax the states," observed Salomon, "when taxation is precisely what we all took up arms to oppose." Until the new government straightened out its relationship with the states, the only way it could pay its bills was to borrow. But it had already borrowed up to the hilt. A new nation already saddled with debt is not an appealing credit risk. No matter, Salomon again went to work. He provided low-interest funds to members of the Continental Congress who were on their last legs. Admitted James Madison, "I have for some time . . . been a pensioner on the favor of Haym Salomon." Most significant of all, Salomon provided a $700,000 loan to the Continental Government, secured by a government promissory note dated March 27, 1782. When Salomon died three years later, his estate still had the bulk of the loan unpaid.

It still does. The note was denominated in depreciating government currency, and Salomon died impoverished. The American government was a deadbeat.

The only admission of the debt owed to Salomon occurred nearly two hundred years later, in the form of a postage stamp. In 1975 the U.S. Postal Service issued a commemorative stamp that read on the back side: "Haym Salomon was responsible for raising most of the money needed to finance the American Revolution and later to save the new nation from collapse." It is probably fair to say that most people never read it before licking the stamp.

❧

In April 1813, at the height of the War of 1812 against Britain, the United States again was in dire straits. This time, unlike in the American Revolution, the United States did not have France to bail it out.

The brilliant secretary of the treasury, Albert Gallatin (treasury secretary under two presidents for thirteen years—a record that still stands), developed a plan to raise $16 million. He secured tentative subscriptions of $5.8 million from the public and $2.1 million from a small group led by John Jacob Astor, the second-richest man in America. Total to date: $7.9 million. Still to go: $8.1 million. Gallatin had only seven days left before the closing date. If he did not raise the balance by then, the offering would fail and the money held in escrow would have to be returned.

Where to go for the $8.1 million?

The only hope was Stephen Girard, the richest man in America. Girard had arrived in Philadelphia as a young French sea captain at age twenty-one and made his fortune in mercantile trading and banking. But there was a slight problem—in fact a very big problem. A year earlier, Girard had turned down the United States Treasury's request for a $500,000 loan because it refused to help him get a charter in his fight with other Philadelphia banks trying to keep him out of the banking business. Since then, the U.S. had upset Girard even further by filing a lawsuit claiming one of Girard's ships had brought British goods into an American port illegally—even though this ship had been given specific clearance by an American admiral.

One imagines that a meeting between a U.S. treasury secretary going, hat in hand, to a civilian being sued by the U.S. government must have been very interesting. Be that as it may, and it would have been most improper to insist that the U.S. drop its lawsuit as part of the deal, Girard readily agreed to help. He imposed no conditions on his adopted country.

There was another obstacle, however, unsaid by both parties: $8.1 million was more than Girard's net worth. To get the deal done, he would have to raise money from others. He would have to achieve what a brilliant treasury secretary, backed by a popular president and the entire U.S. government, had been unable to do.

But Girard had not become America's first tycoon for no reason. He signed an agreement with Gallatin. Putting his considerable credibility on the line, he went to work identifying potential fellow investors and restructured the deal so that payments could be made in installments and interest collected at the beginning or at the end, depending on the investor's circumstances. Within seven days Girard had put $2.5 million of his own money up front and raised the full balance from others. It was the first investment banking deal ever done in the United States, and it saved America.

"Many are willing to risk their lives for their country, but few are willing to risk their fortunes," observed one historian. Girard understood the urgency of the moment, that "there could be no victory, no war, without money." Money for war was desperately needed at the time. When Gallatin submitted his $19 million annual budget to President Madison, he allocated $17.9 million—94 percent—for the War and Navy departments, and only $1.1 million for running the government.

After the war, Girard received no more thanks than had Haym Salomon (though he did get repaid). He was still being hounded by Treasury customs officials over his ship's alleged violation, this time in the form of a penalty. Congress stepped in and absolved Girard from the penalty, but required him to pay double duty plus interest on his cargoes. Congress also failed to make this ruling automatic, meaning that Girard had to go to court to get the ruling enforced. He finally succeeded, but it took him six years. So much for risking his fortune for his country.

❧

J. Pierpont Morgan would not make the same mistake. When the U.S. Treasury came to him during the Panic of 1895 to bail out the government, he made sure he would be repaid in full and have no lingering problems thereafter. Especially since he was quite angry.

Ignored by politicians and journalists after warning that the nation was printing too much money, Morgan got his satisfaction when he got called for an emergency meeting by President Grover Cleveland. After cooling his heels for a day—Morgan was not a man who liked being kept waiting—he finally had his meeting at the White House. Informed there was only $9 million of gold left in the Treasury's vault in New York City, Morgan said, "Mr. President, the Secretary of the Treasury knows of one check outstanding for twelve million dollars. If this is presented today, it is all over."

The treasury secretary confirmed Morgan's statement. The president was cornered—and he knew it. Like Albert Gallatin eight decades earlier, he had no choice but to acquiesce to the financier who sat on the opposite side of the political fence. These were the times of populism and the fiery rhetoric of William Jennings Bryan ("You shall not crucify mankind upon a cross of gold!"). American farmers, burdened by falling agricul-

tural prices, wanted the government to inflate the money supply so they could repay their loans with cheaper dollars. Arrayed against them were the bankers of the East, who wanted a strong, gold-backed dollar to maintain the value of dollar-denominated bonds sold to foreigners. When European investors became nervous that the Populists would prevail and inflate the money supply, they started unloading their bonds for gold. In 1894, U.S. gold reserves dropped more than 50 percent from $100 million to $45 million. In early 1895, gold losses accelerated to almost $2 million a day, raising fears that the government would default and the economy would collapse.

Morgan proposed to President Cleveland a bold scheme whereby he would purchase gold in Europe with the proceeds of a $65-million offering of thirty-year gold bonds. The government would be the issuer, and Morgan would be the underwriter responsible for selling the bonds. To cover the twofold risk of being able to sell the bonds and simultaneously buy back the gold from the Europeans at a price that was affordable, Morgan would have to charge a substantial spread. How much money Morgan netted on the deal, he steadfastly refused to say.

For Cleveland, the deal resulted in political calumny that marked the end of his career. But for the country, Morgan's decisiveness stopped the gold run in its tracks and saved the government from bankruptcy by one day.

Arriving on Time

►**1862** President Abraham Lincoln was scheduled to leave Washington DC on a 6:00 a.m. train to travel 120 miles to Gettysburg, where he was to make short dedicatory remarks at noontime. Lincoln was not pleased; he planned to give a very important speech, and he wanted to make sure he was there on time. With ten thousand people trying to get to Gettysburg for the ceremonies, he knew the roads and train crossings would be jammed. "I do not like this arrangement," he said. "I do not wish to go so that by the slightest accident we fail entirely, and, at the best, the whole to be a more breathless running of the gauntlet."

So he left a day early, and even then the journey took over six hours. Had Lincoln followed his staff's plans, he would have arrived too late to deliver what is commonly recognized as one of the greatest speeches ever given.

The Day That Saved the North—Thanks to the Author of Ben-Hur

►**1864** There are many ways to win a war. One of the easiest is to capture the enemy's capital. As shown when the Vietcong temporarily overran the U.S. embassy in Saigon during the 1968 Tet invasion, the psychological impact can be so devastating that nobody cares that the invasion may

have been a military failure; what matters is the symbolism of capturing the enemy's political headquarters.

In July 1864, General Robert E. Lee concocted a bold plan to humiliate the North and ensure Lincoln's defeat in the upcoming election: capture the nation's capital. (Lee, after all, had a home—Arlington—right across the river from Washington DC and Washington and Richmond were only a hundred miles apart.) Though he needed all his troops to defend Virginia against the approaching army of Ulysses Grant, Lee took a gamble and sent a major portion of his army up north under General Jubal Early. Early's mission: seize Washington, cause panic in the North, and entice France and England to recognize the Confederacy, thereby ending the war.

Standing in his way was Lew Wallace, the man who later in life went on to write the 1880 book *Ben-Hur*. Mention *Ben-Hur* and we all think of the famous 1959 movie based on Wallace's book. In 1864 Lew Wallace was not a novelist, but an obscure major general in the Union army, and it was here that he played the role for which he deserves most to be remembered. At a critical moment he saved the North from losing the Civil War.

Jubal Early was a very aggressive general. As he swept through the Shenandoah Valley heading north into Maryland, it was obvious that Washington DC was in grave danger. Grant immediately dispatched two brigades of men to the nation's capital. Question was, who would get there first? Only one obstacle stood in Early's way: a ragtag group of "hundred days" men under the leadership of Lew Wallace. Recruited on the promise they would only have to serve one hundred days, these men had hardly seen battle. And it showed. When they met the Confederate cavalry at the Maryland town of Frederick, the Confederates drove them out in an hour and even collected a $200,000 bounty for agreeing not to set the town on fire.

Reinforcements from the North arrived, and at Monocacy Junction, three miles away, Wallace dug in his heels. He now had almost six thousand men, but it was hardly a fair fight: Jubal Early had fourteen thousand. And because Wallace didn't know where Early would attack, he had to spread his troops over a defense line six miles wide. But he chose his spots well, concentrating on high points and fortifying selected defense spots. Then came the attack. "Don't fire until you see the whites of their eyes!" was the Union order. In one of the most ferocious battles of the war—it went on all day with much hand-to-hand combat—the Confederates finally won. The Union defenders gave it everything they had, suffering deaths and casualties of 1,900 compared with seven hundred for an invading army almost three times as big. It should have been a rout, but it was not: it was a slugfest. "A crimson current ran towards the river," wrote one Confederate general.

After a day of badly needed rest (half his soldiers were walking barefoot), Early's troops resumed their march toward Washington, only to find that they had arrived a day too late: Grant's reinforcements had just arrived. Exhausted from the fierce battle put up by General Wallace, Jubal Early made the reluctant decision not to invade Washington. He had missed his golden opportunity. Lincoln and Congress breathed a sigh of relief as Early retreated back south, never to appear again, and Wallace returned to the battlefield to supervise burials and to propose a monument to read: "These men died to save the National Capital, and they did save it."

Ulysses Grant agreed fully. In his *Memoirs* he wrote:

> *If Early had been but one day earlier, he might have entered the capital before the arrival of the reinforcements I had sent. . . . General Wallace contributed on this occasion by the defeat of the troops under him, a greater benefit to the cause than often falls to the lot of a commander of an equal force to render by means of a victory.*

House in a Shambles

➤**1879** Seized by the Confederacy and ransacked by Confederate soldiers because its owner had been a U.S. naval officer from New York, this house had been bequeathed "to the people of the United States for the sole and only purpose of establishing and maintaining an Agricultural School for the purpose of educating as practical farmers' children of the warrant office of the United States Navy whose fathers are dead." But with all the problems it had after the Civil War, the U.S. government had more important things to do than run a farm school for navy warrant officers' orphans, and so it rejected the bequest. Subsequently there ensued a lengthy legal wrangle among the decedent's New York relatives, and the house lay abandoned. It looked as though the house would be headed for the wrecker's ball and the great estate subdivided and sold off, like so many other estates.

Finally, in 1879, one of the family members bought out his relatives and took possession. He found the house and grounds "in a dreadful state of disrepair." The orchards, terraced gardens, flower borders, walkways, and roads "had all but disappeared." The outbuildings had collapsed, the lawns were torn up by pigs, the gutters were falling down, the roof and skylights were rotting, windows were broken, and the basement was flooded with water. The once-elegant drawing rooms used by the President of the United States had been used as a grain storehouse.

The rescue of this magnificent house actually was a two-part saga. Back in the 1830s, there existed a naval officer who ever since Jefferson's death had sought to do whatever he could to honor "one of the greatest men in history. He did much to mold our Republic in a form in which a man's religion does not make him ineligible for political or governmental life." While on a trip to Paris in 1832, Uriah Levy commissioned the French sculptor Pierre-Jean David d'Angers to create a full-scale bronze of Jefferson for the rotunda of the U.S. Capitol (where it still stands today). Upon arriving back in the United States with his statue, he learned that Monticello was for sale. He bought it and started to restore it, but then came the Civil War and his death, upon which the family bequeathed it to the U.S. government. Unoccupied and unattended to, the house became a derelict.

To the rescue came another Levy, Uriah Levy's nephew, with the appropriate name of Jefferson Levy. The decrepit hulk available for sale in 1879 needed a total restoration. Fortunately, Jefferson Levy was a wealthy man. He bought the property and invested more than a million dollars during the next thirty years (he also became a congressman from New York). In 1926, on the 150th anniversary of the Declaration of Independence, a private fund-raising effort enabled the U.S. government to finally buy Monticello for $500,000. By the narrowest of margins, thanks to two remarkable men who had a passion for history, we now have a house that is one of America's favorite shrines.

Monticello in 1870, deserted and abandoned

Monticello today

President Because of Two Deaths in the Wrong Order

►**1901** Everyone knows that when the president dies and the vice president dies, the next person in line is the Speaker of the House.

But what if the vice president dies first? The second in line is not the Speaker of the House; in fact nobody knows who it might be. There is no provision in the Constitution for this unforeseen contingency because the Founding Fathers never envisioned it.

In a period of eighteen months, a man came out of nowhere to become president because of two deaths in the wrong order. In November 1899, Garret Hobart, vice president of the United States, died of a heart attack. Because there were only a few months left before the 1900 election, President William McKinley left the position unfilled. He sought as his running mate Senator William Allison of Iowa, who turned it down. He then turned to the prominent lawyer Elihu Root, who also turned it down, hoping for the better position of secretary of war. At the convention, McKinley, against the advice of his campaign manager, Mark Hanna, opened up the floor to the delegates, who nominated the young governor of New York, Theodore Roosevelt. Roosevelt accepted the nomination because he had accomplished pretty much what he could in two years as governor and was making little headway against the powerful politi-

cal boss of New York City, Thomas Platt. Accepting the vice presidency was hardly a promotion; quite the contrary, it was the case of a man being kicked upstairs because he was such a nuisance in his current position. His wife was not happy with the change because they had six children and the vice presidency paid a much smaller salary than that of governor, plus it did not come with a house.

After several months, she feared her husband was becoming bored in "such a useless and empty position." Even Theodore Roosevelt was beginning to admit second thoughts. The position, he said, "ought to be abolished."

The one benefit, of course, is that the job is just a heartbeat away from the big position, which raises the interesting question of just what Theodore Roosevelt's real thoughts were. He might well have known of the misfortune of General Benjamin Butler, the only man to ever turn down the vice presidency—and lose the presidency as a result. In 1864, Lincoln, in search of a "War Democrat," preferred General Butler to be his running mate and instructed former secretary of war Simon Cameron to pay him a visit. Butler, who later become governor of Massachusetts, wondered why anyone would possibly want to be vice president, and drafted a whimsical response. Naturally it did not go over very well: "Tell him I would not quit the field to be vice president . . . unless he will give me bond, with sureties, in the full sum of his four years' salary, that he will die or resign within three months after his inauguration." Six weeks after Lincoln's inauguration, Lincoln died—and the man who took his place was not Benjamin Butler.

Theodore Roosevelt was always guarded whenever he spoke of the presidency. Earlier, when he had been a rising politician as police commissioner of New York, the muckraking journalists Jacob Riis and Lincoln Steffens had asked him if he was actively working to become president someday. TR blew up: "Don't you dare ask me that. Don't you put such ideas into my head. No friend of mine would ever say a thing like that." He continued his rant:

> *Never, never, you must never either of you remind a man at work on a political job that he may be President. It almost always gives up the very traits that are making him a possibility. I, for instance, I am going to do great things here, hard things that require all the courage, ability, work that I am capable of. . . . But if I get to thinking of what it might lead to . . . I must be wanting to be President. Every young man does. But I won't let myself think of it; I must not, because if I do, I will begin to work for it, I'll be careful, I'll be calculating, cautious in word and act, and so—I'll beat myself, see?*

Of course TR—a man who could never sit still—must have thought frequently of becoming president. But he never hesitated to make enemies if that was the price of doing what he thought was right. On one occasion as governor, when he had to decide whether to have a female murderer executed, he was bluntly told, "If you do not pardon this woman, you will never be president." He rejected the advice and went ahead anyway.

In September 1901, eighteen months after a vice president had died, it became a president's turn to die, this one by assassination, and so Theodore Roosevelt became president because of two deaths in the wrong order and two men who turned down the opportunity.

Barely Got Off the Ground

►1939 One of America's favorite movies almost never got funded, was rejected by the director's first choice of male star, and failed to win an Oscar. It is the most famous movie of all time: *Gone with the Wind*. When Louis B. Mayer was considering bidding for the film rights to Margaret Mitchell's novel, his MGM production chief told him, "Forget it, Louis, no Civil War picture ever made a nickel." Clark Gable ended up with the Rhett Butler role only because the first choice, Gary Cooper, turned it down. In the Oscar voting that year, the winner was *Wuthering Heights*.

In the late 1950s, MGM was going bankrupt, so it bet the house on a blockbuster movie, easily the most expensive movie at the time, requiring three hundred sets scattered over 340 acres. The movie was about the life of one man. For this all-critical role, it sought the services of Burt Lancaster. He turned it down. So, too, did Paul Newman and Rock Hudson. Finally, Charlton Heston accepted the part, and *Ben-Hur* went on to win eleven Academy Awards and earn five times its original investment, one of the most profitable movies ever made.

Another of America's cultural icons also was a total "hit or miss": *Reader's Digest*. When Dewitt Wallace came up with the idea in 1920, he prepared two hundred copies of a "dummy" issue and sent it to magazine publishers and other potential backers. No one was interested. Finally, on his wedding day in 1928, he made a final effort and tried a new approach to launching a magazine. Foregoing the judgment of publishing industry experts who scorned the newfangled idea of direct mail, Wallace conducted a subscription-solicitation mailing to several thousand potential readers. Upon his return from his honeymoon two weeks later, he found his mailbox stuffed with 1,500 charter subscribers at three dollars apiece. From then on, Wallace proceeded to build up what has become the world's most popular magazine, published in more than fifty languages.

Going back in history, we find the talented painter of birds, John James Audubon, one of the many people in the trans-Appalachian West who was forced into bankruptcy during the Panic of 1819.

To support his wife and two children, he took up portrait painting and taught school, then embarked by himself on a five-year expedition down the Ohio and Mississippi rivers, looking for more undiscovered birds. Finally satisfied, he envisioned immortality by producing *The Birds of America*. It would be a four-volume, leather-bound set of 400 two- by three-foot engraved, hand-colored plates, accompanied by five volumes of his field notes. Because there was no one in America capable of engraving, hand-coloring, and printing such large plates, Audubon had to go to Europe. He found a printer, and sold advance subscriptions to finance the project. The printing of almost two hundred copies took ten years, and cost $115,640 (equivalent to more than $2.1 million today). The result was a monumental work that today is the envy of collectors everywhere. Today an original complete set goes for $8.8 million.

Emily Dickinson is regarded as one of America's finest poets of the nineteenth century, and many of her 1,775 poems are required reading in literature courses. Yet in her lifetime all she was able to get published were seven poems, all of them anonymously. That her other 1,668 lyrics weren't tossed into the fire after her death is "one of the great miracles of American literary history." But her emergence, while lucky, was no fluke. "Melville and Thoreau," says the historian Don Gifford, "also had their troubles in the lost-and-found department of that century." Herman Melville's *Moby-Dick* was rejected by five book publishers; Henry David Thoreau's *Walden* was rejected by eight publishers, and took him two years to find a publisher.

No subject has a more explicit accepted/rejected ratio than book publishing. Noah Webster couldn't find a publisher for his 1825 book, *An American Dictionary of the English Language*, and had to pay for the first printing himself (it eventually sold 60 million copies). Upton Sinclair's *The Jungle*, the 1906 exposé of the meat-packing industry that eventually resulted in the creation of the U.S. Food and Drug Administration, was turned down by five publishers; Sinclair was down to his last penny paying to have his book self-published before Doubleday came along and agreed to take it on. It became an instant international best-seller. Another major path-breaking book of the twentieth century also had the same trouble: Rachel Carson's *Silent Spring*. In 1962 it finally got published by Houghton Mifflin after several publishers had turned it down.

Even F. Scott Fitzgerald had his share of disappointments. He received more than 120 rejection slips before he got his first short story published ("This Side of Paradise," 1931). "The anger of rejection motivated me to keep going," he said.

The best-selling author of the first half of the twentieth century was Zane Grey, "the man who made the West famous." His ninety-plus books sold 17 million copies and provided the stories for 130 movies. From 1910 to 1930 he had a novel in the top ten best-sellers every year. Yet his first book was self-published. His second book got published, but with only modest royalties. His third book was rejected by several publishers, leaving him totally out of money and living on loans from his brother. Only after he took a trip out west and saw the area firsthand, and wrote a book about it, did he find a publisher and launch his prolific career.

Many writers—especially women—had to publish their early works by themselves. Gertrude Stein, after three years failing to find a publisher for *Three Lives*, had the book printed by a vanity publisher. Before Anaïs Nin finally found a publisher for her best-selling *Diary*, she had to pay a printer to produce her first two books and had her third book published only after eleven rejections. Mae West, earning the second-highest salary in America during the Depression as an actress and screenwriter, never got anything published because the number-one person, William Randolph Hearst, used his influence to make sure no publisher would touch this sex comedienne. Equally thwarted by male jealousy was Margaret Mitchell: William Faulkner, unable to sell his work and annoyed that an unknown writer could produce a runaway bestseller, refused a lucrative offer to write the screenplay for *Gone with the Wind*. Ayn Rand, whose *Atlas Shrugged* was admitted by a poll of Americans in a 1991 survey to be the most influential book in their lives after the Bible, saw her first book rejected by every publisher. When she persevered and transformed the book into a play, she finally found a publisher, thus providing her the income she needed to pursue her literary aspirations. She then wrote *The Fountainhead*, only to be rejected by twelve publishers. *The Fountainhead* went on to become "the greatest word-of-mouth book" in publishing history.

More recent best-sellers that almost never made it include Frank Herbert's *Dune*, the most popular science fiction book ever written, selling 12 million copies (plus millions more of five sequels); twenty publishers had rejected it before it was published in 1965. In 1982 there appeared "the greatest business book of all time": Thomas Peters and Robert Waterman's *In Search of Excellence*, rejected by forty-eight publishers. In 1994 another book phenomenon appeared, one that became the romantic classic of the decade and remained on the *New York Times* best-seller list for 156 weeks and sold 50 million copies: Robert James Waller's *The Bridges of Madison County*. It was rejected by twenty-six publishers.

A Race to the Death

➤**1943**   It was a race to the death, the race between Germany and America to develop the atom bomb. Whoever won the race could win the war overnight.

Germany had the head start. A militarist state, Germany under Hitler commanded people at will and had nine facilities working round the clock to develop nuclear reactors, heavy-water production, and isotope separation. The U.S. had no plan, no strategy, just a couple of university research labs scattered around the country.

The race involved an enormous technological challenge, one for which many members of the American scientific team estimated the chances of success to be one percent. It required finding hundreds of tons of pure-grade ore normally found only in places like the Belgian Congo, then controlled by the Nazis. It required building an entirely new facility—Los Alamos—in a remote site, involving an infrastructure of roads and more than fifty buildings to accommodate tons of equipment and three hundred people—and do so without anybody knowing about it. It required creating a massive new organization and ensuring cooperation between academic scientists and army engineers not disposed to working together. It required integrating scientists of different nationalities, temperaments, and loyalties (two of whom eventually turned out to be spies).

The man chosen to head the project, General Leslie Groves (the man who built the Pentagon), almost didn't get the job because he was considered too "blunt."* In

---

* It was named the Manhattan Project not because of its size or importance, but rather to throw off spies, since projects normally were named for the geographical location of the head engineering firm. German and Russian spies ran around in circles in New York, looking in the wrong place.

a move that astonished everyone, he gambled on Robert Oppenheimer—a brilliant choice in retrospect—but at the time it was a decision that surprised and angered many people worried about Oppenheimer's past affiliation with the Communist Party, and caused Groves lots of headaches.

One percent odds of success? That was just the science part. With all these other problems, try odds of a tenth of one percent.

To put this accomplishment in perspective, compare it with another of America's great technological feats: putting a man on the moon. The moon race, from the time President Kennedy laid down the gauntlet to the time Neil Armstrong landed, took nine years. The Manhattan Project, from the time the scientists started work in earnest until the time the prototype finally was tested (April 15, 1943, to July 16, 1945), took only twenty-seven months.

Yet its success was by the narrowest of margins, aided by incredible good luck possible only in a country free and patriotic like America. Consider two stories from General Groves's 1962 book, *Now It Can Be Told*. Now largely forgotten, they deserve to be retold.

A Lonely Belgian Refugee, Safe Only in America

Were it not "for a chance meeting between a Belgian and an Englishman a few months before the outbreak of the war," wrote General Groves, "the Allies might not have been first with the atomic bomb."

The Belgian was Edgar Sengier, managing director of Union Minière, the largest mining company in the Belgian Congo. Found here was ore containing 65 percent uranium oxide, compared with Canadian ore yielding only two tenths of one percent. The Englishman was Sir Henry Tizard, director of the Imperial College of Science and Technology. Said Tizard to Sengier, "Never forget that you have in your hands something which may mean a catastrophe to your country and mine if this material were to fall in the hands of a possible enemy."

With the invasion of Belgium by the Germans in 1939, Sengier fled to New York. But first, remembering Tizard's warning, he ordered the company's entire stock of 120 grams of radium to be shipped to the United States and England. He also arranged, under false names, for some 1,250 tons of uranium stored in the Congo to be shipped immediately to New York. There, for two years in a warehouse rented by Sengier, the uranium sat while Sengier tried to alert the State Department to the ore's existence and how it could accelerate the country's atomic bomb project.

The problem was, FDR was conducting his own foreign policy for reasons of wartime secrecy, and the State Department never learned about the Manhattan Project until 1945. Fortunately, General George Marshall's deputy Kenneth Nichols heard about Sengier and went to see him in hopes of making a deal. Surprise, surprise: "You can have the ore now," Sengier told an astonished Nichols. "It is in New York, a thousand tons of it. I was waiting for your visit."

So secret was this purchase that unusual measures had to be taken regarding payment. Sengier had to open a special account at his New York bank, receiving funds identified under a specific number. "It was arranged that the reports of the Federal Reserve Bank would not mention any of these transactions," wrote Groves, "and the auditors were directed to accept Sengier's statements without hesitation." After the war, Sengier became the first non-American civilian to be awarded the Presidential Medal for Merit by the United States government.

A Display of Real Patriotism

Ever since ancient times, alchemists have tried to convert metal into gold by converting atoms of one element into atoms of another element possessing different chemical and physical properties. Developing the atom bomb required a similar transformation, this one from uranium to plutonium.

None of the scientists could agree on the amount of plutonium needed for a bomb; estimates varied from ten to one thousand pounds. It was, said General Groves, like being "a caterer who is told he must be prepared to serve anywhere between ten and a thousand guests." What

Groves and the scientists could agree on was that the proposed plutonium plant had better be big—far bigger than what a university lab or a government agency could provide. Only a multinational chemical company like DuPont could handle such an assignment.

DuPont, already stretched to the limit by wartime demands, was less than thrilled about taking on a project as large and dangerous as this one, let alone unpredictable. DuPont's expertise was in chemistry, not physics, and it certainly had no experience whatsoever in the arcane world of nuclear physics. But then, neither did any other company, and Groves argued that if any company could do the job, it was DuPont. Groves added that the president, Secretary of War Stimson, and General Marshall all considered the project to be of utmost urgency.

The risks to DuPont were daunting: the project could be a complete flop, the plant could prove impossible to build, the plutonium could leak and cause serious health hazards to DuPont employees, the factory could explode. In a report to the board of directors, the company's executive committee outlined these risks, concluded there was "no positive assurance of success" and that possible failure could bankrupt the company—yet recommended to the board of directors that DuPont take the job.

Then came the crucial board of directors meeting. On the table, in front of each chair, lay a set of papers, facedown. The president of the company summarized the findings of the executive committee and told the directors that this was a top-secret project, but if they wished, they could read the facedown papers before voting.

Not a single man turned over the papers. They all voted yes.

It was, wrote Groves, "a true display of real patriotism."

DuPont further agreed to do the job at cost, and to receive no patent rights for its R&D. It did insist, however, that the government provide it with disaster liability insurance, and that such insurance carry the personal initials of FDR. This was done, and to make it legally binding, DuPont was required to pay one dollar for the insurance. At the end of the war, though the contract had yet to be fully completed, the dollar was returned to DuPont. Sharp-eyed government auditors caught the discrepancy and asked DuPont to return a third of the refund—thirty-three cents—to the United States. The executives of DuPont did so, feeling bittersweet amusement that this was all the thanks they got for risking their company to help save America.

Worse Things Happen at Sea

►**1945** At 12:14 a.m. on July 30, midway between Guam and Leyte Gulf in the Philippines, the USS *Indianapolis* was hit by two torpedoes fired by a Japanese submarine. The first blew away the bow, the second struck the starboard side adjacent

to a fuel tank and a powder magazine. The resulting explosion split the ship to the keel, knocking out all electric power. She rolled sideways and went down by the bow. In just twelve minutes she was gone.

It was a tragic end for a magnificent warship. Built in 1932, the *Indianapolis* had served as President Franklin Roosevelt's "Ship of State" and personal transport for transatlantic and South American travel before the war. At the battle of Okinawa in late March 1945, the Japanese had identified "the pride of the enemy fleet, the warship *Indianapolis*" as one of their primary targets and had succeeded in hitting her with a kamikaze plane, almost sinking her.

The *Indianapolis* was able to limp back to San Francisco for urgent repairs, then quickly got called to perform a top-secret mission: make a delivery to Tinian Island (near Guam), ten thousand miles away in the far Pacific. The delivery consisted of several wooden crates weighing a total of nine thousand pounds, to be lashed down to the deck and guarded by sentry twenty-four hours a day. In addition, there were two long metal canisters, to be stored in the luxurious private cabin reserved for the commander of the Central Pacific Fleet. Nobody, not even the captain, knew what this was all about. All they were told was that it was "top secret" and "every hour we save [getting it to Tinian] will shorten the war by that much." "Oh sure," joked the seamen, "it's rolls of toilet paper for General MacArthur." And just what was to happen to General MacArthur's toilet rolls if the ship got torpedoed? The Navy's strict instructions: throw the canisters overboard, but make sure—no matter what—that the crates weighing two and a half tons got put on a lifeboat. (How this was to be done in the chaos of a sinking was never discussed.)

The *Indianapolis* raced to Tinian Island in ten days and dropped off her cargo. Inside the crates were the components of an atom bomb; inside the two canisters were the fuel cells containing uranium-235. In five days these components and fuel cells, assembled into a bomb called "Little Boy," would be dropped on Hiroshima.

Having completed her top-secret mission, the *Indianapolis* was ordered to go to Guam and then to Leyte in the Philippines. Although there was no longer any need for secrecy, the ship was to continue traveling without convoy. Not only was this a violation of standard procedure that a warship always have escort when crossing the dangerous Philippine Sea, but the USS *Indianapolis* was particularly vulnerable: she lacked submarine-detection equipment and had a top-heavy superstructure, making her unable to "sustain even one torpedo," according to the commander of the Central Pacific Fleet. Naval intelligence had just learned of the sinking of an American warship on the Guam-Leyte route and believed that several Japanese submarines were lurking in the area, but the Navy never changed the *Indianapolis*'s route nor warned the captain of this danger. The *Indianapolis* must con-

tinue her total radio silence, and no officers at the departing port or the arrival port were informed of this unusual blackout. With these instructions, the ship departed into hostile waters, an orphan.

Two days after leaving Guam, the *Indianapolis* ran into the Japanese submarine *I-58*, waiting for the kill. Two quick torpedo shots at less than 1,500 yards, and down went the *Indianapolis*. Out of 1,199 men, some nine hundred were able to jump into the water. But worse horrors were still to come. As the English say, "Worse things happen at sea." The shark attacks began.

Back in port, nobody paid attention. The frantic SOS calls when the *Indianapolis* sank were so garbled they were ignored. An intercept of a Japanese message bragging of a "hit" was ignored as a ruse. When the ship failed to show up at Leyte on the appointed day, the port commander assumed her orders had been changed—same for days two, three, and four. Back in Guam, the marker on the plotting board for the *Indianapolis* was removed because it was assumed—having received no inquiry from Leyte—that the ship had arrived as expected. When a message was sent to Guam asking why the ship's radio teletype wasn't responding, Guam replied it was probably an equipment failure.

Nobody asked questions because they didn't know what they were supposed to know and not a single officer had any curiosity or initiative.

Meanwhile, men were dying in the

You don't want to run into this submarine on a moonlit night: the I-58

ocean from wounds, dehydration, thirst, and shark attacks. The first day and night went by, no help. Day two, still no help. Day three, still no help. In late morning of the fourth day, a pilot on a routine patrol who happened to go to the back of the plane to check up on a problem looked down at the vast ocean and had the surprise of his life: a few men waving frantically in the water. He immediately sent out a rescue call. Only when a seaplane reached the survivors did the Navy learn they were from the *Indianapolis*. The men drifting in the sea hanging on for dear life were scattered over a line twenty miles long. The first rescue ship didn't arrive until it was completely dark. Despite the danger of attracting the attention of an enemy submarine, it turned on all its searchlights to give hope to the men miles away that help was coming. By then, more than five hundred men had died. Out of an original crew of 1,199 men, 316 were left. Had it not been for the chance encounter of a plane finding men in the water and sending out the alert, everyone would have died. It was the worst disaster in the history of the U.S. Navy.

Clearly, the Navy had a lot of explaining to do. Why no escort? Why no warning of the known danger in the Philippine Sea? Why continued radio silence? Why no notification to the port commanders of two ports? Why no follow-up when the ship failed to show up for four and a half days? The only response the Navy could come up with, as all bureaucracies are wont to do in the glare of bright lights shone on their ineptitude, was to go after an individual, in this case the ship's much-decorated captain. A court-martial of the captain would take the heat off the Navy. The Navy pressed two charges against Captain Charles McVay: first, failure to exercise proper caution in a war zone—i.e., failure to zigzag, and, second, failure to give adequate prompt warning to the crew to abandon ship. On the second charge, McVay's lawyers pointed out that there could be no shipwide emergency order via intercom because the torpedoes had knocked out the ship's entire electrical system. On this second charge, McVay was acquitted. On the first charge, the Navy prosecutors withheld information from the defense that might have exculpated McVay: the Navy's knowledge of Japanese submarines in the area. The prosecutors then pulled a stunt never tried before: it brought over from Japan a surprise witness: the *I-58*'s commander, Mochitsura Hashimoto. Many Americans and congressmen were outraged: How dare the Navy let one of its officers possibly be convicted because of the testimony of an enemy? Little did the prosecutors realize they had a wild card on their hands: Hashimoto, clearly uncomfortable in this situation, defended McVay.

He testified that the clouds had cleared suddenly and it was such a moonlit night he easily could have nailed the *Indianapolis* whether it zigzagged or not. Samuel Eliot Morison, author of the official six-volume history of U.S. naval operations in the Second World War, agreed: "Only a fool could have missed at this short range," he wrote.

Nonetheless, the military tribunal found McVay guilty of not zigzagging. McVay's crew, almost to a man, defended him. To Morison, it all reminded him of the 1757 English trial and execution of one of its admirals, described by Voltaire in *Candide*: "It is found good, from time to time, to kill one admiral to encourage the others."

The charade continued. The pilot who had arrived to drop life rafts for the *Indianapolis* survivors bobbing in the ocean was a man of extraordinary courage. He was Lieutenant Adrian Marks. Violating standing orders never to land his amphibious plane in open sea, Marks managed to bring his plane down amid twelve-foot swells, take on board as many men as he could, then add more men by securing them to the wings with parachute cord. Barely managing to keep the overloaded plane afloat until a rescue ship arrived at nightfall, he saved the lives of fifty-six men. The Navy bureaucracy, however, was more concerned about the loss of one of its seaplanes. It commenced court-martial proceedings against Marks, until higher-ups put a stop to this and gave him a medal for one of the most heroic acts of the entire war.

Might the Interim Have Been Otherwise?

➤**1953**   The Cold War witnessed powerful antagonisms between the United States and the two Communist superpowers, China and Russia. Here are some fascinating might-have-beens:

Two revolutionaries sent a secret message, offering to come to Washington to talk to President Franklin Roosevelt. They were Mao Tse-tung and Chou En-lai, then in the throes of a great struggle with Chiang Kai-shek for control of the world's largest nation. FDR, preoccupied with other things, refused to see them. Acting on the advice of a political crony in China and against his two senior State Department officers (John Davies and John Service), Roosevelt cast his lot with the side that turned out to be the loser, Chiang Kai-shek.

Shortly after he became president, Richard Nixon contemplated opening relations with China, the Communist superpower and ally of North Vietnam, with whom the U.S. was then at war. He consulted with Asian specialists in the State Department and academia; virtually all of them told him to forget it, that nothing could be done until after the Vietnam War was over. But Nixon disagreed and plunged ahead.

"Nixon put himself in Mao's shoes," said former diplomat James C. Humes. "He sensed that the Communist leader might not be too happy about North Vietnam expanding its military might into Southeast Asia, with inroads into Laos and Cambodia. How would the United States react, Nixon thought, if Mexico were taking over the governments of Guatemala and El Salvador?" By appreciating his enemy's self-interest, Nixon was able to establish common ground and achieve a diplomatic breakthrough. Adds historian Barbara Tuchman, "Twenty-seven years, two wars, and x million lives later, after immeasurable harm wrought by the mutual suspicion and phobia of two great powers not on speaking terms, an American President, reversing the unmade journey of 1945, has traveled to Peking to meet with the same two Chinese leaders. Might the interim have been otherwise?"

❧

No one would accuse Winston Churchill, author of the mighty phrase "an iron curtain has descended across the continent," of being soft on communism. Yet when Stalin died in 1953 and the new Soviet leaders signaled interest in the relaxation of tensions, Churchill was interested. "A new hope has been created in the unhappy, bewildered world," he wrote Eisenhower. Eisenhower, however, was not interested. At a conference in Bermuda, the American president told off the British prime minister in no uncertain terms: "Russia was a woman of the streets and whether her dress was new, or just the old one patched, it was certainly the same whore underneath. America intended to drive her off her present 'beat' into the back streets." Against Churchill's advice, Eisenhower refused the Russian overtures, appointed as his secretary of state "the high priest of the Cold War," John Foster Dulles, took a soft line against the McCarthy outrages, and preached concepts of peace that included "going to the brink" and "massive retaliation."

In 1962 the U.S. got into a showdown with Russia over nuclear missiles in Cuba, America's backyard. Yet Cuba was supposed to have been an American colony, not once but twice. Back in the late 1850s, the U.S. was all set to write Spain a $50-million check for "the Pearl of the Antilles" when Congress, fearing President James Buchanan would try to divert some of the money into a personal slush fund, nixed the deal. Then, forty years later, Cuba reappeared at the end of the Spanish-American War of 1898. The U.S. found itself with a lot of new territories: Cuba, Puerto Rico, Wake Island, Guam, and the Philippines. Not knowing what to do with all these places, and more interested in acquiring Hawaii and building a Pacific empire, President William McKinley decided to let one of them go its own way—Cuba.

In 1963, President Kennedy and British prime minister Harold Macmillan negotiated with Khrushchev to implement a comprehensive ban on nuclear weapons

testing. The Russians wanted to allow only three annual on-site inspections, the minimum number technically necessary. The British agreed. The U.S. Joint Chiefs, however, insisted on twenty. President Kennedy got that number down to seven, but the Russians would not go along with what almost everyone agreed was unnecessary snooping, and so the effort had to be abandoned. The result was an arms race of expensive new generations of multi-warhead nuclear weapons.

The "Tipping Point" That Sent America into Two Wars

➤**1963, 2001**   The "tipping point" is a concept used to describe a pivotal turning point at a moment when events could have gone one way or another. Dramatic events like Pearl Harbor or the bombing of Hiroshima and Nagasaki are obvious "tipping points."

But sometimes tipping points are not so obvious. In two cases when America embarked on a drawn-out war fraught with unintended consequences—Vietnam and Iraq—the decision to go to war was made in a flash, on the spur of the moment when America was under attack.

The Single Bullet That Eventually Led Us into Vietnam

Vietnam was getting to be a problem. In early 1963, JFK told Senator Mike Mansfield, "If I tried to pull out completely now, we would have another Joe McCarthy red scare on our hands, but I can do it after I'm reelected." (Similar statements were made to Senator Wayne Morse and to presidential aides Kenneth O'Donnell and Michael Forrestal.) At a September 12 press conference he claimed his policy was "simple" and listed three objectives: win the war, contain the Communists, and bring the Americans home. But after getting battlefield reports from Vietnam that things were going much worse than anticipated, he shifted his thinking dramatically. At a November 12 press conference, he dropped the "winning the war" entirely and made "bringing the boys home" number one: "Now, that is our object, to bring Americans home, permit the South Vietnamese to maintain themselves as a free and independent country, and permit democratic forces within the country to operate." Accordingly he signed an executive order, National Security Agency Memorandum (NSAM) 263, to withdraw one thousand of the sixteen thousand American combat "advisors" in Vietnam and for *all* Americans to be out of Vietnam by January 1, 1965 (i.e., in thirteen months). He had a November 24, 1963, appointment with his ambassador to Saigon, Henry Cabot Lodge, to finalize the details of this withdrawal scheduled for December 3.

The plan never got carried out. To be sure, the thousand advisors made it home on December 3, but that was only because of bureaucratic inertia in executing changes in presidential decrees. The rest—and the 500,000 men later to serve—were not so lucky.

What happened? Two days before his meeting with Lodge, President Kennedy was assassinated. The incoming president, a man with no foreign affairs experience, announced within hours of moving into the Oval Office, "I am not going to lose Vietnam, I am not going to be the president who saw Southeast Asia go the way China went." He summarily rejected Ambassador Lodge in favor of other advisors who warned that "hard decisions would have to be made if Vietnam was to be saved," and issued NSAM 273, canceling JFK's NSAM 263.

Normally, when a new man assumes the presidency because of assassination, you would expect continuity. Indeed, Lyndon Johnson professed as much when he assured reporters, "Let us continue." Only the reality was quite different: within a quick forty-eight hours of taking office, in the midst of all the turmoil over the assassination, he made the single most important presidential decision of the 1960s: massive involvement in Asia.

In his memoirs, *In Retrospect: The Tragedy and Lessons of Vietnam*, Secretary of Defense Robert McNamara provides a photograph with an interesting caption: "Nov. 24, 1963: The First Meeting. Among LBJ's first actions as president—while he was still in his vice-presidential quarters in the Old Executive Office Building and before he had moved into the Oval

Office—was meeting with Dean Rusk, George Ball, Ambassador Lodge, and me to discuss Vietnam. His instructions were clear: Win!"

For a new president with no electoral mandate of his own, such aggressiveness was quite baffling. But not really a surprise. In late 1963, Kennedy and Johnson had their eyes on the upcoming presidential election. They had opposing views on what to do

History books talk about America's long slide into its morass in Vietnam. This is a gross oversimplification. Deeds speak louder than words. Based on the actual deeds—the precise wording of the executive order specifying withdrawal and its abrupt cancellation by another man— there was a defining moment in our Vietnam involvement: the assassination of a president.

Only 48 hours after the assassination: "Win!" (LBJ with Lodge, Rusk, McNamara, and Ball)

about Vietnam afterward. Whereas Kennedy had told his advisers he couldn't pull out until after he was reelected, Lyndon Johnson was now telling the Joint Chiefs, "Just let me get elected, and then you can have your war."

Sending the President Through the Roof

America's other messy war also owed its existence to a certain tipping point. In the aftermath of September 11, George W. Bush unleashed a new policy whereby the

U.S. would take the offensive and attack hostile nations preemptively. However, it did not happen right after September 11, but almost two months later. Look carefully at the facts.

During September, in the aftermath of the attack on the World Trade Center towers, nations throughout the world nodded in agreement with Bush's bellicosity. The president's powerful statement, "You are with us or you are against us," did not raise concerns, nor did his more blunt statement about nations harboring terrorists being equivalent to being terrorists. Obviously the United States was fully justified in going after al-Qaeda and the Taliban in Afghanistan. But the minute Bush announced his intention to go after Iraq, other nations balked. Questions about "weapons of mass destruction" and "chemical warfare" dominated their concern about the legitimacy of Bush's escalation.

Unfortunately they never grasped the real tipping point (which Bush never communicated fully). This tipping point lacked the drama of the Twin Towers falling down, and while it dominated the U.S. news for weeks, it was quickly forgotten.

But the president, the Defense Department, and the Homeland Security Department did not forget the anthrax scare that killed five and caused widespread panic. Nobody could figure out who the culprit was, and to this day the FBI does not know for sure. "There is no greater enemy than the enemy you cannot see," goes the old military axiom. Informed by the CIA chief about the scale of potential damage from chemical warfare, the CIA's report "sent the President through the roof." All of a sudden, weapons of mass destruction—forget low-tech attacks by hijacked planes that could easily be dealt with—became the issue. Iraq was universally recognized to be the number-one hostile country claiming (pretending, it turned out) to possess such weapons. From then on, President Bush ordered nuclear/chemical/biological terrorism to be given top priority. Terrorist groups, he warned delegates at an international conference on terrorism, "are seeking chemical, biological and nuclear weapons. . . . We will not wait for the authors of mass murders to gain the weapons of mass destruction. We act now, because we must fight this dark threat from our age and save generations to come."

The turning point in American foreign policy from coalition to unilateralist was not only September 11, 2001, but also the anthrax scare that caused panic in October. One wonders what the French president's reaction would have been if terrorists had poisoned the Paris water supply. He, too, might have gone through the roof.

TWO

Forgotten by History

Some of our greatest Americans are totally forgotten today. History books do not proclaim their exploits. Yet in their day they were enormously well known—and deservedly so. They were men and women of high achievement. They include a presidential candidate expected to be the next George Washington, a businessman-philanthropist who enriched the lives of millions, and a man who wrote the best-selling book of the nineteenth century—in one night. History has not been kind to them.

Take the man who discovered America, for example. He did all the hard work: importuning Queen Isabella to give him funding, sailing off into the far blue yonder where no one had ventured before, quelling mutiny by his frightened men, and establishing once and for all the New World. Then why is America not called the United States of Columbia?

Columbus missed the history boat—literally—because he was too busy exploring to do his propaganda. His mate Amerigo Vespucci was more aggressive. In 1499, after leaving Columbus's employ, he signed on with another expedition and made four voyages to Brazil. In 1504 several letters appeared, written by Vespucci, claiming he was the captain—which he was not—of the four voyages to *Mundus Novus*, or the "New World." He wrote letters to his Florentine benefactors, offering vivid descriptions of the new continent. "This land is very delightful, and covered with an infinite number of green trees and very big ones that never lose their foliage . . . [the] multitude of wild animals, the abundance of pumas, of panthers, of wild cats . . . of so many wolves, red deer, monkeys . . . so many species could not have entered Noah's ark," wrote Vespucci. Then he moved on to the sexual activities of human beings: "Their marriages are not with one woman but with as many as they like . . . when their children . . . the girls, reach the age of puberty, the first man to corrupt them must be their nearest relative." As for cannibalism, Vespucci had a few words on that subject as well: "One of them confessed to me that he had eaten the flesh of more than 200 bodies."

In 1506 a compilation of Vespucci's letters was published in pamphlet form, titled *The Four Voyages of Amerigo Vespucci*. For the next twenty-five years it was a bestseller, published in some forty editions, and outselling the dull journals of Columbus by three to one. In 1507 a book of geography appeared, *Cosmographiae Introductio*, identifying the new continent as "America." The author eventually realized that Vespucci's claims of discovery were false and soon removed the name

America, but by then it was too late: Vespucci's bestseller had won the day.

Of course, also left out in the naming sweepstakes were John Cabot, who discovered North America (Newfoundland) in 1497, and Juan Ponce de Leon, who in 1513 discovered what would become the state of Florida. Cabotia? Poncedelonia?

History is brutal in who becomes famous and who doesn't. Said Theodore Roosevelt after leaving office in 1910, "If there is not the great war, you don't get the great general. . . . If Lincoln had lived in times of peace, no one would know his name now."

Indeed, we had one president who today is almost totally forgotten for just the opposite: he steadfastly refused to go to war, and was voted out of office because of it. He would have to rank as one of our most courageous presidents, a man who put principle ahead of expediency: John Adams. He belongs in our panoply of forgotten heroes.

History is replete with examples of situations or people who never got their fair mention because it benefited no one to have the truth known. The Spanish-American War, with its rich prizes of Hawaii, Puerto Rico, Wake Island, Guam, and the Philippines, plus the glory of Theodore Roosevelt and his Rough Riders, is well known. Not well known, however, is the postwar aftermath: our war against Emilio Aguinaldo and the Philippine insurgents, an even bloodier conflict than the war against Spain. Or take World War

I: we all know it as a war against Germany. Russia was our ally. Actually, America was waging a secret war against the Bolsheviks, with more than fifteen thousand American troops involved. We won the war against Germany, but we clearly failed in our underground war in Russia, thus leading to a seventy-year Cold War.

A Signature Worth Millions: Button Gwinnett

➤**1776** Today, of course, nobody knows this man with such a delicious name, but we include it here because it is so amusing. He was one of the signers of the Declaration of Independence, appearing near the huge signature of John Hancock.

And who was this man? A nobody, comparatively speaking. But wait! There is more to the story—a story of immense riches made possible by his own obscurity. Born in England, this young man sailed to America in 1765, opened a store, and by good fortune became a delegate to the Continental Congress of 1776 and signed accordingly. Next year he got into an argument, fought a duel, and got killed. So much for Button Gwinnett—a footnote to history.

Years passed, and when it became clear that America had won the war and the Declaration of Independence was now a document of immense historical value, autograph hunters started gathering up all the autographs they could find. All the other fifty-four signers being significant men, they had no problem—except they could find no document ever signed by that ultimate nobody who had died so early, Button Gwinnett. The price of a Gwinnett signature skyrocketed, worth far more than the signatures of his more illustrious colleagues.

Had he been mayor of New York, there would have been at least five hundred documents he had signed. Had he been a major land owner, there would have been numerous land deeds with his signature. Had he been a merchant, there would have been countless bills of lading with his now-precious signature. But there was nothing. American historians and autograph-hunters bid fabulous prices, but to no avail. Where was the autograph of this mysterious man, Button Gwinnett? Without him, no collection of American heritage could be complete.

Then suddenly he reappeared. Not in America, but in England. In the village of Wolverhampton, an antiques collector stumbled upon some committee minutes that included the missing signature, signed long before Gwinnett had emigrated to America. This discovery caused a flutter on two continents: here, at long last, was the missing signature on the most important document in America.

William Shakespeare once said, "Some are born great, some achieve greatness, and some have greatness thrust upon them." One of the last was Button Gwinnett.

Ten Presidents Before Washington

➤**1781**   The creation of the presidency first occupied by George Washington derived from eight years' experience with a presidential office occupied by no fewer than ten men under the Articles of Confederation. Some historians have gone so far as to argue that the first president of the United States was John Hanson. (John who?)

Anyone who thinks the short-lived Articles of Confederation belong in the dustbin of history would be contradicted by no less than Abraham Lincoln. When South Carolina and other Southern states seceded, Lincoln refused their action by referring not to the Constitution but to the Articles of Confederation, whose formal name is "The Articles of Confederation and Perpetual Union." In a hard-hitting speech to Congress on July 4, 1861, Lincoln reminded the South of its solemn oath, saying, "The express plighting [pledging] of faith by each and all of the original thirteen in the Articles of Confederation, two years later, that the union shall be perpetual, is most conclusive."

Prior to 1789, several governments ruled the colonies. The first was the First Continental Congress, of 1774, which asserted the rights of the colonists to be free of absolute British authority; this was followed by the Second Continental Congress, of 1775, which appointed George Washington as General of the Continental Army. The name of this government was "The Continental Congress in the United Colonies of America," best known for passing the Declaration of Independence in 1776. Then, as the war dragged on and it became apparent that conciliation would never be possible, the government adopted a more assertive name by substituting "States" for "Colonies" (drawing upon the Declaration of Independence, which had declared the "United Colonies" to be "free and independent States").

On March 1, 1781, as victory over the British appeared imminent, the "Continental Congress in the United States of America" ratified the Articles of Confederation and changed its name to the "United States in Congress Assembled." This was the beginning of the new nation, defined by the Articles as "A Perpetual Union between the states of New Hampshire, Massachusetts-bay, Rhode Island and Providence Plantations, Connecticut, New York, New Jersey, Pennsylvania, Delaware, Maryland, Virginia, North Carolina, South Carolina, and Georgia."

The British surrendered in 1781. Washington was inaugurated in 1789. During those critical first eight years of independence, ten men ran the country.

The first "President of the United States in Congress Assembled" was Samuel Huntington of Connecticut. But there was a problem. The Articles specified that the president could serve no longer than a year. Because Huntington had been the president of the Continental Congress since

1779, he had been in power well beyond the one-year term limit now mandated by the Articles of Confederation. Huntington solved the problem by accepting the job, then resigning after five months.

The nominee to be his successor, Samuel Johnson, declined the nomination altogether. "Yes, that is correct," says one historian. "Someone actually refused after the ballots were cast to serve as President of the United States."

Quickly replacing Johnson the next day was Thomas McKean, under whom Congress signed the peace treaty with Great Britain. McKean, a signer of the Declaration of Independence, continued in Pennsylvania politics after his brief four-month tenure and is best remembered today as the man who turned down his party's 1804 nomination to be Thomas Jefferson's vice president. His reasoning was simple. In a letter to Jefferson, he wrote: "Presidents of the United States in Congress Assembled in the year of 1781 (a proud year for Americans) equaled any merit or pretensions of mine and cannot now be increased by the office of Vice President." Such were the early beginnings of low esteem for the office of the vice presidency.

Next came John Hanson of Maryland, who, because he took office just after the Revolutionary War ended and served the full one-year term (1781–82) as the first presiding officer of what was now called the United States of America, is given credit by some historians as America's first president.* While historians and legal scholars split infinitives over historical trivia (one historian even going so far as to sue the U.S. government in court for overlooking Hanson), one fact acknowledged by all is that Hanson was the first man to use the presidential title. Whereas his predecessor signed his resolutions, "United States in Congress Assembled, Thomas McKean President," Hanson signed his as "John Hanson, President of the United States in Congress assembled."

He also was called "His Excellency," as were all presidents at the time. But titles and salutations do not a president make. When Washington became president and the members of Congress started addressing him as such, he told them to stop, he would have none of it. "Mr. President" would do, and so it has continued to this day.

After Hanson came Elias Boudinot of New Jersey, Thomas Mifflin of Pennsylvania, Richard Henry Lee of Virginia, John Hancock of Massachusetts, Nathaniel Gorham of Massachusetts, Arthur St. Clair of Pennsylvania, and Cyrus Griffin of Virginia. Of these notables, only two are known today: Richard Henry Lee as the great-uncle of the famous Confederate

---

* For the final word on this dispute, listen to Abraham Lincoln: "A lamb has four legs and one tail. You can call his tail a leg and say he has five legs. However he still only has four legs and one tail. Doesn't matter what you call his tail . . . it's still only a tail." Either Washington was our first president or he was our eleventh—take your pick—but our first was not John Hanson.

general, and John Hancock for his enormous signature on the Declaration of Independence ("big enough for King George to see without glasses!" he roared at the signing).

Why this obscurity? For two reasons: the privacy of deliberations, and the lack of executive power. The members of the Confederation Government had taken an oath of secrecy not to record or publish any of their debates. This oath bound not only the congressional delegates but also the president and his chief officers, the secretary of finance, the secretary of state, and the secretary of war. The United States in Congress Assembled kept journals, but only to record resolutions and a "minuscule amount of official correspondence deemed necessary to enter into the public record." Lost forever were thousands of documents, which nowadays, had they been recorded and preserved, would represent a treasure trove for historians. No documents, no "history."

The presidency in those early days was more like being the head of the UN or NATO, a deliberative job with no real executive power other than that permitted—and voted upon—by the member states. The president could negotiate and sign peace treaties, but could not raise taxes to pay for the Revolutionary War's massive debts. Despite this handicap, all these presidents served their country with distinction, some with considerably greater skill than their successor "presidents." Samuel Huntington, the man who had led the Continental Congress

to ratify the Articles of Confederation unanimously, used his considerable clout to get Congress to go along with Robert Morris's controversial plan to create a national bank and a national budget for the United States. When Congress ran out of money—a frequent occurrence—Huntington stepped in and paid the bills himself.

For an example of presidential character, one need look no further than Elias Boudinot. When John Jay, John Adams, and Benjamin Franklin ignored President Boudinot's instructions that France be included in the 1783 peace negotiations with Great Britain, Boudinot overlooked the rebuff and gracefully accepted what his negotiators had accomplished.

The most distinguished of these unknown presidents has to be Arthur St. Clair. Born and raised in Scotland, St. Clair immigrated to America and became a general in the Continental Army, playing a prominent role in Washington's victories at Trenton and Princeton. In 1783 some three hundred mutineers from the Continental Army marched on Philadelphia and threatened to overthrow President Boudinot's government unless they were paid. When the Pennsylvania militia failed to respond to Congress's plea for rescue, St. Clair personally negotiated with the mutineers and averted the crisis. When another rebellion occurred in 1787—the attack by Daniel Shays and six hundred farmers on the arsenal of Massachusetts—the states quickly called St. Clair to the rescue once again, this time by electing him president. St. Clair put

Arthur St. Clair (painting by Charles Willson Peale)

the rebellion down, but recognized—unlike his predecessor presidents—that any long-term solution required a stronger government. He became the leading advocate of the resolution for a Philadelphia Convention to revise the Articles of Confederation. In another act of leadership, St. Clair initiated and secured congressional approval for what Daniel Webster called the single law that exceeded all others in "the effects of distinct, marked, and lasting character." This was the Northwest Ordinance of 1787, which expanded the United States to include the territories north and west of the Ohio River, but under the strict condition that there be no slavery. This was revolutionary. Upon leaving office, St. Clair became governor of those territories now

occupied by Ohio, Indiana, Illinois, Michigan, and parts of Minnesota and Wisconsin. Those lands, at the time, constituted more than half of the United States.

More important than his leadership in the westward expansion of the United States, including forbidding slavery, is St. Clair's leadership in paving the way for a new, more effective government. What president today would argue for a constitutional convention to redefine his job and create a new form of government? Yet there are those who argue that is exactly what is needed: the Constitution of 1787, created for an agrarian nation of four million people, is out of date for an industrial nation approaching 300 million people, and has resulted in a federal government that is too centralized and powerful. Thomas Jefferson thought that the Constitution would have to be revised every generation or so, just as "a man outgrows a boy's suit." Anyone expecting an Arthur St. Clair to emerge from today's Washington DC culture will be waiting a long time.

A major dilemma facing our constitutional form of government today is excessive presidential power. Almost surely, Thomas Jefferson would be jumping up and down, urging revision of the Constitution: "Time to make a new suit!" He might refer to the eight years from 1781 to 1789—equivalent to two modern terms—when a revolving door of presidents did no great harm. There were no scandals or abuses of power. Given that almost all twentieth-century presidents have had disappointing final years in their second terms, and that the job is "a hard one, a very hard job" (as George W. Bush said in his second debate with John Kerry in the 2004 election), shorter terms and more presidents may be desirable.

Our Nation's Capital

►**1790** The selection of a site along the Potomac River for the nation's capital had nothing to do with the beauty or geographic convenience of the place. It was the result of good old-fashioned pork-barrel politics.

In 1790 the powerful treasury secretary, Alexander Hamilton, was deadlocked in a political struggle with his *Federalist Papers* coauthor and the most powerful member of the First Congress, James Madison of Virginia. Hamilton, trying to force the American "confederation" of states into a tighter union, wanted the national government to have the power to tax and pay off the debts of the Revolution; Congress, consisting primarily of states-righters, balked.

Under a deal with the Jeffersonians, Hamilton agreed to let the national capital, then in his native New York City, go to Philadelphia for ten years, then on to a permanent home in Virginia. Virginia provided the swing votes to change the House of Representatives' 29–33 "nay" vote into a 33–29 "aye," and the bargain

was consummated. Hamilton got his assumption bill, and Virginia got a capital city with all the new construction jobs and other perks that would ensue.

For this city, the Founding Fathers specified that it incorporate a radial layout of the streets from major circles; it must have no rectangular blocks as in Philadelphia (and later New York). Reason: fearful of armed insurrection, the Founding Fathers envisioned the larger circles as military bases for armed soldiers to maintain control of the streets in case of mob violence.

❦

Who designed Washington, D.C.? Everyone will say it was L'Enfant, the French architect who laid out the master plans for the city. In actual fact, the truth is more complicated. L'Enfant, a hot-tempered individual, got fired and went back to Paris, never to be heard from again. Out of spite, he also took all the architectural drawings and maps with him. The situation got so desperate that Thomas Jefferson gathered together the American architects and told them to start all over again from scratch. Fortunately there was a mathematician on the team who had a prodigious memory: a black named Benjamin Banneker. Banneker told Jefferson he remembered everything and could reproduce the drawings. Sure enough, two days later Banneker returned with exact drawings as if L'Enfant had never left. It was a stunning achievement, and so today we have the beautiful city of Washington DC "a monument to Banneker's genius." Who was Benjamin Banneker, and why wasn't he a slave?

Banneker was the man who broadened Jefferson's horizons and helped make Jefferson great. When millions of Americans and foreigners visit the Jefferson Memorial in Washington DC and enthrall themselves with the powerful words "All Men Are Created Equal" and "Life, Liberty and the Pursuit of Happiness," they should remember that Jefferson was a slave owner who once wrote, "Blacks are inferior to whites in the endowments both of body and mind." Jefferson changed his views upon meeting Benjamin Banneker, inventor of the first clock in America, renowned scientist, and author of widely read almanacs. Jefferson entered into a long correspondence with Banneker concerning the mental capacities of the Negro and the whole question of slavery, recommended Banneker's almanacs to the Academy of Sciences in Paris, and got Banneker hired by President George Washington as L'Enfant's surveyor. Upon Banneker's death in 1806, in England William Pitt placed his name in the records of Parliament, and in France—the very country of L'Enfant—the Marquis de Condorcet lauded him before the Academy of Sciences. In his home country, America, alas, Banneker is totally forgotten.

Banneker was not a slave because of an act passed by the Maryland legislature in 1681, whereby children born of white servant women and Negro men were free. Benjamin Banneker's mother was a free mulatto who purchased a slave and then married him. Born of a free mother, he also was free.

Facing Down the Mob

➤**1799**   Not many presidents would undertake a policy that virtually killed their prospects of reelection. But when that policy was the only policy that would prevent other, more hot-headed politicians from plunging the nation into war, perhaps courage is called for. After the deed was done, and he lost reelection, he would look back many years later and say it was his proudest achievement. He wrote, "I desire no other inscription over my gravestone than 'Here lies John Adams, who took upon himself the responsibility of the peace with France in the year 1800.' "

John Adams does not appear on anybody's list of America's great presidents. He served only four years, squeezed in between the two great luminaries Washington and Jefferson. But John Adams did more than just keep good company; he kept his integrity in an impossible situation—a situation far worse than what his predecessor or his successor had to face, a situation almost as dire as what Abraham Lincoln was to confront sixty years later.

America after the Revolution was a weak nation, surrounded by enormous territories controlled by Britain, France, Spain, Russia, and various Indian tribes frequently aligned with foreign powers. Managing those tricky relationships was so important that the second-most-powerful position in the U.S. government was the secretary of state. Recognizing America's weakness, President George Washington developed a policy of strict neutrality that did not always make him friends. He renounced the French-American treaty of alliance, which made the French angry, and sought better relations with the queen of the seas, Great Britain. In 1795, with great reluctance because it was not a favorable treaty but was the best he could get under the circumstances, he signed the Jay Treaty, providing for limited maritime freedom. The treaty was so humiliating that Washington found his house besieged by hundreds of angry citizens, his mail tampered with, and incriminating letters bearing his forged signature being circulated by his enemies. Washington left office almost as angry as Nixon. He gave a "Farewell Address" urging "entangling alliances with none," and quickly retired to the peaceful world of Mount Vernon.

The French, sensing America's weakness, upped the ante and became even more aggressive than the British. In short order, France seized some three hundred American ships, sent a general on a reconnaissance mission down the Ohio and the Mississippi, hired the head of the Creek Indians to become a general in the French army, encouraged Quebec to become a French colony, and began discussions with Spain to take over Louisiana and Florida. When the U.S. sent a new minister to France, the French made their contempt known: they refused to receive him. President Adams then sent a delegation to Paris to seek rapprochement. For several months the delegation members cooled their heels, unable to get a meeting. Finally the French minister, Talleyrand, condescended to receive the delegation, subject to payment of £50,000 and a loan of $10 million for American "insults."

People in America howled with rage. Anti-French war hysteria swept the nation. Congress, acting on its own and sometimes without even consulting the president, voided all treaties with France, raised taxes for a massive naval buildup, and even voted on a resolution to declare war (it fell short by only a few votes). The U.S. Navy—authorized by Congress over the president's strong objections—began an unofficial war with France that lasted more than two years and resulted in the capture of more than eighty French ships.

Trying times. During all this, President Adams refused to yield to "the mob." He trusted his own judgment: "I know more of diplomatic forms than all of you," he told his fellow Federalists—a bluntness that obviously did not enhance his popularity. Adams further angered his party colleagues by continuing to support his secretary of state (and chief political rival), the pro-French Thomas Jefferson. Unable to unify his party, he lost the 1800 election to Jefferson, who continued his policy, which has lasted now for more than two hundred years.

As for the bellicose Federalist Party, it quickly vanished. America, thanks to Adams and Jefferson, survived. Adams's gravestone had the last word.

The Next George Washington?

►**1822** He was so highly regarded he was compared to George Washington. In an age of legislative giants—Clay, Webster, Calhoun—he was ranked the best. "The wisest man in Congress," said Henry Clay. "The most influential member of the House of Representatives," said John Quincy Adams. Offered the position of secretary of war by two presidents, Madison and Monroe, he turned it down for a life in the legislature, where he dominated debates on banking and internal improvements. Chairman of the House Ways and Means Committee at age thirty-two, he was destined to become the youngest-ever president at age forty-two.

Admitted his chief antagonist in Congress: "The highest and best hopes of the country look to William Lowndes for their fulfillment." But William Lowndes never became president. Today he is totally unknown.

How easy it is to forget: to become president of the United States you've got to be alive (!!).* William Lowndes died at age forty, two years before the 1824 election. On top of that, all his memoirs and biographical data were destroyed in a fire. A modest man, he declined to have his features immortalized in marble. When Samuel F. B. Morse was preparing his famous painting of the Sixteenth Congress, Lowndes declined to participate. There is no portrait of him anywhere; the only memory of what he looked like is a caricature done after he refused to sit for a painting. En route to England, he died and was buried at sea, leaving "neither headstone nor common grave to mark his passing."

William Lowndes

---

* And, once elected, to stay that way. In 1900, Mark Hanna, chairman of the Republican National Committee, was scared "that dammed cowboy"—Vice President Theodore Roosevelt—would become president should McKinley die. He sent the newly reelected President McKinley a cable: "Your duty is to *live* for four years." Shortly thereafter, McKinley was assassinated.

Observed one historian of presidents, federal judge Leslie Southwick, "It is as if there existed a conspiracy of obscurity against this statesman. William Lowndes has almost completely faded away, proving that early promise, even the presence of genius, is not enough to preserve a politician in history if he dies too young."

"The Eighth Wonder of the World," Worthy of Ozymandias, King of Kings

My name is Ozymandias, king of kings:
Look on my works, ye Mighty, and despair!
Nothing beside remains. Round the decay
Of that colossal Wreck, boundless and bare,
The lone and level sands stretch far away.

—Percy Bysshe Shelley
"Ozymandias," *1818*

►**1825** Shelley's famous poem is a paean to Osymandias, the Greek name for the Egyptian king Rameses II, whose statue across the Nile River from Luxor bears this inscription: "King of King am I, Osymandias. If anyone would know how great am I and where I lie, let him surpass one of my works."

You don't expect a great idea to come out of a debtors' prison, but that's precisely what happened. Jesse Hawley, a merchant from upper New York State, was sentenced to twenty-four-months' con-finement in debtors' prison. During his stay, he dreamed about a mighty canal that would transform New York's landscape and commerce. Writing under the rather grand name of "Hercules," he produced fourteen essays detailing his vision, even recommending a specific route. Several years later, in 1817, the State of New York executed Hawley's dream and began an ambitious eight-year project to build the world's longest canal, 363 miles. At the time there were only three canals in the United States longer than two miles. A recent twenty-seven-mile canal project had ended in failure. The federal government—thinking the whole enterprise impossible—refused to have anything to do with it, so the New York State legislature plunged ahead and authorized a bond issue with the grandiloquent sobriquet that the canal would "promote agriculture, manufactures, and commerce, mitigate the calamities of war, enhance the blessings of peace, consolidate the Union, advance the prosperity and elevate the character of the United States."

Indeed it did. Finished in 1825, the Erie Canal was the engineering feat of the nineteenth century. Some called it the Eighth Wonder of the World. Certainly it was the only such wonder ever built by the labor of free men, and not by slaves or by forced conscription. Paid eighty cents a day, aided by horses, the workers dug up and removed 11.4 million cubic yards of rock and earth—more than three times the volume of the Great Pyramid of Egypt.

Even more remarkable was the engineering. America had no trained civil engineers then. The project was undertaken by two amateurs, one a judge and the other a surveyor. Asked the Albany legislature: "Who is this James Geddes and who is this Benjamin Wright . . . what canals have they constructed? What great public works have they accomplished?"

Obviously such a project would not attract financing today, but then was then—the age of amateurs—whereas now we live in an era of bureaucracy and professional credentialism. One historian, writing about canals in 1905, identified the key issue when he compared the Erie Canal's founders to the founders of the nation, Washington, Hamilton, and Jefferson: "These men were working for a cause, for the development of their native land, and not for personal gain and aggrandizement. . . . What they did not understand they conquered by diligent study, unwearied zeal, and sound common sense."

The parallel was particularly apt, for the Erie Canal was nothing less than the fulfillment of the Founding Fathers' dream to unify the nation. George Washington's great fear was that the western United States might splinter off from the original thirteen. "The western settlers," said Washington in 1775, "stand, as it were, upon a pivot. The touch of a feather would turn them away." At a time when western America had no choice but to use the rivers running through Spanish, French, and Indian territory, "the whole future of America would be at risk." It was essential to build canals to unify the new nation.

Enter DeWitt Clinton, one of the political giants of the day, called by Thomas Jefferson "the greatest man in America."* Clinton, after narrowly losing the 1812 presidential election to the Republican Party candidate, James Madison, had served as mayor of New York City and was now the governor of New York. Known as "the Father of the Erie Canal," he used his considerable clout to get the state legislature in 1816 to proceed with the canal construction. He did so by addressing head-on George Washington's "touch of a feather" issue:

> However serious the fears which have been entertained of a dismemberment of the Union by collisions between the north and the south . . . the most imminent danger lies in another direction. [A] line of separation may be eventually drawn between the Atlantic and the western states, unless they are cemented by a common, an ever acting and powerful interest. One channel, supplying the wants [and] increasing the wealth . . . of each great section of the empire, will form an imperishable cement of connection, and an indissoluble bond of union.

---

* A most remarkable compliment, coming from an adversary: Clinton was the leader of the Federalist Party, the opposition to Jefferson's Republican Party.

A magnificent achievement

The physical obstacles to executing this vision were formidable. Between the Hudson River and Lake Erie was a rise of almost six hundred feet, requiring eighty-three locks to be filled with water to enable the barges to float up and down from one level to the other. One of the locks is almost as high as Niagara Falls. To cut through the rock, considerable blasting was necessary. But no matter the obstacles, the project got done and became such an economic success that it recouped its cost in nine years. Freight rates dropped more than 95 percent from one hundred dollars to four dollars resulting in an explosion of trade (the volume of wheat trading, for instance, skyrocketed 275-fold in twelve years). The state of New York became known as the Empire State, and New York City quickly eclipsed the larger cities of Boston and Philadelphia to become the dominant city it is today. Thanks to the canal, thousands of immigrant farmers traveled west to settle and develop the rich farmlands of Ohio, Indiana, and Illinois.

Connecting the Great Lakes with the Hudson River and the Atlantic Ocean may be a feat worthy of Rameses II, but as always, Osymandias beckons. Nothing lasts forever. As boats grew in size, the canal had to be made bigger. Designed for boats with a capacity of thirty tons, the canal went through two major renovations, completed in 1862 and 1918, to accommodate boats carrying 250 tons. In the process, parts of the canal were abandoned and the expanded canal rerouted to rivers and other canals to make a larger system of 525 miles, now renamed the Barge Canal.

With the emergence of railroads and trucks, the heyday of the canal was over, and the New York State Barge Canal eventually ceased commercial freight operations in 1994. Today, defaulting back to its original name, the canal and its towpath are used for small boats and bicycles to promote tourism. The U.S. Department of Transportation has a National Scenic Byways Program to "help recognize, preserve and enhance" 126 selected roads of particular historic, cultural, or recreational value, but the Erie Canal apparently is not one of them. A search of the program's website (www.byways.org) yields no mention of the Erie Canal, just part of the canal now called the Mohawk Towpath Scenic Byway (though the Mohawk Indians had nothing to do with building it).

As for DeWitt Clinton, the ten-time mayor of New York who made the Erie Canal possible, his backers planned on a large memorial to be built in front of New York's City Hall. The memorial was never built, and today's bloggers ask the inane question whether he was possibly related to a later Clinton named Bill.

The Crime of the Century, Committed in the Name of God

➤ **1857** A group of religous fanatics pulled out their guns and knives and slaughtered 120 men, women, and children. The outrage included cutting off fingers to get valuable gold rings. "They were not only scalped," said one witness, "but . . . their throats cut from ear to ear and heads severed from their bodies." The killers justified their massacre in the name of a higher being, and gave "thanks to God for delivering our enemies into our hands."

And who were these people? They were the Mormons, who had immigrated to Utah to create a kingdom of God. Their leader, Brigham Young, ran a dictatorial theocracy. He espoused the doctrine of "blood atonement," justifying the killing of people to cleanse their souls of sins, as deemed by him as the tribe's sole judge, jury, and executioner. When a Mormon minister in Arkansas was killed for his polygamous behavior, and rumors ran amok that the United States was sending an army to assert greater control over Brigham Young's theocratic realm, tensions in Salt Lake City ran high. "Woe, woe to those men who come here to unlawfully meddle with me and this people!" thundered Young.

At about this time, a wagon train of 137 people from Arkansas heading for California happened to stop in Utah for a week's rest. The Mormons, fidgety and nervous, resolved to kill them and keep their eight hundred cattle and sixty horses as booty. As a cover-up, they recruited a local Indian tribe, the Paiutes, to lead the attack (with some Mormons, disguised as Indians, participating). When the five-day siege failed, the Mormons resorted to a dastardly ruse: coming forth as saviors and waving a white flag, they offered safe passage out of the valley of Mountain Meadows. The emigrant party members accepted, innocently surrendered their guns, and were promptly massacred. Only seventeen children under age seven were allowed to survive. The bodies of the dead were stripped of all clothes and jewelry, and left unburied for the wolves and coyotes. After hearing of the massacre, Brigham Young claimed he went to God and asked "if it was a righteous thing that my people have done in killing those people at Mountain Meadows. God answered me, that the action was a righteous one, and well-intended."

Three weeks later the corpses were discovered by another wagon train passing through, and the U.S. Army started asking questions. Brigham Young ordered his people to stonewall and put all the blame on the Indians. Anyone who didn't obey would have God to fear: "Unless you . . . will keep secret of all you know, you will die a dog's death and will be damned, and go to hell." Almost everyone obeyed. Two years later, agents of the federal government conducting an inquiry managed to find fifteen surviving children and return

them to their Arkansas relatives, but only after paying ransom to the Mormons, who had the audacity to demand money for feeding the children whose parents they had murdered.

Also passing through the area and hearing the gossip was Mark Twain, who reported the massacre to Eastern newspapers and wrote in his classic, *Roughing It*, "The whole United States rang with its horrors." His report calling Brigham Young "an absolute monarch" who "laughed at our armies" became one of the most widely known stories in the country. But with the Civil War in full rage, the Mormon scandal looked as though it would fade away.

After the war, the U.S. government resumed its investigation. In 1874 a book was published exposing the Mormon Church, *Tell It All*, with a preface by Harriet Beecher Stowe. By 1875 the government had collected enough evidence to go to trial, only to find that putting together an impartial jury in a land of Mormons was nigh impossible. The trial resulted in a hung jury, with the prosecutors accusing the Mormon Church of colluding to prevent key witnesses from testifying. Two years later the government tried again, in what was quickly dubbed "the most important criminal case ever tried in the United States." This time it succeeded. To minimize the inevitable defeat, the Mormons and Brigham Young put up one of their own—Brigham Young's adopted son, no less—as the ringleader of the massacre.

"A crime that has no parallel in American history for atrocity," said the U.S. superintendent of Indian Affairs after visiting the site of the Mountain Meadows massacre (picture from Harper's magazine, 1859)

The man was promptly convicted and executed.

In a land of religious fanatics, the message that the Mormons had committed murder never registered. They were the righteous ones, and for one of them to die to spare the others was in keeping with tribal code. In the words of the modern Western novelist Larry McMurtry, describing the man who had been sacrificed by Brigham Young:

He took the massacre in stride, and so did many of his co-participants. Many of them felt genuinely indignant when they were finally linked to this crime they had committed so long ago. Some may have convinced themselves that they were off hoeing that day. A lie sustained for twenty years can come to seem like the truth.

To this day, the Mormon Church has never fully acknowledged its role in America's most infamous massacre. In 1998, the head of the church spoke at the dedication of a new memorial at the Mountain Meadows site. "It is time to leave the entire matter in the hands of God," he said. "It cannot be recalled. It cannot be changed."

But it can be remembered. There is hardly a history book of the United States nowadays that mentions what was considered at the time the "darkest deed of the century."

It is a day easy to remember: 1857, September 11.

America's Greatest Invention/Innovation

►**1895** The Commissioner of the U.S. Patent Office proposed to Congress that the Patent Office be closed down. His reasoning? All the great inventions had already been made. Preposterous? Actually he had a point:

• The period from the end of the Civil War to the end of the nineteenth century was the "Golden Age of Invention," captured very well by the greatest world's fair of all time, the 1893 Chicago Columbian Exposition. During this thirty-five-year period the U.S. Patent Office issued more than half a million patents. This was the era of the telephone, the camera, the sewing machine, the typewriter, the lightbulb, the phonograph, and the motor-propelled people mover. Steam and electricity replaced human labor, wood, and iron. Crude oil and petroleum came into being. Railroads connected North to South and East to West, heralding an unprecedented age of expansionism and self-confidence.

• When new inventions came along, people couldn't possibly imagine what to do with them. A century ago, many thought a major use of the telephone would be listening to opera in their homes.

What the patent commissioner overlooked was the importance of "innova-tion"—from which almost all "inventions" come. The American experience is replete with examples of ingenuity and creative inventiveness. In the American Revolution, for example, the basic weapon was the simple musket. Only it wasn't so simple. The musket was a handmade weapon, requiring "months for skilled artisans to fashion into a working weapon." Whenever a part broke or malfunctioned—a common occurrence—the musket had to be sent back to the shop and completely rebuilt (every part had to be individually forged and fitted until it worked). To equip an army of ten thousand men, it took years to accumulate enough firearms, plus thousands of armorers to perform the necessary maintenance and repairs once the fighting started. The British Army had a much larger force than did the colonists during the American Revolution, but it also had a major problem: a ten-year backlog of repairs for muskets. Imagine taking your gun into a shop for repairs and hearing the proprietor say to come back in a decade, it should be ready then. No wonder the British packed up their bags and went back home.

In 1798 the U.S. War Department issued a request for ten thousand muskets. Eli Whitney, mired in litigation over his cotton gin, saw a way out of his financial troubles and put in the low bid. He had never made guns before. Lacking craftsmen like the traditional gun manufacturers, he had no choice but to try to find ways to simplify the manufacturing process for nonskilled workers. He never came up with a perfect method, and finally delivered the muskets only in 1809, but he set in process what has become the Holy Grail of manufacturing.

America's greatest commercial innovation is interchangeable parts. It is the key to the production of clocks, cutlery, tools, hardware, sewing machines, printing equipment, agricultural implements, bicycles, electrical equipment, conveyors, elevators, automobiles, and computers. No one brilliant scientist invented it, no one exclaimed "Eureka!" It is the result of thousands of American tinkerers trying to simplify and make things better. The process continues. Nowadays the modern parallel to gun manufacture is the software industry, where handcrafted software is giving way to software created and assembled from components.

The Number-One Bestseller

▶**1899** One evening after dinner, Elbert Hubbard sat down at his typewriter and in an hour banged out a 1,500-word book that became the number-one bestseller in American history.

The day after the book was published, Hubbard got a telegram from the president of the New York Central Railroad, asking for 100,000 copies. The buyer subsequently increased his order to 500,000. The book then spread by word of mouth, was reprinted in more than two hundred

magazines and newspapers, and got translated into thirty-seven languages. A copy of the book was distributed to every railroad employee in Russia. During the 1904 war between Russia and Japan, copies fell into the hands of the Japanese, who concluded "it must be a good thing," and so, by command of the emperor himself, it was given to every person in the Japanese government and military. Over the next ten years *A Message to Garcia* became the book to sell the most copies ever during the lifetime of the author. Over the next several decades, according to the Grolier Electronic Encyclopedia, it became the fifth most widely distributed book of all time (after the Bible, Mao's *Quotations*, Noah Webster's *American Spelling Book*, and Jehovah's Witnesses' *The Truth That Leads to Eternal Life*).

A Message to Garcia sold more than 40 million copies and countless reprints, and influenced the attitudes of a generation of Americans. The book's message: the importance of character. The hero, asked to perform a dangerous mission and deliver a message to a general hiding in the woods of Cuba, did his duty: he did not ask where Garcia was, who he was, what the message was, or "why me?" He simply delivered the message.

Today the book is totally forgotten because it picked the wrong war: the Spanish-American War. Other great wartime books that swept the country and galvanized public opinion—Tom Paine's *Common Sense*, Edward Everett Hale's *The Man Without a*

Country, and Harriet Beecher Stowe's *Uncle Tom's Cabin*—picked more significant wars.

But more important, the book is forgotten because times are different: character is not popular nowadays; personality is. Observes one historian, "At the same time that the number of books emphasizing character has declined, the number emphasizing personality has soared." In the early 1900s, people placed great emphasis on proper attitude. "My heart goes out," *A Message to Garcia* concludes, "to the man who, when given a letter for Garcia, quietly takes the missive, without asking any idiotic questions, and with no lurking intention of chucking it into the nearest sewer, or of doing aught else but deliver it. . . . Civilization is one long, anxious search for such individuals."

It still is. (Because the book is so short—a four-page pamphlet, really—curious readers can find it on the Internet.) In the words of one Amazon.com reviewer, the book "is a quick read and reminder that the world is in desperate need of people who spend less time complaining, pondering, posturing, posing, back-stabbing, you name it . . . but actually get things done."

A Far Cry from Enron

➤ **1900** Today, as we recoil from the incredible greed of Enron, we should remember the three wizards of electricity

Mission accomplished: the messenger, with General Garcia

who gave us a great gift, sacrificed quick riches for their dream, and treated their employees well. They set a standard for modern-day corporate behavior.

Electricity is one of those modern-day conveniences we take for granted. (Electricity as the primary source of lighting for U.S. households skyrocketed from 3 percent in 1900 to 35 percent in 1920 to 79 percent in 1940 to 99 percent in 1960.) But imagine yourself during a perpetual blackout, wandering from room to room holding a candle or a flashlight, lacking the juice that makes possible the computer, the TV, the refrigerator, the air conditioner, the elevator . . . And to whom do we owe this great gift? Not to the well-known Thomas Edison—he developed a technology that never caught on. Our debt is to three men, the first a dreamer who invented the winning technology, the second an industrial entrepreneur who backed the dreamer and won "the war of the currents," and the third a business tycoon who developed the means to distribute electricity cheaply. All of them plowed all their wealth back into their businesses to keep growing. In so doing, they overextended themselves and lost their companies to their creditors; two of them died penniless.

The Dreamer, Ahead of His Time

"Now, my friends, I will make you some daylight." And with that, he would press a switch and the room would be flooded with electronic rays penetrating his body and lighting up the entire room, leaving onlookers spellbound. To this day, nobody dares replicate this feat.

During the 1890s and early 1900s, when the most exciting technology of the day was electricity, the foremost physicist was Nikola Tesla, father of alternating current, the basis of today's electricity distribution system. He was one of the most famous men in the world, a celebrity as well as a scientist. Living in high style in New York, eating lunch every day at his personal table at the Waldorf-Astoria, entertaining such luminaries as Mark Twain, J. P. Morgan, and William K. Vanderbilt, Nikola Tesla made front-page newspaper copy. As far away as London, people were talking about the New Wizard of the West—and they weren't talking about Thomas Edison.

At a critical moment in his career, Tesla threw it all away in pursuit of his dream. "Mr. Westinghouse," he said, "you will save your company so that you can develop my inventions." And with that, he tore up his contract for royalties for alternating current that would have made him a multimillionaire many times over. He paid the price. Always running around trying to finance his myriad inventions, he never fulfilled his potential and died, lonely and penniless, in a hotel room forty years later.

"Tesla is a man who is always going to do something," grumbled Edison. Certainly there was no greater innovator than Edison, a man who developed a huge research laboratory turning out hundreds of products. But science depends on theory as well as innovation, and there was no better theoretician than Tesla. As every patent lawyer knows, there is very little new under the sun; almost every patent is the practical implementation of dreams publicized by earlier, unsuccessful inventors. Hence the common saying among patent-seekers: "Our ancestors were very dishonest. They stole all our best inventions." Nikola Tesla was such an ancestor, the ultimate dreamer whose prodigious scientific experiments form the basis of modern-day radar, tube lighting, X-rays, MRI, robotics, rocket engines, solar energy, and Star Wars. He had 111 U.S. patents and more than seven hundred worldwide.

Tesla never did fulfill his dream of wireless transmission of energy (imagine a motorless car, or a boat being propelled by a signal!). Nor did he realize his other great dream, conservation of nonrenewable resources. Wind and solar power, he argued, should be developed to save coal, wood, and oil. So radical was this idea at the time that other inventors laughed, especially Thomas Edison, who argued that shortages would not occur for "more than 50,000 years." The forests of South America alone, claimed Edison, could support the world for that long.

According to the esteemed *Encyclopaedia Britannica*, only three Americans score among the top ten people whom subscribers call to get more information on. They are Abraham Lincoln, JFK, and Nikola Tesla. (Thomas Jefferson and Benjamin Franklin rank high, but fall outside the top ten.) When *Life* magazine in 1930 did a compilation of the one hundred most influential people of the past thousand years, it included Tesla. A year later he appeared on the cover of *Time* magazine with the caption "All the world's his power house."

Yet Tesla hardly appears in the history books. Look up *radio*, and the inventor named is Marconi, even though the U.S. Supreme Court invalidated his patents as "absurd" and awarded the discovery to earlier patents filed by Tesla. Look up *electricity*, and far more is written about Edison, even though his technology lost out to Tesla's superior technology.

Tesla is not an easy subject for historians. A lifelong bachelor, he lived and worked alone, leaving few witnesses to explain how he achieved his scientific feats. Lacking strong financing, he rarely pursued his demonstrations through to the point of developing workable prototypes that succeeded in the marketplace. When he died, his papers were seized by the U.S. government, concerned that his insights into particle beams and other military matters might fall into enemy hands. What remained after full vetting was shipped off to his birth country, what is now Serbia, many papers missing. He left behind no great scientific treatises or teams of well-trained assistants to carry on his work.

Yet his memory lives on. In 2006 a group of high-powered Silicon Valley investors, led by the two cofounders of Google, announced the startup of an electric car company ready to take on Detroit. Their first car would be a sportscar capable of zero to sixty miles per hour in four seconds—faster than a Ferrari. In naming itself Tesla Motors, the company modeled its vision after a man who thought big.

Inventive Wizard and Industrial Entrepreneur

No other businessman can boast of having beaten *both* Cornelius Vanderbilt and Thomas Edison in their respective fields— railroads and electricity. During his business career he produced an average of one invention every six weeks, backed with 361 patents, all of which he defended vigorously. He formed sixty companies that employed fifty thousand people—making him the largest employer in the United States. Most remarkable of all, in an age of tycoons he was a tycoon as rich as the rest of them, but he was not a robber baron. He was scrupulously ethical, and treated his employees generously.

In terms of immortality, this worked to his disadvantage. Unlike Vanderbilt and other buccaneers of the Gilded Age, George Westinghouse did not crush competitors or flout the law. He was never the subject of any high-profile government investigations. Happily married for forty-seven years, he was never embroiled in any personal scandal—no exciting copy for newspapers here. In fact, just the contrary: he disdained publicity. He rarely gave in-

terviews. He hated to be photographed, and to this day only a half-dozen photographs of him exist. He did not preserve his personal letters or papers. Only two biographies have been written about him, and none since 1926. Over the years his companies disappeared in mergers and takeovers, and when his major company took on the name of its media subsidiary CBS, and was dismantled in the late 1990s, all the historical archives disappeared.

One has to search the history books long and hard to find a great American treated so shabbily by history's benign neglect.

When America's largest life insurance company in 1907 announced the appointment of three new directors, it sent out a press release as follows: "Grover Cleveland, ex-President of the United States; Morgan J. O'Brien, Justice of the Supreme Court of New York, and George Westinghouse."

This man who needed no introduction started his career at age twenty-two, when he filed his first patent in 1869. Putting his creative mind to the great industry of the future—railroads—he invented the first system of using compressed air to bring trains to a halt. Needing money to start a production plant, he went to Cornelius Vanderbilt to try to interest him in investing in his new company. Vanderbilt would have none of it: "If I understand you, young man, you propose to stop a railroad train with wind. I have no time to listen to such nonsense."

Within a year the Westinghouse Air Brake Company became the industry standard, and the biggest customer of "stopping railroad trains with wind" was Vanderbilt. To this day, air brakes based on Westinghouse's technology are still used for railroads, trucks, and buses. Also used today are other inventions of Westinghouse concerned with railroad safety and yard switching equipment. Moving beyond railroads, Westinghouse invented and manufactured equipment for drilling and distributing natural gas. Also at this time, the telephone came into use. All telephone calls were routed through a central switchboard, each call on its own single wire; Westinghouse invented a way to reduce the wiring by creating substations for routing calls; thus the modern switched telephone network was born.

George Westinghouse

Then came the great growth industry: electricity. The problem with getting electricity from the power station to the consumer was that power decreased with distance, meaning that for Edison's invention of the lightbulb to work, houses and offices had to be within fifteen miles of a power station. This meant a lot of business for Edison's company manufacturing the generators (that company today is General Electric), but it was very costly and inefficient, and could only serve areas of high population density. An alternative technology was to send high power over distances, then use a transformer to reduce the power to a safe level at the point of consumer use. Westinghouse resolved that this was the wave of the future, hired Nikola Tesla to develop the technology, and installed the nation's first AC power network. Thereupon ensued "the battle of the currents" between Edison's direct-current system and Westinghouse's alternating-current system, which Westinghouse won conclusively. When the Columbian Exposition world's fair opened in 1893 with its stunning displays of light beams, the company that provided all the lighting and electrical systems was Westinghouse Electric, not General Electric.

Having established his technology as the winner, Westinghouse moved on to actual production. Within two years of his Columbian Exposition coup, Westinghouse set up the first long-range power network, at Niagara Falls. Other innovations pioneered by Westinghouse included an alignment system for enabling turbines, normally working at 3,000 rpm, to work with ship propellers that can do only 100 rpm. Such is the propulsion system used by virtually all ships today.

It is small wonder that an entrepreneur in so many capital-intensive businesses incurred a lot of debt to finance all his companies. In the Panic of 1907, the banks called in their loans and Westinghouse lost control of his company.

Westinghouse's most lasting legacy—one largely lost today—is the notion that a company's foremost obligation is to its employees (as opposed to its top executives). At a time when people worked six days a week, Westinghouse gave his employees a half day off on Saturdays. He paid his people top wages, and built a company town to provide his workers with affordable housing, indoor plumbing, and electric lighting. He was the first CEO to offer his workers a pension plan and paid vacations. His workers were so enamored of his generous compensation policies that they refused to form a union. Even Samuel Gompers, the famous labor leader, extolled Westinghouse: "If all employers treated their employees like Westinghouse did, there would be no need for unions."

Unlike other industrialists like Rockefeller, Carnegie, and Ford who incurred much labor unrest in their companies and re-created their image for posterity by forming large philanthropies to give away money, Westinghouse's priorities were just the opposite. "I would rather give a man a chance to earn a dollar than give him five and make him feel he's a 'charity case,'" he said. When advised that perhaps humanity might be better off if he devoted himself to pure research, he said, "Perhaps so, but think of the many men to whom I give employment. I can't stop now." That he created more new jobs for American workers than any other businessman, before or since, was his stellar achievement. He was the antithesis of today's CEOs who brag how adept they are at "outsourcing" to low-wage countries.

Power for the Masses

"Easy to give away a lot of money when you're rich and successful," cynics might say. To which we offer the remarkable story of Samuel Insull, the father of the electrification of the nation. Regarded in the 1920s as the most powerful businessman in America, Insull stuck to his principles and died a pauper. His social consciousness stands in sharp contrast to that of the executives of Enron, the energy giant of recent memory. For that reason alone, his story is worth telling.

Thomas Edison once said, "We will make electric light so cheap that only the rich will burn candles." Only he couldn't do it, he the promoter with no idea how to make it happen. To implement his vision he had to rely on his young finance manager, the English immigrant Samuel Insull. After twelve years under Edison, Insull left to take over a small electricity company in Chicago. At a most unusual farewell black-tie dinner hosted by Edison, attended by the fifty most powerful men in the electricity industry who were Insull's "most intimate friends and intimate enemies," Insull announced to the tycoons, "My new company will be bigger than General Electric."

Upon arriving in Chicago, he walked through the grounds of the Columbian Exposition of 1893, with its stunning display of electric lighting provided by Westinghouse Electric, and determined to waste no time electrifying the continent. He came up with the brilliant idea to cut prices below the normal cost of production, but still make money by slashing his costs even more through a realignment of the load factor from peak to nonpeak hours. Says the historian and former editor of the London *Financial Times*, Harold Evans, "Insull's concept of load and diversity factors was the single most significant innovation in the single most important technological advance of the twentieth century, the electrification of the continent."

Said Insull, "Here is an industry which supplies convenience and comforts to the day laborer, which kings could not command half a century ago." He provided electricity at one-third the price charged by utilities on the East Coast, yet made enough money to buy more than 250 companies. By 1929 he was providing one-

eighth of the nation's electricity, and gas, and became known as "the power wizard."

He was a financial genius robot, but he was "a robot with a heart." When Chicago's elevated railways went broke, he not only showed them how to reorganize their peak-load traffic capacity and start making money, he personally paid for new coaches and redecorating the stations. He also enforced a universal transfer pricing, and maintained good relations with unions. Unlike the robber barons of the day, he urged more—not less—public regulation: "No monopoly should be trusted to run itself." He helped set up the Illinois State Public Utility Commission to ensure better service to the public and enable utilities to invest to meet future demand—a model suddenly abandoned in the deregulation of the 1980s and 1990s (resulting, in 2003, in the nation's most extensive blackout as well as the nation's biggest corporate collapse, Enron).

As his empire grew, he gave away millions in anonymous gifts to widows, orphans, hospitals, and the Chicago Opera. He treated his employees well, paying them more to work forty-six hours than his competitors did to work seventy. He also gave them free medical benefits, night schooling, and a profit-sharing plan. He went out of his way to hire black workers who could not find employment elsewhere. When the Depression hit, he raised $10 million to pay the teachers, policemen, and firefighters in order to save Chicago from bankruptcy.

But when the Depression continued through 1933, Insull found himself over-extended. Advised to sell his stock short so that every time his share price dropped he could "reap billions and bankrupt every New York bank in the process," Insull blew up: "We can't do that. It would be immoral. We've got a responsibility to our stockholders. We can't let them down."

His decency cost him plenty. On the very day that Samuel Insull raised $10 million for Chicago's poor, the New York banks—angry that he had given most of his business to London banks—abruptly threw Insull's company into receivership in order to grab the best pieces for themselves ("asset stripping" is what it's called today). Insull and all the shareholders in his holding companies got wiped out, whereas the shareholders in his operating companies made out fine. In addition, because Insull had personally guaranteed several recent loans in a valiant effort to keep his companies afloat, Insull lost his homes and personal possessions, too.

A bitter Insull, forced out of his sixty presidencies and directorships, fled to Europe. Indicted by the U.S. government, he reluctantly returned to stand trial. The prosecutors had spent two years preparing their case, and FDR—who undoubtedly didn't know that an Insull company was supplying the power for his Warm Springs, Georgia, retreat—was giving speeches denouncing holding companies like Insull's and implying they had helped cause the Depression. In the city of Chicago, where 700,000 people were out of work, Insull's fate in court looked ominous indeed. It was one of the most celebrated trials of the century, with Insull making a dramatic appearance on the witness stand to clear his good name. The trial took fifty-four days and generated a transcript of 9,500 pages. In deliberations lasting only two hours, the jury found him innocent of all charges. Insull returned to Paris, where he soon died, flat broke. In the meantime, during the Depression when some 40 percent of the stock of America's companies was worth nothing, the stock of Insull's utility companies maintained its value, dropping less than 1 percent. None of his companies went under, none of his employees lost their jobs, and all of his customers continued to enjoy cheap electricity. Even as late as the 1960s, Insull's companies were supplying one-eighth of America's electricity and gas—a remarkable longevity of social and economic performance equal to that of Henry Ford or Thomas Watson.

Compared to today's CEOs, why is Insull such a remarkable man? Because he put his employees and shareholders ahead of his own personal interests. Unlike Enron executives who stashed away money by building $10-million homes in tax-friendly Florida, where one's home cannot be taken away, Insull put up everything he had—and paid the price.

Entangled in Another Nation's Civil War

➤**1917** President Woodrow Wilson once said the Russian revolution was one of the greatest events in the history of mankind, comparable to 1776 in America.

He was referring to the first revolution—the March overthrow of the tsar, not the subsequent October Revolution led by Lenin. At a time of mounting social unrest in Russia, the loss of the tsar was not missed by anyone, including the tsar's many cousins who were rulers in Europe—none of whom rushed to his rescue or tried to save him.

At the urging of the British and French, who were active in Russia trying to support the new Russian government under Kerensky, President Wilson sent a military expedition to the port of Archangel on the White Sea in North Russia. A lot of troubles were soon to come, involving insufficient food and clothing supplies as well as disputes with the local British commander over who was in charge. Most troubling of all was the lack of popular support from the Russian population: the Russian peasants showed little inclination to support the Allied campaign against the Germans.

When the Kerensky liberal regime collapsed, Lenin and the Bolsheviks took over and signed a separate peace with Germany. The United States and the Allies now found themselves facing a Germany that could concentrate all its forces on the western front. They also found the Bolsheviks in a weak position, holding power only in Moscow and faced with opposition from no less than twenty-four separate governments "stretching from the Urals to Vladivostok with no common bond except a hatred of Bolshevism and a distrust of Tsarists." On a more urgent note, there were some fifty thousand Czech-Slovak troops trapped in Russia trying to get home to fight for the liberation of their country. In addition, several million tons of Allied military equipment were stored in warehouses in Siberia. To rescue the troops and equipment, France and Britain begged the United States for more troops. At the urging of the State Department, but against the counsel of his military advisers, President Wilson agreed to send a second expedition, this one to Vladivostok. "Europe and the world," he said, "could not be at peace if Russia was not." The U.S. now had fifteen thousand troops in Russia.

From the beginning, Wilson, a professional historian in his early days, was determined to restrict America's involvement to pure humanitarianism. "Europe had made a great mistake when they attempted to interfere in the French Revolution," he said. "The Russian people must solve their own problems without outside interference."

How fifteen thousand troops could be construed as anything other than interference, Wilson did not say. Lofty words often reflect muddled thinking, especially in international diplomacy. How Wilson and the State Department could possibly think a tiny U.S. force could hold its own against a Red Army of three million men was never explained. Certainly the Bolsheviks of Lenin were hardly about to spare any prisoners in their battle to prevail beyond Moscow. Arrayed against them were the Cossacks in Siberia, known as the White Army, with 250,000 men; they were equally ruthless. All along the Trans-Siberian Railroad, massacres, rapes, and looting were common. Even nurses from the International Red Cross were raped and murdered. Caught in the middle were U.S. troops fighting on one side one day and holding off the other side on another day. Back in Archangel, circumstances were no better. Executions of suspects, individual and wholesale, occurred daily. Prisoners captured by the Bolsheviks were brutally tortured and murdered, terrifying the local population exactly as intended. Unable to defend themselves, the peasant population increasingly blamed the Americans for the chaos. With Germany now defeated and out of the war, American soldiers despaired of being trapped in a never-ending war in a vast wasteland. "What are we here for?" became the popular refrain. One general, sent over from Washington DC to investigate, immediately agreed and urged withdrawal: "Original object of expedition no longer exists. Allies have not been received with hospitality." For the White Russians whom the Allies were

trying to help, intervention was even more disastrous in that it helped the Bolsheviks focus their propaganda on foreign "invaders" and deny the existence of a civil war.

For the Americans it was like Iraq would be eighty-five years later: a war undertaken in a large faraway land and hindered from the start by over-optimism, poor planning, insufficient troops, lack of clear strategy, and angry conflicts between the Defense Department and the State Department (except that in this case it was the State Department that was bellicose). President Wilson in his instructions made it abundantly clear that American troops were not to take one side or another, but in the middle of a civil war, neither local side was going to observe the rules set by an invading occupier claiming to be neutral. American soldiers sent on a humanitarian mission found themselves fighting for their own survival.

Soldiers' letters were censored to prevent any bad news from getting back home, but some letters got through. Said the *Chicago Tribune*, "Our men are dying for a cause, the purpose of which they are no more certain than we in America. America has not declared war on Russia, but Americans are killing Russians and are being killed by them." The isolationist senator from California, Hiram Johnson, famous for his epigram "The first casualty when war comes is truth," jumped into the fray and observed that the U.S. soldiers in Russia "served under conditions that were the most confusing and perplexing that an American army was ever asked to contend with." Some five hundred Americans died in the conflict. The last of the American soldiers came home in 1921, their mission to promote democracy in Russia a shambles. Unable to admit defeat—though it ranks as America's greatest military failure—the United States withheld establishing diplomatic relations until 1934, while Leninism ran rampant. Such was the sorry end of the war formally called the Allied Intervention into Russia, more accurately called by veterans the Frozen War, the Winter War, the Unknown War, the Secret War, the Forgotten War.

The Golden Age of Sport

►**1925** For almost five years he was the best left-handed pitcher in baseball. In his last full season he pitched an incredible thirty-five complete games out of thirty-eight starts, and won twenty-four. He pitched twenty-seven scoreless World Series innings—a record that lasted forty years—and his record for most shutouts in a season by a lefthander still stands. He compiled a lifetime winning percentage of .671 and an ERA of 2.28. Yet his pitching exploits are not recorded in the Cooperstown Hall of Fame. Why?

Because he went on to even greater ex-

ploits as a hitter, the Great Bambino, the Sultan of Swat: Babe Ruth. With a lifetime batting average of .342 and 714 home runs, he has to be the best hitter of all time. But he was also an amazing pitcher, so good in fact that when he announced his plan to become an outfielder and focus on his hitting, Hall of Famer Tris Speaker predicted, "Ruth is making a big mistake."*

The highest-paid athlete of the era was not Babe Ruth, who made $20,000 a year, but bike racer Fred Spencer, who made more than $100,000. The most popular sport in America was six-day bicycle racing, nonexistent in America now, but still popular in Europe. It was the most grueling sport of any, equaled only by heavyweight boxing: for six days, pairs of cyclists would race around an indoor track nonstop day and night, pausing only for naps and a quick meal of steak and eggs. Crowds went wild cheering as bicyclists, exhausted to the core, bumped into each other and sent each other sprawling on the wooden track, generating severe sprains and broken bones. But because cyclists were paid a percentage of the gate, a champion cyclist could earn as much as one thousand dollars a day. It was "a hard way to earn an easy living." In 1925, after a six-day race at Madison Square Garden in New York, a sports promoter arranged a dinner at the Wal-

---

* To amuse fans during pregame warm-up, he would put two baseballs in his left hand and throw them in such a way that the balls remained parallel to each other all the way to the catcher's mitt. No other pitcher in eighty years has been able to replicate this feat.

Dinner at the Waldorf-Astoria Hotel. Standing from left: baseball's Babe Ruth, heavyweight champion Gene Tunney, swimmer Johnny Weissmuller, and hockey player Bill Cook. Seated from left: tennis champion Bill Tilden, golfer Bobby Jones, and bike racers Fred Spencer and Charley Winters

dorf-Astoria Hotel for the eight greatest athletes of the day. Two of them were bicycle racers.

In 1950 the nation's sportswriters voted for the outstanding athlete of the first half of the century. Out of six leading candidates, one received twice as many votes as anyone else.

He was tennis star Bill Tilden. For seven years in the 1920s he was invincible, never losing a single major match anywhere in the world. The runner-up athletes in the 1950 voting were Babe Ruth, Jack Dempsey, Bobby Jones, Red Grange, and Johnny Weissmuller.

In 1950 the Associated Press voted it "the supreme athletic achievement of the century." It was not Babe Ruth's sixty home runs in 1927; by a margin of two and a half to one, it was Bobby Jones winning—with ease—all four major golf tournaments in 1930: the U.S. Open (for the fourth time in a row), the British Open (for the third time in a row), the U.S. Amateur (for the fifth time in a row), and the British Amateur (for the first time). It was such an astounding achievement that the phrase "grand slam" was invented. Weeks afterward, at the height of his career at age twenty-eight, Jones retired. Sixteen of the records Jones set in the U.S. Amateur still stand, more than seventy years since he last played the game. In what has been called "the Golden Age of Sport"—the 1920s era of Babe Ruth, Bill Tilden, Jack Dempsey, Gene Tunney, Red Grange, and Johnny Weissmuller—Bobby Jones stands out as the brightest star.

More than just a superb athlete, he was a gentleman. In a 1928 playoff match for the U.S. Open, Jones accidentally touched the ball as he was lining up to make his shot. Nobody noticed it, but Jones called a foul on himself. When the officials demurred that they had noticed nothing and would not call a foul, Jones insisted they do so. When the match finally ended, Jones had lost by one stroke. Afterward, when the chief umpire commended Jones for his integrity, Jones responded, "Do you commend a bank robber for not robbing a bank? No, you don't. This is how the game of golf should be played at all times."

Most remarkable of all, Jones only played the game three months out of the year. The rest of the time he was pursuing his education, earning a B.S. in mechanical engineering from Georgia Tech, a B.A. in English literature from Harvard, and spending a year in Emory Law School before dropping out because he had already passed the Georgia bar exam and didn't need to be in school anymore.

Never a man of brute physical strength like most great athletes, he explained the secret of his success: "Competitive golf is played mainly on a five-and-a-half-inch course, the space between your ears." He was talking about focus and concentration—exertions that caused him to lose as much as twenty pounds during a five-day match. But he forgot to mention qualities of the heart—modesty, humor, and grace—that won him devoted fans and made him the only man ever to receive two New York City ticker-tape parades. His favorite prize came in 1958, thirty years after he retired, when he was honored as a freeman of the city of St. Andrews in Scotland, the only American so honored since Benjamin Franklin in 1759.

By then he was in a wheelchair. Probably because of his ferocious swinging of a golf club without proper year-round training, he had damaged his spine and contracted syringeomyelia, a progressive disease like Lou Gehrig's that causes muscle atrophy. He accepted the fact that there was no cure. When he finally died in 1971, he weighed less than eighty pounds. Wrote the *New Yorker*, "As a young man he was able to stand up to just about the best that life can offer, which is not easy, and later he stood up with equal grace to just about the worst."

Old champions never die. In its eulogy for Bobby Jones and a bygone era, the *New York Times* wrote, "He is the idol for those who love the game for what there is in it, not for what they can get out of it."

The Towering Giant of the Civil Rights Movement

➤**1937** Not Martin Luther King Jr., but A. Philip Randolph, founder and president of the Brotherhood of Sleeping Car Porters from 1925 to 1968. Long before King became famous, Randolph had paved the way with his successful strike against the Pullman Company in 1937, his 1941 petition to end segregation in the defense industry, his 1948 march demanding an end to segregation in the military, and his facilitating the 1955 Rosa Parks sit-in in Montgomery, Alabama.

"You are truly the Dean of Negro leaders," Martin Luther King wrote to him in 1958. At the 1963 Washington Mall demonstration of 250,000 people—watched by millions of TV viewers around the globe—the lead speaker was not John Lewis or Roy Wilkins or Martin Luther King, it was the pioneer from the pre-TV days, A. Philip Randolph, then a seventy-two-year-old man making his last hurrah. "For more than forty years, he was a tower and beacon of strength and hope for the entire black community," said NAACP president Benjamin Hooks. Awarded the nation's highest civilian honor—the Medal of Freedom—by President Lyndon Johnson in 1969, Randolph faded into obscurity during the highly charged late 1960s and early 1970s. Never one who sought money or personal gain, he spent his last years alone in a Harlem apartment, and got mugged by local hoodlums who had no

idea who he was. Upon his death in 1979 at the age of ninety, his obituary in the *New York Times* appeared not on the front page but on page five of Section B (for metropolitan area news). Commented Hooks, "It's so sad because there are so many young people today for whom that name means very little."

But Woodrow Wilson knew. Many years earlier, his administration had branded him "the most dangerous Negro in America." So, too, did Franklin Roosevelt, who took a quite different posture and invited him to the White House. "You and I share a kinship in our great interest in human and social justice," he said. So, too, did Harry Truman, who agreed to desegregate the armed forces. So, too, did Richard Nixon, who greeted him warmly as "the grand old man of American labor."

Today, young people barely know the name, and they miss the opportunity to draw inspiration from a remarkable life story of determination and sacrifice. They miss the struggle of a man who "had no soles on his shoes. His blue serge suit, he wore it so long it began to shine like a looking glass. He came out sometimes with just his fare, one way. He had nothing else." In 1933, when his friend Fiorello La Guardia became mayor of New York and offered him a job with the city government at a desperately needed salary of $7,000 a year, Randolph turned it down. Regardless of his poverty, he kept his eye on the goal: "Nothing can keep us from winning." Offered the opportunity to run for Congress in a safe district, he declined. His entire life was devoted to advancing the cause of black workers in the labor movement.

Singlehandedly he took on the most powerful company in the United States, the Pullman Company, a fearful union buster. It took twelve years of work, but in 1937 there occurred the most dramatic moment in the history of American labor relations when the Pullman Company entered the negotiating session with Randolph's union and announced, to everyone's shock and surprise, "Gentlemen, the Pullman Company is ready to sign."

It was a defining moment in the fledgling civil rights movement, at a time when jobs and wages were the priority, not equal rights.

Hedy Lamarr

Hollywood with Brains

►**1940** Like Nikola Tesla, this person was one of our great scientists who never got credit because of being too far ahead of her time. Yes, she was a woman—and a Hollywood sex goddess at that. Singlehandedly, she changed the face of the U.S. missile defense system. Her radio-frequency patent eventually led to "spectrum technology," later used for guiding weapons in the Gulf War and now the basis for cell phones and Internet access.

At the peak of her career in 1940, known as "the most beautiful woman in the world," the Austrian-born Hedy Lamarr was at a

Hollywood dinner party, where she got into a conversation with composer George Antheil. She got so excited she left the party and scrawled her phone number in lipstick on his car windshield. Right away they got together, not for a love affair, but to develop her invention to beat the Nazis who had overrun her native Austria. Two years later Lamarr and Antheil got a U.S. patent for a "secret communications system" (filed jointly, but Antheil gave Lamarr all the credit).

In war, the only way a ship can adjust the direction of a torpedo toward another moving ship is by radio signal. The problem with radio communications is that sender and receiver need to send a message on the same wavelength in order to communicate, but a single wavelength can be easily identified or jammed by the target ship. Lamarr's idea was to "hop" from one frequency to another, so that the listener could not figure out what was going on. To do this, she and Antheil devised a system of eighty-eight frequencies, the same number of notes a piano has.

United States Patent #2,292,387 reads as follows:

> *This invention relates broadly to secret communication systems involving the use of carrier waves of different frequencies, and is especially useful in the remote control of dirigible craft, such as torpedoes. . . . Our system . . . employs a pair of synchronous records . . . of the type used for many years in player pianos, and which consist of long rolls of paper having perforations variously positioned in a plurality of longitudinal rows along the records.*

Lamarr's patent goes into great technical detail describing a sophisticated antijamming device for use in radio-controlled torpedoes, whereby a signal is broadcast over a random series of radio frequencies, hopping from frequency to frequency at split-second intervals: would-be eavesdroppers hear only unintelligible blips. The patent design utilized a mix of radio transmitters, modulators, relays, control logic, electric motors, pneumatic actuators, and suction pumps.

The U.S. generals were so dumbfounded by a Hollywood movie star telling them what to do that they ignored her idea and told her the best contribution she could make to the war effort was to give a kiss to every person who bought a war savings bond. This she did: in one evening she raised $6 million. Said the *New York Times*, "She knew what Nazism would do to this country because she knew what it did to her native country, Austria. 'I'm giving all I can because I have found a home here and want to keep it.'"

Alas, Lamarr's invention was so advanced that it could not be commercialized until 1962—three years after the seventeen-year patent expired. Even though her invention formed the basis of the $25-billion U.S. defense communications system, she earned not a dime. Remembered later only for her stunning beauty, she told *Forbes* magazine in 1990, "I guess they just take and forget about a person." Even more might-have-been sorrows were to come. In the 1990s, new patents based on Lamarr's invention led to the explosion of "spectrum wave" technologies that are now used in billions of computers, database systems, and cell phones around the world to ensure privacy. Hedy Lamarr, in the meantime, had gone through six expensive husbands and was reduced to living alone in a one-bedroom apartment in Miami, on a Screen Actors Guild pension and social security. But thanks to efforts of engineers at Lockheed Martin and other contractors who appreciated what she had created, and al-

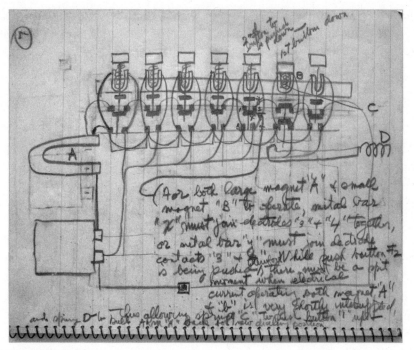

Lamarr's Journal

though she was too frail to attend, she received honors at computer technology conferences before she died in 2000. In 2002 she was inducted into the Electronic Design Hall of Fame (along with twenty-five others, including Marconi, Tesla, Steve Jobs, William Hewlett, and David Packard). Her inscription reads:

Lamarr and Antheil conceived the idea of "frequency hopping" to quickly shift the radio signals of control devices, making them invulnerable to radio interference or jamming. Truly ahead of its time, the system was never implemented by the military, in part because the technology of the time was inadequate. The system finally came into its own in the cellular telephone age. Now called "spread spectrum" instead of "frequency hopping," the basic idea is the same.

Winning Hearts and Minds by Preserving Civilization

➤**1943** "We are barbarians and we wish to be barbarians, it is an honorable calling," said Adolf Hitler. In five years the Nazi war machine had proceeded to loot many of Europe's finest museums and churches. Hitler, the high-school dropout who had failed admission to art school, fancied himself an arts connoisseur. With his sidekick Hermann Göring, he had embarked on the greatest art theft in history.

While the helpless Europeans dithered, the Americans sprang into action. Led by a group of museum curators and a Supreme Court justice, an ad-hoc group of concerned Americans prevailed upon President Franklin Roosevelt to create a committee with the grandiloquent name the American Commission for the Protection and Salvage of Artistic and Historic Monuments in War Areas. Roosevelt, eager to talk about "freedom from want" and "freedom from fear," was quick to add another freedom, saying, "The freedom of the human spirit and human mind which has produced the world's great art and all its science—shall not be utterly destroyed." Soon there was established a most unusual new group in the United States Army: the Monuments Men. Its mission was to protect historic and cultural monuments from war damage. Never before had there been an advancing army whose mission was to protect culture, not just kill.

The American generals fully appreciated this mission. "We are a conquering army, but we are not a pillaging army," said General Omar Bradley. Equally clear were instructions from General Eisenhower to his officers:

Inevitably, in the path of our advance will be found historical monuments and cultural centers which symbolize to the world all that we are fighting to preserve. It is the responsibility of every commander to protect and respect these symbols whenever possible.

"Whenever possible" did not mean "whenever convenient"—it meant: do it!

Enter the Monuments Men (also including several women and Europeans). Consisting of some four hundred museum curators and arts experts, many of whom were to go on to illustrious careers after the war, the Monuments Men were responsible for protecting monuments from bombing and vandalism. They researched areas targeted for bombing, and prepared aerial maps to help the bombers not hit churches and museums. So accurate were their maps that when the Allies bombed the art treasure city of Florence, virtually all the 160 bombs hit their precise targets—in sharp contrast to the retreating Nazis, who deliberately blew up almost all of Florence's bridges. As part of the armed forces, the Monuments Men risked their lives on the front lines to take possession of historical sites and monuments. Signs were put up, saying, "Out of bounds. Off limits. It is strictly forbidden to remove stones or any other material from this site. Souvenir hunting, writing on walls or damage in any form will be dealt with as MILITARY OFFENSES."

As the American troops advanced through Italy, Austria, France, and Germany, they were stunned at the war damage. As in World War I, the Germans had disregarded the Rules of Land Warfare, and used whatever buildings were most convenient for war purposes: bell towers had become sniper positions, churches had become housing quarters and ammunition depots, and bronze statues had been confiscated to be melted down. The Monuments Men took possession of these monuments, arranged to find workmen to begin repair work on the cathedrals, and secured guards to protect the frescoes and statues.

After securing the sites and churches, the Monuments Men shifted their focus to works of art. The condition of the museums was shocking. Anything not part of the culture of Greater Germany had been systematically looted or destroyed by the Nazis. In Florence alone, 50 percent of the art was gone. All over Europe, thousands of valuable art works were missing, including masterpieces by Titian, Pieter Brueghel, Claude Lorrain, Raphael, and Vermeer. Where were they?

Utilizing local contacts, the Monuments Men and Army soldiers scoured hundreds of towns. Venturing into remote castles and underground salt mines, many of them booby-trapped with explosives—one mine had 400,000 tons of dynamite—they uncovered thousands of paintings and art treasures. The volume was enormous: in one German castle alone so many items were found it took forty-nine trainloads to remove them. One mine, called Merkers, had thirty-five miles of tunnels filled to the ceiling with Greek and Roman works,

Byzantine mosaics, Islamic rugs, woodcuts, paintings, gold bars, bags of gold coins, and cartons of currency representing the bulk of Germany's national treasury. The mine was so big that two thousand soldiers had to be called in to guard and remove the contents for safekeeping. In addition, there were hundreds of thousands of other artworks that museum curators had stashed away in safe hiding places to protect them from theft or bombing. Here were found masterpieces by Botticelli, Rubens, Rembrandt, Michelangelo, and Leonardo da Vinci. Stored underground for four years and

Generals Patton, Bradley, and Eisenhower are shocked at what they find in an Austrian salt mine

coated with layers of mold growth, they looked "more like Camembert cheese than works of art."

Taking possession of all these paintings, sculptures, and rare books was one thing; still to be done was identifying who owned them—not an easy task. The Monuments Men set up collection centers for temporary storage and record-keeping. In partnership with the OSS and its newly created Art Looting Investigation Unit, they assisted in the long and laborious process of "identifying, packing, transporting, cataloguing, photographing, archiving, and returning" lost works of art to their rightful owners. It took them six years. By the time they had finished in 1951, they had emptied 1,400 repositories and shipped 3.5 million items.

Why was protecting cultural treasures so important? In a letter to his command-ers in late 1943, Eisenhower answered this question: "We are fighting in a country which has contributed a great deal to our cultural inheritance, a country rich in monuments which by their creation helped and now in their old age illustrate the growth of the civilization which is ours."

In winning hearts and minds, protecting the symbols of civilization counts a lot. After the war, drawing on the proven success of the Monuments Men, one of the Army officers proposed that such a team of arts specialists be made a permanent part of the Army. His suggestion was ignored.

Sixty years later, there occurred "The Rape of Iraq," where, right after the U.S. invasion of Baghdad, the National Museum of Iraq was looted of 15,000 treasures dating back to the days of Babylon.

American trucks returning tons of looted art back to Florence

It was a devastating black eye for the United States at a time when it was trying to win the support of the Iraqi people. In the midst of all the uproar about how the American army could allow such a sacrilege, Defense Secretary Donald Rumsfeld merely shrugged his shoulders and said, "Stuff happens."

Back in World War II, "stuff" didn't happen. In those days the American military did everything possible to help countries preserve their cultural patrimony. It was the right way to fight a war.

Anyone who thinks that history forgotten always stays forgotten, can consider the story of one man who displayed real initiative and get-up-and-go. In the late 1990s, after selling his Texas oil and gas exploration company, entrepreneur Robert Edsel took a sabbatical in Florence to study fine art and enjoy early retirement. But not for long. After learning about the Nazi plunder of artworks in World War II, he read Lynn Nicholas's book *The Rape of Europa*, and jumped into action. He located and interviewed fifteen living Monuments Men and many of their children, and created a foundation to support the memory of the Monuments Men and retrieval of stolen art. He hired researchers to search throughout Europe for pictures of lost art and destroyed museums. After assembling his research, he tried to find a publisher, and when no publisher was interested, he used his own money and published the book himself: *Rescuing Da Vinci*. Edsel subsequently went on to co-produce the 2007 award-winning documentary film *The Rape of Europa* and write another book, *The Monuments Men*.

"Explaining why efforts to save a cultural treasure are worth the risk of a human life is not easy," he says. "Yet history has provided us with the best answer. The cultural heritage of the world belongs to the future. Our future is diminished without them."

In these words he was echoing the spirit of one Monuments Man who was killed in the line of duty in 1945. In a lecture to his soldiers, this Army officer said, "No age lives entirely alone; every civilization is formed not merely by its own achievements but by what it has inherited from the past. If these things are destroyed, we have lost a part of our past, and we shall be the poorer for it."

Bipartisanship at Its Best

►**1941–44** The president was not pleased. An unknown junior senator had taken a campaign tour through the South, visited several military bases where he uncovered graft, won reelection, and was now pushing for a special "Senate Committee to Investigate the National Defense Program"—with himself as chairman. FDR hardly knew the man, and feared congressional interference in his management of the war. He had good history to go on:

there had been Senator Gerald Nye's disastrous hearings into war profiteering in World War I, and the Senate's interference with President Lincoln and the Northern generals, which Robert E. Lee had gleefully called "worth two Confederate divisions."

Reminded that the senator was a Democrat and that his party controlled both the Senate and the House, the president reluctantly agreed: at least it wouldn't be the Republicans doing a witch-hunt. The senator asked for an initial appropriation of $25,000. Lest his investigation "get out of hand," his fellow senators whittled the initial appropriation down to $15,000.

The first thing Harry Truman did once the committee started was go to the Library of Congress and borrow the only copy of a book describing the Civil War committee. He read it carefully, determined not to repeat old mistakes. He then went to the attorney general for help in finding a lead counsel. Finally, he instructed the members of his committee on clear objectives and proper protocol. The key, he told them, was speed—to uncover graft and corruption while the deed was fresh and something could be done about it, not finger-point and gain political points years after the fact. "We were interested in doing a surgeon's job to cure," he said later, "not in performing an autopsy to find out why the patient died." More specifically:

The committee was directed to examine every phase of the entire war program.

It was not organized to tell the war agencies what to do or how to do it. It was not to substitute its judgment for their judgment. . . . I was determined that the committee was not going to be used for either a whitewash or a smear in any matter before it but was to be used to obtain facts and suggest remedies where necessary.

It was a time when tensions were high: Nazi U-boats patrolling the East Coast were eating U.S. tankers for breakfast. The public clamored to know what was taking so long for the U.S. to mobilize and start going on the offensive.

Under the scrutiny of the Truman Committee, no one was spared. Corporations, dollar-a-year executives on loan to the government, military contractors, and labor unions all became culprits. The committee found that no less than sixty-six of the dollar-a-year executives were being paid their full salary on the side, and had succeeded in steering $3 billion of contracts to their companies within a year. It also found a pro-labor bias in the grants handed out by the government's chief agency for managing the war effort, the Office of Production Management. When union workers threatened a walkout at an aluminum mine, the committee exposed their blackmail and averted a showdown. Even government officials got excoriated: "Contract award agencies," said Truman, had become "infested with colonels whose military experience was limited to watching parades."

Within a year, an impressed Senate increased the committee's annual budget to $100,000, and the committee went into overdrive. Its output and impact were prodigious. It interviewed almost 1,800 witnesses, conducted 432 public hearings, held three hundred executive sessions, and issued fifty-one reports. Such high-powered activity put everyone on notice. Asked to explain why his committee was so successful, Truman pointed not to the regulatory reforms that were enacted, but rather to its real-time watchdog function:

A number of suggestions in the committee reports were enacted into legislation by Congress, but the influence of the committee was beginning to make itself felt through other than legislative channels. In many cases the mere knowledge that we were in-terested in a particular subject was enough to cause everyone concerned, whether manufacturers, government officials, or labor, to clear up the problems themselves before the committee could get to them.

The committee worked hard to be even-handed and fair. Before printing a report, Truman sent a copy to the company or agency being investigated and asked for comment—only on facts, not opinions. This prevented the accused entity from trying to claim later that "the Committee didn't know what it was talking about." The overall theme of the investigation was the common good. In settling a coal strike, Truman stated, "It is about time people on both sides of the controversy are giving up what they are clamoring for and think about the

Senator Truman and his committee: nothing like this today to oversee all the money we're spending in Iraq

United States of America." By sticking to the facts and eschewing controversy, the Truman Committee won the public trust. More important, by contributing to public understanding and reassuring the public that the war management was being improved, it helped generate public support for the war effort.

The Truman Committee ended up saving the government $15 billion. In 1943, Harry Truman was on the cover of *Time* magazine. In 1944, *Look* magazine conducted a survey of Washington correspondents and asked them to rate the civilians who had been most helpful to the war effort, after FDR. The winner was Truman. Later that year he became FDR's running mate. In looking back at the Truman Committee, one startling fact stands out: in all its reports, it achieved such bipartisan consensus that its Republican members never once felt the need to issue a minority report.

Fast-forward to America's longest and most expensive war, Iraq, where war profiteering and lack of oversight set new records. Columnist Arianna Huffington wrote in 2005, "With the president preparing to hit up Congress for an additional $80 billion for the war in Iraq, I thought it might be a good time to crack open a history book." Indeed, many people started brushing up on the long-forgotten Truman Committee. In 2007, Senator Charles Schumer of New York wrote:

The lesson of the Truman Committee is sorely in need of relearning today. . . . nothing even close to the Truman Committee has taken root in this Congress. To the contrary, a bipartisan proposal in the House to create a modern-day Truman Committee in the wake of reports of scandal and abuse in Iraq was "blocked from consideration by GOP leaders for more than a year."

Finally, in 2008 Senator Jim Webb of Virginia succeeded in getting an investigation committee passed. In sharp contrast to FDR, who accepted the committee's recommendations and made its leader his running mate, President Bush called the new committee "a threat to national security."

THREE

The Past Was Different Then

"The past is "a foreign country," a place full of surprises, a place quite different from present-day perceptions. This is especially true of technology: the automobile, for example, was once viewed as a useless contraption because it couldn't go over dirt fields like a horse. Same for the telephone: Why would a person in Maine ever want to talk to a person in Texas? Indeed! Why not write a letter?

So whenever we are confronted by change, we limit our ability to perceive reality by standing on the present. Our grandchildren will view us differently. Just go back fifty-plus years, when Detroit ruled the world. It was a time when the "Big Three" controlled more than 90 percent of the American automobile market—plus a good portion of the overseas market as well. The popular magazines of the 1950s "predicted that the world of 2000 would feature commuters traveling to work in atomic-powered cars and personal helicopters," yet they made no mention of personal computers. Go back another fifty years—to 1900—and cars were virtually nonexistent. In New York City, people relied on horses. Long before people had heard of global warming, the key issue of the day was horse waste. Every day horses deposited

2.5 million pounds of manure and 60,000 gallons of urine. Every year some 15,000 dead horses had to be collected off the street and taken away.

Ask people what was the greatest achievement of the twentieth century, and most people will say "the automobile," "computers," "putting a man on the moon," or "the Internet." But go back one hundred years, and different answers emerge. In 1900 the male life expectancy was forty-six years; now it is seventy-three. For females it was forty-eight; now it is eighty. The number of Americans completing high school in 1900 was 6 percent; today it is 85 percent. Would you not agree that the improvement in health care and the spread of education, permitting nearly 300 million Americans to live fuller lives, are the century's stellar achievements?

Go back another forty years, to the outbreak of the Civil War. In 1860, what was the largest industry in America? Flour milling. Go back another twenty years, and what was the biggest? Exporting ice to India and the Caribbean.

If we go back to our early past—to the American Revolution—we might easily wonder why the British walked away after eight years of stalemate. After all, they had lost no major battles other than Yorktown, and still had the world's mightiest army and navy. They could have kept fighting another couple of years if they had wanted to. Then when they waged war again and clearly won the second time (the War of 1812), they still refrained

from pressing their advantage and seizing territory. Why?

America at the time was no prize jewel. Says the historian Gerald Gunderson:

When Britain acceded to independence for the Americans, she yielded them all the territory out to the Mississippi River, most of which was unsettled. Moreover, in the following sixty years, that area was more than tripled as Americans possessed all the land to the Pacific Ocean. The British assumed all this vacant territory would keep the Americans safely preoccupied for a long, long time. Extrapolating from the rate of settlement in the Colonial period, it would take them "three hundred years to reach the Mississippi River, and a minimum of six hundred more to reach the Pacific!"

When Thomas Jefferson consummated the Louisiana Purchase, he never expected the United States would spread across the entire continent: the distances were too great. He predicted it would be a thousand years before the American frontier reached the Pacific Ocean, and that the land might split up into two confederations, one up to the Alleghenies, the other beyond. In looking where the United States might expand, he cast his eyes in a different direction and identified his prize as Cuba: "the most interesting addition which could ever be made to our system of states." The meanderings of a Monticello dilettante? Hardly. Even John Adams, an experienced political pro, viewed the annexation of Cuba as nothing less than "indispensable to the continuance and integrity of the Union itself."

Thomas Hart Benton, the expansionist senator from Missouri, certainly had first-hand knowledge about expansion and Western territory. His view? The U.S. should stop at the Rocky Mountains, and whatever occurred westward of that point should separate itself "from the mother Empire as the child separates from the parent." Daniel Webster agreed, calling for the creation of an independent Pacific Republic.

Understanding the past takes imagination. Continues Gunderson, "It is hard to visualize a time when owning a few books denoted wealth, and donating a thousand volumes was sufficient to have colleges such as Harvard and Yale named for you." Indeed!

Imagine the Bill of Rights, a document taken for granted by all of us, only not always so. For many, the Bill of Rights was too radical, too incendiary, too "un-American." In 1923, Upton Sinclair, the famous author and candidate for governor of California, was arrested by the Los Angeles police for reading from the Bill of Rights and charged with expressing ideas "calculated to cause hatred and contempt" of the United States government. He was held for twenty-two hours before a lawyer got him off.

A question that frequently comes up has to do with American behavior during the Nazi Holocaust. During World War II the Nazi war machine killed more than six million Jews; the response of the Allies was passive at best. At times the Allies even looked the other way. The U.S. War Department was urged by the War Refugee Board to bomb the industrial installations and mass-extermination equipment at Auschwitz. The United States refused because such an effort would be "an unwarranted diversion of planes needed elsewhere."

The War Refugee Board persisted. Armed with secret information from the Czech underground concerning supply routes, key bombing locations, and train schedules, John Pehle, director of the board, proposed that the Allies bomb the railway lines from Hungary to Auschwitz. Assistant Secretary of War John J. McCloy turned it down: "The War Department is of the opinion that the suggested air operation is impracticable. . . . It would not amount to a practical project." When pressed again with a positive example of how Allied pilots had successfully precision-bombed a French prison, McCloy still demurred. Auschwitz and Birkenau, he said, were one thousand miles into enemy territory. "The positive solution to the problem," he wrote, "is the earliest possible victory over Germany."

Many people now criticize FDR's handling of the Jewish rescue question. PBS in the early 1990s aired a TV program indicting FDR for "deceit and indifference." In his defense, historian Arthur M. Schlesinger

Jr. points out that FDR was the strongest and most consistent opponent of Hitler, and had appointed so many Jewish professionals to high positions that some called his administration "the Jew Deal." In addition, FDR continually had to maintain popular support for World War II and keep public attention focused on the main issue: to defeat Germany (not to rescue Jews). Before World War II started, the U.S. had admitted more refugees from Germany and Austria than all other Western countries combined. But FDR was not about to make a crusade out of his quiet efforts to save Jews.

"The attack on FDR," says Schlesinger, "shows a striking disregard of historical context."

For a similar example of how revisionism disregards the historical context, consider the rising reputation of Herbert Hoover today. In the 1932 presidential election, Herbert Hoover never knew what hit him. After having implemented aggressive tax cuts to revive the economy, and having enacted the most progressive legislation in history, he was getting attacked from the left for not doing enough—to be expected, perhaps, at a time of widespread economic crisis and thousands of people losing their jobs. What really flummoxed him was the attack from the right. His opponent, Governor Franklin Roosevelt, accused him of being irresponsible and busting the budget.

If we take Hoover's actions and Roosevelt's words literally, then the argument can be made that Hoover was a progressive and Roosevelt's New Deal was merely an evolution, not a revolution. Indeed, many historians today are seeking to embellish Hoover's reputation, and over the past fifteen or twenty years Herbert Hoover has risen in the ranking of presidents. Yet the fact remains: the voters threw out Hoover because they didn't feel good about a man who, regardless of his humanitarian and administrative skills and his having been the only president ever to donate his entire salary to charity, could utter incredible statements such as, "Many people have left their jobs for the more profitable one of selling apples."

Our First 200 Years: What Took America So Long to Develop?

➤**1600** When America celebrated its Bicentennial in July 1976, everyone knew the nation was two hundred years old. How quaint America was back then, with men wearing powdered wigs and writing with quill pens! How far the nation had come in such a short time!

Actually there was another two hundred years that most people forget: the first two hundred. The Declaration of Independence occurred a full 284 years after Columbus, 189 years after the second Virginia colony, and 169 years after Plymouth Rock. What took America so long to develop?

"The American economy got started late," explains one historian. European governments and trading companies in 1600 were reaping phenomenal returns of more than 200 percent a year from their ventures in India and Russia. America could not match this return, for three reasons:

High Barriers to Entry

Because England and Holland controlled almost all the eastern seaboard, anyone trying to start a settlement needed to get a charter from the home government. This required having a good agent in London or Amsterdam to mount a lobbying campaign. The agent also needed to attract private investment syndicates to put up the money. Because America was a new, highly risky market, investors were demanding in their appraisal. Only ventures headed by an experienced governor, and offering a clear business plan for generating exports to repay investors, got funded.

Lack of Indigenous Trading Opportunities

The East India Company model for making money—shipping manufactured goods to Asia in exchange for local products—did not work in America because tradeable indigenous products did not exist, and the local economy was not sufficiently developed to generate trade in its own right. Instead of being a trading post, a settlement in America had to become large enough

to become economically self-sufficient, including generating its own exports. This took many decades to accomplish.

Lack of High-Value Specialty Items

America had abundant natural resources, but not the kind of high-value items like gold or silks that could justify the cost of transporting them many thousands of miles to developed European markets. The only local product that was profitable was furs—and Canada was a better place to hunt for furs. It was not until the 1700s that the colonists were able to master the trick of extracting concentrated value out of cheap raw materials. Successful colonial innovations included pig iron, potash, barrel staves, whale oil, and tobacco.

❧

In sum, America during the first two hundred years was a struggling territory, rich in land and agricultural resources, but too large and too thinly populated to make economic sense.

In 1763, when Britain signed the Treaty of Paris, obtaining Canada in return for Martinique and Guadeloupe, the British public rose up in rage. They were even more upset when the British government gave away Cuba and the Philippines to Spain in return for Florida and all Spanish territory east of the Mississippi except New Orleans. What did Britain want a North American continent for, with its wild, uncleared land offering little in the way of natural riches? Far more valuable were the Caribbean islands, which offered sugar and trade.

Gory Times

➤**1675** Some forty years after its founding, this training school for the ministry almost went belly-up. Enrollment had dwindled to just twenty students. The school's sole assets consisted of a president's house, a small brick Indian school that was used as a printing shop, and a run-down college hall containing a library, a dormitory, and lecture rooms. Forced to face the reality of the school's "languishing and dying condition," the state legislature terminated all salaried professionals; within a month, seventeen of the twenty students had dropped out. The school went begging to the Massachusetts legislature, but to no avail: the legislature had the Indians to worry about.

In the following year, 1675, there occurred King Philip's War, between the European settlers and the Indians, in which twelve towns were burned to the ground and the state incurred debts that exceeded the value of all personal property in Massachusetts. The college's future president prayed to God to cut off the head of the Indian leader; within a week his prayers were answered, and the Indian chief's head was delivered to the college, where the president-elect's son, a sophomore, took

pleasure in personally removing the jaw. Gory times.

That school became Harvard University.

Colonial Anti-Tobacco Lobby

➤**1700** In America today, the anti-tobacco lobby continues to grow, with more and more government regulations and public buildings insisting on a smoke-free environment, whereas in Europe smoking is much more common.

It used to be just the reverse. Tobacco originated in Virginia, and flourished there to such an extent that there arose the popular saying, "Virginia's prosperity is based on smoke," whereas in Europe the reaction to tobacco was rabidly negative. In the early to mid-1600s, King James I of England wrote a treatise on tobacco in which he called it "a custom loathsome to the eye, hateful to the nose, harmful to the brain, dangerous to the lungs, and in the black stinking fumes thereof nearest resembling the horrible Stygian smoke of the pit that is bottomless." The pope forbade members of the church to use snuff. In Transylvania (now Romania), farmers found to be growing tobacco would have their farms confiscated. In Russia, by order of the tsar, anyone caught smoking had his nose cut off.

The rationale behind these government attitudes toward tobacco—pro in America and con in Europe—had nothing to do with health or polite manners, but with economics. Tobacco is extremely demanding on the soil, and requires ever-expanding amounts of land just to keep production constant. Europe, aware of the need to maintain land to be able to raise sufficient food, recognized the shortsightedness of cultivating tobacco. Colonial America, with millions of new acres available, never had this constraint.

Slow Communication

➤**1777** Slow news shaped history. In the American Revolution, General Burgoyne suffered a dramatic defeat at the hands of the Colonial forces at Saratoga on October 17, 1777. During the month of November several members of the British Parliament pushed a plan to offer significant concessions to the independence movement in the colonies. They got nowhere. Reason? The British had no idea they had just lost a pivotal battle. The news of Saratoga didn't reach London until December 2, by which time it was too late to appease the colonists.

The same thing happened in the Civil War, when the British and the French were relishing the prospect of the South winning. Not only were the two European nations conducting a major smuggling and trading operation with the South, but a divided United States meant less of a threat to them and opened up the possibility of their getting involved in Mexico.

Every day with bad news for the North moved them closer and closer to the point where they could formally intervene on behalf of the Confederacy. Fortunately for the United States, news took several weeks to cross the Atlantic. In August 1862, when Prime Minister William Gladstone was writing to the British cabinet on the hopelessness of the Union cause, and Foreign Secretary John Russell was sarcastically writing "how the Great Republic of Washington degenerated into the Democracy of Jefferson; they are now reaping the fruit," the Union had just suffered a devastating defeat at the Battle of Bull Run. Had Great Britain known about the Bull Run rout when it occurred, it almost surely would have intervened, thus ending once and for all the noble experiment called the United States.

Today we criticize Congress for not being able to make tough choices, hammer out compromises, and get bills passed. We look back with envy on the Constitutional Convention, when fifty-five delegates who barely knew each other met and managed to produce an entire Constitution. What is the major reason they were able to do this, whereas we cannot seem to do it today? "I wonder," says historian Don Gifford, "if a constitution for the United States could have been achieved at the Constitutional Convention in Philadelphia if each of the delegates from twelve of the thirteen ex-colonies had, at the least sign of disadvantage to the interests of his state, been able to pop out into the hall and telephone his home state for instructions? As it was, requests for instructions were infrequent and took days to arrive by courier or packet boat. Meanwhile, the discussions at the convention proceeded both in heat and at leisure. One could argue that the Constitution was achieved precisely because the delegates were and remained discussants, partially incommunicado, not the pawns of immediate instructions from the home office, not pulled up short if a bright compromise occurred to them during a walk in the woods."

People measured time not in hours or minutes, but in months. Said Thomas Jefferson, speaking of the American minister to Spain: "I haven't heard from him in two years. If I don't hear from him next year, I will write him a letter."

Just prior to the War of 1812, the British government announced it would repeal a major irritant to the Americans, namely its policy of searching neutral vessels on the high seas. Many British expected that amicable relations would resume. They were wrong. It took fifty days for the news to reach the United States, by which time it was too late: America, unaware of the British repeal on June 16, had declared war on June 18. The fighting continued. At the end of the war, Andrew Jackson won the hard-fought Battle of New Orleans on January 8, 1815. What he did not know was that the British, two weeks earlier on Christmas Eve, had already surrendered and signed the Treaty of Ghent in Paris.

Oh, for want of a telegram! Lamented the British statesman and philosopher Edmund Burke: "Seas roll and months pass between order and execution."

❧

When news did arrive, it came by messenger—only one copy. This lack of immediate confirmation or follow-up call could allow the recipient to pretend he never got the news—and carry on business as usual. In 1804 the brilliant commodore of the American naval forces attacking the Barbary pirates at Tripoli got word from President Jefferson that he was being replaced as squadron commander. Commodore Edward Preble kept the news secret. In the few weeks he had remaining before his successor arrived, he went on a rampage and quickly won three major sea battles that had the enemy reeling. Despite these victories, no word of his successes reached America quickly, and so he was forced to relinquish command "like a boxer who has his opponent on the ropes, his right hand raised for the knockout blow, only to hear his manager throw in the towel!" He returned to the United States to a hero's welcome, a congressional citation of appreciation, and an invitation for dinner at the White House. But because of the slow news, there was nothing the president could do. Preble and Jefferson must have had a gloomy dinner.

Fast-forward to 1859. For two years Edwin Drake, a former railroad conductor with no experience in geology or engineering, had pursued a wild dream that there was oil deep down beneath the hills of western Pennsylvania. His new technique, deep drilling through rock, had nothing to show for itself but a lot of broken drill bits. "Crazy Drake," everyone now called him. Finally his backers in New York pulled the plug and sent him a letter telling him to quit. The letter was sent by stagecoach, which ran only twice a week and took a week to arrive.

On the tenth day after the date of the letter (which was still in the stagecoach mail pouch, bouncing along muddy roads), Drake finally hit the jackpot: four hundred gallons of oil a day. The Great Oil Rush was on. Oil derricks sprouted up overnight, and America emerged as the king of "the golden flood of petroleum."

Had it not been for Drake's last-minute find, America might not have found oil for another decade, and the Model T and all other automobiles would have been powered by batteries.

A Superior Way to Raise Children?

➤**1782** "How much freedom should children have?" is a question that has faced all parents throughout the centuries. "Spare the rod, spoil the child," said the English maxim. Children in early America were brought up under very strict and even harsh discipline, with hazing and sitting alone in the corner wearing a dunce cap being common.

Hector St. John de Crevecoeur, in his book of 1782, *Letters from an American Farmer*, was fascinated to observe that many white children captured by Indians refused to be reunited with their parents when rescued years—or even months—after separation. He noted about Indians: "There must be in their social bond, something singularly captivating and far superior to anything to be boasted among us." Benjamin Franklin noted likewise: when white children were captured and raised by Indians, and later returned to white society, "in a short time they become disgusted with our manner of life, and the care and pains that are necessary to support it, and take the first good opportunity of escaping again into the woods." He went on to observe, "Happiness is more generally and equally diffus'd among Savages than in civilized societies. No European who has tasted savage life can afterwards bear to live in our societies."*

In fact, so many European settlers after Columbus landed in 1492 had defected to join various Indian tribes that Sir Francis Bacon had written in the early 1600s:

---

* Franklin, who came from Boston, also told the amusing story about some Massachusetts commissioners who invited the Indians to send a dozen of their youth to study for free at Harvard. The Indians said no thanks, already three years ago they had sent some of their young braves to study, and it was a disaster: on their return "they were absolutely good for nothing, being neither acquainted with the methods for killing deer, catching beaver, or surprising an enemy." The Indians offered instead to educate a dozen white children in the ways of the Indians "and make men out of them."

It hath often been seen that a Christian gentleman, well-born and bred, and gently nurtured will, of his own free will, quit his high station and luxurious world, to dwell with savages and live their lives, taking part in all their savagery. But never yet hath it been seen that a savage will, of his own free will give up his savagery, and live the life of a civilized man.

The modern historian Francis Jennings did a comparative analysis of child-rearing habits of Native Americans versus the English and the Aztecs (who were even stricter than the English). He, too, noted that children from English colonies who were captured by Indians would refuse repatriation when the opportunity came. These children appreciated the fact that they "were rarely beaten, a fact disapproved sternly by Englishmen who did not believe in sparing the rod."

Concludes Jennings, "There is much irony in this matter of child rearing. The 'civilized' peoples—Aztecs and Europeans—prepared their children for the cruel side of adult life by making life miserable in childhood. Only among the 'primitive' or 'savage' peoples, which had fierce cruelty enough for outsiders, were children able to grow peacefully."

America in 1800

►**1800** It took six weeks to cross the Atlantic. Traveling from Boston to Washington by stagecoach took ten days, at fifteen to sixteen hours a day. Shipping a ton of goods thirty miles inland cost as much as shipping it all the way to England. America consisted of a lot of small towns. Political argument and brawling was a major source of entertainment; language could become quite extreme. In the election campaign, Federalist newspapers predicted the election of Thomas Jefferson would cause the "teaching of murder, robbery, rape, adultery and incest." Recent presidents have it easy.

The federal government was tiny: 293 people, including members of Congress and the Supreme Court. The president had a salary of $25,000, but "no house, nor carriage, nor servants, nor, indeed, a single secretary." All expenses for protocol, office, travel, and other "business-related" expenses had to come out of the president's personal pocket. When George Washington was president in the early 1790s, this was no problem for him, since he was a wealthy man. But for John Adams in the late 1790s, it was a major problem, so Congress reluctantly allocated a one-time expense budget of $14,000. Vice President Thomas Jefferson chaired the Senate, collected his salary of $5,000 a year, and pretty much stayed home. The capital city was Philadelphia; in November 1800 it was moved to Washington DC—too late for Washington to enjoy the place (he lived just sixteen miles down the river).

The original name for the city was Federal City, D.C. During the construction from 1790 to 1800, the name was changed to honor America's first president. Living quarters for congressmen were sparse, forcing many of them to sleep two in a bed in wooden shacks. Those few who could afford it, mostly wealthy plantation owners from Virginia and the Carolinas, rented mansions in nearby Georgetown and commuted by carriage to the unfinished Capitol building. Next to the Capitol were "a few row houses, a tavern, an oyster market, a grocery store, a washerwoman's establishment, a shoemaker, a tailor and a print shop." The only industry in town was a brewery.

The President's House had no portico (it was added twenty years later), nor was it white. It was gray. Abigail Adams was happy to move out after spending three months in this gloomy, sparsely furnished abode. Originally, the President's House was supposed to be five times bigger, with terraces, fountains, and an enormous garden three quarters of a mile long. Such a palace might be fine for Louis XIV, but not in America, thought Washington, so he had fired the Frenchman L'Enfant and hired a new architect to start all over again, with more-modest specifications. After all, America was a small country, surrounded by powerful enemies claiming the bulk of the North American continent. Even the Atlantic Ocean offered little security, controlled as it was by the British navy.

America's first ship to enter the Mediterranean Sea was the USS *George Washington*. After a three-week journey from Algiers to Constantinople, it sailed into the Golden Horn and asked for permission to enter the harbor. Asked to identify what flag the ship sailed, the captain answered he sailed under the colors of the United States of America. The Turkish harbor captain hurried back to the port to make inquiries, then returned to the American ship and informed him regretfully that no one had heard of such a country, "United States of America."

Tuition at Harvard College in 1800 was sixteen dollars a year—a bargain compared with the more glamorous Princeton (then called the College of New Jersey), where tuition was one hundred dollars a year. And what was the value of one hundred dollars in those days? A pair of shoes cost two dollars. In terms of what economists call "purchasing power parity," therefore, Harvard cost eight pairs of shoes, Princeton fifty. A skilled laborer got paid $1.25 a day, meaning he could send his son to Harvard for thirteen days of work—a bargain. (At Harvard's current tuition of $45,000, the father, to part with only thirteen days of work, would have to be making more than $1 million per year. Skilled laborers today do not make $1 million, which means that either Harvard is terribly overpriced or skilled laborers are being woefully underpaid.)

The U.S. Secretary of the Treasury earned $5,000 a year—not much more than a local postmaster, who earned $4,500. The Chief Justice of the United States made only $4,000—but then lawsuits were infrequent, and really there wasn't all that much for him to do. The real action was collecting customs duties at the ports; this was the predominant source of revenue for the federal government. Accordingly, the collector of customs for Philadelphia got paid $8,500 a year. This was the second-highest-paying job in America.

Because its new form of government included a House of Representatives based on size of population, the U.S. developed the world's first census. It recorded a population in 1800 of precisely 5,308,473 (of which 20 percent were slaves). Immigration was a major source of new labor, but not of voters: the moment immigrants landed on American shores, they had to wait fourteen years before they could get citizenship and the right to vote.

High Educational Standard

➤**1800** Unlike today, when people live to eighty, people in 1800 rarely lived past forty. This condensed time frame made them work a lot harder when they were young. Says historian Bill Adler, "Since childhood was brief, even for those who survived, adolescents lurched into adulthood by age fifteen or sixteen. Parental expectations dictated high performance and productivity to ensure success."

Back then, babies two years of age were speaking fluently, and toddlers of three or four were able to read and write Latin. The record for childhood precocity would have to go to Timothy Dwight, later president of Yale: it was said that by the age of one he had read the entire Bible.*

Clearly, American education has come far downhill since then. One reason for this is information overload. A recent brochure for Harvard University boasts that the school offers no fewer than three thousand courses to choose from. Is Harvard today that much better than when all it taught was the Three Rs? Observes *Time* magazine in an article on information overload, "A weekday edition of the *New York Times* contains more information than the average person was likely to come across in a lifetime in seventeenth-century England."

Abraham Lincoln, running for president at a time when there were no graduate schools in America, admitted that "the aggregate of all his schooling" did not amount to one year. The bulk of his childhood self-education consisted of one or two dozen books. But they were good books, not trash: the King James Bible, *Robinson Crusoe*, Aesop's *Fables*, Shakespeare, Samuel Johnson, even William Scott's *Lessons in Elocution: A Selection of Pieces in Prose and Verse for the Improvement of Youth in Reading and Speaking*. No light reading for this young man. He also read his American history: Parson Weems's *Life of George Washington*, William

---

* One wonders, if he couldn't speak until he was two, how he communicated this.

Grimshaw's *History of the United States*, and the *Revised Statutes of Indiana* containing "the Declaration, the Constitution, the first twelve amendments, the Virginia Act of Cession of the Northwest Territory, the Ordinance of 1787, the act of admitting Indiana, and the first state constitution."

More important than the quality of what he read was the concentration he put into his reading. "Get the books, and read and study them," he advised a law student seeking advice in the 1850s. What few books he read, he reread. So frequently did he reread the Bible and *Macbeth* and *Hamlet* that, even as president, he could cite lengthy passages at heart and startle onlookers with his deep knowledge.

❧

In the early 1960s at Hyannis, JFK and his distant relative Gore Vidal were enjoying cigars over a game of backgammon, pontificating about politics. "How do you explain how a sort of backwoods country like this, with only three million people, could have produced the three great geniuses of the eighteenth century—Franklin, Jefferson, Hamilton?" wondered the president.

"Time. They had more of it," said Vidal. "They stayed home on the farm in winter. They read. Wrote letters. Apparently, thought, something no longer done—in public life."

Replied JFK, "You know in this job . . . I get to meet everybody—all these great movers and shakers and the thing I'm most struck by the lot of them is how second-rate they are. Then you read all those debates over the Constitution . . . nothing like that now. Nothing."

Big Distances: A Barrier to National Development, Solved Only by Private Capital

►**1817** A courier set out from Detroit to deliver U.S. Army documents to headquarters in Pittsburgh, 286 miles away. He rode hard, and at the end of his journey pulled up huffing and panting. How long did his ride take?

Fifty-three days—about as much time as it took to cross the Atlantic Ocean to Europe. America in the early nineteenth century was essentially a collection of isolated settlements surrounded by forests. Much of the nation's subsequent economic growth and political unification were due to basic improvements in transportation. Said John C. Calhoun in 1817, "We are under the most imperious obligation to counteract every tendency to disunion. . . . Let us bind the republic together with a perfect system of roads and canals."

Indeed, the great issue of the 1820s and all the way through the 1850s was not slavery, which became so important in the 1860s, but internal improvements. It cost just as much to send goods thirty miles inland by wagon as it did three thousand miles across the Atlantic Ocean by ship. If the new fledgling country was to grow and stave off the European colonial empires like Britain and France, it had to develop its economy and its size. The "American System" headed by Henry Clay and John Quincy Adams called for internal improvements, land legislation, tariff protection, public works, and a national bank.

The interest in national "economic planning" strikes some as anathema today, but in the first century of the republic it was viewed as absolutely essential if the country was to survive. The transition from an agricultural to an industrial society required enormous amounts of capital to build a transportation infrastructure. Roads, bridges, canals, harbors, and railroads are not cheap.

Yet the benefits could be awesome: after the Erie Canal was completed, the three weeks and $120 it had cost to send a ton of flour from Buffalo to New York City were reduced to only eight dollars and eight days.

And how was the Erie Canal financed? Even though it was "the biggest public works project in the Western World since the Great Pyramid," President James Monroe vetoed the $1.5-million federal government "seed financing" necessary to get the $7-million project off the ground. Unlike today, when virtually every public works project is financed by Washington DC either with money or with a govern-

ment guarantee, this massive project had to make it on its own. The State of New York issued equity shares and bonds for the venture, to be purchased by New York banks for resale to investors in America and England. The Erie Canal succeeded in being built entirely with private funding, as did most of the bridges and roads that eventually reduced distances in America to an economically homogeneous unit. The state played a key role in promoting development of early America, but most of the hard cash came from private individuals. "The primary source of U.S. finance," says economics historian Stanley Lebergott, "proved to be neither foreign nor federal nor state. It was private."

Small White House Staff

➤**1860** Abraham Lincoln, "the most powerful President the United States has ever known," ran the Civil War from the White House and kept on top of every detail of the military campaign, as well as running the national government. Surrounded by hostile congressmen and Southern sympathizers in Washington DC he had to rely almost exclusively on his White House staff to manage the affairs of war and state.

What's remarkable is that he did it with so few people. His White House staff—in sharp contrast to today—consisted of only two people. They were John G. Nicolay, White House chief of staff, responsible for receiving official visitors and maintaining relations with the Senate and House, and John M. Hay,* assistant secretary responsible for the president's daily correspondence. Because the president's White House budget allowed for only one secretary, Hay had to be placed on the payroll of the Interior Department, and both secretaries had to pay for their own pens and paper out of their own pocket, though room and board was free (the two shared a bedroom on the first floor of the White House). In 1861 and again in 1864, another secretary was added, each salary "buried" in the Interior Department.

❧

Today's White House staff totals more than 1,500 people—a bloated bureaucracy. Anyone who thinks that today's needs are more complex than Lincoln's can look to World War II, when America faced its greatest national emergency. Franklin Roosevelt had a staff small enough—fewer than fifty—so he could deal with each assistant personally, and he ordered that his assistants have "no authority over anyone in any department or agency" and should "in no event be interposed between the President and the head of any department or agency." FDR was his own chief of staff (as were Truman, JFK, and LBJ). Sam Rosenman, legal adviser to FDR during World War II, had no assistants at all. The man in that position today has at least fifty. Said Rosenman, "I can't imagine what they all do!"

Back to Abraham Lincoln. Because his staff was small, he had to do his spadework himself. He would hold public receptions twice a week, whereby anybody could come along and offer ideas and complaints to the president. Sometimes as many as fifty people would show up. "I call these receptions my public-opinion baths," he said, "and, though they may not be pleasant in all particulars, the effect as a whole is renovating and invigorating to my perceptions of responsibility and duty. It would never do for a President to have guards with drawn sabres at his door, as if he fancied he were, or were trying to be, or were assuming to be, an emperor."

A Speech Where Every Word Counted

▶**1862** When Abraham Lincoln gave his magisterial Gettysburg Address, it was considered "an oratorical disaster" because it was too short—just two and a half minutes. People were used to long-winded speeches like Edward Everett's two-and-a-quarter-hour oration that preceded Lincoln's remarks; the Lincoln-Douglas debates, which lasted almost four hours; and the Daniel Webster speech to the Whaling Association in Nantucket, whereby he began his talk and

---

* Future secretary of state under William McKinley and Theodore Roosevelt.

suddenly—in a dramatic flourish—raised his arms and delivered the rest of his speech to "the whales of the sea."

Lincoln's short talk left his audience adrift and mystified: Was that all? If the president was going to give a speech, why not talk for hours like everyone else? Hadn't he done his homework?

Indeed he had. Lincoln had worked very hard on his speech. The rumor that he jotted it down while on the train to Gettysburg is totally wrong: he had worked on his speech for days, and wanted fervently for it to be epochal. One is reminded of Mark Twain's famous line forty years later: "I am sorry to write you such a long letter, I did not have time to write a shorter one."

Lincoln had written and rewritten his speech many times until he had the message down just right. He knew the difference between giving a speech in a campaign debate and giving a speech as president: people gave very long speeches—but not presidents. Ever since Washington, the person occupying the nation's highest office was expected to write out his speeches beforehand—not stand at the podium and extemporize ad infinitum. He must maintain the dignity of the office and not make empty promises just because he thought that was what people wanted to hear. Warned the Founding Fathers in the *Federalist Papers*: "Of those men who have overturned the liberties of republics, the greatest number have begun their career by paying obsequious court to the people, commencing demagogues and ending tyrants."

Later, even in the razor-thin election of 1876 where the voter turnout was an astounding 82 percent, both candidates stayed home and focused on strategy, leaving their supporters to do the campaigning. "It was not a contest of personalities," says the historian Lloyd Robinson. "In those days before radio and television, the personalities of the candidates did not matter much to the voters. . . . The voters made their decisions on the basis of ideas and issues—not how a man looked or how warmly he smiled."

Nowadays, of course, we have no Gettysburg Address. In today's endless campaigns, candidates give hundreds of lengthy speeches, resulting in a precious loss of original thought. Since 1920 no president has written his own speeches—"and there is some evidence they can't read them either," says Gore Vidal.

A Near-Fatal Misstep

►**1863** The Emancipation Proclamation, our nation's most revolutionary document after the Declaration of Independence, is heralded today as a bold and courageous act that put the major issue of the Civil War on its pedestal, defined the war's purpose, and set blacks on the path to freedom.

At the time, however, it was not viewed that way. In fact, the Emancipation Proclamation was such a rash move it almost cost Lincoln the war when he released his "pre-official" version in the fall of 1862. Up until then, the purpose of the war had been to save the Union. It was a well-accepted cause that attracted plenty of volunteers. In his pre-release of the Emancipation Proclamation, Lincoln was redefining the war as one to free the slaves. In one quick moment, Lincoln lost much of his volunteer support.

Northern whites had very mixed views about freed blacks. On the one hand they agreed that slavery was an evil, but like today's congressmen who scream NIMBY ("not in my backyard") whenever their favorite social programs or pork-barrel projects get cut from pending appropriations, they didn't want black hordes coming to the North and taking away jobs and creating social unrest.

The immediate result of Lincoln's proclamation was an immediate drop in enlistments. Lincoln had to respond with new conscription procedures that were even more unpopular. Then when he presented the Thirteenth Amendment in 1864, codifying the Emancipation Proclamation in the Constitution, it was quickly rejected by Congress. The Democratic Party was firmly opposed, calling it "unwise, impolitic, cruel and unworthy of the support of civilized people." Feverishly working the back room, twisting arms and making deals, Lincoln persisted. Among those opposed to the Emancipation Proclamation were certain Northern slaveholders. To win their support, Lincoln ingeniously expanded the word "Union" to include

"Union-held areas" in the South such as seven counties around Norfolk, Virginia, and several Louisiana districts (one crucial vote belonging to a Louisiana congressman).

Finally in 1865 he called for another vote. This time it passed, by the slimmest of margins: three votes.

Not as Originally Intended

➤**1742–1900** Many of our leading consumer products were originally intended for different uses from what they later became famous for. Or, as a businessman would say, if a product doesn't catch on with its intended market, try to think of another way to sell your product. Listen to the consumer!

The Franklin stove has a clever design of flues and air vents that reduced the heat lost up the chimney. But that was not how Benjamin Franklin advertised it when he merchandised his product in 1742. He claimed his stove would suppress aging of women's faces caused by harsh, hot air.

The original Levi's blue jeans made for California Forty-niners were made for a very specific purpose having nothing to do with style or fashion or even work clothes. They were made out of hemp sailcloth and rivets so the pockets wouldn't rip when filled with gold panned from the sediment.

In 1886 a pharmacist in Atlanta invented a concoction called Coca-Cola. It was not a soft drink, but a mouthwash and gargle, guaranteed "to whiten the teeth, cleanse the mouth, and cure tender and bleeding gums." When the mouthwash market failed to materialize, the pharmacist repositioned his product as a family beverage to taste and swallow. One problem with this new strategy, however, was the substantial amount of cocaine in the drink (hence the name "Coca-Cola"). In 1903 the formula was altered and the label stated, "Cocaine Removed."

Like pioneer plane designers who all failed because they insisted on designing a plane with moving wings like a bird's, so the typewriter almost never got invented because it was modeled after the wrong example: the sewing machine. The typewriter's inventors positioned it not as a business machine, but as a device to use at home (target market: authors and clergymen). The first typewriter, the Remington #1, appeared in a black case with colored floral ornaments. "The type-writer in size and appearance resembles the family sewing machine," an 1876 ad extolled. "It is graceful and ornamental . . . it is to the pen what the sewing machine is to the needle." Early typewriters were so inferior mechanically to the human hand (like the plane to the bird) that the keyboard had to be designed to a QWERTY format to slow down typists and prevent them from jamming the mechanical keys. The concept of creating a machine so advanced as to challenge humans was never considered.

The Twitter of Its Day

►1872 In New York's Central Park in 1872 a statue was unveiled commemorating "The Master of Our Thought, the Land's First Citizen!" He was called by James Fenimore Cooper "the great author of America," despite the fact that he was not an American. But no matter: Americans have "just as good a right" as any to claim him as one of their own. He was even more popular in America than in his homeland. Virtually every American knew his name, not only in the salons of New York but in the faraway mining camps of California. He was praised by Ralph Waldo Emerson for "addressing those questions which knock for answer at every heart." He was Abraham Lincoln's favorite author. He was a favorite of Mark Twain.

William Shakespeare was the most popular literary figure in America in the nineteenth century. During his travels through the United States in the 1830s, Alexis de Tocqueville was astounded to find Shakespeare everywhere in "the recesses of the forests of the New World." He observed: "There is hardly a pioneer's hut that does not contain a few old volumes of Shakespeare. I remember that I read the feudal drama of *Henry V* for the first time in a log cabin."

Lots of log cabins had Shakespeare. Unlike today where volumes of Shakespeare gather dust on the bookshelf, Shakespeare was a popular poet admired for his oratory and his moral stories about individual responsibility. His stories about heroes and villains appealed to people's need for melodrama. His format—plays—lent itself to mass culture even for those who could not read. On makeshift stages in halls and saloons in small towns throughout the land, short scenes from Shakespeare were performed. They weren't professional recreations of the entire play, they were short adaptations with lots of vitality, performed by bumptious barnstormers, acrobats, singers, orators, and jugglers. Popular audiences included people of all economic strata, especially the lower. Observed Washington Irving in 1802: the noise in the gallery "is somewhat to what prevailed in Noah's ark; for we have an imitation of the whistles and yells of every kind of animal." Because most everyone knew a little something of Shakespeare, they could participate fully—and did. If they didn't like the performance, they got physical in expressing their disapproval. Observed one foreign visitor to America, "The egg as a vehicle of dramatic criticism came into early use in this continent."

Shakespearean episodes helped bring people together. Recalling his days as an apprentice pilot on a Mississippi steamboat, Mark Twain marveled at his master's passion for Shakespeare: "He would read Shakespeare to me, not casually but by the hour . . . he knew his Shakespeare as well as Euclid ever knew his multiplication tables." In a vast, developing nation starved for entertainment, Shakespeare

filled a vital role. During the 1849 California gold rush, a theater seating two thousand opened up in San Francisco and was packed to the roof: "Miners . . . swarmed from the gambling saloons and cheap fandango houses to see *Hamlet* and *Lear.*" Most everyone could relate to at least something from Shakespeare, and they enjoyed the camaraderie of the boisterous entertainment. He was the Twitter of the day, appreciated in short bytes. Everyone related to him.

Even as late as the 1880s, a European visitor observed:

There is, assuredly, no other country on earth in which Shakespeare and the Bible are held in such general high esteem as in America, the very country so much decried for its lust for money. If you were to enter an isolated log cabin in the Far West and even if its inhabitant were to exhibit many of the traces of backwoods living, he will most likely have one small room nicely furnished in which to spend his few leisure hours and in which you will certainly find the Bible and in most cases also some cheap edition of the works of the poet Shakespeare.

It was the beginning of the end for Shakespeare. When people started taking him seriously toward the end of the century, he lost popularity. Shakespeare became highbrow, a literary classic requiring reading from beginning to end—out of reach for the mass market (let's face it,

Shakespeare is not easy reading). Travesties and parodies fell out of fashion, serious theatre took over, and many English Shakespearean actors came to America to perform because the money was better. The result was good theatre—and smaller audiences. Then along came radio, movies, and television at the expense of theatre, transforming people into passive spectators. For many, Shakespeare had now lost his relevance and become a ponderous experience like going to church: "gratified that they have come, and gratified that they now may go."

Transforming the Shopping Experience

►**1877** From the days of the bazaar down to the era of the local general store, shopping was a personal experience. A customer walked into the store and engaged in a conversation with the proprietor. It was well understood that the customer was under an obligation to buy. A lengthy discussion would ensue, the price would be agreed upon, and the transaction consummated. The advantage was all with the retailer.*

Enter the department store, made possible by the availability of a much wider range of goods delivered inexpensively by railroad, along with the growing urbanization of America. In the Gilded Age, America's second-richest man after William H. Vanderbilt was department store magnate Alexander T. Stewart. This Irish immigrant introduced a retailing innovation that had great impact on the way customers shopped and made purchases, and eventually spread all over the world. Singlehandedly he changed the relationship between retailer and customer and made the industry more legitimate.

It had to do with a lot more than the grand department store he opened in 1877 in New York. Certainly this was the first "one-stop shopping" emporium in America, with no fewer than thirty different departments. Stewart's real innovation was far more significant: he threw out the old method of bargaining, and introduced a fixed price for every article offered for sale. He also put a price tag on everything.

For the first time the customer was on an equal footing with the retailer. No longer was shopping a battle of wits, with haggling of the kind seen in an Istanbul bazaar. Thanks to Stewart, a powerful American tradition was launched: the pro-consumer movement culminating in fair-trade regulations concerning conspicuous signs, unit pricing, and content labeling. "Next to the president," it was said at

---

* For an idea of how hazardous shopping could be, consider the story of eight-year-old Ulysses S. Grant. Young and naïve, he was sent by his father to buy a horse. He told the owner, "Papa says I may offer you twenty dollars for the colt, but if you won't take that, I am to offer twenty-two and a half, and if you won't take that, I am to give you twenty-five."

the time, Stewart was "the best known man in America." It can be argued that Stewart probably had more influence and impact than the president did.

A Country of 300 Local Times

►**1883** Nobody thinks of railroads much anymore, but the impact of railroads on the development and unification of a vast country like America was enormous. "The railroad," wrote one historian, "is to American imagery what the church was to Europe . . . in the middle ages."

This takes considerable imagination to appreciate. Go to Europe and spend solemn moments in majestic places like Westminster Abbey, Notre Dame, St. Mark's Square in Venice. Was the "iron horse" truly equal to this?

Since the beginning of civilization, people had traveled at an average of 4.8 miles per hour. The railroads changed everything. Sixty miles per hour meant people arrived at a place long before they were supposed to, necessitating a major change in the concept of time normally measured on a sundial. While there were complaints that America should operate on "God's time, not Vanderbilt's," within a few years the concept of standard time became accepted—with profound consequences for America, hitherto a vast continent of cities and villages far apart.

Originally, God's time was local solar time, based on the number of hours and minutes since noon, when the sun was highest in the sky. A person traveling from Boston to New York by six-hour train ride had to move his clock back by several minutes when he arrived at his destination, because the sun arrived at noon in New York later than it did in Boston. ("Sun time" changes approximately one minute for every twelve and a half miles traveled east or west.)

Throughout cities and villages, the correct time was the time according to the clock on the church steeple; people walked by daily and calibrated their watches to it. For people in rural areas without ready access to correct time, there existed entrepreneurial traveling timekeepers who offered their services, carrying a watch with the correct time to adjust the clocks in a customer's home on a weekly basis. In cities, there emerged the solution of the time ball. On top of a tall building was a large ball, three to four feet in diameter. At official noon, the ball fell and people watching from a mile away could adjust their timepieces with confidence. In large cities like Chicago or Kansas City, the number of people watching every day was in the thousands.

The amount of time required for the sun to traverse a country as large as the United States necessitated some three hundred local times. For the railroads, trying to coordinate connections between an arriving train's time and a departing train's time was chaos. Compounding the problem was the fact that each railroad's timetable keyed off the local time of the city where it had its headquarters or major terminus. The Pennsylvania Railroad, for example, used Philadelphia time, which was five minutes "slower" than New York time and five minutes "faster" than Baltimore time. When it was noon in Chicago, it was 12:31 in Pittsburgh, 12:24 in Cleveland, 12:13 in Cincinnati, 12:07 in Indianapolis, 11:50 in St. Louis, and 11:27 in Omaha. In Pittsburgh the train station used six different clocks, one for each of six major railroads.

Just in the state of Michigan, for example, to go from east to west meant changing your watch twenty times. To ascertain the correct time, each train station would have to call a major urban center to get the correct standard time, then adjust their local time accordingly.

The railroads, not the government, took matters into their own hands to resolve this mess. The leader of this movement was an obscure businessman named William F. Allen, owner and publisher of a widely read, indispensable publication, *The Railroad Traveler's Official Guide*. It was essentially

"Hey, fella, move out of the way!" Until railroads could figure out how to coordinate their times, traffic foul-ups and near-collisions were frequent.

nothing more than a six-hundred-page compendium of timetables, along with a time chart—hardly the makings of a best-seller. The traveler from New York to Pittsburgh, for example, was informed he needed to move his watch back by thirty minutes; from Washington to Albany, forward by two minutes.

Yet Albany, New York City, Washington, and Pittsburgh are very close to each other on the latitudinal scale. Such specificity of time in an era of high-speed transport was a cumbersome and clearly obsolete concept. A much more sweeping simplification needed to be done.

In an 1883 meeting called the General Time Convention, the railroads carried time standardization to its fullest by recognizing the genius of a Canadian, Sir Sanford Fleming, who seven years earlier had proposed that the world be divided into twenty-four time zones separated by one hour, each spaced fifteen degrees of longitude apart. Applied to the United States, the magic number of time zones would be four. Under the plan put forth by William Allen, the approximate longitudinal centers of these zones would be Philadelphia, St. Louis, Denver, and Reno.

At exactly twelve o'clock noon on November 18, "The Day of Two Noons," the U.S. was divided into Eastern, Central, Mountain, and Pacific time zones—on railroad timetables only. But the idea caught on, and within a year 85 percent of American cities with a population greater than 10,000 were using standard time, and in 1918 the U.S. Congress finally got around to passing the Standard Time Act, making railroad time mandatory everywhere. Like the great cathedrals of Europe, the railroads had unified a nation.

Answering the Phone

➤**1893** The advent of the telegraph and the telephone was greeted with considerable skepticism in America, where communications in such a vast country were normally restricted to personal encounters. In *Walden*, Thoreau had written, "We are in great haste to construct a magnetic telegraph from Maine to Texas; but Maine and Texas . . . have nothing important to communicate." Similarly, in a trial conversation between Washington DC and Philadelphia, President Rutherford B. Hayes queried, "An amazing invention, but who would ever want to use one of them?" Nonetheless he bowed to progress and had a telephone installed. In 1893, Grover Cleveland returned to the White House after a four-year interregnum. How was the White House phone answered?

By the president himself: "Grover Cleveland speaking." The telephone was viewed as a medium for emergencies—the equivalent of today's "red button." When you called the White House, you wanted the boss immediately, not some lackey.

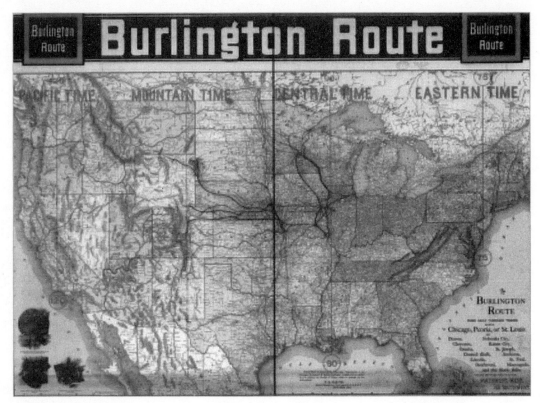

America gets a new map

America in 1900

➤1900 The population was 76 million. The average life expectancy was forty-five years, which is not surprising given that 90 percent of doctors had no college education (they attended what were called "medical schools," widely condemned by the government and the press as "substandard"). Only 4 percent of the population made it to age sixty-five. Almost all births took place at home, and people worked until they died. There was no need for Social Security. The leading cause of death was pneumonia/influenza, followed by tuberculosis and then diarrhea. (Today's leading killers—heart disease and stroke—ranked fourth and fifth; cancer and Alzheimer's had not been diagnosed then.) Local corner drugstores—unregulated, of course—did a thriving business in strange and exotic medicines. Marijuana, heroin, and morphine were all readily available over the counter. Heroin, the most expensive medicine, was cited by pharmacists as "a perfect guardian of health" because it "clears the complexion, gives buoyancy to the mind, and regulates the stomach and bowels."

Hamburgers appeared on the market for the first time, in New Haven, Connecticut. Nobody other than Italian immigrants ate spaghetti.

Only 14 percent of homes had a bathtub. Kitchens were very rudimentary, and of course washing machines did not exist. All was not lost, however: 18 percent of households had at least one full-time servant or domestic help.

Twenty percent of adults couldn't read or write. Only 6 percent of Americans had graduated from high school. Factory workers and coal miners, including children, worked a twelve-to-sixteen-hour day to make one to two dollars. Many workers couldn't survive on such low pay; many immigrants gave up and returned home. The average wage was twenty-two cents an hour. An accountant made about $2,000 a year; a dentist, $2,500; a mechanical engineer, $5,000. Low income and lack of education, however, did not mean a high crime rate as so many sociologists today claim. There were only 230 murders that year in the entire country.

Because there were no income taxes, the federal government was small. Its sole source of income was tariff and excise taxes, primarily on tobacco and alcohol. William McKinley won reelection as president, proving that the key to being reelected is not to be a bold president, but to be a great politician. His running mate

was a brash young politician named Theodore Roosevelt, who got the job only after two other candidates had turned it down. Then, as now, the vice presidency was regarded as a one-way trip to oblivion. Many Americans wondered why the United States, hitherto an isolated country, was sending troops to Nicaragua, the Dominican Republic, and Haiti, not to mention getting involved in faraway conflicts in the Philippines and China. There was a lot to be done in the United States alone. There were only 150 miles of paved roads in the entire country, but progress was in the air: automobiles, phonographs, lightbulbs, typewriters, telegraphs, skyscrapers, automobiles, and the Brooklyn Bridge portended an exciting century to come.

Americans were filled with optimism and faith in technology. Rev. Edward Everett Hale envisioned a time when people would be shot by pneumatic tube from Texas to Georgia (not such a bad idea, given the hassles of airplane travel nowadays). Newspaper mogul William Randolph Hearst predicted a rosy future:

The barbarous races of the world civilized. The powers of the wind, the rivers, and the sun will no longer be fouled with smoke for which men have worn out their lives in coal mines. The deserts will be seats of vast manufacturing enterprises, carried on by electric power developed directly from solar heat.

A 1900 vision of America in the year 2000

The leading automotive technology was Thomas Edison's battery-powered vehicle, leading one person to predict that "the whole of the United States will be sprinkled with electric changing stations." One third of America's eight thousand cars were electric-powered. The major competitive threat to the electric engine was not the gasoline engine, but an engine so successful in propelling trains and boats: the steam engine.

There were only a handful of foreign cars, thanks to a U.S. 45 percent import tax on European car manufacturers. To buy a Mercedez Benz, you went to a New York City department store.

Belief in Infallibility: A Boat with No Bottom

➤**1912** Although the *Titanic* was a British ship, it was largely American-owned (the majority shareholder in the White Star Line was a New York invest-ment trust headed by J. P. Morgan). Most of the first-class passengers who drowned were American; the wireless operator who caught the SOS signal was Ameri-can (David Sarnoff); the rescue ship (*Carpathia*) was American; one of the two government investigations was American; the discovery of the ship in 1985 was made by an American; and the block-buster movie was American. Hence its in-clusion here.

When the ship sank in 1912, everyone demanded to know why the huge ocean liner had carried only twenty lifeboats. Asked whether the *Titanic* had erred in carrying so few lifeboats, the captain of the rescue ship *Carpathia* responded, "No, the *Titanic* was supposed to be a lifeboat itself." More important in creating the un-sinkable ship were tennis courts, grand dining saloons, electric elevators, and Turkish baths.

People also wanted to know why the ship was running at twenty-two and a half knots, full speed, after it had received nu-merous warnings of serious ice conditions.

Incredible though it seems today, the standard practice of ships entering the icy North Atlantic was to maintain their speed and rely on lookouts to spot any icebergs ten miles ahead—plenty of time to take evasive action. After the *Titanic* disaster, the U.S. Senate and the British Board of Trade immediately launched in-vestigations. But the people they called to testify were the survivors and "armchair experts," not specialists in the arcane art of ice navigation. The U.S. Senate investi-gation lasted only four days, and included such silly moments as when the chair-man asked a seaman what an iceberg was made of.

"Ice," the seaman replied.

The British—who one would expect to know how to conduct a serious marine investigation, Britain being a seafaring nation—were more thorough. They took more than thirty days to conduct inten-sive questioning (including asking the surviving senior officer no fewer than 1,600 questions). Still, they accepted the prevailing practice of the day and refused to condemn the British captain for recklessness. Said the inquiry chairman,

> There was certainly no reduction of speed. Why, then, did the Master persevere in his course and maintain his speed? It was shown that for many years past, the practice of liners had been in clear weather to keep the course, to maintain the speed and to trust to a sharp lookout to enable them to avoid the danger. . . . In these circumstances I am not able to blame Captain Smith.

Today, of course, the captain would be found guilty and the lawyers would have a field day. The essential rule of good seamanship is "When in doubt never assume, always confirm." Such were the actions of the captain of the *Carpathia*, the ship that subsequently rescued the *Titanic* survivors. Upon entering ice-filled waters, the *Carpathia*'s captain doubled his lookouts and exercised extra vigilance. When he got the distress call from the *Titanic*, he "added a man to the crow's nest, two more on the bows, and a pair on each wing of the bridge, all chosen for their keen eyesight. This would prove a good precaution: five icebergs were dodged later that night." Another nearby ship, the *Californian*, took the ultimate safety measure: it stopped.

Compare this with the attitude on the *Titanic*, where Second Officer Charles Lightoller told the British Board of Inquiry that slowing the ship down "was not necessarily the most obvious way" to avoid a collision. This statement so stunned the interrogator he then asked, "Well, is it one way?" Lightoller replied, "It is one way. Naturally, if you stop the ship you will not collide with anything."

Out of such insights are great seamen made—assuming they make them.

The two lookouts in the crow's nest had no binoculars (the White Star Line had stopped distributing them in 1895). Asked how fast the ship was going, the sole surviving lookout said he didn't know; asked how large the iceberg was when he saw it, he responded, "I have no idea of distances or spaces." Even worse, they had been on duty for an hour and a half in wind-chill temperature conditions of 5 degrees—brutal conditions affecting the capacity of anyone to reason clearly. When the lookouts saw low-lying pack ice four miles away, they mistook it for haze and did nothing; only when the ice was five hundred yards away did they finally yank the alarm rope.

Many landlubbers jumped on the White Star Line for having such incompetents in such a sensitive position. But were they to blame? No, says *Titanic* historian Daniel Allen Butler: "Based on firsthand experience with 1910-vintage binoculars, I can tell you that their relatively poor optics actually reduce visibility because they absorb so much light. In actual practice, lookouts do not use binoculars to spot objects, but rather to identify them once they are spotted."

Lookouts are not expected to estimate distances, says Butler. Their job is to spot objects and report their findings to the bridge; it is up to the officers on the bridge to make more accurate measurements and decide what action to take. To First Officer William Murdoch the captain had entrusted the ship, believing it to be in good hands. Captain Smith had every reason to be confident. Not only was Murdoch a highly seasoned officer, but the ship itself was a feat of remarkable engineering. This was an age of iron, elec-

tricity, engines, and the telegraph—Man finally conquering Nature. That the technology of the day was still quite primitive occurred to nobody.

Here was a captain who believed the *Olympic* and *Titanic* could be cut in half and still float. Furthermore, he bragged, "If the engines and boilers were to fall through their bottoms, the vessels would remain afloat."

A boat with no bottom?

To this day, no nautical architect has designed such a ship. But who cares? Such was the euphoria of the Edwardian Age in 1912.

Titanic survivors on the Carpathia. When the Olympic's captain offered to come help the rescue, the Carpathia's captain cautioned that "it was not advisable for the survivors to see Titanic's nearly identical-looking sister ship."

The Might of General Motors

➤**1955** How the mighty have fallen! The most powerful corporation in the world in the 1950s was General Motors. No company like it will ever exist again. "General Motors has no bad years, only good years and better years," said president Harlow Curtice. GM made as many automobiles as all its competitors combined, its labor union contracts set the standard for the entire auto industry, and its chairman, on becoming secretary of defense, could say with impunity, "We at General Motors have always felt that what was good for the country was good for General Motors as well."

GM was so powerful that its major concern was not competition but rather the Justice Department. When GM's chairman, Alfred P. Sloan, learned that Ford Motor Company was at the point of collapse, he privately encouraged a team of his top managers to leave GM and go save Ford. Ernest Breech, passed over for the presidency of GM, became number two at Ford. Joining him were the new Ford vice president of finance, three of the four heads of the Ford operating divisions, and the new head of Ford engineering. Dozens of other key positions were also filled with GM recruits.

Wrote management guru Peter Drucker:

Sloan did everything to enable [GM] managers to join the Ford team, helped them work out their pensions and profit-sharing plans at GM so as to be able to move without financial loss, and even, I am told, get word to Ernest Breech, a former GM executive, where inside GM he might find hidden top talent for the Ford management team.

&

By point of contrast, consider this story: Many years ago, this start-up automobile company was tottering on bankruptcy when across the sea a multinational war started. One of the belligerent countries placed so many orders for vehicles and trucks that the company's sales immediately shot up 40 percent. "These orders were our salvation," said the company's chairman. Today, sixty years after the Korean War and the orders placed by the U.S. military, Toyota is the largest automobile company in the world.

Recycling Coca-Cola Bottles

➤**1955** Nowadays there is a great "anti-materialism" push among legislators and environmentalists to recycle our consumer product containers, especially bottles and cans. We look back upon the 1950s as a quaint, boring, terribly materialistic era when there was no sensitivity to eliminating waste or preserving the environment. Just look at the gas-guzzling cars Detroit manufactured then—what behemoths!

Today, as we sort out our soda and

beer bottles for recycling, we congratulate ourselves for being such conscientious citizens.

A note of caution: Back in the 1950s the most popular consumer item was a bottle of Coke, which was recycled regularly— long before people knew what recycling meant. According to the Coca-Cola Company, each Coke was filled, emptied, returned, and refilled thirty-seven times. There is no product on the market today that approaches this remarkable Earth-conservation achievement.

FOUR

American Self-Identity and Ideals

"Jacques Barzun," says *New York Times* columnist David Brooks, "once observed that of all the books it is impossible to write, the most impossible is a book trying to capture the spirit of America."

Said Walt Whitman in his poem *Leaves of Grass*, "Very well, then I contradict myself / I am large, I contain multitudes." The ethnic, social, and economic makeup of America is varied and constantly changing. Alexis de Tocqueville described America as a country of "ceaseless agitation." Such agitation creates an "all-pervading and restless activity, a superabundant force, and an energy . . . which may, however unfavorable circumstances may be, produce wonders."

America is famous for its log cabins; out of many log cabins have emerged many self-made men. Even better, as the saying goes, "He was born in a log cabin he built with his own hands!"

America accomplishes these wonders by being a country obsessed with moving forward. "America is a country of the future," said Ralph Waldo Emerson. "It is a country of beginnings, of projects, of vast designs and expectations." Several of our presidents were very firm about this. John Quincy Adams, when he was Monroe's secretary of state, advised a German baron about immigrants to America, "They must cast off the European skin, never to resume it. They must look forward to their posterity rather than backward to their ancestors."

Equally unequivocal in his advice was President Woodrow Wilson: "You cannot become thorough Americans if you think of yourselves in groups. America does not consist of groups. A man who thinks of himself as belonging to a particular national group in America has not yet become an American." Said Theodore Roosevelt:

> *One absolutely certain way of bringing this nation to ruin, would be to permit it to become a tangle of squabbling nationalities, an intricate knot of German-Americans, Irish-Americans, English-Americans, French-Americans, Scandinavian-Americans, or Italian-Americans, each preserving its separate nationality.*

America's original heritage may be European and partially African, but its character is oriented toward the frontier. George Washington had never been to Europe; when the Marquis de Lafayette proposed to Washington in 1783 that he come visit Europe, Washington declined; if he was going to take a trip, he would rather visit "the New Empire" stretching from the Carolinas via the Mississippi to Detroit. So, too, would Henry David Thoreau: "Eastward I go by force, but westward I go free. . . . I must walk toward Oregon and not toward Europe." But what happened when we reached the end of the frontier, as asked in the 1890s by Frederick Jackson Turner? Other than an eventual inclusion of Alaska and Hawaii, Americans had no choice but to confront and accept their limits. Said Herbert Agar after the end of the Second World War, "We are all descendants of people who fled from Europe. . . . Our instinctive wish is to be left alone by Europe, to stop fretting about Europe, to turn our eyes toward the Pacific. . . . We belong to the West, without which we must perish. We do not belong to Asia."

Americans may belong more to the West than to Asia, but they are not Europeans, they are different. Nobody expressed this better than the great Prussian officer sent by the French to instill some discipline in Washington's ragtag troops at Valley Forge in 1775. He was Baron von Steuben: "The genius of this nation is not in the least to be compared with that of the Prussians, Austrians or French. You say to your soldier, 'Do this,' and he doeth it, but I am obliged to say, 'This is the reason why you ought to do that,' and he does it."

In other words, there's a fundamental difference between Americans and Europeans or Asians: respect for the dignity and rights of the individual. You don't order a person what to do, you persuade him.

The Englishman Thomas B. Macaulay once observed, "Your Constitution is all sail and no anchor." For most countries whose past goes back to the Middle Ages and earlier, the past is a ready anchor. America, on the other hand, never had this advantage and so became entirely different: a forward-thinking nation. When Henry Ford said "history is bunk," he was maligned by historians. But he never said it quite so crudely. In fact, he knew his history better than did most historians, and to prove it he created an enormous replica of the past, the Henry Ford Museum and Greenfield Village in Dearborn, Michigan. Here is what he said, in its full context: "History is more or less bunk. It's tradition. We don't want tradition. We want to live in the present and the only history worth a tinker's damn is the history we make today." Likewise, on another occasion, he stated, "I don't know anything about history. I wouldn't give a nickel for all the history in the world. . . . I don't want to live in the past. I want to live in the Now."

Henry Ford wasn't talking about history; he was talking about progress and the future. So, too, was Benjamin Franklin. Once he was rescued from a shipwreck. After expressing his feelings of thanksgiving and gratitude, he was asked if he planned to build a chapel to memorialize his rescue. "No, indeed not," he responded. "I'm going to build a lighthouse!"

❧

In 1789, after the French revolutionaries had stormed the Bastille, Lafayette sent President George Washington a most unusual gift to symbolize the spread of American democratic ideals to France. It was a key to the prison.

Unfortunately, as the Jacobins took over, it became clear that the spread of American ideals did not match American expectations. In a scene repeated numerous times over the next two hundred years, most recently in Iran, Cuba, Russia, and Iraq, revolts against despotism matured into despotism under new leaders. Yet the dream of America—a house in suburbia with a two-car garage—rings loud and clear throughout the world, propagated by Hollywood movies. Observed a Frenchman in 1932:

The West has thought for a long time, not without a certain naïveté, that it represented spirituality in the world. But is spirituality really the message we have taken along with us everywhere? What has been borrowed from us . . . is our mechanisms. Today, in the most remote, most ancient villages, one finds the automobile, the cinema, the radio, the telephone, the phonograph, not to mention the airplane. . . .

The United States is presiding at a general reorganization of the ways of living throughout the world.

The one really new gospel we have introduced is the revelation, after centuries of passively endured privations, that a man may at last free himself of poverty, and, most fantastic innovation of all, that he may actually enjoy his existence. . . . And so, without our wishing it, or even knowing it, we appear as the terrible instigators of social change and revolution.

The major revolutionary message the world was interested in hearing was not ideological but material. Slogans like "free enterprise" and "democracy" have little meaning in countries without the means to pay for it. In spreading the American gospel to other parts of the world, it is useful to remember the natural abundance we enjoyed as we started our democratic revolution, followed by our technological ingenuity, that created further abundance and growing self-sufficiency. When our system collapsed in the Depression, FDR proposed his Four Freedoms. The first two were political: freedom of speech and freedom of religion. But the second two—freedom from want and freedom from fear—were essentially economic. Democracy and economic prosperity go hand in hand.

❧

One of the perplexing aspects of America is the existence of slavery in a country of freedom and opportunity. "A snake in the garden of freedom," Alexis de Tocqueville called it. How could this happen? According to David Halberstam:

America was the only one of the developed nations that, for a variety of reasons—climate, richness and abundance of fertile land—had experienced its colonial era on native soil. When the age of empire *was finally over in the middle of the twentieth century, all the other colonial powers could pull back, announce they were out of the business of empire, and cut, if it were, the umbilical cord that bound colony to mother country. In America that, of course, was impossible.*

In other words, it was easy for France and England to ban slavery because they never had to live with it. Slavery for them was always offshore. America was different.

In attempting to deal with this issue, one of the benefits of having a Constitution all sail and no anchor is that the Constitution is "what the judges say it is" (Charles Evans Hughes), which is why British prime minister William Gladstone called it "the most wonderful work ever struck off at a given time by the brain and purpose of man." History would support this conclusion: our Constitution and Bill of Rights, by lasting virtually intact for more than 230 years, have set the world record for continuous government. There is not a country in the world that can approach this remarkable feat.

But the beginning was not easy. Of the fifty-five delegates who drafted the Constitution, only thirty-nine signed it. Just to get these votes, the Federalists had to promise they would propose and support a Bill of Rights. That project took another two years, and included a specific provision that any powers not delegated to the new government be reserved for the states and the people.

How the Constitution evolved in actual practice was never a straight line, nor was its survival assured. When President Eisenhower in 1953 chose Governor Earl Warren of California for chief justice, people were astounded that the Supreme Court would be headed by a politician, not a legal scholar. They underestimated what Eisenhower was doing: selecting a man who knew how to bargain and cut a deal. When the new chief justice decided to take on the school desegregation issue presented by *Brown v. Board of Education*, he made a bold gamble: all or nothing. Given the gravity of the decision, the decision must be unanimous. "He wanted no dissents or concurrences that lower courts, legal scholars, the press, and other commentators could pick apart."

It took a politician, working behind closed doors of the Supreme Court chambers, to bring the recalcitrant judges in line and achieve what the Founding Fathers, the Constitution, the Bill of Rights, and countless judges had failed to do. Such was America, a country all sail and no anchor. And what kind of a man was Earl Warren to achieve this? Like Benjamin Franklin and like Lincoln, he was an optimist. Every morning when he got the newspaper, he would read the sports pages first. "They record people's accomplishments," he said, not the failures that made up most of the rest of the news.

There is a famous line in American jurisprudence that says "The life of the law has not been logic; it has been experience" (Oliver Wendell Holmes). Once again, a positive statement, implying progress and improvement—and a use of the past. When Abraham Lincoln crafted his Gettysburg Address, he didn't refer to the beginning of the United States as 1789, when the country was formed, he referred to an earlier time—1776 ("four score and seven years ago"). More important than the country's government was the idealism that created it.

Did Slavery Generate Racism, or Did Racism Generate Slavery?

➤**1700**   Slavery, that "peculiar institution," was not peculiar to America, but what was special was the way it evolved into an institution of ingrained racism according to which blacks were inferior to whites. Only in America could there emerge, as one Afro-American historian wryly put it, "the traditional idea that slaves enjoyed their situation, that Africans looked forward to traveling abroad, and what better way than a free trip on one of Her Majesty's slave ships."

The first blacks to be shipped to America beginning in 1619 were not slaves but indentured servants—as were many whites. This was the practice in Europe, where indentured servants were treated with respect, often as side-by-side equals, with the right to go free after a fixed period of service. But unlike in Europe, land in America was plentiful and dirt-cheap, necessitating the importation of tens of thousands of indentured servants. Africa being the cheapest source of those servants, and also not protected by European laws concerning the natural rights of man, there emerged the practice of servitude for life for blacks. By the early 1700s this concept of indefinite servitude had been stretched further to incorporate the view of slaves as chattel, to be freely sold and traded by their owners. A black man was not a man, he was an inferior man—later codified in the Constitution as three-fifths of a man in apportioning votes.

In less than one hundred years, from 1619 to the early 1700s, slavery had evolved from an economic transaction to being rationalized as a legitimate if racist institution. How could this happen in a nation supposedly devoted to the ideals of freedom and liberty? Why here in America, and nowhere else in the world?

The answer lies in the way slavery and cruelty enslave the master, not just the victim, and bring out the worst in people—a phenomenon witnessed later in the Nazi treatment of Jews in World War II and the Serbian treatment of Muslims in Bosnia. Says former Princeton professor Henry Drewry:

> *I suggest that instead of mistreating black men because they hated them, whites may have come to hate black men because they mistreated them . . . On the one hand Americans were proclaiming liberty, equality, and the rights of man, and on the other they were saying they wanted a system which controlled black men and allowed*

> *whites to have blacks to do their bidding in all things whatsoever. . . . To resolve the conflict whites rationalized that slaves were not entitled to things others were entitled to because they were somehow subhuman.*
>
> *I suggest that it is not in spite of the Declaration of Independence and concern with the rights of man that slavery developed in such a peculiar way; rather, it is because of the Declaration of Independence and the beliefs in liberty and equality that American slavery developed the way it did. If an American was to believe in lofty ideals, he could not believe in them comfortably and deny them to certain men. So the only solution was to believe in these high ideals and at the same time believe that black people who were enslaved and mistreated were not men.*

This idea that slavery enslaves the slaver is not a new thought; it was stated by Thomas Jefferson in his 1783 *Notes on Virginia,* where he admitted that slavery, by "permitting one half of the citizens . . . to trample on the rights of the other, transforms those into despots." Added Henry James in 1863, "It is only the master who . . . seems to have been degraded by it."

In 1852, the *New York Times* had sent Frederick Law Olmsted, later to become famous as the landscape architect of Central Park in New York, the U.S. Capitol Building, and many other famous parks and gardens, on a tour of the South. Olmsted produced a two-volume book, *The Cotton Kingdom: A Traveller's Observations on Cotton and Slavery in the Ameri-*

can *Slave Trade*, that stands as one of the most powerful exposés ever written. This young man did not mince words: in addition to exposing the fallacy that slavery was economically profitable, he identified the root problem: Southern self-rationalization. Nowadays it makes for astounding—if not tragic—reading:

> *The present attitude of the South still finds a mode of justification with many minds, in the broad assertion that the negro is not of the nature of mankind, therefore cannot be a subject of inhumanity. This, of course, sweeps the field, if it does anything. . . .*
>
> *South of Virginia, an intelligent man or woman is rarely met who does not maintain, with the utmost apparent confidence, that the people who do the work of the North are, on the whole, harder driven, worse fed, and more destitute of comfort than are the slaves of the South.*

Olmsted related an encounter with a Northern gentleman on a Mississippi riverboat steamer, talking about a conference of Southerners he had recently attended: "They believed the South the centre of Christianity and the hope of the world, while they had not the slightest doubt that the large majority of the people of the North were much more to be pitied than their own negroes."

Obviously, one of the legacies of slavery was to cause Southerners to sink into a dream world, devoid of reality. In 1994 America's most prominent Afro-American pointed to this truth. At a time when he was touted as a potential presidential candidate, General Colin Powell was asked by *Newsweek* what advice he would give young blacks. He counseled "young blacks not to let racism be *their* problem: 'Let it be a problem to someone else. You can't change it. Don't have a chip on your shoulder, and don't think everyone is staring at you because you're black. . . . Let it drag them down.'"

The Plaque with No Name

►**1774** The Tomb of the Unknown Soldier in Arlington, Virginia, honors a brave World War I soldier of unknown identity. In the Old Cadet Chapel at West Point is another memorial for a brave soldier who fought for his country in the American Revolution. His plaque, too, is nameless.

But we know who he was.

The 1774 Battle of Saratoga was the turning point of the American Revolution, won in large part by the extraordinary bravery of one general who "turned likely defeat into momentous victory." He fell wounded, and today that spot is marked by a monument hailing him as "The Most Brilliant Soldier of the Continental Army." Had the man died, his name would have entered the annals of America's greatest generals. But unfortunately he lived.

Lying in the hospital for weeks with a

leg badly fractured by a musket ball, he seethed with fury that all the glory went to General Horatio Gates, who got a special medal from Congress while he got nothing. Angry at his fellow Americans for failing to give him what he considered his due, and unable to recognize that it was his arrogance and personal vanity that made people dislike him, he sought recognition from others—like the British. Today the name Benedict Arnold is associated with treason.

Twenty-Four Hours That Changed the World

➤**1776** July 2: Up for ratification by the thirteen colonies was the resolution declaring independence. For ratification to pass, seven out of the thirteen had to approve. For a colony to approve, a majority of delegates was required. But in reality, a simple majority of delegates and colonies was not enough; the vote for a move so bold had to be unanimous. Nothing less would do.

Back in June, Thomas Jefferson had learned that six colonies were likely to vote no. If one of the seven likely "yes" colonies changed its vote, the independence movement would be dead in the water. With a month to go, it was essential to garner more support.

On July 1, the day before the showdown, the Continental Congress took a trial vote and concluded that a positive movement was well under way: the vote in favor was now 9–2, with one tie and one abstention. The two colonies ready to vote negative were Pennsylvania and South Carolina, the colony tied was Delaware, and the colony abstaining was New York. With twenty-four hours left to go, the independence supporters, led by Samuel Adams and John Adams of Massachusetts, put the pressure on the recalcitrants led by John Dickinson of Pennsylvania.

How one would have loved to be "a fly on the wall"! But alas, there were no "leaks" in those days, no self-justifying journals by the protagonists. All we know—and some of these stories may be apocryphal—is the following:

• When John Hancock said, "We must all hang together," Benjamin Franklin responded, "Yes. We must all hang together, or most assuredly we shall all hang separately!" Adding to the drama was the giant Benjamin Harrison of Virginia (father and great-grandfather of U.S. presidents), a bull of a man at six feet four inches and 240 pounds. He picked up the diminutive Elbridge Gerry of Massachusetts (later vice president of the United States under Madison), deposited him on a chair, and shouted, "With me, it [hanging] will all be over in a minute. But you, you'll be dancing on air an hour after I'm gone."

• Caesar Rodney, back home in Delaware, hearing he was needed immediately within twenty-four hours, outdid Paul Revere and rode the eighty miles on horseback to Philadelphia to arrive just in time to cast the tie-breaking vote that tipped Delaware into the independence column, two votes to one.

• In an act of remarkable magnanimity, the two Pennsylvania delegates most opposed, John Dickinson and Robert Morris, abstained from voting so as to enable the three pro-independence delegates to carry the state, three votes to two (out of a total of seven).

• The youngest delegate, twenty-six-year-old Edward Rutledge of South Carolina, persuaded his brother-in-law Thomas Middleton to sign, thus putting the pressure on the other two delegates to switch their votes.

• When an alarming message arrived from George Washington, reporting that the British were about to attack New York, the state's four delegates, deadlocked but fearing being abandoned, finally went along.

The final vote of the thirteen colonies on that pivotal day: 13–0. Even the delegates themselves were stunned by their achievement. It was a day, wrote John Adams, that "ought to be commemorated as the day of deliverance by acts of devotion to God Almighty. It ought to be solemnized with pomp and parade, with shows, games, sports, guns, bells, bonfires and illuminations from one end of the continent to the other, from this time forward forever more."

Still to be resolved were some disputes over the wording of Jefferson's Declaration of Independence. It wasn't until two days later that the final document was ready. In celebrating their July Fourth national holiday,* Americans are really celebrating the miracle that took place between July first and July second.

A Nation Legally, But Not Emotionally

►**1783** The concept of a unified nation took many years to catch hold. The English made sure of that by insisting, as a last-minute demand before recognizing independence in 1783, that the thirteen colonies be listed individually under the country name "United States of America." Says historian Don Cook, "The English diplomats believed this would convey that these were not truly *united* states and that England had not yet relinquished those last connections in the capitals once ruled by royal governors." To make sure

---

* Alas, independence wasn't the only topic on people's minds. From Maine all the way down to Georgia, smallpox was a major scare. In Boston the day before the declaration, the hot topic of gossip was the citywide campaign of inoculation compelling people to deliberately infect themselves with a small dose of smallpox to produce immunity.

the rebels got the message, the British foreign minister refused to send an envoy to the infant republic, saying he could not afford to send thirteen.

True to form, the new country behaved like a collection of squabbling states and unclaimed territories, all with different ideas of liberty and equality. For example, in New Jersey but nowhere else, women had the right to vote. In some states, a black man counted as three-fifths of a person in calculating population and number of seats in the House of Representatives; in other states, he counted not at all.

Disagreements among the states were frequent and occasionally bitter enough to provoke talk of secession, new constitutions, and independent nation-states. During the wrangling over the proposed Jay Treaty of 1795, New Jersey and other states threatened to secede if the treaty was not ratified; that the treaty eventually got the necessary two-thirds majority, but just barely, was due only to heavy lobbying by President Washington. During the War of 1812, public opinion in support of the war was so weak in New England that the governors of Massachusetts, Connecticut, and Rhode Island flatly refused to call their state militias into national service. New England politicians got together for a convention in Hartford in 1814, talked of potential secession, and agreed to lend no more money to the national government. The founder of the Massachusetts General Hospital and a leading figure of

the day, a holder of several university honorary degrees, proposed a new constitution for the United States that would recast the map and exclude any people living in the area defined by the Louisiana Purchase.

Unlike the first thirty years of the republic, when the predominant issue had been one of national independence and coexistence with powerful European nations, the major issue after Andrew Jackson became president in 1828 was one of continental expansion. This was a divisive issue, revealing sectional and state loyalties that far overrode national patriotism.

The defining moment of national unity came only in 1863 when Lincoln delivered his Gettysburg Address, advocating "that this nation, under God, shall have a new birth of freedom—and that government of the people, by the people, for the people, shall not perish from the earth." Until the Civil War, the United States had been a collection of states and territories, all with different laws regarding equality and liberty. The name of the country before Gettysburg was usually expressed as a plural: "The United States *are* a free country." After Gettysburg it finally became a singular: "The United States *is* a free country."

Observes the historian Marcus Cunliffe, "America became a nation legally before it was one emotionally." Born of a revolution and more loyal to their particular state or region than to their country, Americans needed almost one hundred years and a civil war before they could think of themselves as one nation. Even as late as 1860, people were coming up with all kinds of strange ideas about how to organize the states. The commanding general of the United States armies and 1852 presidential candidate, Winfield Scott, sent a memo to President Buchanan (with a copy to president-elect Lincoln): "Views Suggested by the Imminent Danger of a Disruption of the Union by the Secession of One or More of the Southern States." In this memo Scott proposed, as a lesser evil to war, that the United States reorganize itself into four countries: the Eastern Northern States, the Old South, the Middle West, and the Far West. Obviously, for such a preposterous notion to be suggested, people did not have much confidence in the concept of a single, unified country.

Religion, the Bane of Freedom

There is no country in the world where the Christian religion retains greater influence over the souls of men than in America.

—Alexis de Tocqueville, *Democracy in America*

►**1789** When James Madison sat down in 1789 to draft amendments to the Constitution to reassure the thirteen colonies that they would not be overwhelmed by the power of the proposed new central government, his first order of business was religion. More than the right to bear arms, trial by jury, and freedom from unreasonable search and seizure, religion was an issue that had to be dealt with forcefully. Out of Madison's proclamations on religion came even broader freedoms. The First Amendment of the Bill of Rights, written by Madison, guarantees not only separation of church and state but also the freedom to worship, freedom of speech and press, and the right to assemble.

Why religion first and foremost? Because the colonies' first experiment with religion had been extensive—and disastrous. There had been no separation of church and state, in fact just the opposite. Every colony had its own official religion. New Hampshire, Massachusetts, and Connecticut were Congregational; Rhode Island was Baptist (although other Protestant sects were still welcome); New York and New Jersey were Dutch Reformed; Delaware was Lutheran; Pennsylvania was Quaker; Maryland was Catholic; and Virginia, the Carolinas, and Georgia were Anglican (Episcopal).

Anybody emigrating to America would have been well advised to check just where the boat was going. Interlopers and infidels were not welcome. Twelve of the thirteen colonies, for example, had strident anti-Quaker laws. When Puritan Massachusetts banished several Quakers and they tried to return to Boston, it hanged them.

"We Think in English"

►**1790** So said Alexander Hamilton, meaning that America was essentially an Anglo-Saxon nation. For one of our Founding Fathers to say this, so soon after a bitter six-year war with the British, may strike people as a bit bizarre. Hardly. "Let us remember," said the American-born Nancy Astor, a member of the British Parliament in the 1930s, "that the American War of Independence was fought by British Americans against a German king and a reactionary prime minister for British ideals."

Americans have long believed that the United States has been unique because of its democracy. This is wrong. While the United States was the first country to break free from its mother country and declare independence, many Latin American countries soon followed. Today all of these countries are liberated, most of them have free "democratic" elections (even if the president acts high-handedly), press freedom is limited, and corruption is commonplace.

What set America apart from other emerging nations was its heritage of British laws and institutions. This should be no surprise: before the American Revolution, the colonies and England were together for almost 170 years. Capitalism, property rights, respect for the individual, due process of law, trial by jury, and right of representative assembly all came from immigrants from England. Mercantile transactions, insurance policies, and credit instruments subject to English law became the basis of American commercial activity. When Hamilton said, "We think in English," he was referring to British common law, rooted in religious principles, and concepts of "Natural Law," which held that a person is endowed by his Creator with a right to life, liberty, and property, and that individual rights are derived from a Higher Power—not from the government.

In Hamilton's view—he was a financier, after all—freedom depended on the security of one's property. He wasn't the only one who thought this way; joining him were Franklin, Washington, Jefferson, Madison, and Adams. Said John Adams, "Property must be secured, or liberty cannot exist."

The key to property was not owning or inheriting it like an aristocrat, but doing something with it. Benjamin Franklin, who spent fourteen years of his life in London—his favorite years—said, "People do not enquire concerning a Stranger, *What IS he?*, but *What can he DO?*" People were expected to improve themselves. Same for property: property rights were sacrosanct but not absolute. The British philosopher John Locke (1632–1704) argued that only "by adding labour to things found in a state of nature" could people "exercise a maker's right that entitled them to articles, including fields." According to the British concept of property rights, squatters and beneficiaries of government land grants must improve the land in order to claim it in perpetuity and enjoy the full protection of due process. In 1844 newspaper editor Horace Greeley made his famous exhortation, "Go West, young man." Less well known is the rest of the sentence: "and grow up with the country." In other words, do something with it, improve it. The American Homestead Act of 1862 was very specific that free land from the government could only be earned by making improvements. In time this concept of improvement expanded to intellectual rights, the source of many trade disputes and legal battles today. Even U.S. patent law draws directly from British concepts of commerce. Also owing a great debt to the British is the limited-liability company, originated by the Dutch in the 1600s and refined by the British in the 1800s, that formed the basis of capitalism. Nicholas Murray Butler, Columbia University president and Nobel Prize laureate, "equated the invention of the limited liability corporation with that of steam locomotion and electricity."

By the later nineteenth century America had started to become a world power. In 1898 Prince Otto von Bismarck was asked the decisive factor in modern history. He replied, "The fact that the North Americans speak English."

Said John Hay, U.S. secretary of state, "The one indispensable feature of our for-eign policy should be a friendly under-standing with England." He wasn't talking about a peace between two nations, any more than was George Bernard Shaw in his glib quote, "England and America are two countries separated by a common language." The basis of common language is shared values, in this case such values being separation of church and state, sepa-ration of government powers, free speech, personal freedom, abhorrence of bribery and corruption, and encouragement of capitalism and the private sector. Years later, Winston Churchill (who had an American mother) talked frequently about America and England having "a special re-lationship."* But it wasn't a relationship of siblings who speak the same language or fight the same war; it went deeper than that, to the point of recognizing con-tradictions. In pamphlets issued to the British people when 1.3 million American soldiers started arriving in England in 1942, the British Army Bureau of Current Affairs emphasized, "Americans are not Englishmen who are different, but for-eigners who are rather like us."

Today English is the world language, understood by 25 percent of the planet. It is the preferred language of computers (invented in America), the Internet (in-vented by the U.S. military), and the World Wide Web (invented by an English-man, now living in America). It is the

---

* His parents got engaged three days after they met—certainly setting the record for Anglo-American affinity.

standard language of international airlines. It is even endorsed by the UN: in 1977 when the *Voyager* I rocket launched a probe into outer space in search of extraterrestrial life, it carried a welcome from the head of the UN—in English.

There is a basic explanation for this permanence. Says one British philologist:

> *Our language and literature and our basic philosophy of government developed in parallel: if the English-speaking people have been writing well for over four centuries, the reason is not simply that they wrote in English but that they have had a lot to write about—and could write it, generally speaking, with relatively little interference from government or anyone else.*

Generosity and Unselfishness

➤**1816** In 1807, Gouverneur Morris, U.S. ambassador to France and writer of the final draft of the Constitution, returned to his landed estate in New York. Never one lacking for ladies, he shocked his friends by settling down and getting married in 1809, at the age of fifty-seven. His choice of a wife, moreover, was even more startling: Nancy Randolph, a young Virginia girl who had been seduced by a brother-in-law and accused of murdering her baby, saved from hanging only by the eloquence of Patrick Henry and his fellow member of the legal "dream team," future chief justice John Marshall. To make ends meet, she was running a boardinghouse in New York City when she was suddenly swooped up and transformed into a lady of one of America's largest manors. But the marriage was a happy one, and upon his death in 1816, Gouverneur Morris left behind one of the most marvelous testimonials of a man's love for a woman. His will stated that she was to receive an ample income for life, and that if she remarried the income should be doubled.*

Black Affiliation with America, Not Africa

➤**1880** Until recently, very few black Americans cared about Africa. If anything, they wanted to forget it. When emancipated blacks after the Civil War chose their last names, they chose American names like Washington, Jefferson, and Jackson—not African names.

The three most influential blacks in American history had definite views as to their real home. "No one idea has given rise to more oppression and persecution toward the colored people of this country," wrote Frederick Douglass in 1880,

---

* As it turned out, she never did; she died twenty-one years later, a widow.

"than that which makes Africa, not America, their home. It is that wolfish idea that elbows us off the sidewalk, and denies us the rights of citizenship." Added W. E. B. Du Bois, "Neither my father nor my father's father ever saw Africa or knew its meaning or cared overmuch for it."

"The Negro is an American," said Martin Luther King Jr., many years later. "We know nothing of Africa."

⤜⤛

Neither, for that matter, did the early black slaves who first came to America—other than their local villages. The irony of the Afro-American identity movement on college campuses today is its severe misreading of history. The Africa they claim would be greeted with a quizzical look by their great-great-great-grandfathers. Were the two generations to get together for dinner, one suspects neither would understand what the other was talking about.

The African continent, since 1400, had been the world center for slavery, with African kings selling slaves to the Middle East and, to a lesser degree, Europe. In northern and northeastern Africa, Islamic wars led to much bloodshed and selling of prisoners for booty. By selling off the male members of a defeated tribe into slavery, the victorious tribe could be better assured of security.

A trading network of African middlemen developed, to meet the availability and demand for slaves. When the demand from America created a large new market, European and American ship captains found coastal African chiefs ready and willing to supply slaves by raiding the interior and bringing back prisoners for sale. Because of the enormous demand, it was not easy: ship captains would take anywhere from one hundred to two hundred days scouring the coast for traders who had enough slaves to fill up the ship. The trading system was a well-organized network of agents and rules: the African coastal traders had to pay tribute to their local king based on the number of bodies seized from the interior. When America ceased to be a market after the 1860s, African trade continued serving other markets in northern Africa and the Middle East.

The whole issue of "black slavery of blacks" is a troublesome one: how could blacks have carried on slave-trading after others had abolished the practice? The answer is simple, and quite similar to the Europeans' experience, though it took longer to take hold. In Europe beginning in the fifteenth century, there grew the concept that only non-Europeans could be enslaved. Slavery was viewed as a punishment worse than death. Eventually, by the beginning of the 1800s, the European concept expanded to all peoples, and so Britain and other European nations abolished the practice for everybody.

The same logic applied in Africa, but within a different definition of race. Unlike Europe, immunity from enslavement was given only to those who belonged to one's own tribe or nation; blacks did not view themselves as "Africans." Rather, they were members of a tribe. Says the late Harvard historian Nathan Huggins:

> *The twentieth-century Western mind is frozen by the horror of men selling and buying others as slaves and even more stunned at the irony of black men serving as agents for the enslavement of blacks to whites. . . . African merchants saw themselves as selling people other than their own. The distinctions of tribe were more real to them than race.*

Adds the Afro-American intellectual Thomas Sowell of the Hoover Institution at Stanford University:

> *Blacks were not enslaved because they were black but because they were available. Slavery has existed in the world for thousands of years. Whites enslaved other whites in Europe for centuries before the first black was brought to the western hemisphere. Asians enslaved Europeans. Asians enslaved other Asians. Africans enslaved other Africans, and indeed even today in North Africa, blacks continue to enslave blacks.*

Even in America up to the Civil War, many free blacks had black slaves. A black in America today is not necessarily a soul brother of a fellow black. Were he to ex-amine his roots, he might find his soul brother to have been his enslaver.

Ban the Book!

➤**1885**   This was the year of *Huckleberry Finn*, acclaimed by Ernest Hemingway as America's greatest novel: "All modern literature comes from one book by Mark Twain. It's the best book we've had. All American writing comes from that. There was nothing before. There has been nothing as good since."

When it came out, however, *Huckleberry Finn* was savaged by critics, to the point that it was banned by the Concord, Massachusetts, public library as "trash . . . suitable only for slums." Fortunately the library ban heightened public curiosity about the book and increased the book's sales dramatically. "They have expelled Huck from their library as 'trash,'" retorted Twain. "That will sell 25,000 for us, sure."*

Public libraries weren't the only ones to censor free speech. In 1838, Ralph Waldo Emerson gave a famous address to the Harvard Divinity School that renounced organized Christianity in favor of personal revelation; he was not invited to speak at Harvard again for thirty years.

Subsequent books banned in America after *Huckleberry Finn* included not only books of the far right or the far left, but

---

* He was wrong. It sold 50,000 copies.

also mainstream books like the *American Heritage Dictionary*, *Webster's Dictionary (Seventh Edition)*, Theodore Dreiser's *An American Tragedy*, William Faulkner's *As I Lay Dying*, F. Scott Fitzgerald's *The Great Gatsby*, Benjamin Franklin's *Autobiography*, Nathaniel Hawthorne's *The Scarlet Letter*, J. D. Salinger's *The Catcher in the Rye*, John Steinbeck's *Of Mice and Men* and *The Grapes of Wrath*, and Walt Whitman's *Leaves of Grass*. Foreign works that felt the censor's wrath included Boccaccio's *Decameron*, Aldous Huxley's *Brave New World*, James Joyce's *Ulysses*, Shakespeare's *Romeo and Juliet* and *Hamlet*, and Jonathan Swift's *Gulliver's Travels*. During World War II, the government forbade the military from distributing any news or books "containing political argument or political propaganda of any kind designed or calculated to affect the result of [a federal] election." Also banned by the U.S. Army was *The Republic* by Plato, a biography of Oliver Wendell Holmes, and Charles Beard's books on American constitutional government. In 1982 James Bamford published a book on the National Security Agency, *The Puzzle Palace*, drawing upon reams of publicly available information. The book became a celebrity, and even made the cover of *Newsweek*. The NSA was not so amused, however, and tried to stop publication of Bamford's book. The book's publisher, Houghton Mifflin, refused. *The Puzzle Palace*, wrote Bamford, "is the only book in history to have been totally unclassified as it was

being written, yet top secret by the time it was published."

Children's books under the gun included *Jack and the Beanstalk*, *Little Red Riding Hood*, *Mother Goose*, and *Tarzan*. Even *Robin Hood* was banned: the story of a man who took from the rich and gave to the poor—obviously a Communist.

Today, with the rise of "political correctness" on college campuses, book-banning has reemerged from its hibernation since the 1950s. Gone are the Communists, as are the various racial and ethnic minorities who feel offended by characterizations in certain books and want these books eradicated. Today, *Huckleberry Finn* is under a new attack: racism. A number of Afro-Americans now accuse America's greatest novel of depicting their race in an unfavorable light, not because of what it says about them, but because they only play a minor role in the book's lineup of major characters. Such is the treatment of great literature in today's ideological wars.

Anybody who doesn't think censorship hasn't returned to America need only look at the curious case of Gore Vidal. One of America's most prolific authors since 1946, with some twenty-five books and five hundred essays and magazine articles to his credit, Vidal needed only scribble in his sleep and book publishers would line up at the door. At least that's the way it used to be, until 9/11.

Many people blame the Patriot Act for the recent fear of censorship. Actually, the problem began with Bill Clinton, not

Bush. Sensitive to being soft on military matters, Clinton had responded to Osama bin Laden by passing an Anti-Terrorism Act that wouldn't pass a first-year course at Yale Law School, it was so vaguely worded. The act defines as illegal and worthy of punishment any actions that "appear to be intended toward violence or activities which could intimidate or coerce a civilian population; or to influence the policy of a government."

Influence the policy of government? Aren't most political speeches and pamphlets written to "coerce the population" or "influence the government"? What else was Samuel Adams doing, stirring up the rebels against the British in 1774?

Gore Vidal's mistake—if it can be called that—was that he spoke out against the patriotic jingoism of post 9/11 and said some unflattering things about America that later, as the war in Iraq dragged on with no end in sight, seemed fairly reasonable. Vidal's essay, "September 11, 2001 (A Tuesday)," was turned down by *Vanity Fair* and *The Nation* for its "anti-American sentiments." Both magazines had been longtime supporters of Vidal. Subsequently, Vidal packaged the article with several earlier essays into a book; again, no takers in America. He then turned to a publishing house in Italy, which published it under the title *The End of Liberty—Toward a New Totalitarianism*. The book was soon translated into twelve different languages and became a European bestseller. Finally a small independent publisher in America took it on, under the title *Perpetual War for Perpetual Peace: How We Got to Be So Hated*, and it became a U.S. bestseller, as did Vidal's sequel.

Imaginative Philanthropy

➤**1888** One of America's most remarkable traits is its enormous amount of private philanthropy, whereby people who have attained great wealth are expected to pay back society by making charitable contributions. No country in the world has produced the foundations America has, nor is the percentage of charitable giving so great. Observed the British politician James Bryce in his 1888 classic, *The American Commonwealth*, "In works of active beneficence no country has surpassed, perhaps none has equaled the United States."

The history of American philanthropy reveals not only enormous amounts of money, but remarkable creativity in using it. How money is given away, by setting a powerful example, can be just as important as the amount dispensed. The history of American philanthropy has many wonderful stories. Here are a few for today's super-rich to ponder, hopefully with a sense of modesty and humility.

Andrew Carnegie gave enormous gifts for schools and libraries. His most interesting gift, however, is a little-known one, for the simple reason that it was rejected by the president of the United States and so never saw the light of day. At the end of the 1898 Spanish-American War, many luminaries such as presidential candidate William Jennings Bryan, ex-president Grover Cleveland, Henry Adams, and Mark Twain were appalled at the prospect of the United States hanging on to the Philippines after "liberating" it from Spain and paying Spain $20 million in compensation. Equally appalled was Andrew Carnegie. "Is it possible that the American republic is to be placed in the position of the suppressor of the Philippine struggle for independence?" Carnegie asked. Backing his words with deeds, he went to President William McKinley and offered to reimburse the U.S. its $20 million in return for Filipino independence. Carnegie was turned down, and so America embarked on a futile guerrilla war costing hundreds of American lives and ending with ten thousand Filipinos dead.

❧

Nathan Straus was a Russian immigrant who founded Macy's, the world's largest department store. But his true passion was children's health: for more than twenty years he financed milk stations so that needy children could get pasteurized milk, and saved the lives of almost 450,000 children. Observed Admiral George Dewey, "If all the little children whose lives Straus saved could mass themselves . . . he would have the most splendid memorial ever made to man." Straus died a bachelor in 1931, leaving an estate of only $1 million.

That's all that was left of his great fortune. His will stated, "What you give for the cause of charity in health is gold, what you give in sickness is silver, and what you give in death is lead." In believing that the true philanthropist should give away his money while alive, Nathan Straus was following a particularly American view of philanthropy.

❧

Spurred on by money-hungry universities, many wealthy people leave money to their alma mater with their name emblazoned on a building—but it didn't used to be that way.

Fascinated by the system of "residential colleges" at Oxford and Cambridge as a solution to making large universities more egalitarian and personal for students, Edward Harkness approached his alma mater, Yale, in 1928 and offered to bankroll a transformation of the campus. Yale dithered, so Harkness went to archrival Harvard—and got an acceptance "in ten seconds." Two years later Harkness and the Harvard president were touring the first two of the Harvard "houses" now completed, and Harkness asked that one of them be named Lowell House in appreciation of the Harvard president's support. "Certainly," said Abbott Lawrence Lowell, "if you will allow another to be named after you."

It was a major miscalculation. "He dropped my arm," recalled Lowell, "and moved away almost as if I had suggested a crime." A year later all seven houses were completed, none of them named for their gentleman benefactor. When Yale, embarrassed at Harvard's good fortune, asked Harkness to reconsider, Harkness forgave his alma mater and bankrolled a similar project for Yale.

❧

Julius Rosenwald, the chief executive who built up Sears Roebuck, gave away $63 million to charity before he died in 1932. Rosenwald was very clever in the way he gave away his money for five thousand schools: the schools were for African-Americans in eleven Southern states. His reasoning? Having experienced segregation as a Jew, he knew that the city fathers would never tolerate letting white schools fall behind Rosenwald-funded black schools. The result was increased government funding of white schools, and the betterment of schools everywhere.

❧

Dr. Laszlo Tauber escaped a Nazi concentration camp and arrived in America in 1947 with seven hundred dollars in his pocket. He was never interested in making money; he simply wanted to practice

surgery. He dreamed of having his own hospital, so in his spare time he got into the construction business, developing office buildings in Washington DC. He practiced surgery all his life, but he also became the U.S. government's largest landlord, with a net worth of $1 billion. Upon his death in 2003, Dr. Tauber's will directed that 20 percent of his estate go to philanthropy and 80 percent to his two children and their children, with the stipulation that they can never touch the capital and can never draw a yearly income greater than that of the president of the United States (currently $400,000). The surplus income, added to the capital, eventually will create one of the world's largest foundations. Upon the death of the last grandchild, the foundation is to be disbanded and the billions are to be distributed, 25 percent to the governments of Israel and the Netherlands, and 75 percent to the government of the United States, "the land of opportunity."

The Eastern View of the Wild West . . . Or, How Others See Us

▶**1900**　It is ironic that the heroic vision of the Wild West we remember today comes to us not from Westerners but from Eastern dudes: Theodore Roosevelt, Owen Wister, and Frederic Remington. Roosevelt and Wister were Harvard graduates; Remington a Yale graduate. After extensive sojourns to the West to experience the life of the cowboy, each returned home to do his creative work. Observes the historian David McCullough:

> *Roosevelt wrote his spirited accounts of roundups and bucking horses at a desk at Sagamore Hill, his twenty-two-room house overlooking Long Island Sound at Oyster Bay. Wister "pegged away" at* The Virginian, *the first true western in American literature, while escaping a Philadelphia winter in Charleston, South Carolina. Remington produced the great body of his work in a studio built to order on his hill at New Rochelle, from where he, too, could catch a glimpse of Long Island Sound.*

If this seems strange, consider that the opportunity to see ourselves as others see us is part of the richness of America's heritage. Not only the West, but also America itself, has been described best by outsiders: the definitive analysis of early America was written by a Frenchman, the best description of the American commonwealth was written by an Englishman, and the most penetrating analysis of American race relations was written by a Swede. The three outsiders were Alexis de Tocqueville, James Bryce, and Gunnar Myrdal.

Probably no man loved America more than a Frenchman, the Marquis de Lafa-

yette. He not only named his children George Washington and Virginie, but took tons of earth with him back to France so he could be buried in American soil.

Immortalized in Granite

➤**1924** America's most famous sculpture is Mount Rushmore, featuring four presidents. Why those four? According to a tourist brochure put out by the National Park Service, "These four figures symbolize the birth and trials of the first 150 years of the United States." Actually, when Gutzon Borglum picked his subjects in 1924, he used a different criterion. Three presidents obviously qualified; the fourth president, however, is unlike the other three and was very lucky to make it. To this day, historians dispute the meaning of his inclusion.

How Abraham Lincoln made it, nobody knows. According to Borglum's widow, Mount Rushmore was intended as a monument to America's expansion across the continent. Washington as a founder of the republic, Jefferson as the force behind the Louisiana Purchase, and Theodore Roosevelt as the local Badlands cowboy who had become the hero of the expansionist Spanish-American War, were obvious choices.* How did Lincoln make it? The lame excuse offered by Borglum's

---

* Other candidates, more fitting than Lincoln, would have been Madison, Monroe, Jackson, and Polk.

widow was that although Lincoln had played no role in the nation's westward expansion, he had been "the savior of the republic" and kept it from shrinking.

Special Consideration for the Handicapped

►**1932** Relations between the president and the press have always been adversarial. Even George Washington felt abused and hounded in his second term, and complained about having to undergo such magnifying-glass scrutiny. Every president has felt this way—with the exception of one. Throughout his tenure, the press made a special effort and displayed an extraordinary degree of courtesy and consideration for his physical handicap.

Have you ever wondered why all photos of FDR show him sitting down or show just the upper part of his body? FDR was a cripple, prevented by polio from ever walking again. According to his grandson Curtis Roosevelt, every day for twenty-four years he "could not get out of bed, get dressed, reach the bathroom or get to his desk without the assistance of another person and a wheelchair." But he wanted no mention of his disability, "particularly any comment that conveyed sympathy. 'Sob stuff,' he called it. He was very much of the stiff upper lip tradition."

The press tacitly agreed not to embarrass the helpless president by photograph-

ing him in an awkward physical effort; the dignity of the man and the office must be preserved. He wanted no pictures of him holding on to other people for support; only photographs taken after he had reached a chair and sat down were allowed. For many Americans, the first inkling they had of the severity of their leader's infirmity was when they saw him hobbling his way on crutches, with aides on both sides, up to the podium to give his first inaugural speech. No photograph was ever printed (one photo was taken; it remained in library archives until recently).

Today, FDR is part of today's cultural wars, with many advocates complaining that the new FDR Memorial fails to highlight his disability. Said a *USA Today* editorial, "The galleries contain not one reference to FDR's greatest feat: achieving all that he did while battling the paralysis of polio. . . . That's wrong. Roosevelt's disability is part of his history."

That may be true today, but it was not then. Says another grandson, David Roosevelt, "FDR guarded his condition closely." Not that FDR was ashamed of it in any way; he simply believed he had to hide his disability to become president and that being recognized as a cripple would diminish his image as a strong wartime leader. He would disagree with today's revisionists who claim his disability was "his greatest feat." For him, it was of secondary importance.

In 1942 Winston Churchill visited the

president at Hyde Park. The president took his guest out for a drive. Because FDR couldn't use his feet on the brake, clutch, or accelerator, he had a car equipped with an ingenious arrangement that enabled him to do everything with his hands. Driving his car with only one hand on its special controls, the president took his visitor on a high-speed spin through the winding forests along the Hudson River. Churchill was terrified. "Don't worry," teased the president, "just feel my biceps." Churchill puts his hands around FDR's upper right arm, and agreed FDR had the arms of a boxing champion.

Yet nobody suggests that for an FDR memorial.

The Word "Impossible" Does Not Exist in the American Vocabulary

➤**1935** Built during the Depression, it is one of America's greatest engineering marvels and major tourist attractions today. Standing sixty stories high, it was built with no prior model for its design—except that it would have to support 45,000 pounds per square foot. "Theories of stress and strain had never before been applied to such immense force."

The tourist attraction is Hoover Dam, twenty miles outside of Las Vegas. Consisting of 66 million tons of concrete (almost as much as all of the twentieth century's previous projects built by the Bureau of Reclamation), and designed as a horizontal curved arch facing upstream (rather than a flat embankment), Hoover Dam has withstood earthquakes and water pressure admirably. The biggest problem in building the dam was trying to pour large amounts of concrete into blocks that would remain stable (the interaction of water, crushed stone, sand, and cement causes wet cement to expand, and then contract as it dries). The dam's size and weight would generate pressures and mass that would heat the concrete to 130 degrees, making the material unstable. "Though the dam would appear solid, it would be, in reality, a pyramid of warm pudding." The engineers therefore devised an ingenious plan to cool the blocks evenly by circulating ice water through a series of one-inch pipes. By lowering the temperature to 43 degrees near the base and 72 degrees near the crest, the engineers cut down the cooling time from one hundred years to a miraculous twenty months.

❧

After its victory at the Coral Sea in 1942, the Japanese navy looked to wipe out the American navy in the Pacific once and for all. The next battleground was Midway Island. They had every reason to be confident. The U.S. Navy, crippled after Pearl Harbor, had been beaten badly at the Coral Sea, losing many ships, including its mighty aircraft carrier *Yorktown*.

Except the *Yorktown* had not sunk. Instead, it had managed to stay afloat and limp back to Pearl Harbor, where American engineers stared in horror and predicted a three-to-six-month repair job to make her seaworthy. Admiral Chester Nimitz had other ideas. He ordered the ship to be refitted immediately to rejoin the fleet already headed to Midway. Observed the naval historian Samuel Eliot Morison:

> Over 1,400 men—shipfitters, shipwrights, machinists, welders, electricians—poured in, over and under the ship; they and the yard shopmen worked in shifts the rest of the day and the next and during the whole of two nights, making the bulkhead stanchions and deck plates necessary to restore the ship's structural strength, and replacing the wiring, instruments and fixtures damaged in the blast.

Less than sixty-eight hours later, *Yorktown* left drydock and headed off to Midway, where its squadrons succeeded in sinking several Japanese aircraft carriers and its firepower attracted the entire Japanese counteroffensive away from the carriers *Enterprise* and *Hornet*, whose firepower won this pivotal battle of the Pacific. *Yorktown* itself sank, but its very existence on the battle scene—thanks to a miraculous sixty-eight hours by American engineers, maintenance technicians, fabricators, and riveters—made victory possible and demonstrated the importance in war of individual initiative all the way down the line from the commander to the lowest worker.

❦

Enter Henry J. Kaiser, the great industrialist of the twentieth century, as George Westinghouse was of the nineteenth: a human dynamo who never stopped and always maintained superb labor relations. Head of the construction consortium that had built the Hoover, Bonneville, and Grand Coulee dams, Kaiser had gone to the White House and told FDR he could build all the ships the country needed to fight World War II. FDR, a former Secretary of the Navy, knew full well Kaiser hadn't an iota of shipbuilding experience. But he was so mesmerized by the man's gall that he threw him a bone: build fifty ships. Kaiser went into high gear.

"Hurry-Up Henry" ended up building 1,383 ships. The first ship took one hundred days to build; "I'll do better," swore Kaiser. Applying assembly-line methods to shipbuilding—though building a ship of thirty thousand components is a lot more complicated than building a car—Kaiser worked incessantly to speed up the process to the point that he set a record of four days and fifteen hours to make a freighter from start to finish (the paint was still wet). His average time to build a ship was forty days. It was probably the most impressive heavy-engineering feat of all time. Kaiser achieved it by applying new methods: making ships in prefab sections, and welding them together (instead of using the traditional method of rivets). An additional benefit of this method was that welding was faster and less laborious, meaning that Kaiser could hire women to make up for the labor shortage caused by so many men sent overseas in uniform. By 1944, 18 percent of Kaiser's workers—almost all of whom had never worked in a shipyard before—were women.

"The fortunes of war were tied to these ships," it was widely acknowledged. To fight a world war that never touched its shores, the United States had to transport everything across an ocean: troops, food, planes, tanks, landing craft, airfield equipment, guns, ammunition, and fuel. Plus, with the U-boats having a field day in the North Atlantic, there was the attrition rate to worry about. The United States needed more than just lots of ships, it needed them "like, yesterday." American shipbuilding skyrocketed from 1.1 million deadweight tons to 8 million in 1942 to 19.2 million in 1943. Only then was it clear that the American shipbuilding program had exceeded the attrition gap caused by U-boat sinkings, making victory a matter of time.

The propaganda value of Kaiser's frenetic shipbuilding feat was enormous. Press and radio headlines all across America trumpeted the launching of every new Liberty ship, and gave Americans hope and pride. Henry Kaiser became so widely admired that FDR even considered him a potential running mate in 1944. By the time the war was over, Kaiser and other shipbuilders had built some 5,500 ships for the U.S. Merchant Marine. It was truly a national effort, "the handiwork of farmers, shopkeepers, housewives, and workers recruited from every walk of life."

America's Most Notable Aristocratic Family

►**1944** America has had many families with money, and other families who were aristocratic in terms of style and "class," but only one such combined family that produced a president of the United States. Most remarkably, this wealthy and aristocratic family produced two presidents, one from each party. And two Medal of Honor winners.

Like other moneyed families that have good taste, the Roosevelts did not flaunt their wealth. They did not live like the Vanderbilts in palatial Fifth Avenue houses or in so-called Newport "cottages." The entourage of Theodore Roosevelt's brothers and sisters lived in small brownstone houses in Union Square and later on Madison Avenue in Manhattan, while the Franklin Roosevelt clan all lived in the farming countryside of Hyde Park upstate on the Hudson River. They lived well. Both future presidents led rarefied childhoods. Franklin was raised by a dominating mother who kept him in curls and dresses until he was six, and forbade him to play with the village children. "The local children touched their hats to him as if he were an English lord." Theodore, too, led an unusual life. In describing himself, he stressed his genealogy: "I was born in New York, October 27, 1858; my father of old Dutch Knickerbocker stock; my mother was a Georgian, descended from the revolutionary Governor Bullock." Until age seventeen, he never went to school—he was taught by private tutors, and twice he went on a year-long Grand Tour with his family, one through Europe, the second through the Mediterranean and Palestine. When he enrolled at Harvard, his oldest sister went up to Cambridge to rent him a luxury apartment (the entire second floor of a house), and spent weeks decorating it with imported furniture and hand-sewn lace curtains to make him feel "at home." No humble dorm room for this fellow. Living in a neighborhood called "the Gold Coast" was fine. Likewise, when Franklin enrolled at Harvard, his mother moved to Cambridge with him to ensure that her son would be living in a comfortable lifestyle, financed by her father, Warren Delano, a giant in the China opium trade. Whenever Theodore or Franklin took a vacation abroad, or moved from one city to another, such movements were duly noted in the *Social Register*, the registry of America's leading "old" families. (But, of course, the drying out of their alcoholic brothers and cousins was not recorded.)

Their wealth, though not enormous, was substantial. Theodore Roosevelt's mother and sisters spent half their time visiting relatives and friends and traveling through Europe in private railroad cars. Theodore Roosevelt could squander much of his inheritance on illiquid investments such as property in the Dakota Badlands. When Franklin and Eleanor Roosevelt married in 1905, their annual unearned income in present-day dollars amounted to almost $250,000, virtually tax-free—plus all their major expenses (their first home and their five sons' private education) were paid separately, by Franklin's mother.

Yet it was these two men "born with silver spoons in their mouths" who turned out to be our most populist presidents: Theodore attacking corporate monopolies and "malefactors of ill-found wealth," and Franklin instituting the New Deal.

Then there's the story of His Father's Son.

When Theodore Roosevelt was growing up, he would see his father leave the house after Sunday dinner and walk over to the Newsboys Lodging House to give moral and financial support to the orphaned boys trying to survive by selling newspapers on the streets of New York. Many years later, living in the White House, he met one of those newsboys— who had since become very successful. The president was thrilled to be saluted by this former newsboy who told him, "I am so pleased to meet you," not as president of the United States, but "as the son of your father."

In a magazine article in 1900, President Theodore Roosevelt wrote, "What we have a right to expect of the American boy is that he shall turn out to be a good American man." Such a son, after making a small fortune on Wall Street, volunteered for service in World War I, became the youngest regimental commander and was awarded the Distinguished Silver Cross and the Silver Star. After the war he founded the American Legion and became assistant secretary of the Navy. Defeated for the governorship of New York, he was appointed by President Taft to serve as governor of Puerto Rico. When a banking crisis hit the island, he did one of the most remarkable things ever done by an American consul: he reached into his own pocket and posted a $100,000 personal guarantee to successfully stop a run on the Puerto Rican banks.

When World War II came, he petitioned to return to active duty as a colonel. Despite his poor sight, fibrillating heart, and arthritis so bad he needed a cane to hobble around, he was accepted and became one of the few fighting generals in the entire army. Promoted to brigadier general after distinguished service in North Africa and Sicily, he begged to command the initial charge of the D-Day invasion. Knowing this man was not one to sit back in the rear and would put himself in the line of fire, his commanding superior voiced hesitation.

"I am Theodore Roosevelt's son!" the man shouted. Knowing the emotional power of a president's son fighting in the middle of his troops, the commander relented, and so the brigadier general got his wish. He led the charge, and for the full day of fighting, was everywhere exhorting his men. "The bravest soldier I ever knew," said General George Patton. Exhausted by the victorious battle, his heart gave out and he died two days later and was buried at Normandy. Six months later he was awarded the Medal of Honor. Asked to name the most impressive exploit he had ever seen in war, General Omar Bradley said: "Theodore Roosevelt Jr. at Utah Beach."

Wrote A. J. Liebling, "Theodore Roosevelt had been a dilettante soldier and first-class politician; his son had been a dilettante politician and a first-class soldier." In 2001 the father also received the Medal of Honor posthumously (for his famous charge up San Juan Hill). Like son, like father.

History 101: Who Says America Is a Democracy?

➤ **2000** When Al Gore won the 2000 election popular vote and was trying to get a Florida recount, he said, "What is at stake here is the integrity of our democracy, making sure that the will of the people is expressed." Several months later, before 9/11, President Bush called for a "Century of Democracy" and the freeing of "captive nations" from dictatorship. In the subsequent war in Iraq, he justified the U.S. presence as "bringing democracy to the Middle East."

Lofty language indeed, if only it were true. Since both a Democratic vice president and a Republican president do not seem to know their basic History 101, despite their Ivy League educations, there is a possibility some readers of this book may be equally misinformed.

The United States is not a democracy, never was, and never was intended to be. It is a republic. The Founding Fathers were very explicit about this. Said Alexander Hamilton, "We are now forming a Republican form of government. Real liberty is not found in the extremes of democracy, but in moderate governments. If we incline too much to democracy, we shall soon shoot into a monarchy, or some other form of dictatorship." Warned Thomas Jefferson (who rarely agreed with Hamilton on anything, but he did here), "The majority, oppressing an individual, is guilty of a crime, abuses its strength, and by acting on the law of the strongest breaks up the foundations of society."

Jefferson and Hamilton certainly had good theory to go on. According to the historian Carl Vipperman:

Because democracy created the kind of system in which numerical majorities exercised power without taking into account differentiations between groups within the body politic and consequently judged the va-

lidity of one measure or another on the assumption that the interests of all citizens were basically the same, Aristotle rejected democracy in favor of a balanced distribution of power among constituent elements of society.

As the current battle between the majority Shiites and the minority Sunnis in Iraq demonstrates, the most difficult part of forming a stable government is protecting the rights of the minority. Dictatorship is rule by one man, democracy is rule by the masses (i.e., the mob). To ensure that the country would not descend into monarchy or mobocracy, the Founding Fathers inserted safeguards against direct election; major checks and balances included a tripartite system of government, the Bill of Rights, and the Electoral College (to give greater weight to the small states). The United States, said Benjamin Franklin, "is a republic, if you can keep it." Said John Adams, "You have rights antecedent to all earthly governments; rights that cannot be repealed or restrained by human laws; rights derived from the Great Legislator of the Universe."

The French had a revolution, too—just a few years after ours. But unlike the United States, they quickly descended into a reign of terror by the majority Jacobins. In two hundred years since, they have had one Directory, one Consulate, two empires, three restorations of the monarchy, and five republics. Not exactly a good track record for a "democracy."

No one doubts for a moment that the current American effort to spread democracy in the Middle East is a worthwhile goal. But when Afghan president Hamid Karzai said "We are committed to the democratic process in Afghanistan," one wishes—"prays" may be a better word— that the political pabulum of democracy would not subvert the need for an underlying constitutional republic.

FIVE

A Warlike Nation, Not a Militarist One

*A*major change happened to America after 1950: A powerful nation became intoxicated by its arsenal. Supported by a strong economy, America could afford a military larger than those of the next dozen nations combined. This is an extraordinary feat. Go back to Xenophon, Alexander the Great, Julius Caesar, and Napoleon, and you will not find a parallel. Forget the memorable scene of a thousand Greek ships invading Troy in the 2002 movie, think of the CNN images of the U.S. bombing Baghdad in 1991.

In 1918 and 1945 the United States strove to maintain the minimum force required and no more. How quaint! Nowadays it acts like it must be the world's policeman. Before invading Iraq in 2003, General Tommy Franks proclaimed that American generals could expect to enjoy "the kind of Olympian perspective that Homer had given his gods." Equally ignorant of the gods was Deputy Secretary of State Richard Armitage, who stated after 9/11, "History starts today." But already the gods had begun their work, lulling America into the dangerous belief she was Numero Uno and could pull the trigger whenever needed. Back in 1993, UN Ambassador (and later Secretary of State)

Madeleine Albright berated General Colin Powell, "What's the point of having this superb military that you're always talking about if we can't use it?"

General Powell was so flummoxed he didn't know to answer: we can't use it because of who we are.

Compared to many politicians, most generals who got their training in combat know the horrors of war and the limits of military power. Also as part of their rigorous training, they know their military history and how war runs counter to the American military tradition. Listen to the farewell addresses of two general-presidents: "Overgrown military establishments are under any form of government inauspicious to liberty, and are to be regarded as particularly to Republican liberty," said George Washington in 1796. Added Dwight Eisenhower in 1961, "In the councils of government, we must guard against the acquisition of unwarranted influence, whether sought or unsought, by the military-industrial complex." Observe also the actions of our third general-president, Ulysses Grant. Known in war as "the butcher," he approved of Andrew Johnson's slashing of military budgets at every opportunity, resulting in the largest military downsizing in history, leaving European militarists astounded. When he eventually did become president, with every unemployed Union general banging on his door to resurrect the war machine, Grant still said no.

Fast-forward to post–World War II. "Democracies," said General George Marshall when he was secretary of state, "cannot fight a Seven Years' War." Certainly, democracies cannot fight insurgencies where rules of decency and controlled firepower are irrelevant, and especially in places halfway around the world, as the British found in 1776. Forgotten in all of today's talk about American military power is one salient fact: America has not had a decisive victory since 1945. Even then, there's a question whether we really "won." Says one historian:

> Because the purpose of war is not merely to defeat the enemy, but to ensure a better and more lasting peace, the war of 1939–1945 ended in tragic failure. The Allies had won not a war but an annihilation. They had over-succeeded. Unconditional surrender had ignored the political truth that today's enemy is often tomorrow's ally. Utterly wrecked and discredited, Germany and Japan could not be immediately enlisted against Russia the moment Stalin began to make his moves to west and east.

Richard Armitage to the contrary, history did not start in 2001, it started in 1776. And it began in the most basic way possible.

⁓

"Where's the money?" General George Washington was beside himself. To get enough soldiers to serve in his army, he wanted his soldiers to sign up for the duration of the war, however long it lasted. Congress, fearful of standing armies and living under the fantasy that the war would be over after one or two campaigns, restricted the term of a soldier's enlistment to one year. Washington knew Congress was pipe-dreaming. To make matters worse, Congress failed to provide the funds necessary to keep his soldiers fully fed and armed. Many a departing soldier was stealing a musket to take home, meaning that there was no musket for his replacement. "Money was useful in the common affairs of life," he told the wealthy John Hancock, "but in war it was essential."

Wars are expensive—very expensive. Anyone who thinks our military history is not significant only has to look at the history of our national debt. Says Harvard Business School professor Thomas Mc-Craw, "The size of the national debt in the United States has almost always been a function of war, including the Cold War." We all know how Lyndon Johnson's strategy of "guns and butter" resulted in the high inflation of the 1970s, and how Ronald Reagan's military buildup—again without the tax revenues to pay for it—contributed to enormous government deficits. Less well known is our much more costly war (in real terms): the American Revolution. The year 1790 found America burdened with a horrendous debt load:

Government debt	$75 million
Government annual income	$5 million
Government debt/income ratio	15:1
Debt per citizen	$25

Twenty-five dollars today sounds like a pittance, but for many people in an agrarian, cashless society at the time it could represent a year's income. Paying off $75 million turned out to be an enormous task: from 1791 to 1797, interest payments on this debt accounted for more than 50 percent of all government expenditures. The $75 million exceeded the total expenditures of the United States government during its first twenty years of existence, from 1790 to 1810. Then when the young nation finally started to get its financial act together, it went to war again with its former adversary—and accomplished little more than to rack up another debt.

Whether we got our money's worth is another matter. While hardly anyone questions the need for the United States to enter World War I or World War II, the Civil War suggests otherwise. In 1850, as the war drums over slavery started to pound ominously in the distance, there emerged the possibility of compensation. It was suggested that the best way to persuade Southern plantation owners to release their slaves would be to compensate them. Thirty-five percent of the entire capital in the South was tied up in slaves, and their total value was $2 billion—equivalent to ten times the entire federal budget. Such an amount, alas, was considered so enormous as to be out of the question. Yet it would have been a lot cheaper than what happened ten years later. Several years after the Civil War, a special commission was formed to look at precisely this question. The U.S. Special Commissioner of the Revenue concluded in 1869 that the war cost was "three times as much as the slavery property of the country was ever worth."

America is a nation born of war, a tradition it has upheld—and paid for—for more than two hundred years. Yet America is not a militarist nation. Indeed, one of the most puzzling aspects about America for foreigners to understand is America's long-standing lack of bellicosity.

At no time was this more true than after the Civil War. After three and a half years of internal fighting, the United States had the world's largest standing army and certainly the most fearsome: more than a million battle-tested men, supported by a giant munitions industry. Everyone in Europe expected the United States to pick a bone and start a fight with either France or Britain—France for its adventures in neighboring Mexico, Britain

for its semiofficial support of the Confederacy. At a time when European nations were embarking upon imperialist scrambles for pieces of Asia and Africa, surely the United States would do the same.

It was not to be. By the end of 1866 the United States Army was down to 25,000 men—the fastest military downsizing in world history.* President Andrew Johnson refrained from seizing Canada, and instead settled America's shipping claims against the British for $15.5 million. He sent General Phil Sheridan to the Rio Grande to remind the French that the Monroe Doctrine still applied to Mexico, but went no further. Observes the historian Robert Leckie, "Europe was astonished . . . she could not understand—as modern despotisms still do not understand—that a nation may be martial without being militarist."

Years later, on December 6, 1941, when Japan broke off peace negotiations, it was suggested to the president that the United States launch a preemptive strike. FDR refused. "This means war," he said. "No, we can't do that. We are a democracy and a peaceful people."

After the war his successor reaffirmed this distinction in the most official manner possible. In 1945, by executive order,

* The second-fastest was the U.S. Army after World War II: It had twelve million men in 1945; by the fall of 1946 it had plummeted to fewer than two million. In the meantime, the Russians had ninety-three divisions in Europe alone and another ten divisions in the satellite countries. In Germany, one or two American divisions would be confronting forty-two divisions of Soviet troops. Clearly, our nuclear superiority was what kept the Russians at bay.

President Harry Truman made a major change to the eagle on the presidential seal: he had the eagle's head turned away from the arrows and toward the olive branch.

Democracy (power to the people) and peace go hand in hand. Whenever the United States embarked on far-flung imperialist adventures, it had to be quick (Santo Domingo, Grenada, Kuwait). Whenever it got bogged down, such as in Korea, Vietnam, and Iraq, voter aversion would compel withdrawal, not because we couldn't win but because the fight was not worth it. In addition, inevitably there would be substantial collateral deaths of innocent civilians, costing us our all-important "moral advantage" and the loss of friends. Said Samuel Adams back in 1775, "Put your enemy in the wrong, and keep him so, is a wise maxim in politics, as well as in war." "Moral advantage" is a little-appreciated but fundamental concept of effective foreign policy. There is a saying, says the historian John Freeman Clarke, that "should be engraved over the mantel of the Oval Office to remind every President: 'We are friends of liberty everywhere but we do not go abroad in search of monsters to destroy.' "

This saying, of course, comes from the Monroe Doctrine (written by Secretary of State John Quincy Adams, not by President James Monroe). Best known for its warning to the European powers to stay away from meddling in Latin American affairs, its more important message is its warning to ourselves. "Why quit our own to stand upon foreign ground?" asked George Washington. "When civilizations take up arms in order to impose their conception of civility on others," said Oliver Wendell Holmes, "they sacrifice their moral advantage."

In 1896, Harvard president Charles Eliot put militarism in its proper perspective: "The building of a navy and the presence of a large standing army mean . . . the abandonment of what is characteristically American. . . . The building of a navy and particularly of battleships is English and French policy. It should never be ours." This principle was reaffirmed in 1947 when the National Security Council was formed. Its charter reads, "To preserve the United States as a free nation with our fundamental institutions and values intact."

Finally, consider the man who was America's greatest military leader. He did not go to Annapolis or West Point. He was not a general. He never fought in war, or killed a man. But when war came, he rose to the occasion with a sterling military performance. The war was the Civil War. When it started, the head Union commander was George B. McClellan—the idol of his troops, second in his class at West Point, author of a text on the art of war, the ultimate professional soldier. If résumés could win wars, the Union had its man.

But even résumés have their limitations: the man has to be the right person for the particular job. Opposing McClellan were Jeb Stuart and Stonewall Jackson, both masters of defense: strike, withdraw, strike again. The Confederate states with their deep forests and valleys offered perfect terrain in which to wage hide-and-seek warfare. McClellan was the master of large confrontations, and therefore kept calling for more reinforcements. When he went in to fight, he usually found that the enemy had slipped away.

The winning strategy was developed by a man with no military experience. But he was observant and curious. He spent hours upon days in the War Department's telegraph office reading and sending telegrams to his generals (the e-mails of the day). He sent an assistant to the Library of Congress to bring him some good books on warfare, which he read at night. After several weeks of reading, he noted that the superior forces belonged to the Union, but that the Confederates had better generals and greater mobility to shift their troops to particular points. The only way to win this troublesome war, he concluded, would be to engage the Confederate forces on many points simultaneously: eventually one or more points would give way and the Union forces could cause disarray.

Most people told him to forget it, that such a policy was amateurish: the war would be over in a year or two, anyway.

What did he know about how to win a war? Who was he to be such an authority from reading a couple of books?

But the man persisted and got his "bookish" ideas implemented by issuing commands and signing his name at the bottom "A. Lincoln." Most historians today rank Lincoln number one among our presidents, for his leadership in preserving the Union and bringing slavery to an end. Major credit, moreover, should be given him for his contributions as a military leader. No president fulfilled the responsibility of commander-in-chief as he did.*

Lack of Imperial Ambition and Expansionism

➤**1772** Lord Clive, the great British military hero who refused to go to America to fight the American rebels, envisioned America as eventually taking over the entire New World: "That the Americans will sooner or later take all of the Spanish possessions and make Cape Horn the boundary of their empire is beyond a doubt." Imagine, from Boston to the tip of Tierra del Fuego!

Four years later Benjamin Franklin was in Paris, outlining various conditions for peace that might be negotiated with England. He demanded more than just

---

* This stands in sharp contrast to Calvin Coolidge. Asked for more planes for the Army Signal Corps, he responded, "Why can't they buy just one airplane and take turns flying it?"

independence; he demanded that Great Britain cede to the yet-to-be-established United States a sum of money for all of Canada, the Floridas, Bermuda, the Bahamas, the West Indies, and even Ireland "if it wished." Of course this didn't happen, but the precedent was set: Americans think big.

At the end of the Mexican War, the U.S. added Texas, Arizona, Colorado, Nevada, New Mexico, Utah, and California to its borders. When President Polk asked the Senate to ratify the treaty with Mexico, a dozen senators objected and said no. Why?

They wanted to annex all of Mexico.

Among the defenders of American aggression in Mexico were Karl Marx and Friedrich Engels. "Was it such a misfortune," Marx asked sarcastically, "that glorious California has been wrenched from the lazy Mexicans who did not know what to do with it?" Engels went even further, saying that "in the interest of its own development, Mexico should be placed under the tutelage of the United States."

In fact, the American expansion across the West and on to the Pacific is not the history of imperialism, but the denial of it. The dozen senators who wanted to annex Mexico were a minority at the time, and also throughout most of the nineteenth and twentieth centuries. America took several territories after 1840, but relinquished most of them. For a clearer picture of American "imperialism," we might try looking not at what America did take,

but rather at the territories it did *not* take. The "glass half empty" suggests a different story from the "glass half full."

Here are American empires that never happened:

From Texas to Mexico

The prospect of annexing Mexico intrigued the Founding Fathers; in 1798 Alexander Hamilton, retired from office after serving as Washington's treasury secretary and most powerful advisor, drew up specific plans for taking over Mexico. His fellow Federalist, President John Adams, said no (Hamilton must be "stark mad," he said). In 1846 the U.S. finally took over Texas, a full ten years after Texas had won independence from Mexico and sought American statehood. The U.S., fearful of starting a war with Mexico, had insisted that Texas remain an independent republic, despite the advice of Marx and Engels. President Polk had his eyes on Mexico, but backpedaled fast lest he jeopardize what little congressional support he had for New Mexico and California. Congress was in no mood for reckless acquisitions.

From Cuba to Canada

The vision of a north-south empire excited many Americans ranging from Thomas Jefferson to Walt Whitman to Henry Cabot Lodge. Jefferson had wanted to seize Canada during the American

Revolution. He also wanted more. "We must have the Floridas and Cuba," he said during his last days as president. When it was proposed that the United States establish a penal colony in Cuba for Negro criminals, Jefferson rejected the idea only because the United States might end up someday annexing the territory.

Said Henry Adams in 1869, "That the whole continent of North America and all its adjacent islands must at last fall under the control of the United States is a conviction absolutely ingrained in our people."

Americans would have none of it. Expansionists salivating about the annexation of Cuba, Puerto Rico, Guam, and the Philippines had to hold their breath while the Senate met to vote on the 1898 Treaty of Paris. The treaty passed—by barely one vote. In 1907 the powerful Speaker of the House, Champ Clark, led the ratification of the proposed reciprocity treaty with Canada: "I hope to see the day when the American flag will float over every square foot of the British North American possessions clear to the North Pole." His loose lips cost him plenty: Canada promptly rejected the reciprocity treaty, and the Democratic chieftains the following year rejected the candidacy of Champ Clark for the presidential nomination.

From the Pacific Coast to Asia

Even in America's most expansionist mood—after the Civil War—Secretary of State William Seward got nowhere. He got Alaska, a frozen tundra the Russians didn't want, but little else. The acquisition of Hawaii and Samoa got nowhere in the Senate.

Even after its overwhelming victory over Spain in 1898, the U.S. refrained from incorporating conquered territories into the Union. Cuba was left untouched, the Philippines were set free forty years later, Puerto Rico remained an affiliate, and it was not until 1960 that Alaska and Hawaii became states.

Nonsupport at Home

►**1776** American soldiers in Vietnam complained bitterly about the lack of support from their fellow Americans at home. But nonsupport for our fighting men is nothing new. Profiteering in war and dodging the draft are long-standing American traditions.

During the American Revolution, almost as many inhabitants of the American colonies fought for the British as for the Continental Army: seven thousand loyalists versus eight thousand patriots. During the brutal winter at Valley Forge, George Washington's troops were starving not because there was no local food available, but because the colonial farmers preferred to go to Philadelphia and sell their food to the British, who could pay more.

Even more treacherous was the War of 1812, in which two thirds of the beef eaten by the British army was provided by American traders. Without this food, the British army could not have survived against the Americans. Rail against this though he might, President James Madison could do nothing: his more basic problem was finding enough men to fight. Out of a vast force of 500,000 men called upon to serve, only 35,000 troops were in uniform at the war's peak in 1814. And this total was achieved only by offering generous bounties to prospective recruits, who rarely served more than a year anyway.

In the Civil War, Abraham Lincoln relied on the states to raise volunteers—an effort derided by General William Tecumseh Sherman as "putting out the flames of a burning house with a squirt gun." When it became clear that the war would drag on and would require longer terms of service duty, President Lincoln resorted to forced conscription. The 1863 Enrollment Act, requiring all able-bodied males to register for three-year service, was not well received: New York City was racked by a bloody four-day draft riot, and thousands of recruits—including a future U.S. president, Grover Cleveland—paid the government a $300 "commutation" fee to escape service. Instead of raising the needed 300,000 troops, the Enrollment Act raised only 150,000—and three quarters of those were paid "substitutes." In the South, conscription problems were even worse. Whereas the Confederacy had a half-million men under arms in 1863,

within a year the number had plummeted to 200,000. The war ended with more Southern troops literally hiding out in the woods and under haystacks than reporting to duty.

Even our most popular war—World War II—had its conscription problems. The United States Army in 1936 ranked twenty-first in the world in size, right behind the armies of Argentina and Switzerland. In 1938 the Ludlow Amendment, requiring that any declaration of war first be subject to popular referendum, fell just 5 percent short of being presented to Congress for a vote as a constitutional amendment. In late 1941, with fighting raging throughout Europe, and China being overrun by Japan, a desperate President Roosevelt urged Congress to renew the one-year draft law. The law passed, but by only one vote.

A one-time freakish period of isolationism? Hardly. During the middle of the war, the U.S. troop contribution was far less than Great Britain's. FDR made continual requests for more troops; most times Congress turned him down.

Not having enough soldiers is a common American dilemma—and a brake against militarism.

In the Steps of Julius Caesar

►**1776–1945** Most historians—and certainly the general public reading the newspapers—think of war as a series of battles. You win the encounters of battle—ergo, you win the war. Trenton, Saratoga, and Yorktown form convenient reference points in the American Revolution, just as Pearl Harbor, Midway, and Normandy do in World War II.

Julius Caesar thought differently. He preferred "conquering the foe by hunger rather than by steel." Combat had its place, but more important was logistics: depriving the enemy by conquering agricultural territory, destroying supply lines, and blocking off areas where potential recruits lived.

There is no glory in logistics, but logistics explains all three of America's great military victories:

The American Revolution

In what was America's longest declared war—eight years—supplies became a critical issue for both sides. In the first year the American rebels had only nine cartridges per man. In the June 1775 fight for Bunker Hill, the colonists were so low on gunpowder they had to combat the British hand-to-hand with the butt ends of their muskets. When Washington took his army out of New York and into New Jersey and Pennsylvania, chased by the British, who were drawn away from their ships in the seaports, both sides ransacked the countryside mercilessly. Jeremiah Wadsworth, a Hartford merchant, earned the sobriquet of "the quartermaster of the Revolution" for his entrepreneurial

ingenuity in arranging for enormous amounts of food, hay, horses, wagons, and teamsters for the Continental Army.

The British counted on their powerful navy to block colonial trade and to keep their own army well supplied. It was not to be. The British navy lacked the resources to bottle up the entire American coast, and American merchantmen—a larger force than the entire Continental Army—harassed British ships all the way from the North Atlantic to the Caribbean. More than two thousand British ships were captured, thoroughly disrupting British supply lines.

The Civil War

Both sides, the North particularly, required massive amounts of food, hay, horses, mules, rifles, gunpowder, hospital supplies, and myriad other items needed for a mobile fighting force.

The Northern generals had the benefit of a secretary of war and a legion of quartermasters and railroad executives who were excellent managers and could deliver goods and supplies to the Northern armies quickly. Their challenge was to provide enough food and equipment to support a massive army invading the thinly populated South. They succeeded admirably; in addition, by upping the ante and wrecking Southern railroads, burning factories and cities, destroying croplands, blocking off Western territories full of potential new recruits, and urging slaves to revolt, they were able to exert tremendous pressure on the South. The massive hardship and 9,000-percent inflation led to the widespread desertion of Southern soldiers going home to support their families. By 1865 the war's-end spectacle was not one of a conquering Northern army, but of a South simply collapsing.

World War II

America produced the greatest war production machine ever devised: 297,000 planes, 86,000 tanks, 12,000 ships, and enormous quantities of trucks and jeeps, arms, and munitions. "Without American

How wars are won: supplying the basics

production," said Joseph Stalin, the Allies "could not have won the war."

Said U.S. Admiral Ernest King, "I do not know what this 'logistics' stuff is that everyone is talking about, but I want some of it."

It is instructive that the man chosen to head the Allied Forces in Europe, and who later became the only five-star general since George Washington and Ulysses Grant, was a staff man with no combat experience. Many people wondered how a lowly lieutenant languishing in the bowels of the military bureaucracy—a man so frustrated that he toyed several times with the idea of quitting the Army—could enjoy such a meteoric rise. Dwight Eisenhower was the man of the moment, promoted over such warriors as Omar Bradley and George Patton because of his planning skills and thorough grasp of logistics. Asked to name the military weapons most essential to his success in North Africa and Europe, Eisenhower named four items remarkable for their simplicity: the bulldozer, the jeep, the two-and-a-half-ton truck, and the C-47 transport airplane.

The Costs of War

➤**1776–2005** For all the hoopla about bravery and courage of men in combat, one fact about war rarely gets any attention: paying for it. Said George Washington, "In modern wars, the longest purse must chiefly determine events." Here is what some of our major wars cost at the time:

American Revolution	$160 million
War of 1812	$105 million
Civil War	$9 billion
World War I	$23 billion
World War II	$325 billion*
Vietnam War	$140 billion
Gulf War	$61 billion

*($54 billion of it paid by the Allies)

To get a perspective on these numbers, consider how little the U.S. paid for the territories of its national expansion during the entire nineteenth century: $140 million.

Louisiana Purchase, 1803	$15 million
Florida, 1819	$5 million
Indian territories (100 million acres), 1828–40	$68 million
California, Texas, New Mexico, 1848	$15 million
Arizona and New Mexico, 1850	$10 million
Alaska, 1867	$7 million
Philippines, Guam, Puerto Rico, 1898	$20 million

A more relevant, modern-day statistic is the cost of America's greatest peacetime victory. The nine-year race to put a man on the moon cost $25 billion.

Note that the war costs cited above are for direct costs. They do not include the hidden expense of pension liabilities. This is where wars get very expensive. This cost first appeared in the Civil War (only for the Northern soldiers—the soldiers of the Confederacy got no pensions). In 1882 the expenditures of the Pension Bureau were $200 million—almost 18 percent of the government budget. In 1889, U.S. (Northern) pension expenditures exceeded the entire government budget before the Civil War.

❧

Wars, if they go on too long, strangle economies. We all know about post–World War I Germany, where hyperinflation got so bad people needed wheelbarrows to carry around enough money to eat. It could never happen here in America, could it? Lest we forget, it has happened—twice.

During the American Revolution, the money used to pay soldiers, called continental scrip, had depreciated to one tenth of one penny per dollar, or $\frac{1}{1,000}$ of a dollar (see Chapter 8, page 239). During the Civil War, the Confederate dollar plummeted in value from ninety cents in June 1861 to twenty cents in February 1863, to one and a half cents in April 1865. The poverty of the South, captured in the movie *Gone With the Wind*, was very real.

❧

Wars not only cause economic havoc and inflation, they cause government debt and personal income taxes.

When James Madison became president in 1809, he inherited a national debt of $57 million. Because of the War of 1812, by 1816 the national debt was $127 million—an increase of $70 million. It took the United States a full twenty years to pay off the $70 million and get the national debt back to the 1809 level. From 1836 to 1845 the national debt got reduced even further, from $57 million to $16 million. Then came the Mexican War, and by 1848 the U.S. had a debt of $63 million. Then came the big explosion: during the Civil War the national debt went from $75 million to $2.8 billion—a thirty-seven-fold increase. In the twenty-four months of U.S. participation in World War I, the national debt grew from $3 billion to $26 billion.

In World War II the U.S. national debt skyrocketed from $16 billion to more than $260 billion, and ushered in a mindset that debts don't matter because we owe it to ourselves. Once it had gotten used to military debt, the U.S. went on a huge military spending spree for armaments and overseas military bases that caused even Dwight Eisenhower to blanch at the growing military-industrial complex. By the time the Cold War ended when Reagan left office, the national debt was $2.7 trillion. When it came to financing something as important as war, the argument went, debts don't matter.

But to finance the debt, even if only the interest, requires income taxes. The first income tax was not, as most people believe, in 1913 when Congress ratified the Sixteenth Amendment, but during the Civil War. The Union government imposed high tariffs, excise taxes, and the first income tax. In 1872 the income tax was eliminated, but the high tariffs and excise taxes remained. In the 1880s under President Rutherford Hayes, the United States undertook a major military buildup. In 1913, on the eve of World War I, Congress enacted an income-tax law. During the war, Congress jacked up the first-bracket rate from 1 percent to 6 percent, and the top-bracket rate from 7 percent to 77 percent. In World War II, Congress raised the first-bracket rate from 4.4 percent to 23 percent, and the top-bracket rate from 81.1 percent on income higher than $5 million to 94 percent on income higher than $200,000. Payroll withholding of personal income taxes was instituted, and the population liable for income-tax payments increased more than threefold. Whereas fewer than 15 million individuals filed income tax returns in 1940, by 1945 the number had escalated to nearly 50 million.

We have had only two presidents who seemed to worry about the impact of the cost of war on America's economy and society. The first was Thomas Jefferson: "The most successful war seldom pays for its losses." The second was James Madison. In 1792 he wrote an article, "Universal Peace," in which he suggested that if every generation had to bear the expense of its own wars, fewer wars would be fought. His article is written in heavy colonial English and makes for difficult reading, but is worth the effort:

> *Of all the enemies to public liberty, war is, perhaps, the most to be dreaded because it comprises and develops the germ of every other. War is the parent of armies; from these proceed debts and taxes, the known instruments for bringing the many under the domination of the few. In war, too, the discretionary power of the executive is extended. . . . No nation could preserve its freedom in the midst of continual warfare.*

Today, as the U.S. winds down its presence in Iraq, that message is abundantly clear. Not even an economy as enormous as the United States's can absorb the costs of a long, drawn-out war costing a potential $3 trillion.

Our Greatest President— at Keeping America Out of War

►**1836** Martin Van Buren does not belong on anybody's list of great presidents, but he certainly belongs at the top of a sublist ranking presidents for diplomacy. Not only did he keep America out of war, but he did it twice, first with Mexico and then with England.

Historians tend to glorify strong presidents, and nothing makes a president stronger than being a wartime leader. In a 1961 collection of scholarly articles on "America's Ten Greatest Presidents," for instance, half the presidents were men who had led the country into war. Yet managing to keep out of war can sometimes be an even greater achievement than rattling the war drums. No one understood this better than the man who led the attack on Pearl Harbor, Admiral Isoroku Yamamoto. In 1941, upon being congratulated for his brilliant attack on Pearl Harbor, Admiral Yamamoto demurred: "A brilliant man would have found a way not to fight a war."

Fortunately for America in 1836, the man who was president was a man whose previous jobs had been secretary of state and then vice president. In addition, he was a consummate politician, saying one thing and doing another, constantly making deals. No thundering bellicosity here, just a man who, as Daniel Webster famously said, "rowed to his object with muffled oars." Another nickname for him was "the little magician."

It took a magician to deal with the Texas mess. In 1836, American settlers in the Mexican province of Texas declared their independence and sought annexation by the United States. Mexico refused to recognize the Texas Republic, and threatened war. Van Buren, despite his eight years of service under the expansionist Andrew Jackson, was less than thrilled about Texas because it was a slaveholding territory and could be the cause of even greater problems. In pursuing sectional peace, he rejected the Texans and upset a lot of Americans salivating at the prospect of a big territory. After a two-year period of diplomacy and patience, he agreed with the Mexican government to accept arbitration. Under the terms of the arbitration, Texas would remain a semi-autonomous entity. Years later, after he had left office and Texas became an issue again, Van Buren explained his reasoning. "We have a character among the nations of the earth to maintain," he said. Whereas "the lust of power, with fraud and violence in the train, has led other and different constituted governments to aggression and conquest, our movements in these respects have always been regulated by reason and justice."

More difficult problems occurred on the northern border of Van Buren's home state, New York. It was as if the War of 1812 had never ended. There, on the Canadian border, rebel "patriots" and anti-British sentiments made for several deadly incidents with the British forces occupying Canada. "Surely war with England was unavoidable," wrote the *New York Herald*. Van Buren quickly issued two proclamations of neutrality, ordered militias in New York and Vermont to enforce them, and sent his lead general, Winfield Scott, on a peace mission to the border to calm things down. But in the meantime an even worse situation erupted in nearby Maine, where

Canadians refused to leave a disputed area and Maine called out the state militia. The state's governor sent a letter to the president that must rank as one of the most insolent ever received by the White House: "But should you go against us upon this occasion," threatened the Maine governor, "or not espouse our cause with warmth and earnestness and with a true American feeling, God only knows what the result will be politically." Congress jumped into the fray with a bill authorizing $10 million and fifty thousand volunteers, and people in Bangor, Maine, burned the president in effigy.

So began the war nobody's ever heard of: the Aroostook War. Once again Van Buren sought compromise and sent General Winfield Scott on another mission to seek "peace with honor." He made it abundantly clear to the people of Maine that they could expect no aid from the federal government if its militia were to provoke an incident. He got the full support of Senator (later President) James Buchanan, chairman of the Foreign Relations Committee: "If there must be war," said Buchanan, "let it be a national war." Most important of all, Van Buren had his own son personally deliver a note to the British foreign secretary in London, Lord Palmerston, stating that he would not countenance being drawn into war by a single state and that peace would be easy "if the wishes of the men in power in both countries were alone to be consulted." Palmerston responded by praising Van Buren's "wise and enlightened course" and conceding that all negotiations be held in Washington. The result, several years later, was a formal treaty with Britain bringing all major questions to a peaceful conclusion.

Going against the wishes of people in New York and Maine cost Van Buren reelection in 1840. A few of his closest advisers even went so far as to advise him to start a war to win back the war vote and distract public attention from the administration's difficulties, but Van Buren refused. In his inaugural address he had stated that while he was ready to resist "any invasion of our rights," he was equally prepared to stay out of the affairs of other nations, domestic or foreign, and to preserve "a strict neutrality in all their controversies."

Odds of Getting Killed

►**1846**   Anytime a soldier gets called up to go fight in a war, the first question that crosses his mind is the odds of his getting killed. (If he doesn't think about it, certainly his girlfriend or mother will.) The last place he would want to be shipped off to would not be Britain or Nazi Germany or Korea—but much closer to home. For sheer carnage, the worst of our wars was the Civil War: 558,000 deaths out of a population of 40 million is equivalent to 4 million deaths today at our current population of 300 million. Or, put another way, suppose Vietnam had produced the kind of carnage the Civil War did: the result would be almost 2.8 million deaths (at

DEATH TOLLS IN U.S. WARS

Engagement	Enrolled (000)	Deaths (000)	Odds of Death: 1 out of . . .
Mexican War	79	13.3	6
Civil War	3,867	558.1	7
WW II	16,354	407.3	40
WW I	4,744	116.7	41
American Revolution	200	4.44	45
Spanish-American War	307	2.5	125
War of 1812	286	2.3	127
Vietnam War	8,744	58.2	150
Korean War	5,764	33.7	171
Gulf War	2,750	0.3	9,483

a population of 200 million). Only the passing away of an entire generation over forty years could heal the wounds of such a war.

Yet there was a war even more deadly, a footnote in the history books because it was so small and comparatively short: the Mexican War. Although the odds of getting killed are virtually identical in the Mexican and Civil Wars (one out of six and one out of seven, respectively), in fact the Mexican War was far deadlier. The average length of service in the Mexican War was thirteen months, or 66 percent of the twenty-month war, whereas in the forty-eight-month Civil War it was seventeen and a half months, or 36 percent of wartime. Being exposed to fighting during two-thirds of the time obviously incurs greater danger than fighting slightly over one-third of the time. The key statistic is "fatality ratio per year of service." For the Mexican War it was 15.4 percent (based on 7,980 deaths and 51,750 enrollees during an average twelve months). In the Civil War it was 9.8 percent. Put another way, in a year of fighting the odds of getting killed in the Mexican War were one out of six and a half; in the Civil War, one out of ten.

Waiting for the battle to start, counting the odds

History celebrates the Mexican War because we won it, we won it quickly, and we won a big prize: much of Texas and all of California. But the Mexican War also has a dark side. "One of the most unjust ever waged by a stronger nation against a weaker nation," said Ulysses Grant. "An instance of a republic following the bad example of European monarchies, in not considering justice in their desire to acquire additional territory."

Continued Grant, "The Southern rebellion was largely the outgrowth of the Mexican War. Nations, like individuals, are punished for their transgressions. We got our punishment in the most sanguinary and expensive war of modern times."

Wars are fought utilizing the lessons of the most recent war, especially tactics and weaponry. Had it not been for the Mexican War, the Civil War would not have inflicted so much carnage. As America learned when financing the anti-Communist Taliban fighters in Afghanistan in the 1980s who subsequently became an enemy fifteen years later, war is the best possible training ground for future combat, and there is the ever-present danger that yesterday's fighters will be tomorrow's enemy (a danger now occurring in Iraq, where insurgents are learning how to fight more effectively in the future). The Mexican War was the training ground for the Union and Confederate generals whose newfound skills enabled a Civil War expected to last a year to become a five-year bloodbath. The Mexican War also spurred the development of deadly weaponry that outstripped the ability to develop proper tactics. At the Battle of Gettysburg, for example, Confederate soldiers with their swords and pistols marched out onto an open field, only to be picked off by Union sharpshooters armed with long-range rifles.

Back to our original question: What war would you least like to be in? Answer: it depends which side you're fighting on. God forbid you were fighting for the Confederacy. The fatality ratio for white Confederate soldiers was 25 percent.

Fighting the Real Enemy

➤ 1862 General George McClellan was unable to advance on Richmond in 1862 and end the Civil War quickly because 100,000 of his men had diarrhea.

Human waste played a significant role in the Civil War. Unlike earlier wars, where the number of troops in a skirmish was only in the hundreds, ensuring proper toilet facilities for huge battalions of men in the Civil War was a logistical and sanitary nightmare. No longer could a soldier take a pee or squat behind the bushes. Quartering thousands of men in a confined area resulted in dung smell, flies, and epidemics that "competed in horror with the battles of war." Wrote a Confederate soldier from South Carolina, "These Big Battles is not as Bad as the fever."

In an effort to combat disease among the troops, the North formed the U.S.

Sanitary Commission, which delivered a report urging proper construction of privies, urinals, and cesspools into which was poured chloride, lime sulphate, and sulphuric and muriatic acid gas to prevent the hatching of flies. To further ensure that soldiers wouldn't catch diarrhea and dysentery, they were issued flannel underwear—even though it hindered their mobility and made them suffer in the sweltering summer heat.

The South had an additional problem besides disease: it was running out of chemicals to make gunpowder. With typical ingenuity, the Rebels resorted to collecting human urine to make nitrate. Confederate women rallied to the cause by saving their urine for pickup by collection wagons headed for munitions factories. (Northern snipers quickly caught on and focused their rifle shots on the urine wagons—not the food wagons.)

Military hygiene assumed particular importance in World War I, with its trench warfare. One thousand men generate six hundred pounds of dung and three hundred gallons of urine a day. Where to put all this stuff? In selecting a trench campsite, commanders looked for an area large enough to locate the kitchen far away from the waste-pit "bathroom." Every two days the waste pit had to be burned with crude oil to kill the flies and larvae. When the campsite proved no longer habitable, the troops picked up and moved on. More often than not, they failed to move fast enough to avoid disease. Before entering battle, commanders ordered all their troops to relieve themselves, because being hit in the abdomen with a bullet was worse if excrement was present.

〜❦〜

In his classic history of epidemics and infectious disease, *Rats, Lice and History*, written in 1934, Hans Zinsser wrote, "Soldiers have rarely won wars. They more often mop up after the barrage of epidemics. And typhus, with its brothers and sisters—plague, cholera, typhoid, dysentery—has decided more campaigns than Caesar, Hannibal, Napoleon, and all the inspector generals of history."

The same could be said of American military history. It wasn't until the twentieth century that a war was fought in which the U.S. lost more lives to actual battle wounds than to disease and lack of proper hygiene and food.

That war was World War II. In the Mexican War, for example, the U.S. lost 13,283 lives: 13 percent in battle, 87 percent to disease. In the Civil War, said Zinsser, the federal army lost 279,659 lives: 16 percent were killed in battle, 17 percent died of wounds and infection, and 67 percent died of disease. In the 1898 Spanish-American War (including the Philippines, not just Cuba), out of 5,660 deaths, 8 percent died in battle, 92 percent died from disease.

In World War I, 53,000 American troops died from combat, 63,000 from disease.

In World War II, the United States went

into overdrive in using the latest pharmaceutical products to save its troops from disease. The greatest problem at the time was malaria. Already in 1937 four million cases had been diagnosed in the United States, especially in the Southern states where most of the U.S. training bases were located. Even worse, all the war theaters—especially North Africa and the Pacific—were in high-malaria areas. When in early 1942 the island of Java fell to Japanese troops, the world supply of quinine was lost to America and her allies. This was an unmitigated disaster: Quinine is the drug of choice not only for malaria, but also for a whole range of other treatments: dysentery, herpes, influenza, meningitis, pneumonia, and typhoid fever.

In an emergency measure never taken before by an army, the U.S. military ordered 100,000 vials of tetanus antitoxin, 40 million quinine tablets, 35 million sulfathiazone tablets, and 10 million sulfapyradine tablets. Another drug, sulfanilamide, reduced the mortality rate from pneumonia from 75 percent to 11 percent and became quickly appreciated as having "dethroned the captain of the men of death." In 1943 FDR signed into law the Pharmacy Corps of the United States Army, giving them power and authority to command desperately needed drugs such as penicillin, glycerin, sugar, and alcohol. Given that it took 65 gallons of alcohol to make smokeless gunpowder for a 16-inch artillery shell, getting hold of alcohol for medical reasons was not easy. The Phar-

macy Corps persevered, and obtained sufficient alcohol and other antibiotics to save countless American soldiers on the battlefield. In 1944, a major American drug company ran an ad: "When the thunderous battles of this war have subsided to silent pages in a history book, the greatest news event of World War II may well be the discovery and development of . . . penicillin."

Great generals have their place in history, but so too do the anonymous quartermasters and doctors who maintain the supply lines of vital health conditions and drugs. They know the major danger in war: not enemy bullets, but lack of hygiene.

Missing: The Ferocity of a Lion

➤**1864** Said Napoleon, "An army of sheep led by a lion will always beat an army of lions led by a sheep."

For more than one hundred years, Southerners have made the excuse that the Civil War was a gallant struggle for a lost cause, that they never had a chance against the powerful industrial North. Said William Faulkner, the South's most renowned novelist, "Who else would have declared a war against a power ten times the area, and one hundred times the men and one hundred times the resources?"

Absolute nonsense. In fact, the two sides were quite evenly matched. The Union armies had a peak strength of about 1 million men; the Southern armies about 600,000. This is a ratio less than 2:1—a far cry from the 3:1 or 4:1 ratio generally considered necessary for an attacking force. The North, as the invader aiming at permanent conquest, had to establish garrisons throughout the South to enforce the occupation. By the end of the war, according to General Grant, more than half the soldiers in the Union armies were involved in garrison or occupation duty as opposed to actual fighting. The South, as the defender, did not have this burden. In addition, 90 percent of the graduates of West Point elected to join the South. The South also had plenty of supplies; whatever it could not produce, it could always import from Europe; never were there any drastic shortages. The *Richmond Daily Examiner* in late 1864 complained of the "well known improvidence of our soldiers who throw away their overcoats and blankets in spring . . . expecting to take new ones from the Yankees before winter." When the war ended, the newly installed Northern war governor of North Carolina was astounded to find ninety thousand Southern uniforms sitting in a warehouse—far better than his own troops had ever enjoyed.

When the war started, the betting money in England—especially that of the powerful British foreign secretary, Lord John Russell—was that the South would win. Even citizens in the nation's capital feared the worst. For Abraham Lincoln to know he was in serious trouble, all he had to do was look out the White House window with a telescope and see the Confederate flag fluttering in the breeze on the other side of the Potomac.

Then why did the South, so close to victory, fail to win?

Wars, like all great endeavors, are essentially won on spirit, determination, willpower, and focus. The South, like America in Vietnam one hundred years later, lacked unity and clear objectives—the ferocity of the lion. When the majority of U.S. naval officers announced they would join the South, before departing for their home states they delivered their ships to their owner, the U.S. government! One admires these men for their sense of duty, but not for their will to win. War is a ruthless business, not a sport for gentlemen.

"The strange conduct of our people during this war!" bemoaned a member of the Confederate Congress in 1864. "They gave up their sons, husbands, brothers and friends, and often without murmuring, to the army; but let one of their negroes be taken and what a howl you will hear. The love of money has been the greatest difficulty on our way to independence— it is now our chiefest obstacle." The plantation owners refused to let their slaves be conscripted, refused to buy Confederate bonds, and refused to pay export taxes on the substantial cotton they were smuggling through the Northern blockade.

Slavery was a dominant institution in the South, but it was not widespread, nor was it a great motivator of troop morale.

Seventy-five percent of all white families in the South owned no slaves. Certain states, less enthusiastic about the war than other states, granted ten times as many draft exemptions on a per capita basis. Besides exemptions, desertions were a major problem. Lee wrote to Jefferson Davis in 1862, "Our ranks are very much diminished—I fear from a third to one half of the original numbers." The situation got so bad that Lee had to send out squads to track down and round up the deserters, many of whom were "wantonly destroying stock and property" and alienating the local population they were supposed to protect.

❧

From day one, the South faced a paradox it could never resolve: it revolted against the North in the cause of states' rights, yet the very autonomy of its members prevented it from forming a single, unified army to fight the North. It was like the Articles of Confederation all over again. President Jefferson Davis, who had been an outstanding U.S. secretary of war under Franklin Pierce during 1853–57, had to contend with his vice president, Alexander Stephens, and many of the Southern senators, who insisted on the primacy of states' rights and that they have a say in how their state militias were used. Presiding over the Confederate Senate was Stephens, a frail ninety-pound weakling who "looked like a freak" and spent most

of his time at home, bedridden. Says the historian David Eicher, Davis knew that "a strong, unified Confederacy under the control of a central government would be necessary if the war that most saw as inevitable were to come." But when war came, there was constant bickering, failure to agree on which generals to appoint, failure to agree on whether they should be ranked by merit or by seniority, failure to agree on suspension of the writ of habeas corpus, and failure to agree on financing. The more Davis meddled in states' rights, the more violent the arguments got, and little got resolved—certainly no way to fight a war.

This breakdown in organization, caused by lack of focus and will, led the South to fail. For a simple example of the South's inaction, consider what one field commander complained to General Robert E. Lee: "Ripley dislikes Pemberton, Pemberton dislikes Ripley, and everything is dysfunctional." Surely one could never make such a comment about the North under Abraham Lincoln.

The General Who Would Have Been Better as President

➤**1868** The great Robert E. Lee, tall and handsome, from impeccable Virginia pedigree, brilliant student and superintendent at West Point, called by his commanding general Winfield Scott in the

Mexican War "the very best soldier I ever saw in the field," the man Lincoln had once tried to hire as head of the Union Army. Turning down the post to join the Confederate Army, Robert E. Lee became the only man in world history to be invited by both of two nations fighting each other to head their armies. Yet he was no George Washington or Ulysses Grant, able to slug it out in a long, difficult, and messy war. Lee was too patrician, too bookish, too proud.

The only way the South could have won the Civil War was to fight a defensive war on its own soil. In this it had significant advantages: better generals, home territory with readily available food and medical supplies, and a more powerful purpose for fighting a war (defending the homeland), whereas the North had an unpopular president, indecisive generals, draft riots, and vast territory to cover. The Confederacy, it is useful to remember, covered a huge area: 750,000 square miles—more than Great Britain, France, Spain, Italy, and Germany combined. In wars of attrition—and that's what the Civil War eventually turned out to be—the defender usually wins. It is a military axiom that the attacker needs three times as many soldiers as the defender (and five times as many if the enemy is strongly entrenched). The North had only slightly more troops than the South when they met head to head, clearly putting it at a disadvantage as an attacker. By playing smart defense, Lee would have repeated

his one brilliant victory—Chancellorsville—where, despite being outnumbered two to one, he divided his army, outflanked the enemy, and delivered a smashing attack like Hannibal's victory over the Romans at Cannae in 216 BC. Another battle or two like Chancellorsville, and the British would have entered the war in support of the Confederacy in 1863, Lincoln would have lost the 1864 election to McClellan, and the North would have asked for a truce.

Longstreet, Stuart, and other Southern generals wanted Lee to use his proven skill in outfoxing his Union counterparts: hunt and prey, retreat into the woods, and attack again (akin to George Washington's strategy of "defensive maneuver"). But Lee felt such skirmishes were personally degrading. When he was assigned to the defense of Richmond and he started digging trenches, he was mocked by the Southern press as "the King of Spades." A proud soldier from the old school, he was hurt by the insult and vowed to redeem his honor by fighting the enemy face to face on the open field. He was tired. He wanted to go for the big win, a decisive Napoleonic battle.

Its name: Gettysburg. When Lee pushed the enemy back on Day One, he continued to press for territory instead of disengaging so he could safely find the best high hill from which to taunt the enemy to initiate a suicidal attack. Willingly giving up hard-won territory was not a concept Lee liked. Instead he engaged in a series of bloody confrontations, and on Day Three he launched a massive offensive across a long, open field that resulted in the obliteration of three days' gains and, in the end, the entire war effort. He relied on "the close-order infantry charge, a method of attack developed in the era of the musket, a gun with an effective range of eighty yards . . . used against defenders armed with rifles, a far deadlier weapon with a range of four hundred yards." In Pickett's Charge, where fourteen thousand Confederate soldiers advanced into the fire of Union rifles, only half came back.

Lee's problem, wrote the British military historian Sir Liddell Hart, was that he always went on the attack. A wiser course might have been to combine offensive strategy with defensive tactics, "to lure the Union armies into attacking under disadvantageous conditions." He was a general who "would rather lose the war than his dignity." Sure enough, he lost the war and preserved his dignity so well that he has gone down in history a martyr, our most overrated general.

Grant, a brutally honest and simple man, had every reason to embellish the skills of his adversary, if only to enhance his own reputation. Yet he did not. To the contrary, he was critical of Lee, and perfectly open about it: "I never ranked Lee as high as have some others," he wrote. "Lee was a good man, a fair commander who had everything in his favor. He was a man who had had sunshine. . . .

Lee was of a slow, conservative, cautious nature, without imagination."

A review of Lee's previous military career is in order: how did he get to be a top general? Until 1861, Lee had had a disappointing career: other than a brilliant stint in the Mexican War, his thirty-two-year career in the army had gone nowhere, to the point where in 1858 he almost quit, he was so discouraged. Like Grant, he viewed his career as a failure. Only in 1861 was he finally promoted to colonel. For him then to get the astounding offer to head the Union army, bypassing numerous higher-ranking officers, was only because he was the protégé of General Winfield Scott. In turning it down, Lee committed a monumental blunder of the highest magnitude. When he went back to his mentor and fellow Virginian Winfield Scott to report his decision, Scott didn't mince his words.

"You have made the greatest mistake in your life."

⁓

Now look at what might have been on that fateful day when Lee turned down Lincoln's offer. Suppose Lee (married to the daughter of George Washington's adopted stepson) had followed the footsteps of his idol Washington and put his country ahead of his state. Suppose he had listened to Winfield Scott, also from Virginia. Suppose he'd had more loyalty to New York—where he went to school and lived for more of his adult life than in

Virginia. How different history would have been! General Robert E. Lee of the Union Army would have been excellent: he would have marshaled the North's superior resources, and pursued the war so professionally that the North probably would have won it in two or three years, as everyone expected. He would have been blessed, as Grant said, in a situation where he had "sunshine."

Not only was Lee in the wrong job (general for the South, not the North), he was in the wrong profession. Back in 1856 he had come out against slavery well before Lincoln did: "There are few in this enlightened age, who would not acknowledge that slavery as an institution is a moral and political evil." To prove his point, he freed his slaves. Coming at a time when many Union generals owned slaves (until finally forbidden to do so by the Thirteenth Amendment in 1868), Lee's act set an example for Lincoln's Emancipation Proclamation of 1863 (which, by the way, only freed slaves in the South, not in the border states of Delaware, Maryland, Kentucky, Missouri, and West Virginia). In 1870, several months before he died, he said:

> *So far from engaging in a war to perpetuate slavery, I am rejoiced that slavery is abolished. I believe it will be greatly for the interest of the South. So fully am I satisfied of this that I would have cheerfully lost all that I have lost by the war, and have suffered all that I have suffered to have this object attained.*

Whereas Grant and Sherman had no compunction about laying waste to farms and doing harm to civilians standing in their way, Lee did. "It is well that war is so terrible," he said, "otherwise we should grow too fond of it." As his armies advanced northward and captured farms, he instructed his soldiers that whatever food they took from the farmers, they pay for it. He, not Grant, won the moral advantage recognized by history.

Had he been the Northern general, Lee—like George Washington, a Southerner presiding over a Northern country—would have been in a unique position to bridge the gap between the two sides and unify a war-torn nation. Worshipped by his men, he exuded calm leadership. Nominated for U.S. President in 1868, he would have made a far better president than his wartime opponent, Ulysses Grant. As it turned out, the bitterness of the defeated Southerners because of Grant's and Sherman's slash-and-burn methods resonated for a full century—a long time for America.

Theodore Roosevelt, certainly a serious student of history and able to see both sides, being a Northerner with a Southern mother, said Robert E. Lee was our greatest American. Winston Churchill, even more adept at history, said the same. So, too, did Eisenhower. In a 1954 speech to the Boy Scouts of America, President Eisenhower cited Lee as one of his heroes.

In 2003, bowing to political correctness, the Boy Scouts of America in central Virginia removed Robert E. Lee from the boys' badges and the regional council name. "It will help our minority recruiting," said one Boy Scout Association officer. (Presumably he had never bothered to learn of Lee's freeing his slaves or that Lee's daughter in 1902 had been arrested for sitting with blacks on a Washington DC train.)

Know Thine Enemy

►**1941** For decades scholars have argued why the U.S. was so caught by surprise when the Japanese attacked Pearl Harbor. While certainly there were many signals and mysterious messages that suggested such an attack was imminent, nobody could put the dots together. The prevalent thinking was that Isoroku Yamamoto, head admiral of the Japanese navy, would attack the Philippines first.

In any guessing game about an enemy's intentions, it pays to "know thine enemy." In Yamamoto, FDR and the American military had a unique opportunity—and they blew it, big time.

Curiously, Yamamoto had studied for two years at Harvard College. Had the White House done some serious background checking about his college days (and certainly FDR, himself a Harvard graduate, would have known how revealing it could be), it would have uncovered some interesting nuggets for a psychological profile. Classmates would have re-

membered Yamamoto well: a hard worker but not a grind, exceptionally curious and imaginative ("a big thinker"). When they introduced him to the game of poker, he became a fanatical poker player who would stay up all night, winning hand after hand. And what did he do with his poker winnings—lead the good life? No, not at all: he hitchhiked around the country during the summer, exploring America.

Clearly a most unusual young man. Years later, as a naval attaché at the Japanese embassy in Washington DC, Yamamoto was asked by younger officers how best to spend their time in America. He told them, "Read a biography of Lincoln to better understand the country, and skip meals so as to have more funds for travel to see various states." He also advised them not to speak any Japanese during their first six months in the United States.

During his stint in Washington, Yamamoto was well known to the U.S. Navy. A compulsive poker player, he became a regular in all-night poker games run by the U.S. military and diplomatic personnel. Spurred on by his victories, he developed contempt for the mental agility of his American naval opponents at the poker table. "The American navy," he said, is nothing more than "a club for golfers and bridge players."

Back in Japan, rising to the top of the naval establishment, Yamamoto strongly opposed the Japanese army's signing the Tripartite Pact with Germany and Italy in

Harvard graduate (young man on the left) with the U.S. Secretary of the Navy

the summer of 1939, knowing this would eventually incur a war with Britain and the United States that the Japanese navy was ill-equipped to wage. Yamamoto became such a target for extremist attacks that the Navy Ministry had to barricade the building with tanks and machine guns, and the morbid joke in the ministry about the threats to Yamamoto's life was for employees to warn each other, "Whatever you do, don't accept a ride in the vice-minister's car!" Eventually, to protect Yamamoto from assassination, the navy minister sent him out to sea as commander of the Combined Fleet.

Now, put yourself in Washington DC in late 1941, with the war drums pounding louder and louder. How would the preco-

cious Yamamoto attack? Knowing the above, ask yourself if the following doesn't make logical sense.

Unlike the home-grown Japanese warriors, Yamamoto had no appetite for wars of attrition, especially with a giant like the United States. He had enormous respect for the United States: it had plenty of oil reserves and manufacturing resources that would enable it eventually to overwhelm Japan. A campaign in Malaya and the Philippines yielding easy but life-costly and time-consuming victories would not be wise. The traditional Japanese naval strategy, to wait for the American fleet to arrive and ambush it in the central or south Pacific, would not work. To beat such a sleeping giant, it was necessary to strike first. Nobody expected Pearl Harbor to be the target—it was too far from Japan for any possible surprise: an armada of ships would be sighted easily. As for planes, Japan had never carried out an air attack before. The logistics were staggering, the risks enormous.

But Yamamoto wasn't a great poker player for nothing. Poker players are gamblers, and when they gamble they go for big stakes. Unlike traditional "battleship" admirals wedded to the old technology, Yamamoto liked the new technology of naval aviation and vowed to go after the U.S. Pacific Fleet with one "all-in-surprise big bet": as in poker, blow the best player out of the game, good and early. Determined to attack Pearl Harbor, Yamamoto told his staff to keep working at the logistics, and be more imaginative and come up with an air attack plan that would work. The staff developed a plan calling for a massive air strike by four of the fleet's six large carriers. Yamamoto told them to be more aggressive; he threw in all six carriers. When the naval general staff complained this was too risky, Yamamoto threatened to resign if he didn't get his way.

It was a gamble, but it was a well-thought-out gamble by a man with a photographic memory for detail. The shame of the American joint chiefs was their lack of imagination in trying to figure out their opponent. They thought of him as a traditional Japanese who would do everything "by the book" (just as they did). They failed to consider that maybe, just maybe,

Isoroku Yamamoto was more American than they were.

Generals for Hire

➤**1942**   Three days into the new year, a most unusual transfer was made. It was payment to an American general working for another nation, in charge of that country's troops.

First, some history. On more than one occasion the United States hired foreign generals to lead its soldiers. The Marquis de Lafayette, vigorously courted by General George Washington, not only provided military leadership but ensured the invaluable support of France's enormous navy. Several decades later, faced with another war against Great Britain, President James Madison tried in vain to rent Portugal's entire naval fleet—ships, admirals, and sailors.

In 1861, President Abraham Lincoln got so desperate to find a general who was an aggressive warrior that he looked abroad. The world's greatest freedom fighter—who happened to be available at the time—was Giuseppe Garibaldi, the hero of the Italian unification who had also fought against slavery in South America. Garibaldi, who had lived in New York during 1850–52, supporting himself as a candlemaker, was eager to lend his martial skills to help America. The two men met, but were unable to reach an agreement. Apparently, Garibaldi wanted a promise that American slaves would be freed. Lincoln turned it down: there was no way at the time he could make this commitment and still preserve the Union.

Even American generals and admirals could be bought. John Paul Jones, in need of money after the American Revolution, went to work for the Russians and became a rear admiral, winning battles against the Turks. General Winfield Scott, victor in the Mexican War, was invited by a group of influential Mexicans to resign his commission and become interim president of Mexico and prepare the country for ultimate annexation to the United States, for which he would be paid $1.25 million (he turned it down). The most surprising example, however—one in the twentieth century—would be that great patriotic drumbeater of "Duty, God, Country," General Douglas MacArthur. He retired from the Army in 1938 to take on a new job as field marshal of the Philippine army. The position not only offered a lavish salary, but also came with a custom-built air-conditioned penthouse atop Manila's luxury hotel. In late 1941, Manuel Quezon, president of the Philippines, begged General MacArthur to evacuate him from the island of Corregidor. MacArthur refused. A month later, MacArthur changed his mind. Why?

On January 3, 1942, Quezon transferred $500,000 into MacArthur's personal bank account.*

Japanese Treatment of Prisoners

➤**1943** The 2004 Abu Ghraib scandal of American soldiers forcing their Iraqi prisoners into compromising positions provoked international outrage, and appropriately so. But arrayed against this is the fact that Americans didn't chop off their prisoners' heads—as the Iraqis and al-Qaeda did.

This dichotomy is not new; it goes back to World War II, when American sailors picked up in the Pacific were questioned ruthlessly and then "disposed suitably." Observes the historian Victor Davis Hanson:

The best hope of a Japanese man in the water was to be rescued by American ships, which meant life and safety in a prisoner-of-war camp in the United States. The worst nightmare of an American sailor or airman in the seas of Midway was capture by the Japanese navy, which spelled a quick interrogation, followed by either beheading or being thrown overboard with weights.

Japanese treatment of POWs violated every tenet of the Geneva Convention. The death rate of POWs in the hands of the Japanese was a staggering 27 percent (in the hands of the Germans, it was 4 percent). When Japan transported some fifty

* The most puzzling thing about this transaction is that MacArthur's superiors (FDR, Stimson, and Marshall) approved it, though it was thoroughly illegal. MacArthur's former assistant, Dwight Eisenhower, suggested MacArthur was "losing his nerve," meaning he needed extra motivation to keep fighting.

thousand POWs by ship from one region to another, it deliberately used unmarked vessels likely to invite attack by American airplanes and submarines; as a result, 10,800 POWs died. Whenever American troops were about to take over a Japanese island where POWs were being held, the Japanese practice was to kill the POWs before they could be rescued. In the Gilbert Islands, twenty-two prisoners were beheaded. At Ballale Island, ninety prisoners were bayoneted; at Wake Island, ninety-six were machine-gunned. At Palawan in the Philippines, 150 Americans were herded into an air-raid shelter, gasoline was poured on them, and they were set on fire.

This brutality influenced the American war policy. A major reason the United States resorted to the quick knockout blow of using the atom bomb, as opposed to the slow process of invading Japan, was to prevent the Japanese from killing the 31,617 POWs they held in their prisons. Says the historian Richard Frank, "Nearly to a man, Allied POWs believed the Japanese would kill them if the Homeland was invaded."

The defining characteristic of a militarist society is that it refuses to admit guilt. After World War II, instead of apologizing for its barbaric treatment of combatants, Japan demanded that the real apology come from the Americans who bombed thousands of civilians in Hiroshima and Nagasaki. The United States, which had dropped the atom bomb to destroy Japanese militarism once and for all, refused.

The people of Japan agreed. In a public opinion survey taken in 1947, asking who was to blame for the atom bomb horror, the Japanese public blamed not the Americans but the Japanese government.

A Battle He Never Fought In

➤1944   George S. Patton was probably the toughest American general who ever lived. When it came time to tell his troops how to win a battle, he got right to the point: "I want you to remember that no bastard ever won a war by dying for his country. He won it by getting the other poor dumb bastard to die for his country." Probably the biggest battle Patton ever won was a battle he never fought in. How could this be?

Patton, whose army caused more German casualties and liberated more square miles of Europe than any other Allied army in World War II, had such a fearsome reputation among the Germans that they were watching his every move. His superiors decided to take advantage of this and use him as a decoy: they created a fictitious "First Army Group," made him the commander, and sent him off into the woods at Calais to conduct diversionary activities and to appear frequently in public, giving speeches. In the meantime, Eisenhower made his preparations off the coast of Normandy. When the Allies launched their D-Day invasion of June 6, 1944, the Germans were caught by surprise: How could the Allies not use their best general?

The Courage of the Common Soldier

➤**1945** Hollywood movies and the Medal of Honor herald our fearsome warriors who fought to the death, often saving the lives of their fellow soldiers. And so it should be.

But there is another dimension of war, often overlooked: the courage of ordinary soldiers trying to maintain their humanity. In World War I, there occurred a memorable event called "A Christmas Peace." There were no Americans involved, just British and Germans. On Christmas Day 1914, a coterie of German and British soldiers came out of their trenches and shared their skimpy rations and gave gifts to each other to celebrate the spirit of Christmas. At the end of the day, they retreated to their positions and resumed killing each other.

A similar event happened at the end of World War II. It was March 1945. The war was drawing to a close. A group of Germans trapped in foxholes were fighting for their lives against a much larger group of Americans, when out of the American side there emerged a man walking toward them. The Germans looked hard and were puzzled: he was not an Anglo-Saxon, he appeared to be a Native American. The Germans were confused—he had no bon-

net of feathers, he had no knife, who was this strange man? The Germans were so overwhelmed by the man's courage that they put their guns down and came out of their foxholes and surrendered. Observed one of the Germans, Karl Schlesier, "In that place, at that time, he must have been the most reasonable man, the most perceptive, the most understanding and by far the most brave. We had not expected to live and he must have seen how idiotic this all was and he acted on his own to save us, risking his own life in the process."

The Germans knew they owed their lives to this singular man. In the prison camp, they all talked about him and how he had demonstrated such initiative. "If he had not come to get us we would have died in our foxholes. His action was a personal one. He was not ordered to do what he did."

So impressed was Karl Schlesier that after the war he immigrated to the United States and became a U.S. citizen, spending the next fifty years as a professor of anthropology in New Mexico. "I never knew to which tribe or Indian nation the brave soldier of March 1945 belonged, or if he survived the war," he said. "I owe him my life and have lived it accordingly." In an article that appeared in the *Albuquerque Journal* newspaper in 2000, he wrote, "I am seventy-three . . . Who was the Indian soldier who saved the lives of German soldiers in an act of kindness and bravery? If you are still out there, let us know."

Our Only Militarist President

I know not with what weapons World War III will be fought, but World War IV will be fought with sticks and stones.

—Albert Einstein

►**1956** While America has had a number of bellicose presidents who talked tough, such as TR, JFK, Ronald Reagan, and George W. Bush, it has never had a militarist president—except one.

First, a distinction: bellicose presidents may engage in skirmishes and wars, threaten other major powers, engage in expansionist policies, and build up the military budget. But they do not talk foolishly or take pleasure in brinksmanship. They do not view war as just another option.

The man who dropped the atom bomb knew exactly what he was doing. One can question whether President Truman was right to do what he did, perhaps, but not that he lacked integrity or self-discipline. President Truman made a conscious decision, and made sure he would never have to make a similar decision again, by giving massive amounts of foreign aid to help Japan and Germany rebuild their economies and democratic institutions. The

bomb to him was an unthinkable weapon, never to be used again.*

Arrayed against Truman were two distinct groups, both with extreme views on the use of the bomb:

• Pacifists who were so frightened by the bomb that they advocated universal disarmament, world government, and sharing of atomic secrets with everyone, including the Russians.

• Militarists who saw the bomb as merely another step up in the development of military weapons, to be used like any other weapon when necessary.

The extreme militarist of the day was General Douglas MacArthur, who wanted to "atomize" China so he could have his military victory in Korea. Truman put him in his place by sacking him. But MacArthur wasn't the only militarist with facile ideas about the bomb; so, too, were the leading Republican standard-bearers, Senator Robert Taft and General Dwight Eisenhower.

Eisenhower may have warned about the military-industrial complex in his farewell address, but his record as president was one of adventurous militarism. No man did more for the military-industrial complex than this ex-general: in

---

* In response to the suggestion that he use the atom bomb to break the Soviet blockade of Berlin, Truman said, "You have got to understand that this isn't a military weapon. It is used to wipe out women and children and unarmed people, and not for military use. So we have to treat this differently from rifles and cannon and ordinary things like that."

1960 his military budget was three times that in 1950, at the height of the Korean War. The 1956 Republican Party platform called for the "establishment of American bases all around the world." By 1958 the United States had alliances and military agreements with nearly sixty countries.

More than a huge military buildup or eagerness to assume imperial worldwide responsibilities, the mark of a militarist is how he behaves. Eisenhower developed two new tools of statecraft: covert action and nuclear brinksmanship. Under Eisenhower, the CIA was transformed from an intelligence-gathering operation into a secret army of the president, dedicated to overthrowing governments in Iran, Guatemala, Egypt, Indonesia, and Laos. The covert-action budget jumped from $82 million in 1952 to $800 million in 1956. When an independent advisory board, the President's Board of Consultants on Foreign Intelligence Activities, issued critical reports in 1957 and 1958 on the CIA's covert activities, President Eisenhower paid no attention. What he did pay attention to were the French. When France became heavily involved in Indochina and asked for American military support, Eisenhower was enthusiastic about getting involved. He backed off only when his Army chief of staff, General Matthew Ridgway, convinced him that any commitment would have to be far more massive than the American public would tolerate.

Unlike Truman, who had opposed any U.S. intervention in Iran to help the British whose oil companies had been nationalized, Eisenhower jumped in wholeheartedly.

In further sharp contrast to Truman, Eisenhower made nuclear weapons an essential component of his military strategy. He elevated the Strategic Air Command, capable of inflicting massive nuclear retaliation, to be the spearhead of American military power. He permitted his generals to consider dropping nuclear weapons on Korea, Laos, Vietnam, and China. He even threatened nuclear blackmail at one of his press conferences: "I see no reason why they shouldn't be used just exactly as you would use a bullet or anything else." While Eisenhower in his later years as president moderated his language, the nuclear buildup accelerated: compared with one thousand nuclear warheads when Eisenhower became president, the U.S. had eighteen thousand when he left.

He personally approved the highly risky and provocative U-2 flights over Russia. When one of the planes finally got shot down by the Russians and the pilot was captured alive, Khrushchev put the issue in true perspective: "Just imagine what would have happened had a Soviet aircraft appeared over New York, Chicago, or Detroit. How would the *United States* have reacted? . . . That would mean the outbreak of war!"

Eisenhower's advice to his successors was that of a war hawk. He advised JFK to invade Cuba and intervene in Laos. He advised LBJ to "go all out" in seeking victory in Vietnam, and if necessary, "to use at least tactical atomic weapons" against China (advice that LBJ found astonishing).* When LBJ announced in 1968 that he was halting most of the bombing of Vietnam, Eisenhower privately called him a coward.

If one were to suggest America's second-most-militarist president, who might that be? The answer is not George W. Bush, who responded to 9/11 with the novel theory of the "preemptive strike." Such a strike was defensive (that the perceived Iraqi threat was based on faulty intelligence and turned out to be nonexistent, is another issue).

Militarism is not defensive; it means aggression against another country for the sake of empire. America's runner-up militarist president is not the bellicose "carry a big stick" Theodore Roosevelt—he never started a war and in fact picked up a Nobel Peace Prize for mediating an end to the Sino-Russian War. Rather, our runner-up would be Woodrow Wilson, who combined lofty ideals with a hair-trigger willingness to use troops whenever necessary in search of peace. He objected to America's entry into World War I, but he certainly had no qualms about picking on small fry. In the words of one historian,

"Wilson created a more benign role for the military while using it as a major agent of his foreign policy." In just seven years, from 1913 to 1920, he kept the armed forces busy by sending them off to ten countries on nineteen different occasions: Mexico, Russia, Haiti, the Dominican Republic, China, Cuba, Panama, Dalmatia, Turkey, and Guatemala. His two armed excursions into Siberia, opposed by his military advisers, turned out to be a losing quagmire and almost got America involved in a full-scale war with Russia.

The Beginning of World War IV

➤**1980**   In this pivotal year, an American president launched the beginning of World War IV.

Since World War II, Truman, Eisenhower, Kennedy, Nixon (with Ford), and Reagan all waged World War III—the Cold War—with grit and determination. George H. W. Bush led the worldwide rescue of Kuwait. Clinton, fearful of his draft-dodging past, indulged the ever-expanding American military and ordered attacks on Kurdistan, Somalia, Haiti, Bosnia, and Kosovo. George W. Bush launched the war on terrorism by attacking Afghanistan and Iraq.

Absent in this lineup of bellicose presi-

---

* "Make no mistake," said LBJ in 1964, "there is no such thing as a conventional nuclear weapon."

dents is Jimmy Carter, the one man with a military career background (albeit short-lived), yet the one who tried hardest to achieve stability through diplomacy alone.

Surprisingly enough, it was this pacifist-leaning president who launched America into the World War IV that the country has been waging ever since, the war to protect Middle East oil from hostile takeover. In his 1980 State of the Union Address, Jimmy Carter announced the Carter Doctrine:

> *Any attempt by any outside force to gain control of the Persian Gulf region will be regarded as an assault on the vital interests of the United States of America, and such an assault will be repelled by any means necessary, including military force.*

So asleep was America at the time (read: Middle East oil as an American birthright) that nobody noticed. But stop a minute and consider: the only previous "doctrine" America ever had in two hundred years was the defensive Monroe Doctrine, forbidding European interference in Latin America. Now, all of a sudden, America was on the offensive, declaring the Middle East as part of the American "lake." President Carter was not about to let any loss of the Middle East threaten the vaunted American way of life, in which cars and plentiful gasoline were taken for granted.

Fast-forward to today. Out of this little-remembered speech emerged American military policy for the next twenty-five years. George W. Bush and Dick Cheney, trying to ensure a steady flow of Iraqi oil to counterbalance an increasingly precarious Saudi Arabia, were following the Carter Doctrine. History moves in trends, not abrupt revolutions. Observes historian Andrew Bacevich in his well-balanced book *The New American Militarism*, "Charging George W. Bush with responsibility for militaristic tendencies of present-day U.S. foreign policy makes as much sense as holding Herbert Hoover culpable for the Great Depression."

Forgotten Victims of War

➤**1990** Whenever you consider buying life insurance, your broker will urge you to also buy disability insurance. After all, what could be worse than death but to be a cripple and a lifetime burden on your family? The same applies to war: the forgotten ones—the soldiers thoroughly maimed and left living a mere fraction of their humanity. War statistics talk about the dead and the wounded, but not about the "living dead." Thanks to advances in efficient helicopter rescue teams and the miracles of modern medical technology, American soldiers are fighting deadlier wars and surviving them—but just barely. They are the "living dead."

According to Dalton Trumbo, author of

the 1939 classic antiwar novel *Johnny Got His Gun*, "Vietnam has given us eight times as many paralytics as World War II, three times as many totally disabled, 36 percent more amputees. Out of every hundred army veterans receiving compensation for wounds received in action in Vietnam, 12.4 percent are totally disabled. Totally."

That was said in 1990. Move up to the Iraq War: the percentage of severely wounded—defined as "having suffered brain damage, loss of limbs, or [having] been crippled for life by their injuries"—was also around 12 percent. In the war's first three years, from early 2003 to early 2006, there were 2,248 fatalities and 16,606 wounded, out of which more than two thousand were severely wounded or totally disabled. In World War II the ratio of killed to wounded was one out of four; in Iraq, one out of nine.

This improved survival ratio was no indication of less deadly warfare. In Afghanistan and Iraq, advances in protective gear, field medicine, and rapid evacuation procedures enabled soldiers to survive injuries that otherwise might have been fatal. American soldiers wore substantial body armor, leaving only their arms and legs exposed. Arrayed against this, however, was the increasingly lethal power of enemy weapons in the form of IEDs (im-

provised explosive devices). Almost half the soldiers wounded in Iraq were classified as "unfit to return to duty," meaning that their wounds were extremely severe. According to Pentagon statistics, the amputation rate of the wounded in Iraq was double that of previous wars. Also much higher than before was the number of mental health cases. According to the commander of the Army Medical Center at Fort Sam Houston in Texas, more than one out of three soldiers returning from Iraq faced post-combat mental-health issues. This was due not only to the physical injuries they may have suffered, but to the particular nature of the Iraq war. "Iraq war veterans," he said, "are more likely to have witnessed someone getting wounded or killed" from roadside explosive or car bombs. "War," he continues, "is sending a normal person into a very abnormal situation. Death and serious injury are very traumatic things to have to deal with."

By military order, the coffins of soldiers shipped back to the United States from Iraq were shipped in complete privacy, with no photographs allowed to be taken. The wounded soldiers, especially the severely wounded ones, received the same treatment: the military planes bringing them home to the U.S. arrived after midnight, when there were few witnesses.

SIX

In Pursuit of Riches

Asked what single book he would put into the hands of a Russian Communist, President Franklin D. Roosevelt replied, "The Sears, Roebuck catalog." So many products! So many choices and varieties! So cheap!

Today, America has a major image problem, especially in the Arab world: it is viewed as a land of gross materialism. What people forget is that the economic success that makes materialism and quality living possible is a strong economy. Democracy—and the patience it requires—does not appeal to people suffering from a hungry stomach and having no home to call their own. Back in 1789, when our Founding Fathers wrote the Constitution, they had no assurance that their project would survive. They needed help from the economy. "The debate over the constitution," observed Chief Justice John Marshall, "was ended not by its ratification, but by the return of economic prosperity."

"In democracies," said Tocqueville, "nothing is greater or more brilliant than commerce. It attracts the attention of the public and fills the imagination of the multitude." No man exemplified this better than

Benjamin Franklin. He held no elective office, he was no politician, he was no military hero. But he was a great common man, a citizen who was both a doer and a philosopher. And, lest we forget, he was a man who could accomplish what he did because he made himself rich in business by the time he was forty.

Of all our presidents, one man in particular recognized the importance of riches in pursuing the American dream. He said, "I don't believe in a law to prevent a man from getting rich; it would do more harm than good. So while we do not propose any war on capital, we do wish to allow the humblest man an equal chance to get rich with everyone else." So spoke a man not normally associated with riches: Abraham Lincoln.

Many foreigners misunderstand this fundamental aspect of America: they accuse America of commercialism, of pursuing Mammon instead of God (though America may be more religious than many other countries). Political stability requires that everyone work hard and do their part—and enjoy the rewards. In 1853 the most prominent senator in the United States was William Seward of New York. He gave a speech to the Senate in which he said, "Multiply your ships and send them forth. The nation that draws most from the earth, and fabricates the most, and sells the most to foreign nations, must be, and will be, the great power of the earth."

Years later, in 1863, when he was Lincoln's secretary of state, in an effort to forestall European powers from supporting the Confederacy, he brought to New York a number of ambassadors from England, France, Germany, and Russia. The point of the visit? To show them "hundreds of factories with whirling wheels, thousands of acres of golden harvest fields, miles of railway trains, laden with freight, busy fleets on rivers, lakes and canals."

And what made all this activity possible? Not the government that encouraged such endeavor, but individuals pursuing personal wealth.

"Robber barons" make for great publicity, even for historians. But such sensationalism is misleading. John D. Rockefeller made hundreds of millions. But more important is how Rockefeller enabled fuel prices to drop 90 percent and workers' real wages to double. Same for Henry Ford, celebrated for creating the first mass-produced car. Henry Ford's great contribution was more than just the assembly line, it was his willingness to pay high wages so his workers could afford to buy a car.

In his masterful work of historiography, *The Historian's Craft*, Marc Bloch had this to say about the short shrift given economics by historians focused on politics:

> *In reproaching "traditional history," Paul Valéry has cited "the conquest of the earth by electricity" as an example of one of those "notable phenomena" which it neglects,*

despite the fact that they have "more meaning and greater possibilities of shaping our immediate future than all political events combined."

Governments prosper or die by the economy. George Washington knew this instinctively. When he took office in 1789, he installed five employees in the newly created State Department, and in the Treasury Department he installed forty. Presidents get reelected or thrown out of office depending on the performance of the economy during their tenure, as George H. W. Bush learned in 1992. He should not have been surprised. His mentor Richard Nixon was once asked why he lost the 1960 election to John F. Kennedy. Nixon could have blamed any number of things: his facial "five o'clock shadow" during the crucial first TV debate, his getting hospitalized during two of the last weeks of the campaign, or his not having in his camp Mafia bosses who controlled Chicago and could deliver the critical state of Illinois. Had any one of these been in Nixon's favor, Nixon might have won. No, Nixon blamed the economy—more specifically, Eisenhower's refusal to pump up the economy in 1959–60, at the risk of incurring a deficit.

Thomas Jefferson wrote many articles and speeches. One doesn't think of his second annual message of December 15, 1802, as being in the league of Washington's Farewell Address ("entangling alliances with none"), Monroe's Doctrine,

Lincoln's Emancipation Proclamation, Wilson's Fourteen Points, Eisenhower's farewell address ("military-industrial complex"), or FDR's ("fear itself") or JFK's ("do for your country") inaugural speeches. Indeed, go through any compendium of great American speeches, and Jefferson's remarks are not to be found.

From the perspective of today, however, Jefferson's remarks take on historical significance. In this particular speech, Thomas Jefferson chose to hammer away at fiscal responsibility and the national debt. After expressing satisfaction concerning the "large and effectual payments toward the discharge of our public debt and the emancipation of our posterity from that mortal cancer," he explained that one generation had no right to bind the next: "The earth belongs to the living generation." Jefferson thought that if it was absolutely necessary for the government to enter into debt for reasons of war or financial panic, those debts should be completely paid off in around twenty years.

"The business of America is business," goes the common saying. Much has been written about the magnificent Statue of Liberty, surely the first sight of America many of our immigrants saw. No, not at all. Long before they caught sight of the Mother Lady, immigrants on the boat deck anxiously looking for their new homeland were greeted by Coney Island's giant illuminated Ferris wheel blazing in the night.

A Bigger Job than the Presidency

►**1785**   In business, one of the criteria that executive recruiters use in looking for a chief executive is "line management" experience, i.e., having many people under his authority responsible for producing the enterprise's products.

We actually had a president of whom it can be said that the presidency of the United States was a demotion in terms of number of civilians under his authority.

George Washington's previous profession was plantation owner. The federal government, with fewer than 350 nonmilitary employees, was smaller than his former organization, Mount Vernon. Mount Vernon was an impressive operation consisting of five farms, each a separate profit center headed by an overseer responsible for providing weekly reports. It was the largest flour producer in the colonies, and was the first plantation to practice serious crop rotation. In addition, Washington developed a substantial fishing industry, imported his own livestock from England, bred a new kind of mule, and started up a loom operation and tanning factory.

Clearly this was an enterprising man, always on the lookout to make small, incremental improvements. A practical man more than an idealist, he was the right man for an entrepreneurial startup: the implementation of a new form of government.

Better than Yum-Yum

►**1789**   The oldest "right" in the United States—the one and only right explicitly mentioned in the Constitution—is not the political right of free speech or liberty, but the economic right of patent protection. Article 1, Section 8, grants Congress the power "to promote the progress of science and useful arts, by securing for limited times to authors and inventors the exclusive right to their respective writings and discoveries." This was written in 1789, a full three years before the Bill of Rights. So important was this "authors and inventors clause" that it became known as the "progress clause"; when presented to the Constitutional Convention, there was no debate and it passed unanimously.

This was no fluke. Already, in the brief period after independence and before the Constitutional Convention, twelve of the thirteen colonies had enacted copyright laws. The men they sent to draft the Constitution were fully aware of the Industrial Revolution in England and how new technologies spurred economic growth. In the midst of their deliberations in Philadelphia, they took an afternoon off to go see John Fitch's new steamboat undergoing trials on the Delaware River. New inventions were a major excitement for them.

Within a year of passing the Constitution, there emerged the Patent Act and the Copyright Act. So important were patents that a patent application was not submitted to a patent office—there

President Washington's handwritten journal of his crops for 1789. Even as president, he kept meticulous records.

wasn't any. Rather, it was submitted to the secretary of state, then reviewed by the secretary of war and the attorney general, and, if approved, signed by the president and the secretary of state.

Fast-forward to 1859. No politician was more cognizant of the importance of patents than Abraham Lincoln: he was a patent lawyer and in fact had been issued a patent (the only president to earn such an honor; his invention was a device to lift boats over river shoals). When asked "What were the three greatest inventions and discoveries in world history?" he responded, "The arts of writing and printing, the discovery of America, and the introduction of Patent-laws."

Were you a Rip Van Winkle who fell asleep and woke up in the nation's capital city at the outbreak of the Civil War, you would find Washington DC a city of dreary mud roads and two-story wooden tenements, dominated by five huge marble-clad edifices: the White House, the Capitol, the Post Office, the Treasury Building, and the Patent Office.

❧

The history of patents in America involves more than superior inventiveness, it involves protracted legal battles in court.* Alexander Graham Bell had to fight more than six hundred patent lawsuits. Fortunately he won them all. Today his telephone patent is known as "the single most valuable patent ever issued in the world."

Others were not so fortunate. Eli Whitney's cotton gin was such a simple invention it got copied quickly. He fought more than sixty lawsuits, and spent so much money on legal fees he never made any money on his invention. Samuel Morse got hit by sixty-two would-be inventors claiming they had invented the telegraph; he, too, prevailed. Thomas Edison had so many problems with patent lawsuits he resolved he would only invent things he could sell.

Coca-Cola executed this resolution to the fullest: it relied totally on sales. Rather than patent the formula and lose it after seven years, the company gambled that no one would be able to figure out the formula. No patent was ever filed. When ordered by the government of India in 1977 to disclose the formula, the company played hardball, said no, and left the country. In the meantime, the company built up a massive international marketing and distribution system that eventually created the world's best-known brand.

In the early 1990s, journalist Mark Pendergrast stumbled upon the original formula in the company archives. Asked

---

* Many people misunderstand what a patent is. Legally, a patent is nothing more than a "negative right"; it does not grant a right to manufacture (which might infringe on other patents), it merely assures the right to bring infringement suits in court. For many inventors, the woes begin with the patent's issue, because then you need a lot of money for legal fees if someone tries to steal your invention. Being a patent holder can be an expensive and time-consuming proposition.

what might be the effect of publishing this secret formula, the executives of Coca-Cola essentially told Pendergrast it made no difference, it was too late to challenge Coca-Cola's position in the marketplace. "Call it 'Yum-Yum'. . . . Now what? What are they going to charge for it? How are they going to distribute it? How are they going to advertise?"

Continued the Coca-Cola executive, "We've spent over a hundred years and untold amounts of money building the equity of that brand name. Without our economies of scale and our incredible marketing system, whoever tried to duplicate our product would get nowhere, and they'd have to charge too much. Why would anyone go out of their way to buy Yum-Yum, which is really just like Coca-Cola but costs more, when they can buy the Real Thing anywhere in the world?"

So much for Yum-Yum.

The Surest Path to Personal Wealth

►**1796** From the founding of America until the Civil War, the major source of personal wealth was not farming or commerce, but investing in raw land. Said George Washington to his real estate agent in 1767, "Any person . . . who neglects the present opportunity of hunting out good lands, and in some measure marking them for his own, in order to keep others from settling them, will never

regain it." Writing to a potential investor about his plan to buy up an assemblage of choice Western lands, Washington urged the utmost secrecy: "I recommend that you keep the whole matter a secret, or trust it only to those in whom you can confide." While president, he borrowed money to purchase three thousand acres in the Mohawk Valley, and quickly sold it for twice what he paid. At the time of his death, he owned 71,000 acres.

All the Virginia planters were interested in making a quick buck in land speculation. They included even Patrick Henry, author of the famous slogan "Give me liberty or give me death!" "Insatiable in money" was how Jefferson described him.

As settlers moved westward, the land they occupied increased in value and enjoyed a ready market of settlers who followed. "All I am now worth," the new secretary of state of America wrote in 1796, "was gained by speculations in land." Ten years earlier he had purchased twelve thousand acres in Pennsylvania for fifteen cents an acre; now his land was worth 2 dollars an acre—a thirteenfold jump. Furthermore, not all speculators paid cash: after the Revolution, military warrants that had been given as payment to soldiers (100 to a private, 1,500 to a general) had depreciated 80 percent. By buying devalued military warrants for twenty cents on the dollar, property speculators could make five times the thirteen times their investment, or 65 times the amount of their original investment.

Robert Morris, signer of the Articles of Confederation and the Constitution, and superintendent of finance during the Revolution, acquired a land tract of more than a million acres, and "flipped" it to a group of English investors for more than three times what he paid for it. (To be sure, he also made lots of bad real estate investments and died bankrupt.)

Everybody benefited from raw land, not just the dealmakers. For the many thousands of immigrants, the abundance of land at reasonable prices meant freedom from Europe's lingering feudal constraints. Said one European visitor, "It does not seem difficult to find out the reasons why people multiply faster here than in Europe. . . . There is such an amount of good land yet uncultivated that a newly married man can get a spot of ground where he may comfortably subsist with his wife and children." On average, a homesteader could buy a plot of land, say fifteen acres, build a house and cultivate the land, and earn enough to pay off his debts in ten years.

When Thomas Jefferson, himself a major landowner, was offered all of France's territory in what became known as the Louisiana Purchase, he knew exactly what Talleyrand meant when he said, "You've made a good deal for yourselves." The $15-million asking price from France worked out to be four cents an acre—at a time when public land was going for two dollars an acre—and rising. That's a fifty-fold return right there.

The key to a growing real estate market, of course, is population. Married women in 1790 bore an average of almost eight children. Between 1790 and 1860 the population increased dramatically, doubling every twenty-three years. This growth, combined with the flow of immigrants, led to enormous demand not only for rural land but for space in cities. From 1820 to 1860, cities went through periods of wild land speculation and building. Many new cities emerged; Cincinnati, Pittsburgh, Memphis, Louisville, Detroit, Chicago, Denver, Portland, Seattle, and San Francisco. The major growth city was New York: in 1800 the population was sixty thousand; by 1860 the population was greater than one million. The city's leading entrepreneur was John Jacob Astor, who made his fortune selling furs—but not for long. Whatever extra capital he had, he used to buy real estate and make an even bigger fortune. Manhattan land he bought in 1800 for $50 an acre, was worth $1,500 twenty years later.

Said Henry George in his powerful 1887 book, *Progress and Poverty*: wealth originated in land. He meant this as a socialist polemic against the rich. What he failed to recognize, however, was that land was a long-term investment, a reward for those who had the foresight to buy in early. Take, for example, the city of Las Vegas, now one of the richest real estate properties in the world. In 1900 the population of this forlorn outpost in the desert was only thirty people. One hates to think what land was going for back then.

Massive Debt Financing for a Subprime Borrower

➤**1803** The United States was offered a deal—take it or leave it—by Napoleon's cash-strapped France: purchase the Louisiana Territory for $15 million. There were a number of legal obstacles involved, but no problem: when an opportunity for sudden riches comes along, most people—even the president and Congress of the United States—are willing to bend the rules a little.

When Thomas Jefferson sent James Monroe and Robert Livingston to Paris, they had specific instructions to try to buy New Orleans and the Gulf of Mexico seacoast for $10 million and not a penny more. Before they could start negotiating, the French put a counteroffer on the table: the entire Louisiana Territory for $15 million. Even though they lacked the mandate to do such a gigantic deal, the two American ministers accepted on the spot and rushed to get it completed and signed before the French changed their minds. It took another month for the news to cross the ocean and Jefferson to hear what happened. When he did, he was delighted. "I very early saw," he said, "that Louisiana was indeed a speck in our horizon, which was to burst in a tornado." Only there was one problem: the Consti-

tution. Nowhere does the Constitution grant the federal government authority to acquire more territory, especially of a size that would double the area of the entire country. To do so would presumably require a constitutional amendment. All his life Jefferson had been a strict constructionist, following the Constitution to the letter and believing that if the Constitution did not give specific permission, he could not do it. His secretary of the treasury, Albert Gallatin, eager to consummate the transaction, kept leaning on him to be more flexible. Finally, Jefferson relented. But he must be very quiet about it. "The less we say about the constitutional difficulties regarding Louisiana, the better. What is necessary for surmounting them," he told James Madison, "must be done sub-silentio." With time running short and Napoleon threatening to back out of the deal, Jefferson pushed for an immediate ratification by the Senate and got it, 24–7.

It may have been the mother of all real estate deals—buying 838,000 square miles for four cents an acre—but good deals are never simple. First there was the question of clear title. The territory had originally belonged to France. In 1782 it was ceded to Spain, then ceded back to France in 1800–1801 in a transaction kept secret so the English wouldn't find out about it. When the Spanish learned that the French were selling to the United States, they objected that France didn't have clear title, that there had been an implicit understanding that the land would never be sold to a third party. Eventually France and Spain reached an understanding, enabling the sale to the United States to go forward. When the closing finally did take place on December 20, 1803, in New Orleans, it would be a most unusual ceremony: the flag of Spain was lowered, then the flag of France was raised, then the flag of France was lowered, then the flag of the United States was raised. Also part of the ceremony was the delivery, on a silver platter, of the keys to the city, relinquished to the French by the Spanish only a few weeks before.

But before this all happened, there was the issue of money: how to pay for it? The United States was a classic "subprime" borrower: it had no cash for a down payment, and no credit rating to speak of. The U.S. Treasury was still paying off its debts from the Revolutionary War. Fifteen million dollars in 1803 was a staggering sum: if adjusted for the relative share of GDP, this amount would equal almost $400 billion today.

According to the opposing Federalist party, $15 million was the equivalent of 433 tons of solid silver that would fill 866 wagons, making a wagon train five and a third miles long. Stacked in dollar coins, it would make a pile rising nine miles into the sky. "We are to give money of which we have too little," said one, "for land of which we have too much." Said Fisher Ames, the most eloquent Federalist, America was "rushing like a comet into infinite space."

The U.S. Treasury retained a British merchant bank to raise the money, a most unusual arrangement because England was on hostile terms with the ultimate beneficiary of the money, Napoleon. But money is money. The British merchant bank had a partnership with a Dutch bank, which in turn routed the money to France in a classic money-laundering scheme. Says one historian wryly, "Thus it was that a London banking firm sold American bonds on an international market to help France finance a renewed war with Great Britain." The London merchant bank, the House of Baring, floated a public bond offering and sold securities to the general public and to banks (the "institutional investors" of the day). The major buyers were not American investors but French and Dutch investors, who bought the bonds at the opening offering price and immediately resold them to other investors for a nice profit ("flipping" is what it's called today on Wall Street).

For the United States, this was a superb deal because the country was essentially financing the acquisition with other people's money, mostly foreigners'. For the foreign investors and speculators, it was a good deal because they were able to quickly resell at a profit. The two merchant banks collected a success fee of $3 million, so they walked away happy. The bonds yielded an interest rate of 6 percent, and all investors got their money back at the end of fifteen years. To be sure, in 1818—several years after a disastrous war with England—$15 million was beyond the capacity of the U.S. to repay in one lump sum. But by then the value of the land was at least fifty times its original cost, thus providing the collateral to underwrite additional financings to repay the original bondholders.

Of course, in all deals there are losers. In this case the loser was France because of its gross mismanagement of the proceeds. A monarchy, France was accustomed to having its queen attired in a manner befitting her rank. "French fashions must be France's answers to Spain's gold mines in Peru," opined the finance minister Jean-Baptiste Colbert in the 1770s. Louis XVI's wife, Marie Antoinette, had an annual clothing budget of $3.6 million, but consistently overran it by commissioning gowns encrusted with diamonds and sapphires that left John Adams, the American consul to Paris, speechless. She was "an object too sublime and beautiful for my dull pen to describe," he wrote. "Her dress was everything that art and wealth could make it." Not to be outdone, Napoleon's wife Josephine took the proceeds of the Louisiana Purchase and spent half of the $15 million on clothes over the next ten years.

Today the Louisiana Purchase is applauded in history books for doubling the size of the country. Less known but even more significant, the success of the Louisiana Purchase initiated for the next two hundred years a much broader view of the Constitution. It also introduced the idea of debt as an easy form of government financing. (And it did establish, to some degree, France's claim to be the world center of fashion.)

Rarely appreciated today is the magnitude of the gamble. Imagine nowadays a president going to Congress and asking for $400 billion to buy territory of which there was no general map and the only information the seller could give him was "Make the most of it." The speaker was Talleyrand, and the United States did do the deal. It takes enormous confidence, but out of such daring are great deals made.

Fool's Gold

➤**1848** Jack London, the famous novelist who wrote *Call of the Wild*, once did a story on the discovery of gold in the Klondike, and arrived at the astounding conclusion that $220 million was spent extracting $22 million from the ground.

"Who has profited? Who has lost? How much has gone into the ground? How much has been taken out of the ground?" he asked. London estimated that some 125,000 gold seekers had rushed into the Northern Eldorado, each of whom "gave a year of his life. In view of the hardship and severity of their toil, four dollars a day per man would indeed be a cheap purchase of their labor. One and all, they would refuse in a civilized country to do the work they did do at such a price."

By multiplying four dollars a day times 125,000 men times 300 days and adding the resulting $150 million to the $75 million that went for their transportation and food, London arrived at the $220 million (actually $225 million). Viewed in its totality, the Klondike Gold Rush was essentially a glorified lottery.

The California Gold Rush of 1848 was not much better. Here, too, the people who made the money were the equipment suppliers and saloonkeepers. Because of the lack of laundry services, for example, gold miners had to send their clothes to Hawaii to be washed. The Hawaiian washer women made more money than most of their California customers.

Even more remarkable about the California Gold Rush was who lost the most money: John Sutter. When the first discovery was made at Sutter's Mill, he must have counted himself the luckiest man in the world: here he was, probably the largest landowner in America, living "like a feudal baron" with his own fort and private army, master of a million acres, when his head carpenter went to one of his sawmills and discovered gold.

However, just as important as making money is keeping it. Within weeks, forty thousand gold-seekers had swarmed into his property, destroying crops, roads, and bridges in their frenzy. Sutter couldn't keep so many trespassers off his property, nor could he sue them in court because by the time his lawsuits got a court hearing,

all the unknown trespassers had long since moved on. Sutter spent the rest of his life trying to win compensation, but to no avail, and finally died impoverished, a broken man.

She Loved Money Too Much

➤**1867**   When Edward Robinson died in 1865, shortly followed by his sister and former partner Sylvia Ann Howland, there was only one family heir left: Edward's daughter Hetty. Robinson left his daughter $910,000 and the income from the balance of his $6-million estate (the money was made in whaling). Sylvia Ann Howland, in turn, left her niece the income from half of her $12.3 million estate. But Hetty was not happy with the income from half of $12.3 million; she wanted more. A thirty-year-old spinster, Hetty Robinson had but one love in life, and she loved it dearly: money. So she did what every American in search of easy money does: she filed a lawsuit.

The Howland Will Case quickly developed a life of its own, and took years to untangle and resolve. The will of Sylvia Ann Howland was written in 1863; everyone agreed she was "of sound mind," and the executor was her (and her brother's) remaining business partner. So far, so good.

In her complaint, Hetty Robinson produced a copy of an earlier will, written a year before the registered will, awarding

her $12.2 million of the $12.3-million estate. Now, normally when there are two
wills, the most recent one takes priority,
not the first one. But Hetty Robinson then
produced two copies of an additional page
to the first will, known during the trial as
"the Second Page," revoking "all wills
made by me before or after this one. . . . I
give this will to my niece to show, if absolutely necessary to have it, to appear
against another will found after my
death." The letter was signed only by
Sylvia Howland; there were no signatures
by witnesses.

Why this strange behavior on the part
of Sylvia Howland? Hetty claimed that
her aunt had become estranged from her
brother/business partner (Hetty's father),
and had made Hetty promise that Hetty's
father would never inherit any money; in
return for this promise, Hetty would get
all her aunt's money. This all came as a
great surprise to the executor, Thomas
Mandell, the business partner of Sylvia
Howland and Edward Robinson. Edward,
as it turned out, had died before Sylvia, so
the need for excluding Edward became
moot, not to mention the fact that Edward, as the managing partner of the family business, had made a lot more money
than his sister and certainly didn't need
any of her share. If there had been an es-
trangement in the family that would have
caused a young woman to turn against her
own father, presumably Mandell would
have known about it.

Regardless of how bizarre Hetty's claim

seemed, the executors still had to contend
with Sylvia Howland's signature on "the
Second Page." Was it real? Or was it a forgery? The executors decided the best way
to beat back Hetty Robinson's challenge
to the will was to claim that the unwit-
nessed signature on the Second Page did
not match the witnessed signature of the
first will, which everyone agreed was legitimate.

The fight was a vigorous one. The evidence before the court took a full year
to compile and consisted of more than
one thousand pages. Handwriting experts
from all over the country and even from
France were called in by the plaintiff to
argue that the two signatures matched.
Hetty Robinson's lawyers even produced
110 samples of the signature of the late
President John Quincy Adams to show
that a person's signature was consistent, to
which the defense argued that John
Quincy Adams was famous for his scrupu-
lous handwriting.

In what must have been the only time
John Quincy Adams ever got called a
horse, the defense leaped at the opportunity to hoist the plaintiff on her own
petard: "Are not the improbabilities of a
race horse, impossible for a draft horse?"
Sylvia Howland, they argued, had been
too infirm to write anything but her
name, so how was it possible for an infirm
old woman to write so clearly unless the
signature was not hers? To rebut the alle-
gations of forgery, Hetty Robinson's
lawyers reached into the bowels of the

Harvard faculty and retained the renowned scientist Louis Agassiz and Oliver Wendell Holmes Sr. (father of the future Supreme Court justice). Holmes testified that he had examined the signatures under a microscope and found no traces of lead on the paper that would have been used for tracing, nor had he found any squiggles in the penmanship that suggested the work of a nervous hand. He was followed as an expert witness by the equally venerable Louis Agassiz, who treated the court to a lengthy and undoubtedly most edifying discourse about the microscopic interactions of ink and paper fiber.

Not to be outdone, the estate recruited the leading mathematician of the day, professor Benjamin Pierce. Now shifting gears, the estate argued that the two signatures indeed matched—too perfectly, in fact, for a human hand. Benjamin Pierce's son Charles began with a discourse on the mathematical probabilities of loops and strokes. He described how he had analyzed forty-two samples of Sylvia Howland's signature, superimposed them on top of each other, and found that one out of five downstrokes coincided. But in the case of the first will and the Second Page, all thirty downstrokes coincided exactly. He counted the number of times the formation of a letter requiring a downstroke coincided. The number of available comparisons was 831, which, when multiplied by the thirty positions in the signature, yielded 25,830 possibilities. The question

then became, What are the odds that each position will match exactly? Was it even remotely possible that the very exact identicalness of the two signatures could have been achieved by chance? Or was it obvious that more sinister motives were at play?

Enter the father, Benjamin Pierce. He presented a table with the number of coinciding downstrokes on the left column, from three to twelve. On the right column he assembled the number of cases of actual coincidence for each number (ninety-seven in the number-3 row, 131 in the number-4 row, etc.). Multiplying all the numbers, Professor Pierce informed the court that he had calculated the odds that Sylvia Howland could have produced two signatures in which all thirty downstrokes coincided. The answer was one out of five for each downstroke. But there were thirty downstrokes, so the total answer was one out of five to the thirtieth power, or "one out of 2,666,000,000,000,000,000,000"—clearly impossible.

The estate won.

With the specter of a criminal fraud charge hanging over her head, Hetty Robinson changed her name by getting married and moving to London to lie low for eight years. After a proper interlude, she came back to America, settled in New York, and began her prodigious investment career. "Buy cheap and sell dear!" was her investment philosophy (though exactly how she did this, she never revealed). She wore a beat-up black petticoat lined with pockets to hold the bonds, stock certificates, and large sums of cash for the day's trading, earning for herself the sobriquet "The Witch of Wall Street." A fierce competitor, she once warned another trader, "When I fight there is usually a funeral, and it isn't mine."

Hetty Robinson

She took no prisoners: she once foreclosed on a church. She hated to spend money: when her son hurt his leg in a sledding accident, she put the boy in a charity ward and refused to pay for a doctor; eventually the boy's leg had to be amputated. During her lifetime she constantly moved from one apartment to another to avoid establishing a residence permanent enough to attract the attention of the New York State tax authorities. Over a thirty-year period, Hetty Green parlayed her $1-million inheritance into $125 million (equivalent to $17 billion today). When she died, the *New York Times* called her the richest woman in America.

Had it not been for Benjamin Pierce, she might have started out with $3 million—and died worth $375 million, making her richer than any other man. The only reason she did not is that she loved money too much.

When the Will Got Read

➤**1877** He was the world's richest man, worth more than the U.S. Treasury— $104 million.* In the delightful phrase of the time, he was "puffed with divine greed."

He didn't write his will until he was

---

* Take a moment, if you will, to imagine how this wealth compares with Bill Gates's wealth. Nothing can compare to Vanderbilt's. On paper, $104 million represented more than 10 percent of all American currency in circulation at the time. Furthermore, Bill Gates—like virtually every entrepreneur—is only a one-shot wonder: he made his fortune in software. Vanderbilt, on the other hand, was that rare two-shot wonder: he made his first fortune in ships, then sold everything and went into a new field, railroads. For Gates to equal what Vanderbilt did, he would have had to jettison Microsoft and start Google—plus some.

eighty-one. When he became ill a year later and his family gathered around for the last rites, he showed the stamina that had made him rich. He battled death for eight more months, exhausting everyone in the process (including two of his physicians, who died). Every day the newspapers carried stories about his various ailments, his net worth, and what the impact of his death would be on the stock market. Hardly a week went by without some newspaper announcing he was dead. "Commodore Vanderbilt dying!" some newsboys yelled one day outside his bedroom window. The next day, when a reporter came to his house, he crawled out of bed and screamed from the top of the grand staircase, "I am not dying!"

His deathbed would have merited a scene in *Macbeth* or *Hamlet*. Lying helpless in the sweltering summer heat, he was besieged by his eight daughters, each seeking a bigger slice of his fortune. "Get out, Ethelinda!" he roared. "Leave me alone, Sophia! Enough of you, Phoebe!" He had already made out his will, he said, and he would not change it. Everyone had been taken care of: his wife, his ten children, and fifty-two grandchildren and great-grandchildren.

Except for his young second wife, who had signed a $500,000 prenuptial agreement, no one had the faintest idea how much he or she would get. The only person to learn anything was one of the physicians, Dr. Jared Linsly, to whom the sick man confided, "If I had died in 1835 or 1836 or even 1854, the world would not have known that I had lived, but I think that I have been spared to accomplish a great work that will last and remain, for I have taken care that it is to be secured in such a way that the stock cannot be put on the market after I die. . . . Had I given one daughter $3,000,000 and another daughter $5,000,000 . . . in six months the stock would have been down to 40."

Called "Commodore" because he once owned so many ships (this was before he bailed out of shipping at age sixty-nine and went into the railroad business, where he made 80 percent of his money), Cornelius Vanderbilt was a cold, imperious man who demanded total obedience from his employees and wife and children. When his first wife objected to moving from their bucolic farm on Staten Island to a townhouse in New York, he had her put away in an insane asylum for two years until she relented. He gave the same treatment to one of his sons who had run up a string of gambling debts. He paid scant attention to his daughters, and treated them with the same disdain he did his wife. His was a man's world, where men were supposed to be athletic and virile. Like George.

George was George Washington Vanderbilt, his youngest son, a youth of powerful physique like his father. Except that the son was better: he could bench-press an unbelievable nine hundred pounds. That's my boy! But George was dead. He had gone to West Point to become a professional soldier, then contracted malaria during the Civil War. For the Commodore this was a double tragedy: the best of his sons had chosen not to enter the world of business (at least not yet), and the boy had died when it would have been so easy to hire a "substitute" as so many others had done during the Civil War. The Commodore never got over it, and for the rest of his life he paid quacks and charlatans to help him communicate with his son through séances.

With his first two boys the Commodore was much tougher. William, the oldest, was an acquiescent, gentle person, incapable of saying an unkind word about anybody. His thorough decency would irritate his father and provoke him to yell, "Bloody fool! Idiot! Blatherskite!" But as the Commodore grew older, he showed the same mellower attitude toward William that he did toward George: he gave him a chance. When William turned his modest Staten Island farm into a thriving operation, the Commodore was impressed. He invited William to join him at the New York Central, and quickly promoted him to vice president. William was a man whose judgment could be trusted. The only concern was—and it could be a major one—did William have fire in his belly? William's true love in life was his family and his horses: his idea of a good time was to spend an evening at home with his wife and children and grandchildren, whereas the crusty Commodore

preferred to stay out all night playing whist with "the boys."

The Commodore had a clear view of human nature, which he applied to his sons: "If a boy is good for anything you can stick him down anywhere and he'll learn his living and lay up something: if he can't do it he ain't worth saving, and you can't save him." Early on he had warned each of his sons not to expect any of his wealth until the son had demonstrated his capacity to support himself on his own. Certainly the middle son, "Corneel," could never pass the test. Forever incurring gambling debts and borrowing money on the strength of his father's name, Corneel caused his father to despair, "I would give $10,000 were his name not Cornelius!" The Commodore refused to pay his son's debts, but on one occasion he made an exception. Corneel's biggest creditor was the kindly newspaper editor and 1868 presidential candidate Horace Greeley. When Greeley died in 1872, leaving behind a mountain of bills, the Commodore sent $10,000 checks to each of Greeley's daughters.

Now, in 1875, at the age of eighty-one, as he sat down to write his will, he had to decide what to do with his money. He had little interest in philanthropy, other than some gifts to please his wife, who wanted to help her church and found a university (now Vanderbilt University). He had his enormous brood of children and grandchildren, but like many self-made men he felt they were taking advantage of him.

He was not interested in leaving them a lot of money. "A million or two is as much as anyone ought to have," he said.

The one thing that consumed his attention was his railroad empire, threatened every day by the jackals and speculators of Wall Street, not to mention ruthless competitors all ganging up to short the stock at the slightest whiff of weakness. True vigilance was required. "What you have is not worth anything unless you have the power," he said, "and if you give away the surplus, you give away the control." He therefore resolved that control of his empire would rest in the hands of one man. For lack of anyone better, that man would have to be William. To be sure, William's two oldest sons, Cornelius Junior, age thirty-one, and William K., age twenty-four, were fine young men and hard workers, but it was still too early to tell how they would turn out. After making some quick calculations, he called in three witnesses and dictated a simple three-page will. He signed it on January 9, 1875.

He died on January 4, 1877. Four days later the will was read. Leaving out the ninth and last point, which deals with the appointment of executors, the will is constructed in a logical format obviously designed, like a mystery novel, to lead up to a powerful surprise ending. That it certainly did.

Point 1 left the New York townhouse and $500,000, as agreed, to his wife. Point 2 left $250,000 apiece to daughters Phoebe, Emily, Marie Louise, Sophia, and Mary Alicia. Point 3 dealt with trust funds for other children: $400,000 to Ethelinda, $300,000 to Eliza, $500,000 to Catharine, and $200,000 to Corneel. Point 4 gave small annual stipends to his sister and niece, and Point 5 made numerous $5,000 bequests to grandchildren and other relatives. Points 6 and 7 addressed certain procedural details concerning the purchase of bonds and the modest payment of taxes.

What about all the rest of the money? And where was the tenth, still-unnamed, heir, William?

One imagines the deadly silence in the room as Point 8 starts to be read: "All the rest, residue, and remainder . . . of the property and estate, real and personal, of every description, and wheresoever situated, of which I may be seized or possessed, and to which I may be entitled at the time of my decease, I give, devise, and bequeath unto my son, William H. Vanderbilt, his heirs, executors, administrators and assigns, to his and their use forever."

William H. Vanderbilt had inherited 97 percent of the world's greatest fortune.

Living Well (on $1,000 a Day)

►**1880**   William H. Vanderbilt sold $50 million of his New York Central stock and reinvested the money in government bonds. That very day, he spent the rest of the afternoon scrutinizing a janitor's luncheon bills and disallowed a charge of forty cents.

"I am the richest man in the world," he said. He started spending money in a big way. He built two $3-million mansions on Fifth Avenue in New York, one for himself and his wife, the other for two of his daughters. He took frequent trips to Paris, coming back laden with paintings and artifacts for his new palace. He treated French artists better than his janitor: whenever he would have a picture painted to order, he would offer a higher price than was asked, telling the surprised artist that he wanted him to do the very best he could.

While accumulating a $1.5-million art collection for his palace nearing completion, his wife expressed reservations about leaving their own home at Fifth Avenue and 40th Street. "We don't need a better home, and I hate to think of leaving this home where we have lived so comfortable," she told a friend. "I have told William that if he wants a finer place for his pictures, to build a wing to which he could go whenever he felt inclined; this is too good a house to leave. I will never feel at home in the new place. I remember the first picture we ever bought. We paid ninety dollars for it, and we were afraid to let our friends know how extravagant we had been. I have the picture yet, and there is more pleasure to me in looking at it than all the Meissoniers and other great pictures in the house."

Other multimillionaires agreed the big house was a waste of money. One day two gentlemen from Pittsburgh were visiting New York and were cruising up Fifth Avenue in their carriage when they came to the Vanderbilt mansions. "I suppose these are really the best residences in the city," surmised Henry Clay Frick.

"I think they are so considered," agreed his companion, Andrew Mellon.

"I wonder how much the upkeep of the one on that corner would be?" wondered Frick, pointing to the father's house. "Say $300,000 a year? I should think that would cover it."

"It might," conceded Mellon.

"That would be six percent on five million, or five percent on six, say a thousand dollars a day," calculated Frick. "That is all I shall ever want."

Fiddling with the Clock to Get a Pension

➤ **1885** When General Ulysses Grant became president, he was advised to take a "leave of absence" from the Army so he could be sure to receive his Civil War pension. Grant would have none of it: only by resigning could he create a vacancy and allow General William T. Sherman to move up the army hierarchy and take his place.

Seventeen years later, forced into bankruptcy after investing in a Wall Street swindle, Grant was destitute. He had no pension to draw on. (Ex-presidents didn't get a pension in those days, and he got no

Army pension because he had "resigned," not "retired.") Sherman and other friends lobbied Congress for Grant's reinstatement on the regular Army retired list, which would allow Grant to collect his former salary without blocking the career advancement of another general. They got their bill through the Senate, only to be turned down by the southern representatives in the House. "Thus," the *New York Times* editorialized, "four Confederate brigadiers, eleven colonels, one lieutenant colonel, one major, five captains, two lieutenants, and twelve enlisted men did to Grant what they couldn't do in the field."

Taking advantage of growing public sympathy for Grant, now dying of cancer, Sherman and his friends made one desperate last effort. On the morning of March 4, 1885, when Grover Cleveland was to be inaugurated as president at noontime, Samuel J. Randall, the Democratic Speaker of the House, tried to get his colleagues to focus on the Grant issue and forget all the various appropriations bills on the table. At around 11:45 he finally got them to vote, and the Grant bill passed easily. Ulysses Grant could now relax; he had his pension.

The only problem was the Senate also had to vote, and time was running out— only fifteen minutes left. Most senators were off in the Capitol rotunda, getting ready to march in the inaugural procession. Randall ordered them to come back to their seats. In the meantime, he had one of the Senate clerks turn back the Senate clock—which had just run past noon. The senators voted, President Chester Arthur ordered a congratulatory telegram to be sent to Grant, and the senators finally arrived at the swearing-in of Grover Cleveland, twenty minutes late.

"Where have you guys been?"

Midas

➤**1887** His was the most amazing achievement in the history of American wealth, far more so than Bill Gates or Warren Buffett today. A few people have inherited $100 million, and a lot of people have made $100 million, but no man has done both—except for one man. Most remarkable of all, he made even more money than his father. "Any fool can make a fortune," he said. "It takes a man of brains to hold on to it after it is made." (A sentiment subsequently echoed by Andrew Carnegie: "Even a fool can make a million dollars, but it takes a sage to keep it.")

Asked why he didn't buy himself a yacht even though he spent $200,000 a year, he offered this keen insight on money: "No yachts for me!" he said. "No yachts for me, no sir! They are easy to buy, but they are hard to sell."

This Midas, of course, was William H. Vanderbilt, son of the world's richest man, Cornelius Vanderbilt. After inheriting $100 million out of his father's $104 million fortune in 1877, he had to contend with some very unhappy brothers and sisters. The result was "the will trial of the century"—which he won conclusively. This gentle man, no great genius or domineering buccaneer, proved his father's judgment to be correct: in just eight years he added more than $110 million to the family fortune. He, too, died the world's richest man.

Believing that the burden of such a fortune was too great for one man to bear (indeed, he literally died of overwork), William Vanderbilt divided his fortune among seven of his eight children. His will attracted international attention. Observed the *New York Sun*:

> *Never was such a last testament known of mortal. Kings have died with full treasuries, Emperors have fled their realms with bursting coffers, great financiers have played with millions, bankers have reaped and sowed and reaped again, great houses with vast acres have grown and grown and still exist; but never before was such a spectacle presented of a plain, ordinary man dispensing, of his own free will, in bulk and magnitude that the mind wholly fails to apprehend, tangible millions upon millions of palpable money. It is simply grotesque. The numerical significance of a million is incomprehensible; it can only be measured relatively and by illustration, and when it comes to dealing with hundreds of millions, the understanding is overwhelmed and helpless. Mr. Vanderbilt gave them right and left, as if they were ripe apples.*

The apples did not stay ripe long. William Vanderbilt's children and grandchildren embarked on a high-velocity spending spree that dissipated even the Vanderbilt fortune. By 1923 the family fortune had been chopped up into nineteen parts. Out of seventy-four Americans with annual incomes higher than $1 million, only two were heirs of William Henry Vanderbilt, and only one ranked in the top ten.*

Further decline was still to come. In 1973, 120 heirs met at Vanderbilt University for a family reunion, only to discover there was not a single millionaire left among them.

Cash-Flow Miracle

➤ **1904** In the early 1900s he was widely considered a crackpot. His two previous business ventures had gone bankrupt. Third time around, he had a nearly impossible time raising money for his latest, "best" new venture. "Come on, Henry, you've failed twice," many investors told

---

* He was William's son, Frederick, the one and only smart third-generation Vanderbilt. After graduating from Yale, he went out and amassed a $78-million fortune and served as a director of many companies, including twenty-two railroads. He had no children. Angry that he inherited only a pittance compared with his two older brothers and appalled at his siblings for their lavish spending, he left his Vanderbilt relatives nothing.

him. "Why don't you forget it and just get yourself a job?"

But Henry persevered, and started the Ford Motor Company with an initial capital investment of $28,000 to pay for twelve workmen and a tiny 250-by-50-foot assembly plant. Over the next forty years, how much additional capital was invested in the company?

None. Thanks to the amazing speed of the assembly line,* the Ford Motor Company was profitable from day one and financed its growth entirely from operations. Parts makers sold their components to Henry Ford on thirty-to-ninety-day credit; because Henry Ford could assemble a car in just ninety-three minutes and sell it in a few days, he was able to build his company on supplier credit.

Rent, Don't Sell

➤**1908** America's first billion-dollar fortune was amassed by Howard Hughes in the 1950s through his acquisition of Trans-World Airlines and RKO Pictures, his buildup of Hughes Aircraft into a major military electronics contractor, his real-estate development in Las Vegas, and his sole ownership of the Hughes Tool Company, which he had inherited from his father.

His father's fortune came from a stroke of financial acumen. In 1908 the father invented the drilling bit that enabled oil exploration companies to finally cut through the bedrock that lay above Texas's huge reserves of oil. But unlike most inventors, the elder Mr. Hughes refused to sell his products; rather, he rented them. Oil exploration companies and wildcatters paid $30,000 per well for the use of a Hughes bit; once oil was struck, the bit had to be returned to the Hughes Tool Company, where it was cleaned, sharpened, and rented out again for other drilling attempts. "Sheer genius," said the president of Standard Oil (which rented fifteen thousand bits in the first decade alone). "Highway robbery, of course, but genius all the same."

Renting to 75 percent of the world's oil wells provided a nice "cash cow" income stream to the Hughes empire for the rest of the century.

Today's most successful investor is Warren Buffett, the world's second-richest man after Bill Gates. Mr. Buffett is a man who knows his history. "Successful investing," he says, "means knowing when to buy, when to sell, and when to rent."

Acres of Diamonds

➤**1915** By popular demand, the most influential motivational speech of all time

---

* A popular joke of the day told the story of a worker fired by Ford "for incompetence." What had he done? He had dropped his wrench, and stooped down to pick it up. When he stood upright, he found himself sixteen cars behind.

was finally published: "Acres of Dia-monds" by Russell Conwell, a Baptist minister in Philadelphia. Having first de-livered the sermon during the Civil War, Conwell traveled the country and deliv-ered it six thousand times before his death in 1925. It's a parable about a successful Persian farmer named Ali Hafed, "the man who would be rich." It seems that Ali was a man of some wealth, but he was un-happy because he lusted to possess the richness of diamonds. Told there were dia-monds in a faraway land, Ali Hafed sold his farm and set off in search of diamonds. Years later, after thousands of miles and poor and despondent, he threw himself into the sea, never to be seen again. In the meantime the man who bought Ali Hafed's farm took his camel out for water one day, and saw something flashing in the sunlight. It was a diamond. Looking fur-ther, the man found the place was filled with diamonds greater than the diamonds of Golconda, greater than the diamonds of the Kimberly Mine. Poor Ali Hafed! Says Conwell, "Had Ali Hafed remained at home and dug in his own cellar or in his own garden, instead of wretchedness, star-vation, poverty and death [in] a strange land, he would have had 'acres of dia-monds'!" Continues Conwell, "Acres of di-amonds are to be found in this city, and you are to find them. Many have found them. And what man has done, man can do. They are not in faraway mountains or in distant seas, they are in your own back-yard if you will but look for them."

The moral of the story: stick with what

you know, don't give up so easily, don't be swayed by the allure of greener pastures, the seeds of fortune are close at hand. Dig in your own backyard! Using Conwell as an inspiration, here are some stories of in-vestors and businessmen who missed the diamonds lying in their gardens:

Henry Comstock, an illiterate miner who staked a claim to the Nevada mine that bears his name, sold all his holdings for $11,000 so he could open a trading-goods store. The store went belly-up and Comstock ended up putting a gun to his head. In the meantime the Comstock Lode turned out to be the biggest mine in North America, far richer than the Cali-fornia Gold Rush. Between 1859 and 1878, the Comstock Lode yielded $400 million in silver and gold (equivalent in GDP terms to $600 billion today).

In 1878, after eighteen months in busi-ness, the Bell Telephone Company ran out of money and Alexander Graham Bell of-fered to sell out to Western Union for $100,000. Western Union's president turned him down: "What use could this company make of an electrical toy?" West-ern Union's lead investor Cornelius Van-derbilt agreed: why would people want to talk when they could use Western Union's telegraph and get a printed message? With no investors in sight, Bell turned to fran-chising, and within a year was self-financing with 185 franchisees. "Ma Bell" eventually became the second-largest company in the United States, and was on its way to becoming number one when the government broke it up in 1982.

In 1888, in Atlanta, a brilliant chemist named John Pemberton—who had earned his medical degree at age nineteen, gone on to start up eighteen companies, and owned a research lab that was recognized as the best in the state of Georgia—invented a wine drink that he changed into a mouthwash and finally into a soft drink that tasted pretty good. After incorporating the company, he became discouraged by first-year sales of seventy-five dollars—incurring a personal loss of fifty dollars—and, in need of money to pursue other interests, he sold the Coca-Cola company to one of his employees for $2,300. Within ten years Coca-Cola was the number-one drink in the United States.

In 1894 Alvah Roebuck, cofounder of Sears, Roebuck, sold his half-share to Richard Sears for $25,000. Years later, at the beginning of the Great Depression, after he had squandered the money and was flat broke, he went back and got a menial job at the company that once had been half his. Richard Sears, in the meantime, had recently died, leaving an estate of $25 million.

In 1906 Alex Malcolmsen, founding partner and chairman, sold out to his partner Henry Ford for $175,000; fifteen years later that stake was worth $63 million. Down the road at General Motors, an equal debacle took place. In 1910 Will Durant, the founder of General Motors, got turned down by J. P. Morgan as a "visionary nitwit" for predicting that there would soon be fifty thousand automobiles on the road. Durant went to another investment group and finally got a $15-million loan. But the terms were stiff. The investment group demanded control of the board and all the company's assets pledged as security. The lawyers who drew up the agreement considered General Motors so shaky they cut their fee in half just to get all cash, no stock. From 1913 to 1919 the share price rose from thirty dollars to $850.

Lenin once said that "of all the arts, the cinema is the most important." Yet few industries have been so out of touch with the public as the movie business. When the technology of sound became feasible in the mid-1920s, Harry Warner of Warner Bros. dismissed the idea: "Who the hell wants to hear actors talk?" Equally shortsighted was Darryl Zanuck of 20th Century Fox. Offered the opportunity in 1946 to bankroll a company starting to manufacture television sets, Zanuck turned it down: "Video won't be able to hold any market after the first six months. People will soon get tired of staring at a plywood box every night."

An inventor named Chester Carlson came up with a new process to make photocopies of a document on plain paper. He went to the predominant image company in America, Eastman Kodak, and offered to sell them his patents for a cheap price if they would commercialize his invention. Kodak, fearful of antitrust problems, turned it down. Carlson then went to a much smaller company called IBM; IBM, too, gave him the cold shoulder. Finally, in the late 1940s, a small company making photographic paper agreed to acquire the patents and give Carlson the platform he needed. The company's name was Haloid, later changed to Xerox, and an industry was born.

At about that time, 1948, the Ford Motor Company was offered the opportunity to buy Germany's largest auto manufacturer, Volkswagen. The offer was simple: just take over the company. Don't pay anything. Yet Ford turned it down. The Englishman in charge of Ford-Europe opposed the deal because he feared the Ford German subsidiary might eventually become stronger than Ford in England. Asked by Henry Ford II what he thought of the German offer, he retorted, "I don't think what we are being offered here is worth a damn!" By 1954 Volkswagen had become the world's fourth-largest automobile manufacturer (after the Detroit Big Three), and in 1972 the Volkswagen Beetle surpassed the Model T to become the best-selling car of all time. To this day, Volkswagen remains the most powerful auto company in Europe. Even greater errors were still to come. In the mid-1950s the Ford Motor Company was approached, hat in hand, by two Japanese auto companies, seeking an alliance of some sort. Ford blew them away as makers of "tin cars." Today, Toyota is a lot bigger than Ford, and Nissan is more profitable than Ford. Admits a former Ford CEO: "[We] made some strategic

errors . . . by not properly assessing the strength of the Japanese."

In 1955 every bank in town turned up their noses at the businessman seeking a loan for his young company, even though it was already profitable. Getting desperate, he offered to sell half the business for $25,000; there were no takers. Today that $25,000 would have made one a multibillionaire. The company, of course, was McDonald's. The businessman was its founder, Ray Kroc.

In the late 1970s two college students developed a prototype personal computer for the general public. They went to Atari with this offer: "What do you think about funding us? Or we'll give it to you. We just want to do it. Pay our salary, we'll come work for you." Atari said no. The young men then went to Hewlett-Packard, who told them, "We don't need you, you haven't got through college yet." The two entrepreneurs never did finish college; instead they went on to bigger things. Steve Jobs and Steve Wozniak founded Apple Computer.

❧

We close with a quintessential all-American story Ben Franklin would have liked, a story with a happy ending.

In 1924, forced to sell the family farm after his father died, and mired in debt, he dreamed of striking it rich in the Kansas oilfields. Teaming up with two partners and borrowing money from his mother, he headed off to Kansas. He and his partners

Harry Truman: He quit too early.

acquired a 320-acre site and commenced drilling. After several false starts, they got down as far as nine hundred feet when their funds ran out and they had to stop. They parted ways, and the dejected young man trudged back to Missouri to face his mother and his fiancée. The man who bought the property resumed drilling and immediately hit a gusher. His company went on to become Cities Service, one of the largest oil companies in the United States.

As for the young man, he started another business—a store—but it went bankrupt. The only thing good in his life was that his fiancée stuck with him. Finally, at the urging of a friend, he entered politics. Many years later, sitting in the Oval Office, Harry Truman admitted had he struck it rich in the Texas oilfields he never would have become president of the United States.

A Model Businessman– Philanthropist

➤**1929** "He should be the most thanked man in the world," said the *New York Times* on his seventy-fifth birthday. No buccaneer like many self-made moguls, this enormously wealthy man sought more than money. He was George Eastman, founder of Eastman Kodak, the pioneer of roll film and the simple box camera. His company slogan: "You press the button, we do the rest." By creating an affordable product that helped preserve memorable moments, George Eastman richened people's lives.

Long before it became a recognized management tool for improving productivity, George Eastman provided his employees with high-quality working conditions.

What the *New York Times* was referring to was not just his consumer product, but the way he ran his business. George Eastman's treatment of employees set the standard for enlightened capitalism. He recognized that his greatest challenge was recruiting, training, and retaining the highly skilled workforce needed to make Kodak a success. He reduced employee working hours and introduced strict safety standards on the factory floor that cut worker accidents 80 percent in just three years. Other medical innovations included a Fresh Aid Fund, a medical department, and a disability benefit plan. He also insti-

tuted an employee profit-sharing plan, a savings system, a retirement program, and a life insurance program. This had never been done before in the United States—or anywhere else, for that matter.

He was an equal-opportunity employer. Many of his employees were women. When MIT recommended one of its professors for a senior position at Kodak, Eastman hired her on the spot. When asked to contribute to the all-black Tuskegee Institute, he made "by far the largest single contribution ever made to Negro education." He then made an equivalent contribution to another black school, the Hampton Institute. Believing every man deserved a second chance, he instructed his staff to take extra measures to hire handicapped workers and ex-convicts. Compared with most businessmen, then and now, who believe the purpose of a business is to serve the stockholders, Eastman took a broad view and included other constituencies such as workers and the community. "Mr. Eastman," said one associate, "was the only man I ever knew who started out a conservative and wound up a liberal."

He was a liberal, but not a bleeding heart. Money must be earned. He was dead set against "gift stock": he dug into his pocket and made cheap stock available

George Eastman, progressive capitalist

to employees, but on the condition that they contribute 2 percent of their earnings. When he took his company public and became a rich man, he set aside 18 percent of his personal profit and distributed it to his workers, with the following note: "This is a personal matter with Mr. Eastman and he requests that you will not consider it as a gift but as extra pay for good work." Such fairness stood in sharp contrast to other corporations such as Ford, which in 1913 had a staggering 370-percent annual employee turnover, or Andrew Carnegie's United States Steel Corporation, where the modus operandi was "I have always had one rule: When a workman sticks up his head, hit it."

Looking for a young man to strengthen his business, Eastman went to Harvard Business School and asked to recruit its top MBA student. The man was Marion Folsom. Folsom joined Eastman Kodak and rose to the position of treasurer. Together, Eastman and Folsom structured Kodak's groundbreaking pension and retirement plan. (Folsom, because of his work with Eastman, served on every advisory committee developing the Social Security Act, and eventually became Secretary of Health, Education, and Welfare.)

Eastman could be as hard-nosed as any of his fellow industrialists: "In business it is war all the time," he once wrote. When a friend complimented him for being so organized and disciplined, he responded, "Yes, one has to be hard, hard in this world. But never forget, one must always keep one part of one's heart a little soft." This included his sales to the War Department in World War I—a time when wartime profiteering, as in most wars, was rampant. Not for Eastman: he voluntarily refunded $335,390 to the U.S. government, representing the profits made by Eastman Kodak on war contracts. $152,620 of this was returned in 1919, $182,770 in 1922. Recognizing Eastman's extraordinary gesture (unequaled in all of America), the president of the United States wrote him this letter:

THE WHITE HOUSE
WASHINGTON

February 7, 1922.

My dear Mr. Eastman:

Secretary Weeks reported to the Cabinet today the very unusual experience of your return to the government, on behalf of the Eastman Kodak Company of $182,770.00 which had been paid the company on war contracts in excess of the contemplated profit provided in the contract. I had heard of this pleasing incident informally at the time I had the pleasure of personally greeting you and some of your friends, and had also the satisfaction of seeing the incident noted in the columns of the press. I have no doubt that becoming expression has already been conveyed to you, but I cannot resist adding my own appreciation of this very prompt and considerate action on the part of your company in making a wholly voluntary adjustment after the close of a great war service.

With very best wishes, I am,

Very truly yours,

Warren G Harding

Mr. George Eastman,
c/o Eastman Kodak Co.,
Rochester, N. Y.

Eastman's social innovations "attracted the attention of visitors from every state in the United States, from England, Australia, South America, Mexico, China, and Japan." Finally he gave away 75 percent of his fortune to philanthropy while he was alive. This, too, was unusual. Most magnates, such as Ford, Guggenheim, and Rockefeller, kept accumulating their money and left it to foundations to manage after their deaths. Not Eastman. "Men who leave their money to be distributed by others are pie-faced mutts," he said. "I want to see the action during my lifetime." With that, he resigned from day-to-day management of Kodak to supervise his gifts to educational institutions and the city of Rochester, New York. A number of these gifts were given anonymously, under the name of "Mr. Smith."

He was a totally unselfish man: at the age of seventy-seven, starting to suffer from a spinal ailment that threatened to cripple him, he shot himself so as not to be a burden to others. His suicide note read, "My work is done. Why wait?"

The Year the Stock Market Recovered

►**1936** Rarely have the history books gotten so much so wrong.

On October 29, 1929, the stock market lost $10 billion in share values—more than twice the amount of currency in circulation in the entire country at the time.

Bernard Baruch, the renowned financier and presidential economic advisor, sent a cablegram in November to Winston Churchill: "Financial Storm definitely passed." In June 1930 President Herbert Hoover received a delegation requesting a public-works program to help speed the recovery. "Gentlemen," he said, "you have come sixty days too late. The depression is over." Indeed, many investors who prided themselves as "bottom fishers" proceeded to jump into the market and scoop up bargains. How did they fare?

They lost most of their money. Despite five 30-percent rallies, the market kept falling back to new lows. The Depression (now—with the benefit of historical hindsight—spelled with a capital *D*) was beginning to accelerate into an abyss. By year's end of 1932, after three years of falling share prices, 80 percent of the stock market's value had been wiped out. According to historical stock charts, the stock market didn't recover its 1929 level until 1954—twenty-five years later.

But wait! This assumes that investors dumped all their stocks in 1932. Suppose they had held on to their stocks? They would have recouped all their losses by late 1936—not 1954. How can this be?

Sophisticated investors don't take simple numbers at face value—they look at all numbers in context. According to investment adviser Mark Hulbert, historical stock charts are misleading because they oversimplify the reality by ignoring other factors such as deflation, dividends, and

the index itself. The early 1930s economy was characterized by 18-percent deflation, thus calling for an upward adjustment in real purchasing power. Dividend yields, to compensate for the drop in share prices, were a handsome 14 percent. Finally and most important of all, the Dow was a skewed measure, consisting of only thirty stocks. Which stocks are selected has a major impact on the Dow average (fast-growing IBM, for example, was excluded from the Dow for forty years during 1939 to 1979). According to research firm Ibbotson Associates, by using the overall market index rather than the Dow, and taking into account the factors of deflation and high-yield dividends, the stock market had fully recovered by 1936.

Investors who panicked and dumped their stocks obviously got killed. Those who were patient and held on, however, saw their depleted holdings bounce back fivefold and made out like bandits. This is a useful lesson for Americans who saw their stock market portfolio collapse 30 to 40 percent in 2008. What goes down, must come up.

Economic Boom

►**1945**　Between 1945 and 1950, the U.S. GNP grew almost 50 percent—the greatest five-year boom in economic history. This is a remarkable performance, coming right after an artificially stimulated wartime economy. Usually after a war, the economy goes into a serious recession (as it did in 1780 and 1865). Post–World War II was expected to do the same. Testifying to Congress about the effect of the end of World War II on the economy, U.S. Secretary of Commerce Henry Wallace warned, "During the next four years . . . unless drastic steps are taken by Congress, the U.S. will have nearly 8 million unemployed and will stand on the brink of a deep depression."

Even the Russians got into the act. They offered to be the recipient of $10 billion of American aid in the form of capital equipment. The benefit to America? The manufacture of so much equipment would rescue capitalist America from its postwar economic woes. Needless to say, President Truman was not amused.

"There should be no mincing of words," said the Truman administration's ranking postwar planner. The end of the wartime military spending would cause "an immediate and large dislocation of the economy," with the "severity of this shock . . . increased by the sudden ending of the war." In August 1945, 53 million people were in the employed labor force. Twelve million of them were in the armed forces, most of them scheduled for swift mustering out. Where would these people go?

What the government planners failed to recognize was the stimulus provided by excess capital. During the last two years of the war, Americans had saved almost 25 percent of their take-home pay. By mid-1945, Americans' liquid assets (savings accounts and war bonds) totaled an astonishing $140 billion—three times the entire national income in 1932. Add 1945 individual income of $120-plus billion, and Americans had more than a quarter of a trillion dollars to spend during the first year of peace.

Instead of greeting this liquidity as a blessing, government planners fretted about the inflationary consequences. In fact, they were terrified about an avalanche of disposable cash crashing down on a tight consumer economy—enormous inflation would ensue. It would take many months, possibly years, for industry to convert to making washing machines, autos, radios, and other consumer items to soak up the surplus purchasing power.

Needless to say, it did not happen.

America's Best-Kept Secret

➤ **1981** In a single word: inheritance.

Americans have always had an obsession about the self-made man and how he pulled himself up by his own bootstraps to make a success of himself. The favorite stories in nineteenth-century America were the tales of Horatio Alger: work hard, and thou shalt succeed. Yet Horatio Alger—though he always downplayed it—was himself a Harvard graduate with a nice inheritance to carry him along.

The American yearning for a rich daddy is a long and consistent one. "Thrift," said Mark Twain, "is a wonderful virtue, especially in an ancestor." Indeed. Asked why his son gave more money to charity than he did, John Jacob Astor replied, "My son can afford it. He has a rich father." A similar story is told about JFK. In the early 1960s, when John Kennedy was president of the United States, his father, Joseph P. Kennedy, the man who made all the money, held a meeting of his eight children and berated them for their high style of living. "Every one of you, with the exception of young Teddy here [Edward Kennedy, future Senator from Massachusetts], is spending far more than the income from your trust funds. Now what do you propose to do about it?" All the younger Kennedys looked crestfallen—including the attorney general and the president of the United States. Then JFK spoke up and offered a cheerful solution. "Dad," he chirped, "I guess the only solution is you got to work harder and make more money!" One of the richest men in America in the 1930s was Adolph Lewisohn. "Father, you're spending your capital!" his son cried. "Who made it?" he replied.

More successful at increasing their inheritance were the heirs of Collis Huntington, one of the California tycoons who built the transcontinental railroad. When he died, Huntington left half of his $75-million estate to his young wife, Arabella, and the other half to his nephew Henry. Thirteen years later Henry doubled his inheritance by marrying Arabella.

Kids always know where the money is.

The teenage Alice, daughter of President Theodore Roosevelt and his deceased first wife, had a big inheritance coming her way, an amount so large that the president joked to his second wife, the first lady, that they "should be good to Alice because they might have to borrow money from her." Now, most readers of this book may not know the difference between *per stirpes* and *per capita*, but young Alice certainly did. Under a per capita inheritance, all grandchildren inherit equally. Under per stirpes, the grandchildren inherit all of whatever their mother or father gets. Because Alice was her mother's only child, she would inherit her mother's entire estate and not have to share it with her half sister and half brothers. As Alice recalled, "I constantly reminded my grandfather of it. 'Remember, Grandpa,' I would say, 'per stirpes, not per capita.' I must really have been an odious child . . . Anyway it worked."

❧

Now let us look at the hard numbers. All household wealth in America comes from two sources: lifetime earnings and savings, and inheritance.

Larry Summers, national economic adviser under Obama and former secretary of the treasury under Clinton, coauthored a study on this topic in 1981. He and Laurence Kotlikoff analyzed these two sources of wealth and figured out the percentage that came from each. What percentage would you ascribe to each?

Only 19 percent comes from earnings and savings; the rest—81 percent—comes from inheritance. Using the year 1974 as an example, they calculated the total net worth of the U.S. economy to be $4.154 trillion. After subtracting $270 billion consumed by institutions, the non-institutional household-sector economy became $3.884 trillion. Life-cycle wealth (i.e., accumulated savings) was only $733 billion, or 19 percent. By subtraction, then, the 81-percent balance of $3.151 trillion had to be transfer wealth.

The reason for this is simple: for most of their lifetimes, Americans consume more than they earn. "Growth rates of real earnings slightly exceed growth rates of real consumption over the lifetime." More specifically, from ages eighteen to forty-eight, average per capita consumption exceeds earnings; during the ages forty-eight to sixty-two, earnings exceed consumption; during the ages sixty-two to seventy-five, earnings plummet.

Conclusion? "The pure life-cycle component of aggregate U.S. savings is very small. American capital accumulation results primarily from intergenerational transfers."

SEVEN

Running for President

Every four years we get treated to the great American carnival: a presidential election. Said Theodore Roosevelt, long before he became a candidate himself, "I am now recuperating from the Presidential campaign—our quadrennial Presidential riot being an interesting and exciting, but somewhat exhausting, pastime. I always enjoy it and act as target and marksman alternately with immense zest; but it is a trifle wearing."

Today, despite the massive publicity and the best efforts of newscasters and political parties to build up voter excitement, voting has become largely a spectator sport. In the forty years since 1960, when voter turnout was 61 percent, voter turnout has remained well below 60 percent (53.2, to be exact). Only in 2008 did the turnout rise to more than 60 percent.

Early elections were a far cry from today's carnivals. Take, for example, our first presidential election, in which the "godlike" George Washington won by a unanimous electoral vote: hard to believe, but the popular-vote turnout was a mere 5 percent. In terms of voter mandate, George Washington was our weakest president. Of course, in reality he was our strongest president: for the previous thirteen years he had been the most powerful man in America, and during his presidency he didn't have a troublesome Congress or Supreme Court to worry about. By the way, were you to meet George Washington and try to shake hands with him, you would get an icy stare. Washington did not shake hands with anybody, not even with Hamilton or Jefferson. He bowed.

Prior to 1880, candidates didn't "run" for elective office; they "stood." Compare that to today's marathons in which candidates travel millions of miles, at enormous expense, eating countless chicken dinners and shaking millions of hands, kissing babies and giving pep talks just to convey some sense of urgency and excitement to the voters. We once had an election race, in 1911, where a candidate seeking reelection as president found time to write and publish a one-hundred-page essay that is still regarded to this day as an outstanding treatise. It was Theodore Roosevelt's "Revealing and Concealing Coloration in Birds and Mammals." (TR lost to Woodrow Wilson.)

Winning was not "the only thing" in those days; fair play and integrity also counted. When a man approached Grover Cleveland with documents containing "dirt" on his Republican opponent, James G. Blaine, Cleveland paid the man on the condition that there were no copies—and then promptly burned the documents. In 1940, FDR's campaign advisers brought him evidence that his opponent, Wendell Willkie, had been carrying on a lengthy affair with a well-known woman columnist in New York; FDR told his advisers to drop it. Eight years later, running far behind Thomas E. Dewey, and desperately in need of campaign funds, President Harry Truman got a call from a wealthy businessman offering a substantial infusion of money in return for Truman's carrying out certain policies; Truman told him to go take a hike.

It is common today to lament the quality of our presidential leadership—where are the Jeffersons, the Lincolns, the FDRs?—but we forget that FDR probably could not be elected today: the press would have mercilessly photographed him in his wheelchair, looking helpless. Fortunately for America, the leading media at the time was radio, and nobody had a voice like FDR's. Jefferson's alleged relations with one or more of his "employees" (slaves) would have doomed his candidacy today, and Lincoln would never have been elected in today's rigid two-party format. Even John Kennedy, burdened with Addison's disease and other massive health problems requiring daily doses of cortisone, could not be elected today.*

---

* He was such a physical basket case that his entire medical history, stating what a miracle it was he was still alive, appeared in the *Journal of the American Medical Association* in 1957, without his name. It just called him "the thirty-seven-year-old man."

Whenever we confuse presidential "popularity" with "greatness," we should remember that the only twentieth-century president as popular as Ronald Reagan was not TR, Wilson, FDR, or JFK—but Calvin Coolidge. Over the past two hundred years, says the historian John Lukacs, the presidential election has declined from a character contest to a popularity contest to a publicity contest. Whoever hires the best campaign manager and the best "spin doctor" to craft his press releases and policy positions is obviously someone—as Andrew Jackson would say—of presidential timber. Just look at our TV-led presidential debates: candidates have to limit their answers to journalists' questions to less than three minutes. Such debates, complained candidate Senator Paul Simon in 1988, are "as different from the Lincoln-Douglas debates as a Beethoven symphony is from a radio jingle."

Anyone seeking the presidency, as in any top job in business or government, would be advised to have clear-cut career goals and objectives. At the tender age of five, he was ushered into the Oval Office by his parents to meet the president of the United States, Grover Cleveland. This enormous man towered over the little boy and told him: "My little man, I am making a strange wish for you. It is that you will never be a president of the United States."

The little boy, mesmerized no doubt—who would not be?—eventually had other ideas. From the time he was in law school, he laid out his career path to the White House. First he would be elected state senator, then he would become assistant secretary of the navy, then governor of New York, then president. His model was Theodore Roosevelt. Despite a bout with polio that put him out of action for several years, Franklin D. Roosevelt followed his cousin's career path perfectly.

Certainly nobody put more effort into winning the presidency than the master kingmaker, Joe Kennedy. The year: 1955. Joe Kennedy wanted his son to become president in 1960, but how to position John for the limelight? Very simple: have John run as vice president behind Lyndon Johnson, who would almost surely lose to Eisenhower; this would finish off LBJ and clear the coast for Kennedy in 1960. To get Johnson to run, Joe had one of his political aides go to Texas and offer to bankroll the full $10–12 million needed to launch a presidential campaign. But Johnson was not fooled. He knew a trap when he saw one, and declined, putting his hopes on beating Kennedy in 1960.

Turn the clock back to 1824, to a very clever, conniving plan to win the presidency. The candidate, John C. Calhoun, desperately wanted to be president of the United States. But he had a slight problem: there were four other men in the race, all better known than he: John Quincy Adams, Andrew Jackson, Henry Clay, and William Crawford. What to do?

A brilliant thinker, he devised a plan daring in its audacity. And, scary to say, it almost worked.

Betting that the four leading candidates

would be so evenly split that neither the Electoral College nor the House of Representatives would be able to reach a decision, Calhoun figured the congressmen would have no choice, as inauguration day loomed, but to turn to the vice president–elect and name him president. So Calhoun dropped out of the presidential race and offered his support to Adams in return for the vice presidency; Adams accepted. Calhoun then went to Jackson and made the same deal; Jackson, too, accepted. Calhoun was now halfway home; all he had to do was pray for an impasse.

As Calhoun predicted, neither Adams nor Jackson won enough votes to clinch victory. But when Henry Clay threw his support behind Adams, Adams secured just enough votes to win the presidency and deprive his vice president–elect of the presidency by default.

An aberration? Hardly. Move up the clock to our nation's most pivotal election, 1860, when a man who wasn't even running—Joseph Lane (ever heard of him?)—almost became president of the United States. The game plan was as follows: with the Republican candidate, Lincoln, sure to win the free states and most likely the Electoral College, the southern states and the Democrats all banded together to make a last-ditch effort to win the biggest state, New York. Had they done so, the election would have been thrown into the House of Representatives, where the winner would have been a wild toss-up: Lincoln, Breckenridge, or—most likely—a tie, in which case there would be no winner and the election would have to proceed to the Senate to elect the winning vice president, who, because there was no president, would automatically become president. Because the Democrats controlled the Senate, the new president would not have been the Republican candidate for president, Abraham Lincoln, but the Democratic candidate for vice president, Senator Joseph Lane of Oregon.

So much, thank God, for diabolical plans to win the presidency. But as we shall now see, further surprises were in store.

The Electoral College: More Democratic than You Think

➤ **1789–2004** Every four years political columnists toss up the ultimate horror: the possibility of a popularly elected president not winning because of the "archaic" Electoral College.

Actually, this has only happened twice: in 1888, when Grover Cleveland won a majority of the popular votes but lost the electoral vote to Benjamin Harrison, and in 2000, when Gore lost to Bush. (The other two controversial elections were 1824 and 1876, when the popular-vote winner also had the majority of electoral votes and still did not get to the White House: the problem lay not with the Electoral College, but elsewhere—namely, with conniving politicians.)

In every other election the Electoral

College winner and the popular-vote winner have been the same, and have gotten into the White House. Even for Grover Cleveland, who might have felt he got a raw deal, the system worked. He simply waited four years and ran again in 1892, beating Harrison in the second go-round. (As for Al Gore, the same might have happened for him given Bush's declining popularity ratings in 2004, but he chose to withdraw from politics, thereby revealing the one trait that caused him to lose in the first try: being too cautious and risk-averse, as when he eschewed Bill Clinton's help in his campaign.)

What, then, does the Electoral College accomplish? According to the historian Kenneth Davis, the Electoral College "makes it almost impossible for a third-party candidate to mount a serious challenge to the major party candidates."*

If so, then the Founding Fathers would have been very pleased. The issue for them was not political parties—there were no parties then—but rather that the presidency be occupied by a man representing the will of the people. Other than George Washington as a candidate, there was little else to go on. Said Benjamin Franklin to his fellow Constitutional Convention delegates, "The first man at the helm will be a good one. Nobody knows what sort may come afterwards."

Indeed, the Founding Fathers were terrified about two possibilities: that an obscure politician would come out of nowhere and win the presidency, or that the office would be occupied by someone who was not popularly elected.

History has proven their worst fears true on several occasions—none of them having to do with the Electoral College:

• In 1852 and in 1976, an obscure politician won the presidency by taking advantage of weak requirements for winning the party nomination: Franklin Pierce and Jimmy Carter (in both cases, the parties subsequently changed the rules to prevent a recurrence).

• In 1974, there being no vice president, and the president having to resign in disgrace, Gerald Ford was "appointed" president by his disgraced predecessor (and to turn the Constitution even more upside-down, the new vice president also was unelected— appointed by the appointed).

Before we pass judgment on the much-maligned Electoral College—"it is impossible to explain to foreigners; even Americans don't understand it," says Arthur M. Schlesinger Jr.—we should remember its historical purpose and what

---

* In 1856, Millard Fillmore had 22 percent of the popular vote, but got only 2 percent of the electoral vote. In 1912, William Howard Taft (not a third-party candidate, but he came in third) got 23 percent of the popular vote and only 1.5 percent of the electoral vote. In 1992, Ross Perot got 19 percent of the popular vote but none of the electoral vote.

has been accomplished. The Founding Fathers did not think one man could win a majority against several candidates, and therefore the election would have to be determined by a vote in the House of Representatives (again, the idea was to choose a clear, popularly elected winner). When the rules were changed in 1800, separating the voting for the president from that for the vice president, the House of Representatives assumed particular prominence in the "crooked deal" of 1824, when it elected Adams over Jackson. But Jackson, like Cleveland sixty-four years later, got his revenge in the proper manner: he ran again in another four years and won.

In sum, the presidency has been taken by three people who lacked the popular following the Founding Fathers desired. In addition, the office has been denied to three other people who should have been given it because of their popular vote. However, two of them did eventually get it (and so, too, might have the third one, but he got sick and died: Tilden).

Many people will be surprised, but a careful reading of history shows the following statement to be true: *In no case has the Electoral College mechanism failed to prevent a determined man from reaching the White House.* If a candidate feels he got a raw deal, he should try again, like Grover Cleveland.

In the meantime we can thank the Electoral College for what it has really accomplished in balancing the lesser power of the small states against the clout of the large states. This conflict between the will of the majority versus the rights of the minority is the most difficult challenge facing any government (witness post-Saddam Iraq). The genius of our Founding Fathers in creating the longest-lasting continuous government in the past three thousand years was their ability to address this conflict. Along with the tripartite form of government and bicameral legislature, stands the Electoral College. Cumbersome, yes, but it works.

Critics of our Electoral College focus on the wrong danger. They should look at the possibility that the best candidate might not get the nomination in the first place, thereby depriving the electorate a chance to choose between the two most qualified individuals. "Tweedledum and Tweedledee" may be bad enough (or good enough), but what about other candidates in the wings?

It is fun to weigh the qualifications of the two nominees and wonder if the American people (and the Electoral College) made the right choice. Irving Wallace wrote a magnificent book on this subject in the 1960s, titled *They Also Ran*, exploring many presidential races and suggesting that in quite a few cases it was the lesser candidate who won. Significantly, almost all these unfortunate cases occurred in the nineteenth century, when no doubt we had a string of mediocrities before and after the Civil War. But that was well over a hundred years ago, when nominations were in the hands of political bosses and therefore not applicable today. In the twentieth century, out of a choice of two, it can be argued that the better man has won in almost all cases.

There was one election, however, in which the clear best candidate never got a chance to run. Despite his impressive résumé of relevant work experience, his high visibility among the voters, and his obvious vote-getting power (he had won every political office he'd run for, including the presidency), he was rejected by the bosses of the Republican Party and denied the nomination. Had the nomination been his, he would have won the presidency again.

He was Theodore Roosevelt in 1911. Unable to dislodge William Howard Taft, he ran as a third-party candidate and came in second, ahead of Taft, with 27 percent of the vote. Had he been renominated by his party, he would have beaten Wilson.

Second-Choice Candidate

➤**1792** Our first president was very fortunate to get the nod as the lead standard-bearer. He didn't get it because of his widespread popularity; to the contrary, he barely squeaked through, making it only because he came from a pivotal state.

After the skirmishes of Lexington and Concord in April 1775, the colonists found themselves in total disarray in their rebellion against Britain. The Army of Massachusetts succeeded in surrounding the British army in Boston, but lacked enough troops to capture the city. General Artemis Ward called for reinforcements from the seacoast towns of the four New England provinces; all said no, they were saving their local militia to defend themselves against possible invasion by the fearsome British navy.

The Southern colonies were no more anxious to send troops. Yet if a war was to be fought, said Benjamin Franklin, it had to be fought by all thirteen colonies acting together.

The immediate task facing the Continental Congress in Philadelphia was to choose a commander-in-chief. The leading candidates were John Hancock, Charles Lee, Horatio Gates, and Artemis Ward. Hancock was the leading politician of the day, and Lee, Gates, and Ward were outstanding generals. Also in the running, but merely as a dark horse, was a colonel from Virginia named George Washington. A member of the Continental Congress, Washington started showing up for sessions resplendently dressed in his military uniform, sending indirect messages to his fellow delegates: "Choose me! Choose me!"

Not everyone bought his act. Observed one of the other delegates from Washington's state of Virginia: "Although a decent man, he had lost every battle he had been in."

The kingmaker of the congress was John Adams, the spokesman for New England and the one most desperate for help. He chose Washington for one reason and one reason only: Washington came from a colony vital to the New England revolutionary cause.

❧

Move the history reel forward, to late 1859 and early 1860, and a similar story unfolds. An ambitious former congressman aspired to higher office: the Senate seat of Stephen Douglas in 1864. Abraham Lincoln had few illusions about seeking the presidency—he was no national figure. Anyway, the presidency was an administrative job; Lincoln wanted to join the Senate, where the great orators of the day plied their craft: men like Daniel Webster, John C. Calhoun, and especially Lincoln's hero, Henry Clay. As an orator, Lincoln could push favorite moral causes such as popular government, free labor, and containment of slavery. As an executive, he could not.

When the Republicans met for their national party convention and Lincoln's name was thrown into the ring as a potential "dark horse," Lincoln continued to insist that he preferred the Senate to the White House. "I declare to you this morning, General, that for personal considerations I would rather have a full term in the Senate—a place in which I would feel more consciously able to discharge the duties required, and where there is more

chance to make a reputation, and less danger of losing it—than four years of the presidency."

The Republican delegates, however, had other concerns—namely the pivotal "border states." In an election that looked increasingly confusing and rancorous, the Republicans needed the support of Kentucky and Illinois. After concluding that the front-runner, William H. Seward, could not win the election, the delegates on the third ballot turned to Lincoln.

Running for First Lady

➤**1838** There is not a single president who, as a young boy, publicly announced that he would grow up to become president of the United States. Every one of our presidents had modest aspirations in their childhoods.

Not so one woman. A young girl of no particular stature, she told many of her friends that she hoped to marry a man who would become president. They all giggled.

When she reached maturity, she had a few boyfriends, but no one special. Her biological clock was running out: lest she become an old maid, she needed to marry quickly. Any man would do. Her prospects were slim: there was Edward Speed, but he was interested in Matilda Edwards. There was Edwin Webb, but he had two little children who were more than she could handle. There was a rising-star politician with whom she "flirted outrageously"—a man who eventually became the Democratic candidate for president. But he was too busy with his career to be bothered. Time was running out.

There was a fourth man, very shy and awkward. Her family objected, but she gave it her best shot and so dominated her evenings with the young man that he could hardly get in a word edgewise. He finally proposed, then broke it off. She was devastated.

Spinsterhood loomed.

"Be patient," her friends told her, "he'll be back." Months later, the ungainly young man—a recluse with no other girlfriends—re-proposed and she finally landed her catch. Twenty years later Mary Todd Lincoln entered the White House as First Lady.*

❧

A quarter-century later, Rutherford Hayes became president of the United States. Dining at the White House one evening was a sixteen-year-old girl, the daughter of his former law partner in Ohio. The girl told the president she liked the White House so much she must marry someone destined to become president. One imagines Mr. President had a good chuckle.

But the last laugh belonged to the young girl. No great beauty, and very demanding and intense, she found it difficult to socialize with men. Her chances of catching a young man headed for great things were slim. If she could not catch a president, she would have to help make one. So, when a local judge came courting, she examined him carefully. He came from a prominent Cincinnati family and had gone to Yale, but he was enormously fat. Did this mean he lacked the burning fire of ambition? In their two-year courtship, he agreed he needed to be goaded and pushed, and she saw a talent that exceeded her own. When they married in 1886, he joked to her that the prime requirement for being a good husband was obedience.

Three years later, at the age of thirty-two, William Howard Taft became the youngest-ever solicitor general of the United States, responsible for representing the federal government before the Supreme Court. Enjoying his life in Washington DC, the jovial Taft, aided by his ambitious wife, made many friends and political allies, including the young assistant secretary of the Navy, Theodore Roosevelt. When the opposing political party won the presidency, and Taft (and Roosevelt) had to leave Washington, Nellie Taft was beside herself: "My darling," she said, "it will put an end to all the opportunities you now have of being thrown with the bigwigs."

The next eight years found Nellie and

---

* The Democratic politician who rejected her was Stephen Douglas, Lincoln's opponent in the 1860 election.

her husband back home in the political wilderness of Cincinnati, where her husband contentedly served as a circuit-court judge. But when his fellow Ohioan William McKinley became president and his good friend TR became vice president, Taft returned to Washington to meet the president, who offered him a position as civil administrator of the newly acquired Philippines. "Take this job," the president advised him, "and you shall not suffer."

The Philippines was probably the last place Taft wanted to go, but Nellie recognized the value of being in a high-profile position. Certainly a lot better than being a judge! She immediately departed for the Far East to spend several months learning about Asian culture, then joined her husband in Manila to help him in his lonely post. Taft became so esteemed by the local people that when he departed three years later, he was sent off by cheering crowds in the streets of Manila, expressing their gratitude. He was the most successful administrator of an occupied country America ever had.

Nellie Taft could not make her husband want to be president, but Theodore Roosevelt could. He made Taft his assistant, then pushed him to be his successor. When he asked Taft what position he wanted, expecting him to say "the presidency," and Taft responded "Chief Justice," Nellie informed the two men that her husband had misspoken, he should be president. When Taft finally did become president, his progressive-minded wife went into high gear, insisting she be the first wife ever to participate in the inauguration ceremony and ride to the White House with the new president. Nellie Herron Taft had finally arrived home.

First Steps First

➤**1844**   Many people aspire to be president, but usually the hardest part is breaking into politics in the first place. There is little glory in local politics, but without a beginning there can be no end.

Among the finest groups of candidates ever to compete for a congressional seat were the three candidates from the Seventh Congressional District of Illinois in 1844. Two of them later became war heroes, one of them—touted in his early days as a future president—dying for his country, and the survivor moving on to senator. The third eventually did become president.

Problem was, here they were—friends and members of the same party—in their early thirties, ambitious to get into national politics—and there was only one opening. What to do? Edward Baker, John Hardin, and Abraham Lincoln had a meeting. History does not record what was said, but the aftermath would suggest that it was every man for himself.

In a rough campaign marked by personal attacks and alleged vote-stealing, Baker won the county nomination over Lincoln. But Lincoln bore him no ill will:

he spoke well of his opponent's integrity, and three years later named his newborn son Edward. In the subsequent go-round at the district level, Baker and Hardin ended in a tie, putting the last-place finisher in a position where he "possibly could have beaten both candidates." But Lincoln refused to try to cut a deal for himself, saying, "I should despise myself were I to attempt it." Moving on as a Baker delegate to the party convention where Hardin finally won, Lincoln proposed a resolution, which passed, recommending that his party support Baker in the *next* congressional election. In this bizarre move, Lincoln foreclosed any opportunity to become congressman after Hardin's term expired. Hardin would be the congressman now, to be followed by Baker. Lincoln's political career looked bleak.

Actually it was a very shrewd move, thinking of the long term. By conducting himself honorably, Lincoln was gambling that by getting the party to limit the front-runner Hardin to one term so that the runner-up, Baker, could also have his moment in the sun, Baker in turn would be morally restricted to only one term, thereby opening the door for Lincoln the third time around.

Which is exactly what happened, but with one complication. After Hardin served his term in Congress and Baker served his term, Baker kept his word but Hardin did not. Lincoln's gamble had failed: he was in for a rough fight with

a well-known ex-congressman. Hardin mounted a vigorous campaign of dirty tricks, even trying to get the nomination rules changed that would assure his re-election. But the party leaders, impressed that Lincoln never said anything negative about Hardin ("talented, energetic, usually generous and magnanimous," Lincoln would say), would have none of it. They persuaded Hardin that he should withdraw—it was now Lincoln's turn. Abraham Lincoln had finally won his dream: he was now a national politician.

After serving as congressman for one term, it was another twelve years before Lincoln won a second public office, but when he did, it was the big one.

How Lincoln won the presidential nomination is a virtual recapitulation of his winning the congressional nomination. In 1855, in his eager bid to become senator, he saw his dream diminish as several backers, led by Norman Judd, switched to Lyman Trumbull. Despite cries of "Treason!" from his wife and his campaign manager, Lincoln maintained cordial relations with Judd and eventually backed out of the contest, recognizing that Lyman Trumbull probably had a better chance of winning. But it was a bitter blow. In 1856, Lincoln was again proposed as the Republican Party nominee for a high state office, this time for governor, and once again in the spirit of party unity he backed off, proposing the name of William Bissell.

Both Trumbull and Bissell won. When

the Illinois delegation to the 1860 Republican convention put forth their choice for presidential nominee, they put forth not the state party's two senior officeholders, but the man who had played an instrumental role in putting them there. The politician who presented Lincoln's name was none other than the former ally whose defection in 1855 had cost Lincoln the senate contest: Norman Judd.

Said Lincoln several years later, his losing against Trumbull was "the best thing that could have happened."

Luck

➤ **1860** He was the luckiest man to run for president: He won with only 39.8 percent of the popular votes cast—the smallest percentage ever recorded. He had no help from his running mate: he only met his vice president Hannibal Hamlin on Election Day. How did Abraham Lincoln manage to win?

The remaining 60.2 percent was split among three other candidates: Stephen A. Douglas (29 percent), John C. Breckenridge (18 percent), and John Bell (13 percent). Had it not been for the presence of *two* "third-party" candidates—Breckenridge and Bell—Lincoln might not have been elected. (In that year there were four candidates because each of the two parties had nominated an upstart Southern candidate as well as an official Northern one.) Says the historian Jay Winik:

Lincoln's victory "was in many ways a fluke and nothing more."

Naturally, lacking a strong "popular mandate," Lincoln had a difficult time leading the country. In 1864, with the Civil War going badly, Lincoln made preparations to go home, fully expecting General George McClellan to be his successor. "You think I don't know I am going to be beaten," he told a friend, "*but I do* and unless some great change takes place *badly beaten.*" It was only when Lincoln finally found two generals who could win battles—Ulysses Grant and William Sherman—that his popularity began to rise, and the ideas he fought so hard for began to receive a fair hearing.

Still, Lincoln's popularity was never great. Lucky to be elected president, he was even luckier to be reelected. Observes the historian James McPherson, "If the election had been held in August 1864 instead of November, Lincoln would have lost." Not only that, but he would have lost in the *friendly* half of the country. The Southern states had seceded, meaning they couldn't vote. According to Lincoln biographer David Herbert Donald: "Fifty-four percent with your enemies not voting is not such an overwhelming vote."

❧

If Abraham Lincoln was the luckiest man to run for president, who was the unluckiest? This man was probably the most impressive man to run for president and not make it. What's more, he lost by only the narrowest of margins at the last minute, after everyone thought he had won. In fact, he had gone to bed thinking he had been elected president.

When late returns came in with an unexpected loss in California in the 1916 election, a reporter called to ask Charles Evans Hughes to comment on his surprising defeat. "The president has retired," said Hughes's valet.

"When he wakes up," the reporter snapped, "tell him he's no longer president." Hughes, whose résumé included a college Phi Beta Kappa, highest honors from law school, the governorship of New York, and the post of justice of the Supreme Court, eventually went on to an even more illustrious career as a self-made millionaire, secretary of state (ranked among the three greatest), and chief justice of the Supreme Court (ranked as the greatest since John Marshall). Oh, if only he had been elected president!

If Wilson were to run against Hughes today, the winner definitely would be Hughes. Imagine a full medical history of Woodrow Wilson falling into a rival campaign manager's hands (like the Thomas Eagleton blow-up in 1972). It would have read as follows: Woodrow Wilson has been "in frail health all his life, easily tired, not able to work more than five hours a day, and unable to cope with stress. In student days the strain of study was too much for him; severe indigestion forced him to drop out of college and out of law school, and headaches and nerves caused

breakdowns in graduate school." The report would go on to reveal that beginning in 1906 Wilson had lost the use of his right arm for a while owing to a neuralgia attack, followed by a stroke that destroyed central vision in his right eye, followed in turn by a series of small strokes, plus continuing hypertension and arteriosclerosis. This explosive information, of course, was covered up—just as occurred later, when he suffered a massive stroke as president.

Anybody who thinks luck doesn't play a pivotal role in presidential elections should look again. In the 1960 election, the front-runner was Vice President Richard Nixon, confronted by a young senator of no great distinction. Trailing Nixon, John Kennedy (long before he was "JFK") took a gamble in agreeing to the first-ever presidential debate against an experienced opponent who had been a champion debater in college. Kennedy arrived at the debate suntanned and immaculately dressed, but so nervous his arms were dripping with sweat.

As bad luck would have it, Nixon had just gotten out of the hospital. He was pale, he had lost so much weight his collar was a full size too big, and he refused to have any makeup applied to spruce up his appearance. Worse things were to come. He arrived first and was sitting under a microphone in the control room when Kennedy arrived. Jumping up to greet Kennedy, Nixon banged his head into the microphone, totally disoriented. After the debate, Nixon rushed out so fast he forgot to pick up his coat and briefcase.

Present at the debate was Chicago mayor Richard Daley. Recalled CBS president Frank Stanton, the man who organized the debate, "Daley asked me if I wanted a ride downtown. As we walked down the hall he said, 'You know, I'm going to change my mind and tell my men to go all out for Kennedy.' He meant that he hadn't been supporting Kennedy with any enthusiasm until that debate. And his support made an enormous difference, because Illinois determined the election."

Doing What It Takes to Get Reelected

➤**1864** No one would associate Abraham Lincoln with the ruthless tactics of campaign managers like Mark Hanna or Karl Rove, but to put him far above the fray would be a mistake. Lincoln, too, could play hardball when he had to.

In the middle of an unexpectedly long war that had—in Walt Whitman's memorable words—turned the nation into "one vast central hospital," the president needed all the help he could get in his faltering reelection bid. His primary support came from soldiers and those who continued to believe in the war.

Of the twenty-five states of the Union, only fourteen permitted soldiers to vote in the state they happened to be in while fighting. Soldiers from the remaining eleven states would be out of luck because they were not home. One of the critical states was Indiana. The state's Republican governor went to Secretary of War Edwin Stanton and told him that without the support of Indiana's fifteen thousand soldiers, Lincoln would lose. How about giving the soldiers "sick leave" so they could come home to vote?

A letter immediately went out, signed by the president, to General William Tecumseh Sherman: "Indiana is the only important State victory in October, whose soldiers cannot vote in the field. Anything you can do to let her soldiers, or any part of them, go home to vote at the State election will be greatly in point." Never in the history of warfare had soldiers been permitted to go home to vote, thought Sherman when he read the letter, but then, this was different. "Our armies vanish before our eyes and it is useless to complain," he wrote his wife, "because the election is more important than the war." (He also knew if Lincoln lost, he would be out of a job.)

Acting on Lincoln's instructions, General George Thomas issued an order one week before the election granting furloughs to all enlisted men "who are in hospitals or otherwise unfit for field duty: Pennsylvania, Indiana, Illinois, Michigan, Wisconsin, Ohio, Connecticut and Massachusetts . . . transportation to be ordered to and from their homes."

The Democrats were furious when they heard what Lincoln had done, but there was nothing they could do, lest it impugn the patriotism of their fighting men. They became even more frustrated when they saw what happened on Election Day. From every direction, thousands of soldiers got off the train to vote and sweep Lincoln to victory. Exactly who these thousands of troops were, nobody could be sure. It was, in the words of one historian, "the day that Michigan, Illinois, Pennsylvania, and Ohio voted in Indiana."

Mailing a Letter to Himself

➤**1881** What president mailed a letter to himself? This is not a trivia question, it is actually a very serious one. Think again: What president mailed a letter to himself, and why did he do it?

Chester Alan Arthur never intended to run for president of the United States. He reluctantly accepted the role as running 'mate with James A. Garfield because as vice president he wouldn't have to do much work, at least no more than he did as chief of the New York City Customs Office. Ever the dilettante, Chester Arthur was known for his good cheer and dapper clothes. But to everyone's surprise, when circumstances changed, Chester Arthur rose to the occasion and became a serious man.

As Garfield lay on his deathbed for several months after being shot, Arthur had time to reflect on his potential responsibilities. "I pray to God that the President

will recover," he said. "God knows I do not want the place I was never elected to."

When Garfield finally died, the vice president, at home in New York City, decided he should take the oath of office immediately, rather than wait until he got to Washington. His friends went out into the street looking for a judge, and at 2:15 in the morning Chester Arthur was sworn in as president. Unable to sleep that night, the new president got up and wrote a proclamation summoning the Senate to a special session to choose a president pro tempore. Because there was no vice president, and Arthur was concerned what might happen if he was assassinated before he got to Washington, he wrote this important letter to ensure an orderly line of succession. Fearful that the letter might fall into the wrong hands if he sent it to Congress, Arthur decided the safest course was to send it to himself at the White House. That way, should he be killed, the letter surely would be read.

The Questionable Virtue of Youth

➤**1896** Of all the presidential candidates, one man fit the description "Boy Wonder of American Politics"—William Jennings Bryan, the thirty-six-year-old Democratic Party candidate in 1896, who uttered the powerful words, "You shall not press down the brow of labor this crown of thorns; you shall not crucify mankind upon a cross of gold!" Bryan lost to William McKinley by 600,000 votes out of 13.6 million cast. Bryan ran again in 1900 and 1908, with declining results, and was "washed up" at the age of forty-eight.

After Bryan, the second-youngest candidate was the Republican Thomas E. Dewey, in 1944. He was forty-two. Four years later, at the age of forty-six, he blew a sure-win race against Truman by acting complacent and not campaigning vigorously. A more mature and seasoned Dewey would have won.

Harry Truman, Dewey's opponent, had every reason to be skeptical of bright, flaming youth. In 1960 he accused the forty-three-year-old John F. Kennedy of not being mature or experienced enough to be president. Kennedy's response: "To exclude from positions of trust and command all those below the age of forty-four would have kept Jefferson from writing the Declaration of Independence, Washington from commanding the Continental Army, Madison from fathering the Constitution, Hamilton from serving as secretary of the treasury, Clay from being elected Speaker of the House, and Christopher Columbus from discovering America."*

A clever response, but writing the Declaration of Independence or discovering America isn't the same as being president of the United States. Looking back on our past, we see another bright flaming youth who rose like a rocket, then crashed because of youthful poor judgment. A college graduate at seventeen, a lawyer at twenty, a congressman at thirty-one, and vice president of the United States at thirty-six—the youngest man ever to hold that office—John C. Breckenridge ran for president at forty, lost the party nomination to Stephen Douglas, and ran as an independent, finishing third. That was as far as he got. At the pivotal decision point in his life, he switched sides and joined the Confederate Army, rising to the position of Confederate secretary of war; at the end of hostilities, forced to flee for his life as a traitor to the Union, he made his way to Cuba and spent the next three years in exile. Pardoned by President Andrew Johnson in 1868, Breckenridge returned home and died six years later, at the age of fifty-four, still under the cloud of treason.

Harvard professor Harvey Mansfield offers this shrewd insight on age and political wisdom:

> *If you're not a famous mathematician by the time you're twenty-five, I suppose you won't be one. But philosophy, especially political philosophy, depends on or uses experience. You have to learn what*

* Observed speechwriter Ted Sorenson, who had helped JFK craft his response: "Kennedy wisely struck out the other name I had on the list—Jesus of Nazareth."

human beings are like. That's one point. And then another point is that with something like mathematics or different branches of science, you're on a frontier. Everything that's being done now is the best that's ever been done. But with political philosophy, that's by no means the case. What's being done now is not as good as what used to be done in the great books or in the classics. It takes a long time to develop a mature understanding of these books, reading them over and over, and teaching them helps as well. So you'll get better. And you would be at your best, I would say, in your fifties or sixties, even.

Campaign Cover-Up

➤**1904** When the Barbary pirate Sherif Mulai Ahmed ibn-Muhammed er Raisuli had the temerity to kidnap a wealthy American living in Tangier, Ion Perdicaris, President Theodore Roosevelt was delighted. With a troublesome presidential election coming up, he needed a headline-grabbing cause around which to rally the nation. An American held for ransom by a ruthless pirate—how perfect! "The President is in his best mood," said the French ambassador. "He is always in his best mood."

Putting America's honor and prestige on the line, TR dispatched seven warships to the scene, got the French to prop up the reigning sultan, and, after weeks of pointless negotiating, sent the electrifying demand, "Perdicaris alive or Raisuli dead!" The Republican Party delegates, after hearing the telegram read aloud, stomped their feet and renominated Roosevelt by acclamation. In the meantime, back in Morocco, Raisuli finally released Perdicaris and American prestige was saved.

What was not known, and was kept secret until 1933, was that Perdicaris was not an American! Apparently, during the Civil War he had become a Greek citizen to avoid being drafted by the Confederacy, and had never bothered to reclaim his American citizenship. For the president, who only found out about it during the middle of the crisis, it was most embarrassing. "It is bad business," murmured the secretary of state; "we must keep it excessively confidential for the time present." No word of this secret leaked out, and Roosevelt went on to win the 1904 general election by the largest popular majority ever given to a presidential candidate.

From Secretary of State to the Presidency

➤**1912** In this election, the incumbent president had so much respect for his challenger that he was prepared to leave office immediately if he lost, and not wait around for the four-month interregnum between administrations.

He therefore concocted the following plan: he would order his vice president and his secretary of state to resign immediately, then replace the secretary of state with the newly elected president, and then resign himself. There being no president or vice president, the secretary of state would automatically become president. An ingenious idea, but it never happened. Because President Woodrow Wilson won a surprise victory at the last moment (by a scant 3,775 votes in a pivotal state), the issue of whether Charles Evans Hughes would have accepted this unusual offer never came up.*

Farfetched? Hardly. It almost happened again—in 1946. Harry Truman had been thrust suddenly into the presidency. In the midterm congressional elections of November 1946, all six Democrats seeking reelection were routed. "The New Deal is kaput," said the *New York Daily News*. "It is finished. It is over. Historians to come will lift it out to study as a species, as they study the Thirty Years' War or the Black Plague and other disasters." The *New York Herald Tribune* did a conversion of congressional votes to state electoral votes and computed that if the midterm elections had been a presidential election, the Democrats would have been clobbered 357–174 (as opposed to their 432–99 landslide win in the 1944 FDR-Dewey election).

Leading Democrats hung their heads in shame. Why postpone the inevitable? Marshall Field, the Chicago newspaper magnate, and Arkansas senator J. W. Fulbright were Truman supporters. They both advised Truman to appoint a Republican as secretary of state, then resign. There being no vice president at the time, the Republican secretary of state would become president. Senator Fulbright even suggested a specific individual: Senator Arthur Vandenberg, chairman of the Senate Foreign Relations Committee.

Truman, of course, went ballistic, and once again this novel theory of presidential succession never occurred.

Could it happen again? Yes, in slightly different form, using the vice presidency instead of the secretary-of-state position. The Succession Act of 1947 changed the third in line of succession from the secretary of state to the Speaker of the House. But the 1967 Twenty-fifth Amendment specified that there must be a vice president at all times, and gave the president the power to nominate the occupant of the position, subject to confirmation by both houses. (This is what happened in 1974.) If Wilson were president today, he could have his vice president resign, and then appoint Hughes to the vice presidency. Same for Truman: he could follow Senator Fulbright's advice and appoint Vandenberg to the vice presidency, then resign.

---

* Hughes eventually did become secretary of state, five years later, but it was in a standard hierarchy, with a president and vice president firmly above him.

It Helps to Stay Alive

➤**1919** It seems like a non sequitur to say that a key qualification of a presidential candidate is that he stay alive—except that it has happened three times in our history that we have been denied a likely president because of premature death.

The first, as mentioned in chapter 2, was William Lowndes. A second instance was Bobby Kennedy, assassinated in 1968 while on the verge of winning the Democratic nomination. Both candidates had as good a chance as anyone to make it all the way.

There is a third candidate: he definitely would have made it. His sudden death shocked and traumatized millions of Americans: they knew what they had lost. In March 1919, they woke up and were stunned to hear that their senior statesman who everyone expected to win the presidency again in 1920—eight years after losing a three-way race to Wilson—had died of a pulmonary embolism in his sleep: Theodore Roosevelt. He was only sixty years old.

Secret Deal for the Presidency

➤**1951** The two top Republican contenders for a sure-win victory against a lame-duck Democratic administration had a secret meeting. The leading Republican was the powerful senator from Ohio, Robert Taft. Eisenhower, the victorious general from World War II, was the popular candidate. But Taft was the one who had the upper hand: Eisenhower came to him, not he to Eisenhower.

In their private negotiation in the spring of 1951, Eisenhower offered to stay out of the campaign and let Taft be the nominee, if Taft would support the principle of collective security in Europe. All Taft had to do was compromise.

Son of the only man to hold the top two positions in the U.S. government—President and Chief Justice William Howard Taft—Taft was a man one would think had good political instincts. He did not: he refused the offer.

Eisenhower entered the race, painted Taft as an isolationist who didn't know what he was doing, and won the nomination and then the election against Adlai Stevenson.

Rarely has a front-runner blown it, fair and square. William F. Buckley once said he would rather be governed by the first two thousand names in the Boston phone book than by the Harvard faculty. The same can be said of Robert Taft,* first in his class at Yale and first in his class at Harvard Law School: too smart to be president.

---

* The same was to be said almost fifty years later, not so much about the president of the United States (a Rhodes Scholar), but about his wife, Hillary Clinton, when she and her husband pushed the ill-fated healthcare plan: "She was always sure she was right."

Sexual Time-Bomb

►**1960** John F. Kennedy's wild philandering—with as many as four hundred women, complete with many photographs showing him naked with a lovely broad—provided ready grist for the tabloid mill. Any one of these flibbertigibbets could have been a walking time-bomb had she opened her mouth during the close election contest with Richard Nixon. Kennedy won the election by only 118,000 votes out of 68.3 million ballots cast. According to a *Life* magazine poll in 1984, "A third of Americans say that if they had known of his [Kennedy's] affairs, they would not have voted for him."

Kennedy was lucky to have Nixon for an opponent. Warned by his aides that Nixon might use one of the photographs against him, John Kennedy responded, "He won't use it."

Kennedy was also lucky to have a compliant press. Said one former Associated Press reporter, "There used to be a gentlemen's agreement about reporting such things." Even Ben Bradlee, the Washington bureau chief of *Newsweek* and later the editor of the *Washington Post* who helped bring down Nixon during the Watergate scandal of 1974, was surprised when news of Kennedy's womanizing began to come out after JFK's death. The prevailing moral ethic of the 1960s was, "You don't talk about my private life and I don't talk about yours." Kennedy knew the score perfectly, and played it to the hilt: "They can't touch me while I'm alive," he once said, "and after I'm dead, who cares?"

Presidential Training Ground: The Vice Presidency?

►**1972** Anyone who thinks the vice presidency is a good training ground for the presidency should look at the only time in our nation's history when both office-seekers were former vice presidents: 1972 (Richard Nixon and Hubert Humphrey). "That fact alone," says one historian, "should have tipped off the nation that the executive branch was about to enter its darkest hour. By the time the next presidential election came around, neither Nixon nor Agnew would be in office, both having been forced to resign in disgrace."

The real benefit of the vice presidency, for ambitious men seeking the presidency, is practice running for national office—and not winning the prize (lest the poor fellow waste four years of his life, with nothing to do). This was the route taken by FDR in 1920 and JFK in 1956. The national exposure they gained, and the subsequent freedom to pursue their real objective after losing, served them well.*

---

* This assumes, of course, that they do a good job campaigning. As the VP candidate in Gerald Ford's 1976 campaign, Bob Dole's disastrous performance as a hatchet man in the vice-presidential debates—where he tried to cast the Republican Watergate scandal as no more a campaign issue than "the Vietnam War, or World War I, or World War II, or the Korean War—Democratic wars"—may have cost Ford the election.

Serving as vice president is not a good training ground for serving as president. Running for vice president, however, is a good training ground for running for president.

The Common Touch

➤**1980** Two of our leading presidents rose to power largely on the basis of their public speaking ability. They wrote most of their speeches themselves, practiced their delivery many times until they got their rhythm and cadence right, and always endeavored to close their speeches with a strong summing-up statement.

Even rarer, they both were masters of the homespun anecdote. At a moment's notice they could draw upon a wealth of pithy yarns to disarm their audience and make their point, be it one-on-one or in a formal debate or in a speech. They could relate to people easily.

In 1980, when Ronald Reagan was running for president, he was told that only three chief executives of America's largest five hundred companies had endorsed his candidacy. He voiced no concern: "I've got to be the candidate of the shopkeeper, the farmer, the independent, the entrepreneur—there are a lot more of them."

This common touch, developed after years in the public speaking arena, molded his campaign strategy when he sought the presidency. In so doing, he was following the example of Abraham Lin-

coln. "Don't shoot too high," said Lincoln; "aim lower and the common people will understand you. They are the ones you want to reach."

What Our Presidents Say About Presidential Greatness

➤**1789–2000** Every four years, Americans enter the polling booth, pull the lever for their candidate, and hope for a man with the qualities that made some of our earlier presidents great.

Brains is not one of them. If intellectual dexterity were the criterion for judging presidents, the winner would be James A. Garfield. This classical scholar not only developed an elegant proof of the Pythagorean theorem, he could write Latin with one hand and Greek with the other, simultaneously! Or Herbert Hoover, who also spoke several languages. (Whenever he and his wife wanted privacy in the White House, they conversed in Mandarin.) Or Calvin Coolidge, whose idea of relaxation was to read Dante's *Inferno*—in medieval Latin. Or George H. W. Bush, who breezed through Yale in two and a half years, Phi Beta Kappa. Our most intellectual president was not John F. Kennedy, who won a Pulitzer Prize for *Why England Slept*—his rich father's ghostwriters deserve most of the credit. For original authorship, we have to credit the president with a Harvard Phi Beta Kappa,

The two Georges

Theodore Roosevelt. He wrote forty books, including a multivolume history on the winning of the West that still stands today as a work of fine scholarship. Still, though he prided himself on his intellectual achievements, he was the first to put it in proper perspective. "I am only an average man, but by George, I work harder than the average man!" Or, as Oliver Wendell Holmes said of TR's distant cousin Franklin D. Roosevelt: "A second-rate mind with a first-rate temperament."

And what makes for a good temperament? A happy family life? If that were the model, the winner would be George H. W. Bush, who once said the achievement he was most proud of was that his children always came back home for the holidays. The same cannot be said of his predecessor Ronald Reagan, whose daughter wrote a book depicting her First Lady mother as being a witchlike "Mommie Dearest."

Many presidents, it seems, have come from rather unhappy if stable family backgrounds. When this man died at age twenty-eight, his name appeared on at least four marriage licenses, two divorce decrees, and three birth certificates—including one of a future president of the United States. Who was his son? An even better one: A hard-driving entrepreneur, with a thriving business in three states, he had six children, including a ne'er-do-well son who could never hold a job for long and was always borrowing money. He left his son out of his will. Seven years later his son became president of the United States.

The first son was Bill Clinton; the second, Ulysses Grant. Grant had a hard time not only with his father, but also with his father-in-law. When the Civil War started and "Sam" Grant needed to borrow money to buy his Union Army uniform, both his father and his father-in-law turned him down, they thought so little of him. Harry Truman also had a confidence problem: when he married his local sweetheart, his fiancée's mother warned her in no uncertain terms, "You don't want to marry that farmer boy, he is not going to make it anywhere." At least that wasn't as bad as what Warren Harding had to go through: when he got married, his father-in-law was so angry he disinherited the bride and tried to drive him into bankruptcy.

We don't know what Abraham Lincoln's father thought of his son, but we know what Abe thought of his father. Lincoln, probably the most compassionate man ever to occupy the White House, did not invite his father to his wedding, never visited the man, and declined to attend his father's funeral in 1851. George Washington wrote more than a thousand letters in his lifetime, but mentioned his father in only two of them.

People looking to marital bliss as a clue to presidential greatness are also likely to be disappointed. One of our leading presidents spent his pre-inaugural night alone, while his wife spent the night down the hall with her girlfriend, to whom she was to write some 2,300 letters during her lifetime. The president was Franklin D. Roosevelt in 1932. After his death in 1945, Eleanor admitted she and her husband hadn't slept together for twenty-nine years.

If obvious qualities like brains and family happiness are not harbingers of presidential success, what ideals should voters look for? Rather than answer this impossible question directly, let us look at examples of modesty, statesmanship, and perspective that suggest wisdom. Asked whether the responsibilities of the job worried him, FDR said, "If you had spent two years in bed trying to wiggle your big toe, after that anything else would seem easy!"

That Thomas Jefferson was a remarkable man goes without saying. Who else "could calculate an eclipse, survey an estate, tie an artery, plan an edifice, try a cause, break a horse, dance a minuet, and play the violin"? Who else could read the Bible in four languages? Said President John F. Kennedy to a group of Nobel Prize winners at a White House dinner, "I think this is the most extraordinary collection of talent that has ever gathered at the White House—with the possible exception of when Thomas Jefferson dined alone."

When Thomas Jefferson died, he requested that his three major life achievements be inscribed on his gravestone.

Being president of the United States was not one of them. His gravestone reads, "Here was buried Thomas Jefferson, Author of the Declaration of American Independence, of the Statute of Virginia for Religious Freedom, and father of the University of Virginia." No presidential library for this fellow; compared with today's presidents, who save every scrap of paper for posterity, Jefferson's modesty is alluring.

Equally modest about the presidency was John Quincy Adams. Two years after losing reelection in 1828, he returned to the House of Representatives, where he served his finest years of public service until his death in 1848. "No election or appointment conferred upon me," he said about his return to the Hill, "ever gave me so much pleasure." And just think, this came from a man who had been not only president, but, prior to that, a brilliant and much-acclaimed secretary of state (then the second-most-powerful position in America). Also extremely modest and down-to-earth was Harry Truman, who, when asked what was the first thing he would do upon arriving home after leaving the White House, responded, "Take the suitcases up to the attic."

Most studies of presidential leadership focus on the issue of "power." In a less bureaucratic era, several of our presidents were quite subtle and indirect, using a "feminine" form of control as opposed to a "masculine" one—as when Abraham Lincoln admitted, "I claim not to have controlled events, but confess that events have controlled me." Lyndon Johnson's sudden decision not to seek reelection in 1968 shocked the nation, but it should have come as no surprise to the student of history. Even our one president above reproach, George Washington, may have bailed out in time. "The President," wrote Thomas Jefferson, "is fortunate to get off just as the bubble is bursting, leaving others to hold the bag." Sure enough, when his own time came, Jefferson saw the handwriting on the wall and declined to run in 1796. Let John Adams take the heat, he figured; he would wait until 1800 and win at that time—which he did. Our most bellicose president, Mr. Bully Pulpit himself, Theodore Roosevelt, declined to run in 1908 for a second elected term: "It would be better to have some man like Taft or Root succeed me in the Presidency than to have me succeed myself . . . they would be free from the animosities and suspicions which I had encountered, and would be able to make a new start and would have a much greater chance of achieving useful work."

Politicians get elected to the presidency, but once elected they must become statesmen. Suggests one historian, "A politician thinks of the next election; a statesman thinks of the next generation." For another definition of this important distinction, consider the description of William

Lowndes, the leading candidate for the 1824 election (before his premature death): "There was a singleness in his character and a chastity in his intentions which politicians find cumbersome but which statesmen will venerate for all future time."

Or Abraham Lincoln. In the midst of the Civil War; a delegation of Methodist ministers called on the White House to assure the beleaguered president that the Union cause would prevail because God was on their side. But Lincoln was a wise man and knew what to say. "Gentlemen, it is not a question of whether God is on our side. It is a question of whether we are on his side."

The issue is not one of God or religion, but morality in general. Observed Harry Truman, "I wonder how far Moses would have gone if he'd taken a poll on Egypt? What would Jesus Christ have preached if he'd taken a poll in Israel? . . . It isn't polls or public opinion of the moment that counts. It is right and wrong."

Presidents need to communicate their vision to the public in a persuasive way. No one was better at this, of course, than "the great communicator," Ronald Reagan. But a Hollywood résumé, while helpful, isn't necessary. When the famous actor Orson Welles visited President Franklin Roosevelt in the White House, FDR told him, "There are two great actors in America, and it is a fine thing we have now met." When the British sent one of their emissaries to George Washington in the summer of 1776, the general put on his most elegant uniform, refused to receive the hand-delivered letter from London addressed to "George Washington, Esq., etc. etc.," and made it abundantly clear that he was the leader and would accept no letter addressed to "etc. etc." Present in the room watching the general's magisterial performance was John Adams, who called Washington "one of the great actors of the age." And it wasn't because Washington was a "natural." He worked at it. Washington's great passion and love in life was the theater.

To execute their vision, presidents need to manage carefully the selection and handling of subordinates. When Abraham Lincoln started his term in office, he picked "perhaps the strangest cabinet ever formed, yet one of the most able." None of the men had specific experience for his particular position, five of them were former adversaries of Lincoln, and they all disliked one another. Warned that "they will eat you up," Lincoln replied, "They will eat each other up." In one particular case, rarely had a relationship started off so poorly. As the favored candidate who lost the presidential nomination on the third ballot, he was not a happy man. He arranged for a major newspaper story saying that the nominee, being unfit for the presidency, would require someone to run the government for him, and that he would be pleased to fill this role. After being appointed secretary of state by his opponent, he persisted in his fantasy and wrote a memo titled, "Some Thoughts for a President's Consideration." In it he suggested that the recipient was not fit to be at the executive head of the government, and that the recipient should turn this task over to him. Who was this impudent politician?

William Seward. After seeing Seward's memo, Lincoln was appalled and wrote an angry note, but did not send it. Instead he met privately with Seward and informed him in no uncertain terms who was the boss. "Whatever policy we adopt," Lincoln told Seward, "I must do it." Seward calmed down and went on to become Lincoln's strongest ally over the next five years of his administration. "Executive force and vigor are rare qualities," Seward later wrote his wife. "The President is the best of us." Another of Lincoln's adversaries was Salmon P. Chase, governor of Ohio, who ran for president five times from 1856 to 1872. Chase suffered from a particularly American disease known as "presidential disease—a troublesome ailment and sometimes fatal to the peace of mind and moral equilibrium of the persons attacked by it." Appointed secretary of the treasury by Lincoln, he used his position to further his presidential ambitions: he had his face put on the millions of low-denomination bills printed to finance the Civil War (Lincoln got put on the scarcer high-denomination bills). Lincoln was not pleased, but he bore no grudge and later appointed Chase as chief justice of the Supreme Court.

It is no coincidence that our other "great" president—George Washington—also had this quality of being magnanimous to his adversaries. On one occasion when a close personal friend and a political enemy were under consideration for the same position, he selected the enemy. His reasoning? "My friend I receive with cordial welcome to my house and welcome to my heart, but, with all his good qualities, he is not a man of business. . . . His opponent is, with all his politics so hostile to me, a man of business; my private feelings have nothing to do in this case. I am not George Washington, but President of the United States."

How a president deals with his friends is a true test of his independence. "I love to deal with doctrines and events," said James A. Garfield; "the contests of men about men I greatly dislike." Garfield, who was assassinated before he could make any real impact, knew the danger of political friends and influence-peddlers "bent on boot and booty." Whatever they felt was their just reward for helping him get elected, it was inappropriate now that he was a president. He must now fight them, but do so shrewdly. "They must not be knocked down with bludgeons," he said. "They must have their throats cut with a feather."

There is one final quality, lest we forget: decisiveness. "When he became president," Harry Truman said of James Madison, "he was like every other man of considerable brain power and education.

He found it difficult to make decisions." No matter how wise and good the president may be, it does him no good unless he acts on it. For the last word, we turn to Abraham Lincoln. At the end of a disagreement with his cabinet, he announced, "Seven nays, one aye; the ayes have it."

The president is the boss.

❧

So much for great men speaking about great men. But even presidents can be wrong. Theodore Roosevelt once called Thomas Jefferson America's worst president because Jefferson tried to lead by ideas and was not much of a hands-on doer: "Jefferson . . . was perhaps the most incapable executive that ever filled the presidential chair."* After TR's death, there was a widespread popular movement to build a large monument for TR in Washington DC with a specific site picked out.

Decades later, a monument was built on that site. But it was not for Theodore Roosevelt, it was for Thomas Jefferson.

---

* Woodrow Wilson, who disagreed with TR on practically everything, certainly agreed on this one. Asked to list his own candidates for American greatness, he cited Benjamin Franklin, Robert E. Lee, and Abraham Lincoln—and made it clear that he excluded his fellow Southern idealist Thomas Jefferson.

EIGHT

Simple Mathematics, My Dear Watson

Historians rarely show proper appreciation of statistics and mathematics. In business, when investors look at a deal, they "run the numbers." Of course, not everything can be quantified, but whatever numbers are available, they analyze. When analyzed in excruciating detail, numbers frequently "come alive"; that is, they tell a story.

In the 2008 presidential election, many people questioned whether John McCain, at seventy-two, was too old to be a president. The answer is, of course, it all depends. Our "oldest" president would have to be Andrew Jackson: at a time when the life expectancy for white males was below forty, he was sixty-one when he began his first term.

For a deft use of perspective, consider the story of Enrico Fermi, the great atomic scientist. Fermi once asked General Leslie Groves how many generals might be called "great." Groves said about three out of every hundred. Asked to define what made a general "great," Groves defined it as a general who had won five major battles in a row. Fermi thought about it for a moment, did a calculation of mathematical probability, and came up with a different explanation. He reasoned as follows: the odds are one in four that a general will win two battles in a row, one in eight for three victories, one in sixteen for four victories, and one in thirty-two for five. "So you are right, general, about three out of every hundred. Mathematical probability, not genius."

In 1751, Benjamin Franklin observed that the colonists were twice as likely to get married as the English, they married at average age of twenty, and they had eight children. Thus, he predicted, America's population would double every twenty years, meaning that in a hundred years America would have more people than England. So sound were Franklin's calculations that they were cited in Adam Smith's *The Wealth of Nations*, and used by Thomas Malthus to justify his views on overpopulation and mass hunger.

Franklin's calculations were correct: by 1851 America had a larger population than England did. But the implication that America would become poorer was wrong. Franklin predicted that America would not become poorer as it grew because productivity would keep ahead of population growth. He also predicted that Americans, as they became richer, would have fewer children, enabling them to become even richer.

Predicting the future is never a matter of plotting a straight line from the past, for the simple reason that the factors that made up the past are constantly changing and interacting. Malthus was wrong because he failed to look beneath Franklin's numbers, and only took them literally. Historians, also, not knowing basic statistics, frequently oversimplify history. One

historian, for example, stated, "In the two hundred years between 1800 and 2000, real per capita GDP in the U.S. increased thirtyfold, a remarkable accomplishment."

Thirty times sounds big, but over two hundred years? A financial analyst would look at it more thoroughly. Divide 3,000 percent by 200 years and you get 15 percent per annum—i.e., 15 percent "simple" interest. But this is oversimplistic, because it assumes a static base, whereas in Year 2 the base is increasing to 1.15, then in Year 3 to 132.25 (1.15×1.15), then 152.09, etc.—i.e., compound interest. That is why, when investors look at a deal, they use a Hewlett-Packard 12C calculator to compute "internal rate of return" (IRR) reflecting the real annual rate of interest given the growing base each year. If 1 is the U.S. GDP in the year 1800 and 30 is the GDP in the year 2000, what is the U.S. IRR? The number 1 becomes a -1 (the "present value"), 30 is the "future value," and 200 is the "number of years." The interest, according to the HP calculator, is 1.72 percent!

Not very remarkable.

When you apply mathematics to history, be careful what numbers you use. Pay attention to "net" numbers as opposed to "gross" numbers, do not be misled by a large number taken out of context, and look at "the big picture." As Sherlock Holmes would say, "Elementary, my dear Watson!"

Finally, just run the numbers. Big numbers—a billion here, a billion there—are meaningless. Break them down into simple numbers, and history becomes much more meaningful. In World War II, for example, America spent $325 billion. This money enabled it to kill 500,000 enemy soldiers. Each enemy soldier killed, therefore, cost American taxpayers a whopping $650,000.

Pretty expensive war, wouldn't you say? Such is the price of maintaining our freedom and democracy.

Consider the following numbers:

• More innocent Americans died at the hands of the Ku Klux Klan during Reconstruction than at the hands of Osama bin Laden.

• The number of Americans killed in the entire thirteen-year war in Vietnam is lower than the number of Americans killed each year by drunk drivers.

• The number of conventional bombs we dropped on Vietnam and Cambodia was equivalent in force to 641 Hiroshimas.

Historical dates by themselves rarely mean much, but subtracting later dates from earlier dates gives a number that tells a story. That Harvard was founded only twenty-nine years after the Pilgrims landed on Plymouth Rock says much about the Pilgrims: they didn't just live off the land, they tried to build something. Numerous other colleges soon followed. How many second-generation societies in any civilization have done this?

For a sense of historical perspective, consider that Great Britain emerged in 1763 "from the Seven Years' War as the most powerful empire the world has ever seen." If 1763 marks the rise of the British Empire and the end of World War I marks its demise, then the British Empire had a lifespan of 155 years. The United States did not achieve this distinction until 1945 (and for several decades afterward, it was challenged and threatened every step of the way by the Soviet Union). For the United States to match the reign of Great Britain, it must remain predominant until the beginning of the next century (1945 + 155 = 2100). The British Empire, like most great empires, did not fall because of military defeat, it imploded through imperial overstretch. For the United States, already stretched to the limit with its global responsibilities and fiscal debt, a lot can happen between now and 2100.

A Venture Capital Investment

►**1624**   The Dutch bought Manhattan Island from the Indians for sixty guilders (twenty-four dollars). We all know that Manhattan eventually proved to be a bonanza, the most valuable urban real estate in the world. But what the history books don't tell us is what happened to the actual twenty-four-dollar purchase. How did the Dutch make out on their investment?

They got clobbered. Manhattan Island was a lemon of an acquisition: by 1645 it had run up astronomical losses of 550,000 guilders (almost ten thousand times the original investment); most financial advisors in Holland were urging that the settlement be closed down. At a special meeting on March 3, 1645, the Directors decided to stick with the venture and pump in more money. "Notwithstanding the discovery that their North American province had fallen into ruin and confusion, and that this same province had, in place of being a source of profit, actually cost over five hundred fifty thousand guilders above the returns—they evidently felt that it was not entirely beyond hope, and that they need not and ought not to abandon it."

The Dutch poured in more money, but the venture eventually failed because of bad management. Unlike the English governors of New England and Virginia, who gave away thousands of small land grants to attract rapid immigration and settlement, the Dutch were interested in trading. In pursuit of short-term profits, the West India Company divvied up the land among a few wealthy Dutch landowners (patroons) and paid only subsistence wages on the company-owned farms. It was a shortsighted policy: only a few Dutch settlers immigrated to such a place; most settlers had to be recruited from other countries. Worker productivity and loyalty sank to an all-time low.

In 1664, Charles II of England gave his brother, the Duke of York, a territorial grant stretching from Maine down to the Delaware River. Four English frigates sailed into New Amsterdam harbor and persuaded the unhappy Dutch and non-Dutch settlers to accept the patronage of the English. The English picked up Manhattan for nothing—then proceeded to lose it themselves in a hostile takeover in 1776.

History does not tell us what the Indians did with their twenty-four dollars, but at least they got twenty-four dollars and no headaches—plus they were New Jersey Indians, with no real claim on Manhattan anyway. If anything, they were looking for an "exit strategy": the Manhattan trading market was undeveloped, the labor force was unskilled, and the capital requirements were enormous. By getting out of a bad situation and taking whatever they could get, the Indians made the right decision.

In a newspaper column written in 1999, the humor columnist Dave Barry wrote, ". . . purchased from the Indians for $24, plus $167,000 a month in maintenance fees." He got the idea right: the Dutch invested a lot of money—and lost it all. Pity they didn't pay more attention to the name of the place they were buying. The Indian word "Manahactanienk," translated into English, means "the island of general intoxication."

Mathematical Coincidences of Presidential Relatives

➤**1776–2008** The mathematician John Allen Paulos once figured out that the odds of a fellow American passenger on a 747 plane knowing someone you know, out of a nation of nearly 300 million people, were one out of one hundred, but that the second-level odds of one of your friend's acquaintances knowing one of your fellow passenger's friend's acquaintances were ninety-nine out of one hundred. It should come as no surprise, therefore, that many of our presidents were related. Mathematics, not aristocracy, is at work.

Especially when the American population was 10 million or 50 million.

John Tyler was the son of Thomas Jefferson's college roommate. He had no presidential relatives at the time, but he did in 1945, when his great-great-great-nephew became president (Harry Truman). Zachary Taylor was not only James Madison's cousin; he also was related to Thomas Jefferson and James Monroe, as well as to Chief Justice John Marshall and General Robert E. Lee. The second Adams president and the second Bush president were sons of a president; the second Harrison president was a grandson. First prize in the mathematical president "family," however, would go to FDR: he was related to no fewer than eleven other presidents. On his father's side he was related to John Adams, John Quincy Adams, Martin Van Buren, and Theodore Roosevelt. On his mother's side he was related to George Washington, James Madison, William Henry Harrison, Zachary Taylor, Ulysses Grant, Benjamin Harrison, and William

Howard Taft. Also, thanks to his mother, he was related to both Jefferson Davis and Robert E. Lee. Robert E. Lee was related to Thomas Jefferson, James Madison, James Monroe, Martin Van Buren, William Henry Harrison, James K. Polk, Ulysses Grant, Zachary Taylor, and then later on to Grover Cleveland, Benjamin Harrison, Theodore Roosevelt, and Franklin D. Roosevelt. He also was related to Patrick Henry, John Marshall, Jefferson Davis, and eventually to Queen Elizabeth II. Within the Confederate Army, Lee's relatives were generals Stonewall Jackson, Albert Sidney Johnston, Joseph E. Johnston, and J. E. B. Stuart.

Every father, especially if he's a very successful man, worries about his daughter when he gives her away at the wedding ceremony. Imagine how an ex-president of the United States must feel: How can the young man possibly equal him?

Yes, we actually had an ex-president who gave away the bride to a young man who eventually became president of the United States. Theodore Roosevelt gave away his late brother's daughter, Eleanor, to Franklin D. Roosevelt. "It's a good thing to keep the name in the family," he quipped. (As for a nice house to live in, of course, he had no idea.)

One would be hard-pressed to describe the meeting of the three heads of state at Yalta in 1945 as a "family reunion," but two of them were cousins, related to a famous American general in World War II who later ran twice for president. The general was Douglas MacArthur, who ran for president in 1948 and 1952 (and got nowhere). He was a sixth cousin once-removed of Sir Winston Churchill and an eighth cousin of President Franklin Roosevelt. (Churchill and Roosevelt shared a great-great-great-great-grandfather.)

George W. Bush has the distinction of having presidential relatives on both sides of his family. His father, of course, was president; so, too, was his mother's distant, long-ago cousin Franklin Pierce. As for Jeb Bush becoming president, the odds are one out of 150 million adults. But like your fellow airplane passenger knowing someone who knows someone you know, his odds are a lot better than yours or mine. From George Washington to the present, there have been seventy-eight presidential sons; two have become president, so with good odds like that (one out of forty), why not a third? Problem is, Jeb Bush also has a brother who became president. The odds of a president, Papa George, having *two* presidential sons is so remote it won't happen. People fearful of a "dynasty" can sleep at night.

Statistics mavens may appreciate that the 2008 presidential election had its full share of presidential relatives: John McCain was a sixth cousin of First Lady Laura Bush, and Barack Obama was a ninth cousin once-removed to Vice President Dick Cheney—a most unlikely match. Obama also included as his presi-

dential relatives the two George Bushes, Gerald Ford, Lyndon Johnson, Harry Truman, and James Madison. (Obviously, if he was related to Truman, he had to be related to Tyler, too.)

George Washington's Compensation

➤**1776** When George Washington took over as commander-in-chief of the Continental Army, he had two choices of compensation: a monthly salary of five hundred dollars, or full reimbursement of all expenses at the end of the war.

Washington chose the latter, and when the war was over he sent a bill for $449,291.* Although the bill was paid promptly, Washington had made the wrong choice.

Here are the facts; you decide:

• He was betting everything that his side would win; had his side lost, he would have had to flee for his life.

• The war lasted a lot longer than anyone thought it would—six years. At $500 times 12 months times 6 years, his total earnings would have been $36,000—with no inflation adjustment.

• The war's hardships invoked a bout of hyperinflation, making his $449,291 virtually worthless.

---

* Naturally, the bill was audited. After going over all the accounts, the government auditors found that Washington's figures were off by less than one dollar.

"A bird in the hand is worth two in the bush," investors will say. Indeed, Washington should have taken his $36,000 while it still meant something (if you plot $500/month on the graph, you arrive at a total value of almost $1 million). Washington was so short on cash when he was elected president that he had to borrow $2,500 just to get to New York for his inauguration.

An aberration, a sign of poor financial management? Hardly. George Washington was a methodical, shrewd businessman; at least he managed to hang on to Mount Vernon. Most other plantation owners got wiped out. Thomas Jefferson, for example, was constantly in debt, had to sell all his books to pay his living expenses, and at one point tried to sell Monticello—but there were no takers.

The Mathematical Formula that Shaped America's Landscape ($22^2 \times 10 = 1{,}760^2/640$)

➤**1785**   It is hard to imagine an obscure Englishman who died in 1609 as the father of the spatial and legal development of the New World landscape. His name was Edmund Gunter. His conceptual mathematics was to determine the

Price Inflation, 1776–1780

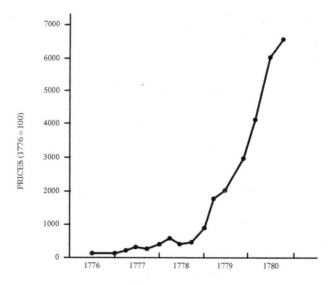

During the American Revolution, the money used to pay soldiers, called continental scrip, had depreciated to one-tenth of one penny per dollar. By 1780, what had cost $100 in 1776, now cost $7,000. (Graph from Stanley Lebergott, The Americans: An Economic Record. *W.W.* Norton & Company, 1984, p. 42.)

spatial organization of two thirds of the entire United States.

After the Revolutionary War, the American government was so short of funds it had to sell western lands to farmers to avoid bankruptcy. To speed up the process, it passed the Land Ordinance Act of 1785, authorizing the division of the western territories into six-square-mile townships consisting of thirty-six square sections of 640 acres each. Overnight, surveying became a highly sought-after skill, just as computer programming is today.

The convenience of 6/36/640 owed its existence to "Gunter's Chain," consisting of one hundred links of 0.66 feet each. Such a chain is twenty-two yards long: ten square chains make an acre, and 640 acres make a square mile. Thus Gunter synthesized the acre, the mile, and the decimal system.

Take out your calculator and try this one:

$$(100 \text{ links} \times 0.66 \text{ feet}/3) \times 22 \text{ yards} \times 10 = 4{,}840 \text{ square yards} = 1 \text{ acre} = (5{,}280 \text{ feet}/3 \times 1{,}760 \text{ yards})/640$$

The advantage of Gunter's mathematics was that 640 acres was large enough to survey easily, and 640 could be readily divided into small plots to be sold to the poorer farmers—how democratic! Nobody had to worry about titles, boundaries, or lots; a farmer simply told a government land officer he wanted to buy section *x* in township number 4 in range number 2 in the Ohio Territory, and the official ac-

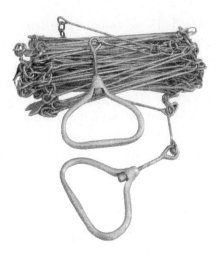

Why a chain? Because unlike rods, the chain's links made it flexible enough to easily carry around.

cepted the money and issued a deed. No lawyers or hassles. It was all very simple. Thanks to the grid, American westward movement proceeded smoothly.

Of all values transformed from Europe to America, none was more important than the absolute, antifeudal ownership of land. Striving to own property was the American dream.

The sale of more than a billion acres of land, made possible by Gunter's Chain, which enabled government surveyors to stay abreast of settlers and squatters heading west, financed the entire expenditures of the U.S. government for 150 years. It was only when expansion reached the Pacific, and there was no more land to sell, that the U.S. government resorted to income taxes.

❧

But the chain did not die. Every time we watch a football game, there is a moment of high drama every time the referee carries out the ten-yard chain to measure whether the offense team got a first down. Now that we have laser video-beam technology to measure precisely, many people are calling for the abolition of the chain. But football purists demur: the chain has worked well for a hundred years, why change it? Just as most of America's landscape was determined by the chain, so many a football game's victory or defeat has rested on the verdict delivered by a chain.

America's other great national pastime, baseball, is treasured as "a game of inches." But so, too, is football. National sports reflect a nation's character and values. There is not a country in the world that has a sport—let alone two sports—so dependent on exactness, precision, and measurement.

A "Third World" Nation

➤**1800** There is considerable rhetoric today about the widening gap between the developed countries and the Third World. But this gap is to be expected, just as it happened to Britain and America in the early 1800s. Simple mathematics, says economist Jeffrey Williamson: "Consider two countries, one with income per person of $100, and the other $1,000. Let the poorer of the two grow much faster, 10 percent per year, than the richer, 2 percent per year. The gap widens by $10!"

Indeed, 10 percent of $100 is $10, and 2 percent of $1,000 is $20. Eventually, of course, the gap narrowed and finally collapsed in the early twentieth century as America's faster economic growth rate enabled it to catch up to and bypass Great Britain. But from the founding of the republic in 1789 to the 1830s, the United States was like most Third World countries today: it was getting poorer and the mother country was getting richer.

200,000 Afro-Americans in One War, Not in Another

➤**1861** When the Civil War started, slaves were a secondary issue: the key issue was union versus secession. On a quiet May night in 1861, near Fort Monroe in Virginia, a small event occurred that was to trigger the eventual enlistment of nearly 200,000 black troops and laborers in the Union Army. This enlistment would strike, in the words of General Ulysses Grant, "the heaviest blow yet given the Confederacy." Unforeseen by anyone, it was to prove a critical factor in determining the outcome of the war.

Three slaves, working on a Confederate fortifications project, slipped away and sought refuge behind Union lines commanded by General Benjamin Butler, also a lawyer and politician (later 1864 potential running mate with Lincoln, then governor of Massachusetts). When a Confederate officer sought the return of the runaways based on the Fugitive Slave Law,

Butler refused. His reasoning was twofold: (1) since Virginia had seceded from the Union, the Fugitive Slave Law was inapplicable; and (2) since the slaves had been used for military purposes, they were contraband of war and therefore subject to confiscation.

The Confederate officer went away, dumbfounded. Then Butler went one step further in accelerating history: he hired the slaves to work for the Union Army.

In one fell stroke, says the historian Gabor Boritt, "three slaves and Benjamin Butler had struck a monstrous blow for freedom and the Federal war effort." Once the secretary of war endorsed Butler's rationale—which he did promptly—the North progressed from giving military slaves their freedom to hiring them for military purposes, to promoting them from menial service jobs to becoming actual combat troops. As Afro-Americans proved themselves to their suspicious Northern captors to be loyal and diligent workers, they broke down racial stereotypes to the point where Lincoln could gamble on rescuing the flagging war effort by issuing the Emancipation Proclamation.

History again turned to Butler. At Lincoln's request, he became the first general to lead ex-slaves into battle, thus paving the way for Afro-Americans to join the Union army en masse. Jefferson Davis was so outraged he issued what must have been the first and only *fatwa* in American history—long before Americans knew what this Islamic term meant. Davis ordered that Butler be executed on the spot, should the Confederates be so lucky as to get their hands on him.

How significant was the contribution of Butler's recruits to the Northern victory? Simple numbers tell the story. In his defense of the Militia Act of July 1862 authorizing Afro-American troops, Lincoln said:

> *The slightest knowledge of arithmetic will prove to any man that the rebel armies cannot be destroyed by Democratic strategy. It would sacrifice all the white men of the North to do it. There are now in the services of the U.S. near 200,000 able-bodied colored men, most of them under arms, defending and acquiring Union territory. . . . Abandon all the posts now garrisoned by black men; take 200,000 men from our side and put them in the battlefield or cornfield against us, and we would be compelled to abandon the war in three weeks. . . . My enemies pretend I am now carrying on this war for the sole purpose of abolition. So long as I am President it shall be carried out for the sole purpose of restoring the Union. But no human power can subdue this rebellion without the use of the emancipation policy.*

Some 110,000 Afro-Americans served as troops at the war's end, and no fewer than twenty-one were awarded the nation's highest award, the Medal of Honor. Another 90,000 served in a support capacity as laborers, cooks, carpenters, for-

Black regiment in New York, getting ready for war

tifications builders, spies, scouts, and guides.

Even the Confederacy recognized their impact. In early 1865 it did the unthinkable: it passed a law calling for the enlistment of its slaves as soldiers. Out went the slave-owning society; in came a last-ditch attempt to woo slaves to fight to save their masters. Obviously it didn't work, and a month later the South surrendered.

Now let us look at what might have been, a story told to us not by American historians, but by two British historians who obviously have a quite different take on American history.

The first to recognize the military value of liberated slaves was not Benjamin Butler in 1861, but John Murray, Earl of Dunmore, in 1775. In most Southern states, blacks outnumbered whites. Forced to flee when the Revolution started, this loyalist governor of Virginia knew how to hit the plantation owners below the belt: emancipate the slaves. He knew full well, in the historian Simon Schama's words, that "the majority of slaves wanted nothing to do with the new American republic of bondage."

The reaction of the Southern slaveholders was vicious and swift. "A most diabolical scheme!" fumed the Virginia House of Burgesses. "Hell itself could not have invented anything more black than this design of emancipating our slaves," added a

Pennsylvania planter. "If that man [Dunmore] is not crushed before spring," wrote General George Washington, "he will become the most formidable enemy America has; his strength will increase as a snowball is rolling; and faster, if some expedition cannot be hit upon to convince the slaves and servants of the impotency of his designs."

The so-called expedition to convince the slaves was a reign of terror. The Virginia planters quickly issued strong warnings to their slaves, and, to make sure they got the message, executed any runaway slaves who got caught. Massachusetts, Rhode Island, New York, New Jersey, Pennsylvania, and Delaware all passed acts prohibiting the enlistment of blacks, to keep their Virginia colleagues happy. Unable to recruit more than six hundred runaways before the Southern planters retaliated, the Dunmore movement never caught on, and so one fifth of the population never had the opportunity to declare their preference. Given that the Loyalists had been guaranteed continued possession of their Negroes, the number of blacks deserting to the British side came solely from the patriots and would have been lower, say one-third of the population, or 200,000. Considering the closeness of the fight and the fact that it was only won by the Americans at the very last minute, 200,000 Afro-Americans would have made all the difference.

Imagine: hauled away in chains while Afro-Americans celebrated, Washington, Jefferson, and Madison became footnotes in history, while Benjamin Franklin, president of the Pennsylvania Society for Promoting the Abolition of Slavery, finally got a full hearing and advocated that even the Loyalists not continue their slaveholding. When Britain abolished the slave trade in 1807 and slavery in 1833, the few remaining slaves in the South finally became free. There was no Civil War, and Abraham Lincoln continued his practice as a small-time lawyer in Springfield, Illinois.

Fake Government Surpluses

➤**1866**   Anyone looking at the history of the federal debt would be impressed by the twenty-eight-year performance from 1866 to 1893. In an effort to pay off the massive Civil War debt, seven consecutive administrations from Andrew Johnson to Benjamin Harrison all ran budget surpluses without fail.

However, statistics can lie—especially when government budgeting is involved. During this time the U.S. government embarked on the most profligate "giveaway" program in its history: land grants from the public domain. Between 1866 and 1933, the government gave away 500 million acres to individuals, railroads, and states, and sold another 70 million acres at below-market prices. Observes the economist Gary Anderson, "Over the same period that the federal government was

FEDERAL SURPLUS AS % OF EXPENDITURES	
1865	-74.3%
1866	7.1%
1867	37.2%
1868	7.5%
1869	14.9%
1870	32.8%
1871	31.2%
1872	34.8%
1873	14.9%
1874	0.4%
1875	4.9%
1876	10.9%
1877	16.6%
1878	8.8%
1879	2.8%
1880	24.4%
1881	38.4%
1882	56.4%
1883	50.1%
1884	42.8%
1885	24.4%
1886	38.7%
1887	38.6%
1888	41.6%
1889	29.3%
1890	26.7%
1891	7.3%
1892	2.9%
1893	0.6%
1894	-16.6%

acting with supposed excess zeal in balancing the budget by running huge apparent surpluses, it was 'spending' and therefore liquidating a major portion of its fixed capital assets."

If the capital value of the land given away during the budget surplus years of 1866–93 is subtracted from the recorded surpluses, the surpluses would vanish and the result would be a substantial net deficit. But because the federal government made no distinction between operating budgets and capital budgets, it could pretend to be balancing the budget while at the same time it was looting the store.

Today, as the United States faces a severe government deficit problem, much is often made of the fact that the United States for 143 of its first two hundred years managed to keep its house in order and balance the budget. To be sure, "balancing the budget" was always an important political objective, treated with far more reverence than it is today. But also part of the equation was shoddy accounting practices.

What Immigration?

▶**1907** Our largest migration is not the 140-year immigration of 47 million Europeans and Asians to our shores from 1820 to 1960, but rather the forty-year migration of more than 30 million Americans from the farmlands to the cities and suburbs from the mid-1920s to the mid-

1960s. But how could this be? Forty-seven is greater than thirty, right? Yes, but forty-seven is a "gross" number, not a "net" number. Plus, it covers 140 years, not 40.

In reality, less than two-thirds of immigrants stayed in America, whereas the number of migrants was entirely "net." Of the 47 million immigrants, some 18 million went back home, leaving a net immigration of 29 million. The return rates varied widely among ethnic groups, from 3 percent for Russian Jews and 10 percent for the Irish, to 55 percent for Japanese (in Hawaii) and 60 percent for Italians. In the last decade of the nineteenth century, for every one hundred immigrants there were thirty-seven emigrants.

There were two kinds of immigrants: permanent immigrants, and migrant workers known as "birds of passage" (after migratory birds who move from place to place frequently). These were immigrants who intended to work in America for a short time, then return home to their families and villages. The introduction of the steamship in 1880 reduced the length of a transatlantic crossing to ten days, making it possible for workers to return home in the winter when unskilled labor was in short demand in the United States. Many of these workers, after saving enough money to buy substantial land back home, did not return to America.

Getting a handle on the exact numbers is difficult because the U.S. Census Department didn't keep records of emigration until 1908. On the next page are the sta-

tistics of immigration/emigration for the three decades from 1910 until the beginning of World War II, drawn from the Statistical Abstract of the United States.

This is the most famous photograph ever taken of American immigrants: The Steerage, by Alfred Stieglitz, 1907.
    Except for one thing: the boat was not going to America, it had just left America for Germany. The "poor and huddled masses" on the deck are emigrants returning home.

From 1910 to 1919, 6.3 million people immigrated to the United States, and 2.1 million went back home. But not every-

FOREIGNERS ENTERING AND LEAVING THE UNITED STATES

	Resident Visa		Tourist Visa		Total	
	IMMIGRANT (m)	EMIGRANT (m)	ADMITTED (m)	DEPARTED (m)	ADMITTED (m)	DEPARTED (m)
1910–1919	6.3	2.1	1.4	1.8	7.7	3.9
1920–1929	3.8	1.3	2.3	1.6	6.1	2.9
1930–1939	0.7	0.5	1.6	1.8	2.3	2.3
	10.8	3.9	5.3	5.2	16.1	9.1
	100%	**36%**	**100%**	**98%**	**100%**	**57%**

body answers the entry/exit form correctly, nor do they report an overstay or change in intent, which explains why there are 400,000 more departed than admitted in the "tourist visa" column (1.8-1.4=0.4). Obviously, there were a lot more than 2.1 million emigrants—2.5 million to be exact. In the following decade we see a different anomaly: 700,000 more visitors arriving than leaving (2.3-1.6=0.7). Some of these people stayed on and became residents; others were simply double-counted (an immigrant who made four trips home would frequently show up in immigration records as five immigrants).

The real figure to use is not the total gross immigration or total net immigration, but the annual velocity of immigration. The velocity of permanent immigration, at 7 million over the thirty-year period from 1910 to 1939, was 233,000 people a year; for domestic migration, it was 750,000 people a year—more than three times as much. More than being a nation of immigrants, America is a country of people relentlessly on the move in search of greater opportunities within the vast borders of America.

The Ally We Chose to Forget

➤**1940** American histories of World War II focus on our fighting in Europe and the Pacific, but there was a whole other arena where the war was really decided—the Eastern Front. More than America, the Soviet Union was the country that saved the West from Nazi barbarism. Look at who was doing most of the fighting.

In 1940—a good two years before the U.S. got into the war—the Soviet Union was fighting the Germans. The invasion and liberation of Western Europe, observes John Lukacs, was feasible because "nearly four-fifths of the German Army were fighting in Russia. Had he a larger reserve army, Hitler could have sped it to Normandy and driven the invaders into the sea."

WAR PARTICIPATION		
Theater	Anglo-American Divisions	Soviet Divisions
Northern Africa (1941–43)	9–20	0
Italy (1943–45)	7–26	0
Western Europe (1944–45)	56–75	0
Eastern Front (1940–45)	0	190–266
Number of German divisions destroyed by	176	607
Percentage of German casualties inflicted by	29%	71%

The United States never really got going with lots of troops until 1944. The number of Anglo-American divisions finally reached a maximum of seventy-five only at the end of the war, whereas the Russians had a minimum of 190 divisions on the field ever since 1941.

Had the USSR and the United States remained allies after 1945,* the former's contributions would have been acknowledged. But it was not to be. American soldiers could not recount their experiences fighting alongside Soviet soldiers without being branded traitors or Communists. A survey conducted in the mid-1980s found that 40 percent of Americans had forgotten that the U.S. and the Soviet Union had fought together in World War II. "The Cold War," says one historian, "made a significant past inaccessible to many Americans." Indeed, Americans felt that they—not the Russians—had won World War II.

Says the investment banker Peter Peterson (former secretary of commerce under Nixon):

With our typical American hubris, we concluded we had won the war. Some years later, I was to find that others had a very different view of how that war had been won. In 1972, while I was representing our government in its negotiations with the Soviet Union on trade and Lend-Lease payments, Secretary General Leonid Brezhnev took me aside for a rare one-on-

---

* It should be noted, however, that the USSR was an ally only insofar as it served its own self-interest. Take Pearl Harbor, for example. While there were numerous warning signals that the Japanese might attack, the White House was uncertain where and when it might occur. Russia, on the other hand, knew the exact hour of the Pearl Harbor attack from its master spy Richard Sorge—and kept quiet.

one exchange. "Does not your President understand that while you ask for cold cash interest payments on Lend-Lease," he said, "we already have paid far, far more, with the blood of twenty-one million human Russian lives?" That's seventy times the number of Americans who lost their lives in battle in World War II!

Lucky to Be in Port

➤**1941** One would be hard-pressed to see a silver lining in the horrendous disaster of the Japanese surprise attack on Pearl Harbor. Certainly the damage to the U.S. Navy was awesome.

But it was not as much as you might think, given all the vivid photographs of burning ships and explosions. In fact the Japanese sank only eighteen out of the ninety-six warships docked at Pearl Harbor. To be sure, eight of these eighteen sunken ships were battleships—the backbone of the Navy. But six of them were later salvaged, making the net loss only two. In addition to the seventy-eight warships still afloat at Pearl Harbor, the U.S. Navy had plenty of other ships in the Atlantic and South Pacific: 168 destroyers, 112 submarines, fifteen heavy cruisers, eight light cruisers, and—most important of all—all of its six aircraft carriers (soon to be the dominant fighting ships of the war). As a percentage of the total U.S. fleet, eighteen out of 405, the Navy had lost only 4 percent of its ships during

Pearl Harbor. Furthermore, the Japanese failed to knock out the enormous fuel tanks that supplied the entire Pacific Fleet. "Had the Japanese destroyed the fuel supply," observed Pacific Fleet commander-in-chief Chester Nimitz, "it would have prolonged the war another two years."

The greatest stroke of luck, however, concerned the ships. "It was God's mercy that our fleet was in Pearl Harbor on December 7, 1941," said Nimitz.

So they could be sitting ducks and get bombed easily? In the larger sense, yes. Had they been out at sea, they would have been bombed anyway and gone down to the bottom of the Pacific, with thousands of sailors drowned. But by sinking in the shallow waters of Pearl Harbor when most of the sailors were off duty, many deaths were avoided and most of the ships eventually resurrected. "We would have lost the entire Pacific Fleet and eighteen to nineteen thousand men," said Admiral Nimitz, "instead of the ships and 3,300 men we did lose."

The shock value of the December 7 attack, of course, was enormous—but far out of proportion to actual damage done. As America was to rediscover later, in Vietnam, massive bombing raids have little military value: they fail to knock out the enemy, and only serve to harden enemy ingenuity and resolve. Whereas the U.S. had only six aircraft carriers in 1941, for example, by 1945 it had more than one hundred.

Saving American Convoys in the North Atlantic

➤**1942** German submarines were inflicting terrible losses on American ship convoys trying to deliver supplies to Britain, then tottering on its last legs. The British Air Command was having little success in attacking and sinking the U-boats. As soon as a U-boat spotted an attacking British plane, it dived as deep as possible to avoid getting hit. Because it took a plane two minutes to arrive at the precise dive site, by which time the German submarine had descended to one hundred feet, the British set their depth charges at one hundred feet.

For reasons no one could understand, the results were meager at best. It took one British physicist, Patrick M. S. Blackett, to realize the problem. Blackett, who later went on to win the 1948 Nobel Prize in physics, was a specialist in cloud chambers, cosmic rays, and paleomagnetism. During the Second World War he had been recruited by the British Admiralty to apply his fertile mind to the emerging field of study now known today as "operations research." Blackett looked at the data and saw what others couldn't see: the combat data on German submarines was an *average* figure—useless in targeting a U-boat in a vast ocean (like looking for a needle in a haystack). What mattered was specificity, not all-inclusiveness. The goal was not to achieve the impossible by hitting *all* the U-boats, but to be realistic and

hit *some* of them. Furthermore, observed Blackett, the warning time in some cases "was much less than two minutes, and the U-boat could descend only about twenty feet before an aircraft dropped its load; in those cases the sub could still be located and hit. Therefore, if the depth charges were set at twenty feet, instead of one hundred, the percentage of submarines actually damaged or destroyed would be much higher."

Result? The number of hits increased so dramatically the Germans lost more submarines than they could produce. This attrition, combined with the astonishing growth of U.S. ship construction (from 1.2 million gross tons in 1941 to 13.7 million in 1943), enabled the United States and England to win the U-boat war.

The Japanese City We Bombed into Oblivion

➤**1945** Was the atom bomb necessary? Ever since President Truman made the decision to drop the atom bomb, people everywhere have argued passionately whether such a brutal act was necessary.

What people forget is that Truman's predecessor, FDR, had just recently bombed a Japanese city into oblivion—with no signs of submission by the Japanese. The city was Tokyo, fire-bombed on the night of March 9, 1945. Conventional bombs were used, and it was the greatest single destruction in the history of warfare: in just a few hours, 84,000 people burned to death and one million people were wandering the streets, their homes and apartment buildings reduced to rubble. Fifteen square miles were totally destroyed.

Yet Japan did not surrender; it continued fighting. Five months later, with the knockout weapon finally perfected and made available, Truman must have reflected on how the destruction of Tokyo had failed to get the message across.

Certainly it was not for want of trying. Before bombing Tokyo, the United States had sent planes over the city to drop leaflets warning civilians to evacuate the city immediately. Entitled "Appeal to the People," the leaflet stated: "You are not the

Tokyo after the fire-bombing. For ten years the Japanese government, ashamed of its lack of defense against a conventional air raid, refused to let this picture be published.
Photographs of Hiroshima and Nagasaki? Absolutely.
But Tokyo? No.

enemy of America. Our enemy is the Japanese militarists who dragged you into the war."

But militarist nations do not go down easily. "Practically all Germans deny the fact that they surrendered during the last war," Franklin Roosevelt said, "but this time they are going to know it. And so are the Japs." Only it didn't work. Back in 1920, the Englishman A. G. Gardiner observed about Germany, "Wars do not always end with the knowledge of defeat. They only end with the admission of defeat, which is quite another thing." In the case of Japan in 1945, the country was defeated, but the country's leaders wouldn't admit it.

The man who planned the bombing of Tokyo was General Curtis LeMay. "If this raid works the way I think it will, we can shorten the war," he said. Years later, after the war was over, LeMay was asked about the moral considerations of dropping the atom bomb. He responded:

Everyone bemoans the fact that we dropped the atom bomb and killed a lot of people at Hiroshima and Nagasaki. That I guess is immoral; but nobody says anything about the incendiary attacks on every industrial city in Japan, and the first attack on Tokyo killed more people than the atomic bomb did. Apparently, that was all right . . .

At Hiroshima, the death toll was 78,000; at Nagasaki, 64,000. We remember Hiroshima and Nagasaki, but not the 84,000 dead at Tokyo.*

The purpose of the atom bomb was not so much the damage but to deliver a colossal shock. Explained Gen. George Marshall to the head of the British Military Mission in Washington: "It's no good warning them. If you warn them, there's no surprise. And the only way to produce shock is surprise."

Viewed in this context, the atomic bomb is a military tool of limited utility. Bombed nations will always fight back. The key is shock and surprise, which the United States achieved in its "Shock and Awe" bombing of Baghdad in 1991. And which al-Qaeda achieved on 9/11.

The Most Controversial Number in American History: A Million Lives

► **1945** An anonymous document, written by "a prominent economist" recom-

---

* Nor do we remember the European city that suffered equivalent "total destruction": Cologne. There, in under thirty days, the Allies dropped the equivalent of one and a half times the Hiroshima bomb. A single B-29 plane delivers a bomb payload of ten tons of TNT, meaning that a single raid by five hundred planes unleashes five thousand tons. The power of the Hiroshima bomb was 12,500 tons, or 2.5 raids. The Nagasaki bomb was 22,000 tons, or 4.4 raids. Cologne suffered the equivalent of 3.8 raids.

mended by ex-president Herbert Hoover, arrived on the desk of Secretary of War Henry Stimson. Among its conclusions was an estimate that an invasion of Japan to end the war would cost "500,000 to 1,000,000 American lives."

It was a number totally out of the blue, a wake-up call. Who this economist was, Hoover would not say. Yet this secret memorandum developed a life of its own and became the major rationale used by Stimson and Truman to justify using the atom bomb.

Today, nine out of ten Americans believe the bomb was justified because it saved a million American lives. Critics of the bomb have jumped on this figure and accused Truman of fiddling with the truth, to the point of being dishonest. Defenders of the bomb, for their part, have used it to come up with their own greater estimates. Never has a simple number played such a pivotal role in history: it brought America into the atomic age.

The first to cite this number was Winston Churchill. When he heard the news of the bombing of Nagasaki, he applauded the news and said it had saved 500,000 lives. Two weeks later, he used the higher number, one million. (In two weeks?)

There it lay quiet for another year or two while the world rejoiced over long-awaited peace. Then, when more and more questions were raised over the morality of using the bomb, Harry Truman defended his action by citing "half a million," "a million," or "several million." You

would think, given the importance of his decision, that a president would have his basic numbers straight.

The confusion all started with General George Marshall. In developing the two-phase plan to invade Japan—an attack on Kyushu in November 1945 followed by an attack on Honshu in March 1946—he cited losses of twenty thousand at Kyushu (subsequently updated to forty thousand), and made no prediction what would happen at Honshu if the war lasted that long. Other military planners were not so sanguine. They noted that it took eighty-two days of fierce fighting to capture the island of Okinawa, resulting in 200,000 fatalities (12,520 of them American). They also noted how the Japanese at Luzon and Iwo Jima had been willing to use kamikaze attacks and "fight to the death," committing suicide rather than surrender. Growing evidence emerged about Japanese plans to mobilize women and ten-year-old children to defend the homeland at all costs, and to execute the 31,617 Americans being held in Japanese prison camps. General Douglas MacArthur feared a worst-case scenario: "If the Japanese government lost control over its people and the millions of former Japanese soldiers took to guerrilla warfare in the mountains, it would take a million American troops ten years to master the situation."

Trying to get a grasp on all these

numbers, Stimson sought the advice of Justice Felix Frankfurter. Frankfurter advised him to stick with the simple one-million-lives figure: "The longer a sentimentally appealing error is allowed to make its way, the more difficult it is to overtake it." Stimson, admitting that "history is often not what actually happened but what is recorded as such," went along with the figure.

Caught in the fog of war, U.S. Army planners had no degree of certainty how many American lives would be lost. But the picture looked grim. The U.S. invasion of Kyushu alone, code-named Operation Olympic, expanded to 650,000 troops. Compounding American concerns was the morale of the U.S. armed forces: five years of fighting had stretched manpower resources thin. When Stimson visited the military bases in Georgia, he was stunned by the low morale and tired condition of the troops. Human resources for fighting the war were diminishing rapidly. A quick victory was vital.

Problem was, the U.S. Army Air Force had run out of military targets to bomb. The crusty General Curtis "Bombs Away!" LeMay, cigar in his mouth, complained that his planes were reduced to "bombing garbage cans." The only targets left were civilian cities. Intense bombing of Tokyo

had devastated the city, but had not worked. The atom bomb looked like the only solution.

That it worked, there is no doubt. Even the emperor himself—the only man who could bring Japan to the peace table—admitted that the primary reason for surrendering was the atom bomb. A national poll taken of Japanese in 1946 revealed a startling fact: the Japanese people blamed not the Americans for the devastation of Hiroshima and Nagasaki, but their militarist leaders for wanting to fight so long.* Hard to believe, but even after the two bombs had devastated Japan, the vice-chief of the Japanese navy, known as the "father" of the kamikazes, was running around Tokyo trying to take over the government. He told the army minister and the army chief of staff, "Let us formulate a plan for certain victory: if we are prepared to sacrifice 20 million Japanese lives in a special attack [kamikaze] effort, victory will be ours!"

Viewed in a larger context, whether Truman's decision saved forty thousand lives, or a million or several million, pales beside the fact that in more than sixty years no lives have been lost to a cataclysmic bomb. It all began with the man who wrote that secret memo; to this day we do not know who he was.

---

* What if we go backward in time rather than forward? Such was physicist Robert Oppenheimer's approach to the "million lives" issue: had his team succeeded in building the bomb two years earlier, he said, well over a million lives would have been saved.

More Important Than the Amount of Money Is How It's Used

►**1948** Every time there's an international crisis that calls for massive nation-building, pundits call for another "Marshall Plan." Just send in a couple of billion dollars to rejuvenate Eastern Europe or Iraq or Africa or wherever, and the money will be well spent.

No question, the Marshall Plan for rebuilding post–World War II Europe was America's most successful aid program. But people who think that the amount of money was what made the difference are in for a surprise.

Look at the numbers. In the three years from 1945 to the beginning of the Marshall Plan in 1948, the United States spent more than $9 billion in various aid programs for Europe—$3 billion per year. The 1948–52 Marshall Plan was $13.4 billion—$2.7 billion per year. Hard to believe, but the United States spent *less* money on the Marshall Plan than it had on previous aid programs. In fact, when Marshall announced his plan, it was no big deal: the *New York Times* printed only a modest headline. Why, then, was the Marshall Plan so successful?

Rather than continue giving away billions of dollars to individual countries, General Marshall and his advisors created a comprehensive multilateral plan, managed by the Europeans themselves, for economic rehabilitation of the entire re-

gion. This insistence on self-help was based on the recent American experience with New Deal welfare programs, the wartime Lend-Lease program for the UK, and the postwar aid programs for European countries, which had all started as short-term projects but later seemed to develop lives of their own. The United States was determined to avoid another large, self-perpetuating scheme.

"The critical difference was in the conditionality attached to the aid, which required Europeans to help themselves by dismantling the restrictions that had been blocking their mutual trade . . . the revival of intra-European trade launched the European recovery."

But make no mistake about it, the Marshall Plan also had conditions. Said the U.S. ambassador to France, if the Communists got into the French government, France could not expect "a single dollar bill."

Today, as the United States gives away enormous amounts of money in foreign aid, there is no Marshall Plan. In 1994 the *Wall Street Journal* delved into history to see what could be learned in order to give aid effectively to the Eastern European countries emerging from the shackles of communism. It concluded:

The Marshall Plan involved more than just rebuilding, it sought to transform Western Europe into a unified trading bloc. . . . The Marshall Plan had three things that today's Western attempts to aid the East don't have. It had a headquar-

ters—the Talleyrand mansion in Paris. It had $13 billion. . . . And the Marshall Plan had a plan.

Definitely it helps to have a plan. After allowing for inflation, $13.4 billion in 1948 is equivalent to $115 billion today. But that figure greatly underestimates the percentage burden on the economy. The gross national product has increased sixfold since then, so an equivalent burden now would be almost $700 billion—a large number, but still far less than what the U.S. spent trying to promote democracy in another part of the world: Iraq.

Not the Right Asterisk

➤**1961** When Roger Maris hit sixty-one home runs, breaking Babe Ruth's 1927 single-season record of sixty home runs, the baseball commissioner ruled that Maris's record be marked with an asterisk. The rationale was that Maris had had an unfair advantage in that he had played in an expanded, 162-game season, whereas Ruth had played in a 154-game season (indeed, Maris's total at the end of his 154th game had been fifty-nine—one short of Ruth's record).

However, baseball in the 1960s was a different game from the baseball of the 1920s. "Ruth, not Maris, should have an asterisk," says the baseball columnist Alex Patton. "Anyone who played in the majors before 1947 wasn't competing against the best players available."

Baseball in Ruth's day was a white man's sport; blacks played in the Negro Leagues. The Negro Leagues had outstanding ballplayers, as witnessed by the level of play quickly introduced to the majors by Jackie Robinson, Monte Irvin, Roy Campanella, Ernie Banks, Willie Mays, and Hank Aaron. By not having to play against great players like these, Ruth had an advantage. "Baseball instantly became a better game when blacks were given the opportunity to show their hustle, determination, and smarts to their white peers," says one historian writing about the Negro Leagues.

"Imagine if Maris had faced only white pitchers like Ruth did," says Patton. "He might have hit seventy home runs."

"Add an asterisk next to Babe Ruth's career," says the *New York Post*'s baseball columnist, Mike Vaccaro, "because every one of his 714 home runs was hit against pitchers with white faces." But race was not the only cause for an asterisk. Consider, if you will, the greatest pitching feat of all time in baseball, "a game of inches": Afro-American Bob Gibson's 1968 season, in which he completed twenty-eight out of thirty-four starts and had an ERA of 1.12. Unheard of. Said Joe Torre, later manager of the New York Yankees, "Trying to hit Bob Gibson was like trying to hit a pebble with a piece of string." Gibson was helped by the fact that in those days the pitcher's mound was raised six inches— "as tall as a three-story building," said Torre. "It seemed that way to a lot of hitters."

❧

"I don't believe I ever broke Jim Brown's record," said Walter Payton when he topped Brown's NFL career rushing yards in 1984. "I didn't do it in the amount of time Brown did. I had more games and I played longer. So I didn't break it."

One would expect nothing less of Walter Payton, whose nickname, given to him by his teammates, was "Sweetness." Payton, unlike most sportswriters and fans, was not obsessed with statistics. He easily could have argued that even though he played in more games, for almost his entire career he had played on a losing team and confronted much bigger linemen than Jim Brown did. It didn't matter. What mattered was paying tribute to a great athlete, Jim Brown.

Statistics can take one only so far. Viewed in context—the impossibility of "comparing apples with oranges" (professional sports in an earlier era with the high-powered, big-money sports of today)—most sports records probably need an asterisk of some sort. Just whose record deserves the asterisk is a subject that fuels many a heated beer-party debate among sports fans.

The Warren Commission Botched Up, Big-Time

➤**1964** History gets filtered down to us through the interpretations of many people, including those who were present. One only has to look at the assassination of President Kennedy to see how unreli-

able most witnesses are—victims of the "Rashomon effect" (named for the Japanese story and film *Rashomon*), in which observers of an event offer contradictory but thoroughly plausible accounts of what they saw. To this day, despite several massive investigations and the help of numerous on-site photographs and hundreds of witnesses, many people disagree about how many bullets were fired, from where, or by whom. Yet if the Warren Commission and subsequent historians had used their imaginations and paid closer attention to the number of seconds *before* and *after* Oswald's alleged three shots in 4.6 seconds, they would have figured out how Oswald did it—and put to rest many years of conspiracy theories.

The members of the Warren Commission concluded that JFK had been killed by a lone gunman. But they couldn't figure out how a lone gunman could do the job, nor could they establish any political motive for such a horrendous crime—just that Oswald was a nut with marital problems.

The American people didn't buy it. Since the Kennedy assassination, there has been an outpouring of more than two thousand books and tens of thousands of articles each year, raising more and more conspiracy theories. Compared with 1964, when 56 percent of Americans believed the Warren Report, now 70 percent of the public believes there had to be some kind of conspiracy involved.

"Conspiracy" is what people resort to when they want an easy answer. Professional investigators don't give up so easily.

Had the Warren Commission been more thorough, it would have saved Americans a lot of aggravation.

The Physical Evidence

Forget esoteric conspiracy theories and shadowy "second gunman" figures lurking in the grassy knoll; let's focus on the hard evidence: the Zapruder film. Thanks to the latest computer technology, it is now possible to time the sequences of individual pictures of the film with exact precision.

The key issue dominating the lone-gunman-versus-conspiracy dispute was the issue of timing: how could a man fire three bullets and hit his target twice in just five seconds? The last shot, which almost everyone agreed hit the president's head and caused the fatal wound, appeared on frame 313. Two other bullets were fired, one missing and the other going through Kennedy's throat and Governor Connally's chest. Of the first two shots, everyone figured it was the first shot that hit, and the second one that missed. The reasoning was that firing three shots in a hurry was such a difficult exercise that obviously the most accurate attempt would be the first one,

when the assassin had all the time in the world to get ready and poise his aim.

The time between the two hits—shots one and three—was 4.8 to 5.6 seconds. But the time required to operate the bolt of Oswald's Mannlicher-Carcano rifle was almost 2.3 seconds. This meant that shot number one took place at second 0, shot number two at second 2.3, and shot number three at second 4.6 (actually 4.8 to 5.6). Possible. Likely? No way. Professional Army sharpshooters tried to duplicate the feat and failed to hit two out of three. Critics thereupon scoffed at the Warren Commission's claims that Oswald—no super marksman—could have pulled off such a feat, and looked at possible conspiracy theories of a second gunman.

When lawyer Gerald Posner reexamined the issue in 1993, he took a fresh approach. He rephrased the question: suppose it was the first shot—the "easy" shot—that missed? Under this scenario, the first shot appearing on the Zapruder film, which hit the victims in frames 160–166, was not the first shot but the *second*. This would make the time for the three shots 8.0–8.4 seconds—enough "for even a mediocre shooter to aim and operate the bolt twice."*

---

* Two other factors made the assassination relatively easy to accomplish: the distance, and the behavior of the car. The fuzzy newspaper photographs of the presidential motorcade give the impression of faraway distances, whereas in reality the distances were quite short. When Oswald fired his second shot, the president was only 150 feet away, equivalent to forty-five feet with the aid of a 4X rifle scope. It does not take a super marksman to hit a visual target forty-five feet away. By the time Oswald got off his final shot (the fatal one), Kennedy was 265 feet away (sixty-six feet through the rifle scope). In behavior that defies every rule of presidential security, the limousine driver responded to the second shot by slamming on the brakes to see what was going on. The vehicle came to a virtual halt, thus giving the assassin a stationary target. With four seconds to aim at a target sixty-six visual feet away, Oswald had strong odds in his favor.

The logic is reasonable. Most athletes will admit that the first try, when the whistle blows to start the game, is often sloppy because of nervousness. Only after the first kick/hit/throw do they calm down and become more precise and accurate. The first rifle shot is not the easiest to do—as the unathletic Warren Commission members assumed—it is the hardest. The second and third tries are much easier.

The Motive—Covered Up

Despite the proof of the above numbers, assassinations also need a justifying motive to make them credible. In a letter to the *New York Times* in 1993, William Manchester, author of *Death of a President*, identified the key source of the public's skepticism that Oswald was the sole killer:

> To employ what may seem an odd metaphor, there is an esthetic principle here. If you put six million dead Jews on one side of a scale and on the other side put the Nazi regime—the greatest gang of criminals ever to seize control of a modern state—you have a rough balance: greatest crime, greatest criminals.
>
> But if you put the murdered president of the United States on one side of a scale and that wretched waif Oswald on the other side, it doesn't balance. You want to add something weightier to Oswald. It would invest the president's death with meaning, endowing him with martyrdom. He would have died for something.

> A conspiracy would, of course, do the job nicely.

There *was* a conspiracy involved, but it had nothing to do with the assassination; it had to do with certain government agencies misleading the Warren Commission and the American public. In an intelligence cover-up at the highest levels, the CIA and FBI failed to inform the Warren Commission about John and Robert Kennedy's covert operations to remove Castro. "Such information," the agencies reasoned, "would not contradict the central conclusion and therefore could be, and was, kept secret."

In thinking this information was not important and could be kept secret, the CIA and FBI were astoundingly naïve. Every crime needs a motive, and until there was one, Americans wouldn't believe that a loser like Oswald could have been the lone killer. Twelve years later this Cuba information all came out when Senator Frank Church's Select Committee on Intelligence revealed the anti-Castro plots and the fact that "the CIA and FBI had lied by omission to another arm of government." The conclusion was clear: "The Kennedys' fixation with Castro had inadvertently motivated a political sociopath."

Vietnam: Fudging the Numbers

►**1965** How America got itself involved in the Vietnam War is a topic that stirred much puzzlement at the time, and continues to do so to this day. In February 1962, a three-star general and a new field command called MACV (Military Assistance Command, Vietnam) took over U.S. operations in Vietnam, and proceeded to airlift troops and supplies, build jungle airstrips, coordinate artillery fire and air support, fly helicopter rescue teams, and fight alongside South Vietnamese troops in the field. Attacked at a press conference for being "less than candid with the American people" about the growing involvement in Vietnam, President Kennedy tried to wiggle his way out: "We have not sent combat troops there—in the generally accepted sense of the word. We have increased our training mission and our logistics support."

Many members of the press were not fooled. James Reston identified the key issue and wrote a column about it that day: "The United States is now involved in an undeclared war in South Vietnam," he wrote. "This is well known to the Russians, the Chinese Communists and everyone else concerned except the American people."

What followed were several developments not known to the American people. After the fighting started in earnest in 1965, the U.S. Army found itself overwhelmed trying to cope with the hordes of refugees created by the Army's burning of peasant villages in search of the Vietcong. In 1966 the U.S. Army changed the count from 1.4 million to 268,000 by simply changing categories. When the number of refugees climbed back by the end of 1967, the United States initiated a bold new program that succeeded in reducing the number of refugees to 205,000.

Presto! By abolishing the term "refugee" and substituting a new term, "war victims," the number of refugees dropped dramatically. More distortions were soon to come. In 1967, General Earle Wheeler, chairman of the Joint Chiefs of Staff, received a report of 600,000 Vietnamese troops—far more than the previous estimate of 371,000. Wheeler cabled the report to General William Westmoreland: "If these figures should reach the public domain they would, literally, blow the lid off Washington. Please do whatever is necessary to insure that these figures are not, repeat, not released to news media or otherwise exposed to public knowledge." Shortly afterward, President Lyndon Johnson asked Westmoreland for a status report. Westmoreland told the president that the U.S. had reached the crossover point—which of course was not true. A year later, after receiving more reports promising the same, the president threw up his hands and quit. Let someone else solve this bloody war. Just as George Orwell had predicted in *1984*, a society—the U.S. armed forces in Vietnam—had descended into a "doublethink" world of systemic falsification of reality, in which "body counts," "refugees," and "pacification" took on bizarre meanings.

The charade over body counts never seemed to end. Arthur Goldberg, the U.S. ambassador to the UN, attended one of the briefings and asked how many of the enemy had been killed before Tet. The answer was eighty thousand. With a ten-to-one ratio of wounded to killed, and only 230,000 estimated Vietcong in the field, Goldberg did a quick mental calculation and responded that all the enemy must be either dead or wounded. "Who the hell are we fighting?" he asked. Next day, when General Wheeler admitted that the United States could not achieve a classic military victory in Vietnam, former secretary of state Dean Acheson blew up: "Then what in the name of God do we have five hundred thousand troops out there for? Chasing girls?"

The same obfuscation applied even to the enemy. To hide the number of deaths they were suffering at the hands of the U.S. military, the North Vietnamese Army developed a unique military tool known as the body hook, to quickly drag a dead comrade away from the scene and bury him, before the conquering U.S. soldiers could do their body count. This had the double benefit of denying satisfaction to the enemy and concealing bad news from their own people. When the U.S. left South Vietnam in 1975, the standard assessment of enemy soldiers killed by the U.S. was around 700,000. Twenty years later, in a press release addressed to the Agence France-Presse, the North Vietnamese government admitted that the number of NVA deaths was far greater: 1.1 million. That figure, said the memo, had been "deliberately falsified during the war to avoid demoralizing the population."

❦

For reality to sink in, it should occur in one sharp focal point—like scoring a touchdown or hitting a home run. Everyone notices, whereas continuous two-yard gains or Texas League singles go unnoticed. We all know Hiroshima or Nagasaki, but we know little about our later bomb warfare. American military commanders in Vietnam, making little progress in Vietnam and Cambodia, had every reason to be frustrated. "Bomb 'em back into the Stone Age!" cursed General Curtis LeMay. The only problem was that we did—and it didn't work. From 1965 to 1973 the United States dropped 8 million tons of bombs. By contrast, President Harry Truman, much castigated for dropping the two atom bombs on Hiroshima and Nagasaki, had only used 12,500 tons of bomb power. The ratio of LeMay versus Truman was 640:1. Yet Vietnam to this day is still called "a limited war."

So long as they are the right numbers, statistics—being much more precise—don't lie like words do. Out of Vietnam have emerged a number of left-wing myths that do not stand up to scrutiny. One is that Afro-Americans served in disproportionate numbers and suffered disproportionate deaths. In fact, Afro-

Americans—who made up 12.5 percent of the U.S. population—constituted 10.6 percent of the Americans serving in Vietnam and 12.1 percent of the deaths. Same for the antiwar movement: most of the protesters were objecting not to the war, but to the prospect that they might be drafted. Yet the war was not a massive draft program. Only 25 percent of those who served in Vietnam were drafted; the rest were volunteers.* Contrary to most media stories, Vietnam was probably one of the most democratic wars Americans ever fought in response to Uncle Sam's "We Need You."

Unraveling the Archaeological Mysteries of the *Titanic*

►**1985**   When the ship went down after grazing an iceberg and was described by one survivor as "not a tremendous crash, but more as though someone had drawn a giant finger all along the side of the boat," everyone assumed the cause had been a freakish gash long enough to flood six compartments (i.e., 249 feet long).

What you see is what you see, right? Not always. Numerous movies and books and articles have been written about the *Titanic*—plus two government investigations. You would think that by now everyone would have their basic facts straight.

Yet if anyone had bothered to do the simple mathematics—mathematics you or I could do—he would have realized that there was no way the *Titanic* could sink by scraping an iceberg. Consider: a 249-foot gash would have sunk the ship in thirty minutes. For the ship to stay afloat as long as it did, the gash would have to have been a sliver only three-quarters of an inch from top to bottom along all 249 feet—an impossibility of physics.

Little wonder, then, that when Robert Ballard discovered the wreck seventy-three years later and examined the hull closely, he found no such gash.

In the early 1900s a Cunard sailor named John F. Curtain suggested that the *Titanic* had not struck an iceberg, but had simply self-destructed from the heavy vibrations of her twenty-nine massive boilers, causing hull fatigue. Nobody paid attention to this farfetched theory until 1985, when Robert Ballard observed "very clear evidence of where the plates had 'popped,' leading him to think that the fatal damage was really caused by separation of the plates. This discovery was unexpected." Curtain was wrong in saying there was no iceberg, but he was right to point at the ship's self-destruction.

❧

Question 1. Why Did She Sink So Quickly? Indeed, the real question is not why did the

---

* This is in sharp contrast to our "good" war, World War II, in which two-thirds were drafted, and only one-third were volunteers.

Titanic sink, but why did she sink so fast? Only by examining how the ship could sink so quickly can one begin to surmise how the "unsinkable" ship could sink at all. This, remember, was a ship designed to stay afloat for three days under the worst possible adverse conditions. Yet she survived less than three hours in a situation where none of the night watchmen saw huge icebergs, and where the only noise heard by any of the crew or passengers was "a thud": obviously, something terrible and unexpected had gone wrong. What was it?

To figure this out, look again at the evidence. It doesn't take much to sink a big ship. In his testimony before the 1912 British Board of Inquiry, *Titanic* naval architect Edward Wilding had said all that was required was an aggregate of holes totaling "somewhere about twelve square feet."

The underwater square footage of the *Titanic*, at 850 feet length times 15 feet height times two sides, works out to be 25,500 square feet. Divide Wilding's estimate of twelve square feet by 25,500, and you get 0.0005, or $\frac{1}{20}$ of one percent. Because of the watertight bulkheads, these 12 square feet couldn't be in one place, but in several. Stated Wilding, "I cannot believe that the wound was absolutely continuous the whole way. I believe it was a series of steps." Obviously he had to be right. But nobody believed him, and so the public hung on the fantastic image of the gash (just like a conspiracy—very dramatic: imagine the side of the *Titanic* as one long zipper).

Eight decades later, Wilding was proven correct. In 1996 a Discovery Channel expedition—the first expedition devoted solely to marine forensics—visited the site. Using the modern technology of sonar imaging to analyze the starboard side of the wreck buried under fifty-five feet of sediment (caused by the hull crashing to the bottom of a 12,500-foot plunge at thirty-five miles per hour), the scientists identified six openings, total damage size 11.4 square feet.

Now look at the picture on the next page.

Any one of these plates is a lot bigger than 12 or 11.4 square feet. It doesn't take much to make several of these plates separate when a collision occurs and the vital forces consist of the enormous weight of a ship times its 25-knot speed times the counterweight of an immovable iceberg times the water resistance of the ocean when the two objects collide. We're talking big numbers here.

Several recent books on the *Titanic* have posited various theories implying criminal liability by the White Star Line for building a ship allegedly unsafe because it had brittle steel and hand-driven rivets. They ignore the fact that no ship—not even a ship today—could survive this one-in-a-million coincidence that happened on April 14, 1912. Simple probability theory tells you that when you have thousands and thousands of ships crossing

Would you entrust your life to this ship? The Titanic *starboard bow plates where the ice hit.*

dangerous oceans, anything can happen— and eventually will (which is why we will always have airplane crashes in the years ahead, no matter how hard the airlines and governments try to make flying 100-percent safe). "Standard operating procedure," says historian Daniel Allen Butler, "is a disaster waiting to happen."

"God himself could not sink this ship," its makers had said. The *Titanic* boasted an array of safety features never seen before on the high seas: a double hull, sixteen watertight compartments, and an electrical system that could close every door simultaneously. The *Titanic* was an impressive ship, but God moves in strange ways.

Question 2. Why was it so hard to find the wreck? As the *Titanic* floundered, it gave out its CQD (Come Quick, Danger) position as 41°50'N, 50°14'W. For seventy-three years people used this reckoning to try to locate the underwater wreck, with no luck.

When the wreck finally was found, the location was 41°43.9'N, 49°58.8'W— some thirteen miles away. Yet the fact remains that on that morning of April 15, 1912, when the *Carpathia* arrived at the site of the lifeboats, one of the first things the rescuing captain said to the *Titanic*'s fourth officer was: "What a splendid position you gave us!"

How can a huge ship sink two and a half miles and end up thirteen miles away? One answer: a lot can happen in seventy-three years. The ocean is not static, nor is the seabed a peaceful place. The Gulf Stream moves at the rate of 0.5 to 0.8 knots. If the *Titanic* remained intact as it sank—a view stated by *Titanic*'s surviving officers—it probably had plenty of trapped air and drifted eastward under the effect of the earth's rotation, a phenomenon known in marine geology as Coriolis force (this is why, for example, the ocean's surface is a slope, not flat— causing water in the mid-Atlantic to be forty-eight inches higher than the water on the Atlantic seacoast). Finally, on November 18, 1929, there occurred a huge underwater earthquake that generated a two-hundred-mile tsunami, causing massive destruction to the coast of Newfoundland. "Such an underwater force," suggests one marine expert, "more than likely moved the *Titanic*'s wreckage from its resting place, some miles east of the CQD position, to the one discovered by Dr. Ballard."

Such a theory seems farfetched. The *Titanic*'s passengers, disagreeing with the officers, testified that the ship broke in half as it slipped beneath the surface. This would have eliminated any trapped air that might cause Coriolis drift. Also, the ship's massive boilers were found outside the ship, resting nearby. Such boilers are so heavy they would have plummeted straight down after breaking loose from the hull. Clearly the ship landed very close to where it went down.

How, then, to explain the discrepancy between the two locations? Obviously the CQD position was wrong. But if the position was wrong, how did the *Carpathia* find the lifeboats? Pure luck. When the *Carpathia* arrived at the scene, with all the excitement and confusion going on, it did not bother to take a fix to determine its actual position (certainly no such evidence was presented at the post-sinking official inquiry). In the meantime, during the two hours since the sinking, the *Titanic*'s lifeboats, carried by the prevailing ocean currents, had drifted four miles south of the sinking site, directly into the path of the *Carpathia*, coming up from the southeast toward the position given out by the *Titanic*. In his relief at finding the lifeboats, it is easy to understand how the *Carpathia*'s captain would say, "What a splendid position you gave us!"

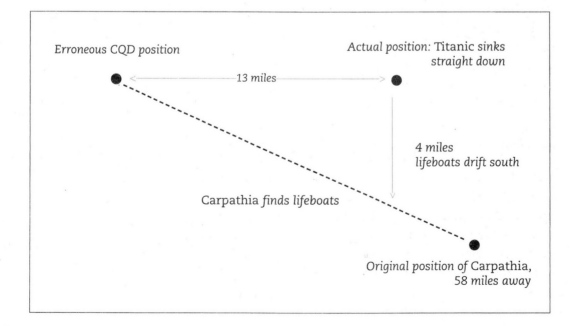

Erroneous CQD position

Actual position: Titanic sinks straight down

13 miles

4 miles
lifeboats drift south

Carpathia *finds lifeboats*

Original position of Carpathia,
58 miles away

If the *Titanic* was thirteen miles away from where it was thought to be, how did Robert Ballard manage to find it? "Thinking outside the box," he answers. Like Patrick Blackett who solved the problem of how to attack the German U-boats, Ballard understood that easier than finding the ship was to look for any of the numerous pieces of debris, then follow the path of the debris.

Question 3. What Happened to the Bodies? After Robert Ballard came back from discovering the *Titanic*, he was besieged with questions about where the bodies were. Strange thing is, he couldn't find any.

The answer to the question is, nobody knows. How can human bodies simply disappear in the deep of the ocean? Skulls and teeth are pretty indestructible, and you would think that some traces of bones and skulls would be found on the smooth sea bottom where the *Titanic* rests. After all, small glasses and silverware were found easily. Even pairs of shoes. In fact, one pair of shoes rests on the sea bottom just as if someone had laid them down perfectly.

Except that there is no way two matching shoes would end up two and a half miles down, where a thunderous underwater maelstrom broke a mighty ship in half, exactly six inches apart. This is a history book, not an anthropology book, so we let you, dear reader, figure out the answer. There was a man in those shoes once.

The Magic Number of U.S. Troops Needed to Win Iraq

Better to let them do it imperfectly than to do it perfectly yourself, for it is their country, their war, and your time is short.

—Lawrence of Arabia

►**2020** Ten years from now, people may look back and find themselves repeating the 1950s question, "Who lost China?"—only this time the country is Iraq. They would point to the fact that the United States didn't have enough troops to provide sufficient security and quell the insurrection. They may ask why President Bush and Secretary of Defense Rumsfeld failed to heed the warnings of the Army chief of staff, General Eric Shinseki, who had predicted the number of necessary soldiers to be "something on the order of several hundred thousand."

Such is history taken out of context, the use of history for political ends. The instinct of every general is to ask for more troops than he needs, just to be on the safe side (witness McClellan during the Civil War). When General Shinseki appeared before the Senate Armed Services Committee in 2003 and was asked how many troops would be needed for the impending operation, he responded in vague generalities ("several hundred thousand"), and refused to be more specific, for the simple reason that he had no idea what would happen any more than Donald

Rumsfeld did. The senator who asked Shinseki the question was a liberal Democrat who had voted against the war resolution and presumably was looking for whatever political ammunition he could find; yet he chose not to pursue Shinseki. With the war about to start in another month, everyone's attention was focused on how to overcome Saddam's powerful army. The general calling the shots was not Shinseki, but Tommy Franks, head of Central Command. Because of concern for civilian casualties and the prospect that Saddam might try to blow up the oil fields as a last hurrah, General Franks resolved to capture Baghdad as quickly as possible. This required a light fighting force, which Franks determined to be 175,000 men, not a huge force of 300,000–400,000 with cumbersome supply lines and logistics. Certainly he knew Shinseki's opinion—and he overruled him. (He also overruled other generals who argued for a smaller force.)

It was a daring gamble, and it worked, resulting in a military rout even more stunning than General Norman Schwarzkopf's victory in the 1991 Gulf War. The "how many troops?" naysayers held their tongue and President Bush landed on an aircraft carrier proclaiming "Mission Accomplished." All along, the U.S. strategy had been to win the war quickly and get out quickly, and not get involved in the messy business of nation-building and risk becoming labeled as "occupiers." Said Donald Rumsfeld, "We are going to go in, overthrow Saddam, get out. That's it." Iraq was to be a war of liberation, not occupation. "Time," as T. E. Lawrence had warned, "is short."

The subsequent looting and total breakdown of civil order in Iraq caught everyone by surprise, not only the Defense Department but also the State Department, the National Security Council, and the CIA—none of whom had envisioned such a contingency and prepared a plan for it.* "The 'plan' was to be out of Iraq by the end of August," admitted one staffer. At the time when Saddam's statue fell in April, this seemed like a reasonable assumption.

But hopes and objectives do not make a plan; alternative scenarios also need to be developed, especially a worst-case one. "Better forty years of dictatorship than one year of anarchy" goes an Arab proverb. Despite this warning, serious contingency planning for anarchy was never done, not even by the State Department. Said General Colin Powell in a rueful admission after the fact, "A judgment was made by those responsible that the troop strength was adequate." Even Saddam Hussein— who presumably knew Iraq better than

---

* This stands in sharp contrast to FDR's administration. In planning for the occupation of postwar Germany, for example, the U.S. Army prepared a 400-page manual and followed it to the letter. On the other extreme is America in World War I: it didn't even have a battle plan, let alone a postwar plan. It sent General John J. Pershing to France with 300,000 troops and basically told him, "Start fighting!"

anyone—was stunned by the magnitude of the collapse and ensuing anarchy.

The following statistics of American occupations may be instructive. Certainly it was all the U.S. military planners had to go on:

Number of U.S. Soldiers per 1,000 Inhabitants

Germany	1945–50	100
Japan	1945–51	5
Balkans	1998–2003	20
Afghanistan	2003–	**1**
Iraq	2003–	**7**

All the first three occupations were successful.

But every situation is unique, and none of these experiences necessarily applied to Iraq, a country in far worse shape than anyone thought. If Kosovo were used as a model, 500,000 troops were needed to secure Iraq. But the United States did not have 500,000 troops, so this number could not be the "magic number." Nor could it be 2.5 million troops, following the German example. Whatever the number, Iraq would have to conform to American reality, not the other way around.

In the end, it may be that there was no magic number. In a 2006 *Time* magazine cover story on the chaos in Baghdad, journalist Aparisim Ghosh wrote, "Conventional military tactics don't work in an asymmetrical conflict. Sheer numbers and firepower count for very little."

NINE

Not What You Think

Sometimes, I am not sure of what I absolutely know is so!

—Richard Rodgers and Oscar Hammerstein,
The King and I

H ere is a story that appears regularly in history books:

He was only one of many men who gambled everything they had for the cause of freedom. Thomas Nelson, educated at Eton and Cambridge University, returned home to Virginia to take over the family plantation, sign the Declaration of Independence, and succeed Thomas Jefferson as governor of Virginia. Appointed commander of the Virginia militia, he provided the money to supply and arm his soldiers. At the Battle of York-town, where his Virginia militia provided a third of the rebel army, he recommended to Washington that they unload artillery fire upon a stately house that Cornwallis had made his military headquarters. "Whose house is that?" Washington asked.

"Sir, it is my house," Nelson replied.

Nelson lost everything, not just his house. After the fighting stopped, Nelson was unable to repay the $2 million in debts he had incurred arming his men, and his political enemies in the Virginia legislature re-fused to indemnify him, even though George Washington had written, "To Governor Nelson, the highest praises are due." His health failing,

Nelson with his wife and eleven children moved to a small farm where he died eight years later. He was so poor that his sons were forced to bury him secretly in an unmarked grave, lest his ˙creditors seize his body as collateral for their unpaid loans. Yet despite his riches-to-rags saga, he never regretted his efforts in the Revolutionary War. "I would do it all over again," he told a friend.

A wonderful story, except it's too good to be true. It was presented this way on the Internet, where so many unchecked facts appear, to get people feeling patriotic. But not for long: within days, history bloggers cleared the air with their more extensive research on what actually happened.

Go back to the story and read again: do you really think a patriot so esteemed by George Washington could be sabotaged and abandoned like this? Hard to believe.

Obviously there is more to the story. Nelson's colleagues knew full well he had been "gilding the lily"—and they didn't like it. The house being shelled was not his house, but his uncle's. The artillery firing on the house was not Washington's, but the French artillery's (which Washington and Nelson had no control over). The house was not demolished, it was only grazed, and it stands today, fully restored and open to the public as part of the Colonial National Historical Park. While it is true that Nelson was cash-poor and flat broke, so, too, were Washington, Jefferson, and just about every other Southern patriot. Nelson died as one of the largest landowners in Virginia, and regardless of how his dead body was disposed of by his sons, after all the debts were paid, they still managed to inherit several plantations.

That Thomas Nelson was a true patriot, there is no doubt. But there is no need to embellish the story with myth—the story is powerful enough as it is. One of the reasons Thomas Jefferson and John Adams spent much of their waning years writing to each other was to set the record straight and leave a written record of what had actually happened during the Revolution. They recognized the "distinction between history as experienced and history as remembered." If they neglected to put down on paper what they had experienced, later historians might be tempted to add layers of fiction to make a better, but not quite accurate, story. According to the historian Joseph Ellis, "Adams realized that the act of transforming the American Revolution into history placed a premium on selecting events and heroes that fit neatly into a dramatic formula, thereby distorting the more tangled and incoherent experience that participants actually making the history felt at the time."

❧

"History," said Tolstoy, "would be an excellent thing if only it were true."

The use of history as propaganda is

widespread—"the invention of tradition," Eric Hobsbawm called it. American history books for young children extol the revolution of the thirteen colonies against a tyrannical British empire. In fact, the colonies were essentially ruled by small cliques of white Protestants and wealthy landowners. The "free" society was not found in the colonies, it was found in England. Women in England had more rights than women in the colonies; Catholics and religious minorities also had more rights, and slavery was already illegal.

Or take the Boston Tea Party. We all know the image of patriots dressed up as Indians throwing crates of tea overboard. A great panorama, but it misses a deeper, more interesting "real" story. The patriots did not dress up as Indians so they could whoop and holler while they performed their task. To the contrary, they were obsessively secret and quiet about it all. They deliberately recruited fifty youths who didn't know one another, painted their faces so they couldn't recognize one another lest they chirp when subsequently interrogated by the British, and told them to keep their bloody mouths shut. They waited until low tide, so the boxes wouldn't make a lot of racket splashing into the water. When the boxes landed on the sand or in shallow water beside the ships, the youths stomped on the tea to make it unusable. And they instructed that no "collateral damage" be done whatsoever. Explained one participant, "Entire silence prevailed, no clamor,

no talking. Nothing was meddled with but the teas on board. Having emptied the whole, the deck was swept clean, and everything put in its proper place. An officer on board was requested to come up from the cabin and see that no damage was done except to the tea."

When the angry British tried to round up the "terrorist" rebels, they couldn't find anybody; they had vanished. All in all, a masterfully planned guerrilla operation, one rarely equaled by the U.S. military in more than two hundred years. Is not this brilliant operation more interesting than the patriotic superficiality of most books? Is it not more germane to the first-year teachings of our cadets at West Point?

In the early 1980s, Americans were transfixed by the TV miniseries *Roots*, the epic story of Alex Haley's maternal ancestors' progress from Africa to American slavery to the present. It all made for an engrossing story—but not altogether accurate. One wishes Haley had had the courtesy, in relating the story of his mother's ancestry, to tell us something about his father's side of the family. Going back twelve generations, he would have arrived not in Gambia but in Ireland.

Before we rush to conclusions that may be unwarranted, it pays to observe carefully. What we think we see or understand, may not be so. Said cowboy actor Will Rogers, "It ain't what you don't know that hurts you. It's what you do know that ain't so!" In the 1800s, the regional coalition that constituted half the states of America met to discuss their growing desire to secede from the national government in Washington. In a dispute over the overriding issue of the day, there could be no reconciliation; despite the coalition's desire not to have to go to war, the national government, headed by a strong-minded president, seemed determined in its point of view, even to the point of hostilities. The tension got so bad that many states felt they had no choice but to leave the Union and set up an independent republic.

It didn't happen. We are talking not about the Civil War, but about New England in 1812. The issue was whether to go to war against Britain. New England was antiwar, but finally relented and joined President James Madison and the congressional leaders such as Henry Clay who wanted war.

Another example of rushing to conclusions concerns the military contribution of Afro-Americans. In one particular war, laws in America forbade blacks to bear arms, though they were perfectly free to serve in the military as cooks, gravediggers, and other menial functions. America's commander-in-chief, careful about such distinctions and nervous about arming former slaves, refused to accept them into his army. As a result, hundreds of them signed up with the enemy. Caught by surprise that Afro-Americans were fighting on the side of the British, General George Washington changed his mind and started recruiting them at the end of 1775. The result was many hundreds of badly needed recruits.

Before we say, "Oh yes, I know what you're talking about," it pays to listen and observe carefully, lest we be fooled. This was the mistake made by the Germans at a critical moment in World War II. They were so impressed by one American general, and followed him so closely, that they ignored warning signals that General George Patton was not the one who would be the commanding general of the invasion of France. As a result, they were completely fooled when General Eisenhower landed at Normandy.

Still another example of narrow-mindedness: We think we (the United States) won World War II, right? Wrong, it was one of our allies that did most of the fighting. By looking at our past from our own narrow perspective, we often miss out on the truth. In any endeavor, it pays to look at all the evidence carefully. Often the clues can be quite basic. Take Pearl Harbor, for example. Hundreds of books have been written about the debacle, seeking a rational answer to how America, despite numerous hints and intercepted messages, could be caught so flat-footed. More important than the narrow Watergate-style question "What did FDR know and when did he know it?" is the character of the man himself. Back in 1923, "writing with the authoritativeness of one who had been assistant secretary of the navy," FDR had written an article for *Asia* magazine in which he argued that it was "technologically impossible for Japan to attack America's Pacific coast."

The Bible says, "He hath ears but he hear not, he hath eyes but he see not." Consider the strange case of Lyndon Johnson, former antiwar congressman. In 1954, Secretary of State John Foster Dulles arranged a private meeting with eight key congressional leaders to inform them that President Eisenhower wanted congressional approval to send military support to the French, who were about to lose Indochina. The congressmen, anxious to avoid another Korea, asked a spate of questions about whether this would mean another war, and how much it would cost. One congressman, the leader of the group, was particularly adamant and argued that America should not go it alone if no other allies would join America in supporting the French. Upon his urging, the group of eight congressmen turned down the president's request. They would not go to war.

Ten years later this man who kept us out of Vietnam would become president and plunge America into full-scale hostilities.*

Such are the surprises of history. But equally surprising is the present, the new global world the United States now lives in. Consider how the rest of the world disagrees with Americans in rating our greatest presidents. In the United States, Lincoln consistently ranks number one.

But travel abroad, and one sees that it is Washington the doer, the man who overthrew a colonial power, who is revered. There is no statue of Abraham Lincoln in cities outside the United States (except in London). But go to London, Paris, Buenos Aires, Rio de Janeiro, Budapest, and Tokyo, and you will find statues of the founder of our country. His achievement is the one the world celebrates.

Muzzling the Radical

►**1787** The members of the Constitutional Convention had a problem: the elderly Benjamin Franklin, who had the unfortunate habit of speaking his mind whenever he felt like it. Whereas Thomas Jefferson and James Madison were always reasonably circumspect in their words, here they had a loose cannon.

Jefferson, in a moment of reflection, had gone on record that a new constitutional convention might be necessary every twenty years or so. His fellow constitutional delegates, struggling in the heat of a long Philadelphia summer to produce a lasting document, were less than thrilled. Cool it, they told Jefferson, and so Jefferson never said a further word about what would have been the most in-

---

* Obviously something happened to LBJ over the next ten years, though exactly what has to be one of the great mysteries of history. One warning signal of his abrupt about-face occurred in 1961, when he took a diplomatic trip to meet President Ngo Dinh Diem, and came back with this impression: "Diem is the Winston Churchill of Southeast Asia."

teresting insight of the entire summer (our loss, certainly). But worse was still to come. From Benjamin Franklin they heard that "our people would drift into so deep a corruption that only despots could rule them."

Horrors! Standing high in the name of righteousness, the Convention members ordered that Franklin be followed at all times, and be accompanied by a chaperone to "make sure he held his tongue."

So much for free speech in the founding of America. Political correctness was the byword even then.

Alternative to War: Hard Cash

➤**1860** The weeks after Lincoln's election found the nation adrift. In the intolerable five-month interregnum between Lincoln's election and taking of office the following March—that's how long it was in those days—radicals were pounding the war drums. South Carolina, followed by Kentucky and Alabama, were making loud noises to secede. The victorious Republicans, committed to the moral evil of slavery, failed to take the secession threat seriously. As James G. Blaine noted, it was as if the Republicans, having gained the object of their efforts, were surprised and aghast at the reaction their success had produced. "We all dealt in a fool's Paradise," lamented Charles Francis Adams, a leading Republican. All people, he said,

were "of average blindness. . . . We knew nothing of the South, and had no realizing sense of the intensity of feeling which there prevailed; we fully believed it would all end in gasconade"—i.e., bluster and hot air.

Even Lincoln, sitting home in Illinois and out of touch with the mood of the South, viewed secession as the talk of a few hotheads. When South Carolina seceded on December 20, he dismissed the news as "loud threats and muttering."

Into the foray stepped the most senior member of the Senate, John Crittenden of Kentucky. First elected to the Senate back in 1825, Crittenden had served as governor, U.S. attorney general under three presidents, and four-term senator. If peace had its chance, it had found its man.

Like everyone else, Crittenden knew slavery was a dying institution. Its demise was inevitable. What the South needed was time: more time for the inefficiencies of slavery to work their way through the economy. "The peaceful laws of trade may do the work which agitation has attempted in vain," he observed. Because the North was much wealthier than the South, the obvious solution was for the North to buy out the slaves. Indeed, such a "buyout" was the solution proposed by Henry Clay in 1850. Clay's proposal got nowhere, but remained on the table for Northerners to consider as a last resort.

Under the Crittenden Compromise, slavery would be preserved south of the 1820 Missouri Compromise line of 36°30' latitude while cooler heads prevailed and tried to work out appropriate compensation for the slaves. The idea was that the longer the talks dragged on, the more isolated the Deep South states would become. But such a compromise would have included the new state of New Mexico (though everyone knew the arid land of New Mexico would never support a cotton plantation). The president-elect—in the most momentous decision of his presidency—rejected it out of hand. "Have none of it, stand firm," he said. So out the window went the best chance for peace, though in the meantime hundreds of petitions supporting Crittenden's plan had descended on Congress. Observed Horace Greeley, "If a popular vote could have been had on the Crittenden Compromise, it would have prevailed by an overwhelming majority." All the Southern states agreed to Crittenden's proposal, but the victorious Lincoln Republicans—acting as if they had a mandate when they most assuredly did not—refused to support it and filibustered it to death. Even William Seward, the number-two Republican and the leader of the moderates, went apoplectic: "Not one word said to disarm prejudice and passion . . . mad men North and mad men South, are working together to produce a dissolution of the Union by civil war." In the Senate, one day before Lincoln's inauguration, Crittenden's proposal lost to the mad men, nineteen to twenty.

In his inaugural address, believing there would be no civil war, Lincoln gave the seceding states an ultimatum: rejoin the Union, or fight. He miscalculated. When he sent relief supplies to Fort Sumter, the South took this as a provocation and launched shells at the fort. No lives were lost. But Lincoln treated it as a declaration of war and called up 75,000 soldiers for ninety days, and so the fighting started. The four Upper South states, led by Virginia and North Carolina, refusing the president's order to invade the Deep South, made the fateful choice to secede.

The result was the loss of 558,000 lives and a hundred years of hostility between North and South. Was it worth it? At 2 million slaves at four hundred dollars apiece, the $9-billion Civil War cost more than eleven times what it would have cost for the U.S. government of the North to simply indemnify the Southern plantation owners for their slaves and give each Afro-American family "40 acres and a mule."

Ironically enough, Lincoln himself eventually came around to the idea of a buyout. In 1862, with the war dragging out a lot longer than the expected ninety days, he offered a buyout for Delaware, Maryland, Kentucky, Missouri, and Washington DC at the rate of four hundred dollars per slave for 432,622 slaves. Lincoln calculated that the $173,048,800—compared with the war's daily cost of $2 million—was a bargain "nearly equal to the estimated $174 million needed to wage war for eighty-seven days." But by then, with the war in full fury and the

Might the rebellion have been avoided?

South having won most of the battles, it was too late. Still, Lincoln did not give up. A month later he succeeded in signing a law outlawing slavery in the District of Columbia and paying slave owners three hundred dollars per slave. Washington DC was the only place in the United States where compensated emancipation took place. Then, in early 1865, as the war was winding down, Lincoln considered using compensated emancipation as a means of shortening the war. Calculating that the war was costing $4 million a day, he drafted a proposal to Congress to pay the South $400 million as compensation for the economic loss of their slaves, in return for immediate cessation of hostilities. Lincoln shared his draft with his Cabinet members, but they all objected, so Lincoln dropped the idea.

Today, buyouts are a common practice in helping institutions rearrange their workforce to cope with new economic and political realities. Might not hard cash, given cooler heads in the 1860 Republican Party, have avoided a bloodbath?

Unpopular War

➤**1863**   The war was of no direct interest to the vast majority of the population: why go fight and get shot at? Especially when wealthier young men could get an exemption and stay home to pursue professions considered vital to the national interest. People complained bitterly about how it was becoming "a rich man's war but a poor man's fight." As the number of casualties escalated to more than a quarter million, the war became so unpopular that many citizens considered revolting against the government and leaving the country.

In the year of an upcoming presidential election that would serve as a referendum on whether the war should be continued, further hostilities were opposed by as much as 80 percent of the population. The U.S. president up for reelection faced daunting prospects, and had to contend with peace demonstrations and draft riots in the streets.

By 1864, alienation from the Confederate government and its zeal to preserve slavery had reached overwhelming proportions. Whites made up only 60 percent of the South's population, and only 5.5 percent of them owned slaves. Slave owners who held more than twenty slaves automatically were exempted from the draft. For the Confederate government of Jefferson Davis to wage a costly, deadly war for the benefit of this rich minority, was not popular. In addition to widespread demonstrations, riots in Richmond, and massive desertions, many Southerners carried out guerrilla operations against the state and offered active military support to the enemy. One state, for practical purposes, went over to the other side (West Virginia). The 40 percent of the population held in slavery posed a continual threat of massive internal insurrection.

The Civil War is always seen as a war between the North and the South. This is a mistaken impression. The war was really between the North and the Confederate administration that ruled the South.

The Two Generals Who Ended the Civil War

➤**1865**   Not Lee and Grant, but Johnston and Sherman.

"Ending a war," wrote the late historian Barbara Tuchman, "is a difficult and delicate business. Each side must become convinced at the same time and with equal certainty that its war aim is either not achievable or not worth the cost. The certainty must be equal, for if one side perceives a slight advantage or disadvantage it will not offer terms acceptable to the other." For Lee and Grant, ending the war was easy. The Army of Northern Virginia, starving for food and down to fifteen thousand muskets and sabers, was being hunted down by eighty thousand well-armed, well-fed federal troops. Lee,

General Joseph Johnston

General William Sherman

of Joseph Johnston, the man rated by Grant as the South's best general.

Then came the assassination, just five days after Appomattox. Whatever peace deal was in the cards went out the window. Terrified Northern mobs rampaged through the streets screaming, "Conspiracy! Revenge!" The acting chief of the Union in the heat of emergency and near panic was not Vice President Andrew Johnson but the bellicose secretary of war, Edwin Stanton, acting as "president, secretary of war, secretary of state, commander in chief, comforter, and dictator." To such a man, in an obviously apoplectic state of mind, anarchy loomed: the

although imbued with deep Southern chivalry about noble sacrifice, wasn't about to contemplate unnecessary mass deaths. Nor was Grant, who, exhausted by victories that had cost the North so many lives he was being called "the butcher," felt it was time to stop.

Lee may have been the head general of the Confederacy, but he did not have control of all his generals, especially when President Jefferson Davis wanted to launch a guerrilla war and fight it out for another twenty years. In surrendering to Grant, Lee was surrendering only the Northern Virginia army. Still out in the field were several other armies, under the leadership hated Confederacy had a president who wouldn't concede and who had at his disposal several armies ready to hole up in the mountains of Tennessee and Georgia and fight on for years. The reputation of these cavalry generals was legendary. Already Jeb Stuart, John Mosby, John Hood, and Nathan Bedford Forrest had wreaked havoc with their hit-and-run raids on the Union forces. Forrest, in particular, was so successful that William Tecumseh Sherman had ordered an expedition to flush him out "to the death, if it costs ten thousand lives and bankrupts the treasury." And for good reason: in the summer of 1862, with a force of only 2,500 men, Forrest had pinned down a forty-thousand-man Union army, sixteen times his size. Rampaging through Alabama, Mississippi, and Tennessee, Forrest regularly defeated Union forces twice his size. "There will never be peace until Forrest is dead!" said an exasperated Sherman.

Forget the meeting of two gentlemen generals at Appomattox, the war had now taken an ugly turn. Stanton and Grant turned to the only man who could save the situation: the ruthless William T. Sherman, the general the South hated—and feared—the most.

The man he had to deal with—his only hope for a quick resolution—was the commander of the Army of Tennessee who had beaten him at Kennesaw Mountain, General Joseph Johnston.

The two adversaries now met, the former victor representing the losing side, the former loser the winning side. They conducted private negotiations at a shabby roadside house and barn known as Bennett Place, and developed a lifelong admiration for each other. The deal they worked out was a perfect example of generals having more common sense than politicians about how to achieve peace.

Both generals had their hands tied, being under orders from their respective presidents to reject any proposals that would define civilian peace terms. But Johnston attempted an end-run around Jefferson Davis by proposing that all of the Confederate armies surrender, and Sherman attempted an end-run around Andrew Johnson by accepting this proposal and offering peace terms even more generous than Appomattox to make it stick. "The point to which I attach most importance," he wrote to the Army chief of staff, "is that the dispersement and disbandment of these armies is done in a manner as to prevent their breaking into guerrilla bands."

The civilian superiors on both sides went ballistic. Andrew Johnson and Edward Stanton sent an embarrassed Grant to see his friend Sherman and tell him to renege on the deal, and Jefferson Davis ordered Johnston to resume fighting. Johnston refused. Instead, he and Sherman reconvened at Bennett Place, and finally came up with a document that Sherman could get his government to sign. Ignoring Jefferson Davis, Johnston urged his own men and the other Confederate generals to "observe faithfully the terms of pacifi-

Here at Bennett Place—not at Appomattox—is where the Civil War finally ended

cation agreed upon; and to discharge the obligations of good and peaceful citizens. . . . By such a course, you will best secure the comfort of your families and kindred, and restore tranquility to our country." To Sherman he wrote, "The enlarged patriotism exhibited in your orders reconciles me to what I have previously regarded as the misfortune of my life, that of having to encounter you in the field."*

Over the next thirty days the other Confederate generals all agreed to lay down their arms and the unrepentant Jefferson Davis was captured and put in prison. The war, finally, was now over.

The Cruel South

➤**1870** Only 30 percent of blacks could read and write. The reason for this, for some strange reason, has never been publicized. Yet it is all very obvious and simple.

Most of the Southern states during slavery had laws prohibiting anyone from teaching slaves to read and write. The results could be brutal. One of the most brilliant black scientists, Percy Julian (1899–1975), was the inventor of cortisone and other valuable drugs. Julian recalled the days of discrimination when he left the cotton fields of Alabama for De-

---

* In an interesting bit of historical irony, the two generals who ended the Civil War also died together. In 1891, standing in the rain as a pallbearer at Sherman's funeral, Johnston caught pneumonia and died.

Pauw University, from which he graduated Phi Beta Kappa, and Harvard University, from which he graduated with top honors. As he left home to enroll at De-Pauw, "there stood his ninety-nine-year-old grandmother, who once had picked a record 350 pounds in one day; his grandfather, waving a hand from which two fingers were missing—cut off because his master discovered he had learned to write."

Did He Really Say It?

➤**1882** Every day brought William Vanderbilt, the world's richest man, stacks of hate mail, pleas for money from strangers, and dubious business deals from acquaintances. When he graciously gave an interview at the end of a tiring afternoon, he got goaded into uttering his infamous epithet, "The public be damned!" From then on he was cast into the irons of history as the penultimate cold-blooded robber baron.

But did he really say it? Or did he get goaded by a pestering reporter into saying words that, taken out of context, look intemperate? Read the interview carefully and judge for yourself:

Reporter: Why are you going to stop his fast mail train?

Vanderbilt: Because it doesn't pay. I can't run a train as far as this permanently at a loss.

Reporter: But the public finds it very convenient and useful. You ought to accommodate them.

Vanderbilt: The public? How do you know they find it useful? How do you know, or how can I know, that they want it? If they want it, why don't they patronize it and make it pay? That's the only test I have of whether a thing is wanted—does it pay? If it doesn't pay, I suppose it isn't wanted.

Reporter: Mr. Vanderbilt, are you working for the public or for your stockholders?

Vanderbilt: The public be damned! I am working for my stockholders! If the public wants the train, why don't they support it?

Many years later, another corporate tycoon got hoisted onto the Pillar of Arrogance for a similar statement. The man was Charles E. Wilson, chief executive of General Motors and author of the infamous quote "What's good for General Motors is good for the country."

But that's not exactly what he said. Nominated by President Eisenhower in 1953 to be his secretary of defense, Wilson was in Washington DC for his confirmation hearings before the Senate Armed Services Committee. Wilson was asked if he would sell all his GM stock, worth a considerable sum; Wilson reluctantly agreed to do so. In the course of several heated exchanges between Wilson and the senators on this point, Wilson was asked if, as secretary of defense, he would ever make a decision adverse to the interests of GM. Wilson responded yes, sure he would, but went on to say that he could not conceive of such a situation "because for years we at General Motors have always felt that what was good for the country was good for General Motors as well."

Juicy sound bites have always been red meat for hostile media lions. Like Henry Ford, who got nailed for saying "history is bunk," Wilson was the victim of having his words taken out of context: "gotcha!" Certainly he meant well: he was speaking as a patriot, not as a corporate bully. After winning confirmation, he went on to be probably the toughest secretary of defense of the twentieth century, constantly battling with the military—and with the big defense contractors like GM—for reduced defense expenditures. When he left, nearly everyone agreed he had worked for what was best for the country.

In 2009, General Motors careened into bankruptcy and had to plead to Congress for repeated bailouts. Its car sales were down 40 percent—but so were almost everyone else's, including the German, South Korean, and Japanese car companies. The major problem was not GM making bad cars, but the financial collapse affecting all of America. Because the economy had tanked, nobody could get the bank credit they needed to purchase any car—not just a GM car. Sixty

years after Wilson had made his statement, he was proven right: what's good for the U.S. is good for General Motors as well.

Freemen Yet Slaves Under "Abe" Lincoln's Son

►**1904** The largest employer of blacks in the late nineteenth and first half of the twentieth century was the Pullman Company, the largest hotel chain in the United States—its rooms being on moving railroad cars. The company insisted that all its porters be black because they would be subservient and provide exemplary service to white passengers traveling in Pullman's luxurious cabins. To his credit, George Pullman opened the way for hundreds of thousands of blacks for the first time to earn a steady living, save money, and enter the American middle class. But he paid them low wages and forced them to rely solely on tips (to ensure full customer service). Working hours—away from home for weeks on end—were long and brutal, often involving only three to four hours of sleep a night.

When employees went on strike in 1894 seeking better wages and working conditions, Pullman crushed them, making it clear he tolerated no dissent. It left such a bad residue of ill will that Pullman, on his deathbed in 1897, feared angry employees might try to dig up and mutilate his body. He instructed that his coffin be lined with lead, then wrapped in tarpaper, covered with quick-drying asphalt, then covered with another layer of concrete reinforced with heavy steel rails interlocked at right angles, and buried ten feet under the ground, leaving him "more secure than the pharaohs of ancient Egypt."

His fellow director, Abraham Lincoln's sole surviving son, Robert Todd Lincoln, liked the idea so much he had his father's grave disinterred and reburied in the same manner.

He also became good friends with George Pullman and eventually the next president of the Pullman Company. Now, one would think that the son of Abraham Lincoln would be magnanimous toward blacks, but such was not the case. He was a man who took more after his mother than his father. Under his direction, the Pullman porters continued to be paid subsistence wages. Called before a congressional committee investigating the condition of Pullman porters, and asked whether $27.50 a month was enough for a porter to support his family in comfort and decency, Lincoln responded, "Absolutely not. I want to say that situation annoys me very much indeed."

Yet he did nothing. Coasting on his family name—very powerful in those days—he ignored whatever he didn't want to hear. Hauled before another congressional committee investigating Pullman's industrial relations, he denied hearing of any bids by porters to unionize, "not the slightest." In the meantime, Pullman's enormous profits continued to grow. Lincoln became one of the richest men in America, and built himself a huge, fifty-room summer home in Manchester, Vermont.

Summer home of Robert Lincoln

In 1904, a former porter wrote a book complaining that the Pullman Company was forcing black porters to work double the hours of other (white) train staff for half the pay. He titled his book *Freemen Yet Slaves Under "Abe" Lincoln's Son.*

The early home of Abraham Lincoln

Five years later, there occurred the hundredth anniversary of Abraham Lincoln's birth. It was the largest commemoration ever of any person in America. Celebrations were held everywhere—almost all of them segregated. The biggest was in Abraham Lincoln's hometown of Springfield, Illinois, where a gala dinner was held, "a lily white affair," blacks excluded. Robert

Todd Lincoln was there, the guest of honor.

Simultaneously, a more poignant celebration took place in Kentucky: the dedication of the so-called Lincoln Cabin. Seven thousand people attended, blacks as well as whites, to hear the keynote speaker, President Theodore Roosevelt. Abe Lincoln's son chose not to attend.

Dark Side of a Liberal President

►**1913**   As a college president and then U.S. president, Woodrow Wilson established himself as one of the world's most progressive leaders, a man of compassion for the masses.

Not so well known, however, is that Woodrow Wilson was a racist, the only true racist ever to occupy the Oval Office. Historians looking at our long line of presidents for their treatment of blacks have focused on non-issues like Jefferson's relationship with Sally Hemings or Abraham Lincoln's early views on colonizing blacks by sending them back to Africa. These are non-issues because they have absolutely nothing to do with their performance as president. With Woodrow Wilson, however, it is a different story. His racist views pervaded his entire term in high office. In public, he was very willing and eager to espouse liberal principles and "Fourteen Points" for mankind; in private, he could be brutal toward "the darkies" in his own

American backyard, and also to Italian, Hungarian, and other non-Anglo-Saxon immigrants.

As a young man in the 1880s, Wilson complained about the influx of immigrants from southern and Eastern Europe—"men out of the ranks where there was neither skill nor energy nor any initiative of quick intelligence," he called them. In 1901 he wrote an article in *The Atlantic Monthly* describing Negroes as "a host of dusky children untimely put out of school." Conditions in the South since the Civil War had approached "ruin" until "at least the whites who were the real citizens got control again." One wonders whether this Princeton professor had ever read the Constitution. Still more of Wilson's Southern heritage was to come. After becoming president, Wilson arranged that the first movie to be shown in the White House was a movie glorifying the Ku Klux Klan. He ordered federal civil service workers to be segregated by race in their employment, with separate eating and toilet facilities. When a Negro leader protested this segregation, Wilson called his words "insulting" and sent him packing. Getting the clue, U.S. Post Office and Treasury officials in the South used Wilson's order as an excuse to discharge or downgrade black employees. Afro-Americans working in the Post Office found themselves suddenly "relegated to separate and lesser facilities for everything from break rooms to restrooms." In Atlanta, twenty-five blacks were fired from their post office jobs to create job openings for whites. Said the Georgia head of the Internal Revenue Service in 1913, "There are no Government positions for Negroes in the South. A Negro's place is in the cornfield."

A Gift to the Moon

➤ **1919**   In World War I the British captured several large German battleships and took them to the Orkney Islands in Scotland, to a place called Scapa Flow. While moored there, the German sailors aboard the vessels managed to sink them so they couldn't be used in the war. There they remained for decades, a monument to German determination and British carelessness.

In the meantime, the Americans developed the atom bomb and used it on Hiroshima and Nagasaki to bring World War II to a quick end. One of the consequences of this act was that it coated the earth with a tiny film of radioactivity. Now, normally this wouldn't be a problem—radioactivity comes from many everyday sources and doesn't cause harm—but it did become a problem in the 1950s when the United States needed radiation-free metal for its massive atomic-bomb-testing program in Nevada. During this time the U.S. government exploded eighty-six atom bombs at its Nevada test site, killing lots of local sheep and sending radioactive dust as far as New York.

Scapa Flow, Scotland: radiation-free metal under the water

German battleship turret housing retrieved from Scapa Flow. U. S. Atomic Bomb Testing Grounds, Nevada

Because all steel made after 1945 was inherently contaminated (it takes a lot of air to make steel), the American atomic scientists had a problem with their measurements of radioactive fallout—until, that is, some smart fellow remembered his history and came up with the idea of using steel from sunken pre-1945 battleships. Luckily, the harbor at Scapa Flow in northern Scotland is quite shallow, so it was no problem for British divers to dismantle one of the German battleships and deliver several large pieces of radioactivity-free metal to the Nevada test site. In one case, they dismantled an entire turret from a German battleship. That turret then was reassembled in Nevada to house sensitive testing equipment. (For special effect, the scientists added a long gun barrel consisting of empty paint cans.)

In 1963, after the United States and Russia signed a treaty banning atmospheric testing, the Nevada test site was closed down. But radiation doesn't fade away, it lingers. In the late 1960s, when preparing to land a man on the moon, the United States once again ran into a problem. The scientific instruments and electronics used to guide the landing module are extremely sensitive and need to be totally free of any magnetic interference caused by radioactivity, no matter how slight. No American-made metal would do. Back to Scapa Flow went the divers to bring up some more radiation-free ore. That metal, crafted into the form of a lunar landing module, now rests on the moon.

Today, other remnants of the German navy, now in the form of the U.S. Pioneer probe, have passed the orbit of Pluto and are on their way to distant star systems.

Fierce Opposition to the ERA

➤ **1920** When Alice Paul of the newly formed National Women's Party proposed the Equal Rights Amendment, prohibiting discrimination against women in the workplace, she set off a storm of controversy. Members of one sex rose up to take a strong position on the measure. Politically active groups of this sex formed marches and political action committees, organized rallies, and hounded their congressmen to block this radical measure. The Democratic Party and the labor unions also took a strong position on the ERA. Taking the totally opposite position were employers and Republicans.

Who was opposed, and who was in favor?

Opposing the ERA were the League of Women Voters, the American Association of University Women, the Women's Bureau of the Department of Labor, the Parents and Teachers Association, the Women's Christian Temperance Union, and the National Council of Jewish Women. The dispute was so bitter it came to be called the "women's war." Also opposing the ERA were the Democratic Party and labor unions that didn't want women taking away jobs from their male members.

The reason women activists were so opposed to the ERA was that they saw it as a direct threat to their cherished "protective labor laws" limiting excessive hours, requiring special facilities for women workers, and forbidding the employment of women in certain physically demanding occupations. The ERA, by its implicit demand that the right to work was a paramount right, threatened to undermine these protections.

Those in favor of the ERA were many men, employers, Republicans, and members of the political right, who welcomed the competition of women in the marketplace and who supported the constitutional right of a person—female as well as male—to choose one's place of employment.

Today the debate still rages: how best to promote greater well-being for women? Right-wing opponents of the ERA use many of the same collectivist arguments used by the earlier left-wing opponents: that women are a special group. If that is so, then one's support of women's rights revolves around whether it is fair to give preference to a particular group, for whatever reason. Supporters of the ERA, both now and back in the 1920s, make the individualist argument that women are no different from men, do not need special protection, and should have the right to self-determination.

A Hidden Motive for Appeasement

▶**1935** United States foreign policy has an almost paranoid fear of appeasement, resulting from our disastrous policies of the 1930s, when we let Nazi Germany seize territory after territory, resulting in World War II. Whenever upstarts like Saddam Hussein or Slobodan Milošević invaded neighboring countries, images of Neville Chamberlain were evoked in many newspaper editorials as a spur to U.S. intervention. This is a misreading of history. First, let us review the facts:

1935: Germany introduces the draft, creates the Luftwaffe, and builds a navy—all in flagrant violation of the Treaty of Versailles.

1936: Mussolini invades Abyssinia; Hitler invades the Rhineland; a Fascist military putsch takes over Spain.

1938: Hitler seizes Austria; Chamberlain "sells out" Czechoslovakia.

1939: Germany seizes Czechoslovakia and Poland.

1940: Nine months after doing nothing in response to a war declaration, France and Great Britain start fighting Germany.

What we have here is a lengthy, consistent pattern of appeasement so breathtaking as to defy belief. No one in his right mind would tolerate such aggression—unless he had a hidden agenda. One or two incidents of appeasement could be called stupidity. But not five years.

Why did the nations of the West—including the United States—do nothing? Because they were hoping Nazi Germany would strike eastward and destroy the menacingly socialist state of Stalinist Russia. Said Winston Churchill in 1927, to Benito Mussolini, "If I had been an Italian, I am sure that I should have been wholeheartedly with you from start to finish in your triumphant struggle against the bestial appetites and passions of Leninism."

American fear of Bolshevism and socialism had existed even before Lenin arrived on the scene. No fewer than 900,000 people had voted for socialism and Eugene Debs in the 1912 presidential election (won by Wilson against TR and Taft). In the meantime the Industrial Workers of the World had issued their warlike manifesto: "Abolition of the wage system! It is the historic mission of the working class to do away with capitalism." In the 1920s, the "Back to Normalcy" Harding administration conducted a hunt for radicals and aliens suspected of subversive activities, and rounded up 150 of them for quick deportation to Russia. The municipality of Cambridge, Massachusetts, passed an ordinance making it a crime to own a book containing the words "Lenin" or "Leningrad." As one reporter observed, America was "hag-ridden by the specter of Bolshevism. . . . Property was in an agony of fear,

and the horrid name 'Radical' covered the most innocent departure from conventional thought with a suspicion of desperate purposes."

It was in such an environment that the U.S. and European nations welcomed the Nazi power as a buffer, and viewed its aggression with concern—but not with alarm. U.S. Brigadier General Charles Sherrill, defending the U.S. Olympic Committee's controversial decision to participate in the 1936 Games in Berlin despite the obvious propaganda value it would give the Fascists, said he wished Mussolini had an opportunity to come to the United States and "suppress Communism as he had done in Italy." Said Lord Halifax a year later, "I and other members of the British Government fully realize that the Fuhrer has achieved much not only in Germany itself but, as a result of having destroyed communism in his country, he has barred the latter from Western Europe. And Germany may therefore be considered the West's bastion against Bolshevism."

Tougher Peace Terms than World War I

➤ **1945** The victors in World War II imposed tougher peace terms than did those in World War I. This stick—followed by the carrot of the Marshall Plan—enabled the victors to ensure a peace that survived for more than sixty years, as opposed to the earlier twenty. But the important thing to remember is not the successful carrot, but the powerful stick that made it possible.

You wouldn't know this from reading John Maynard Keynes's *The Economic Consequences of the Peace*, a polemic lambasting the British and Americans for imposing stiff terms on the defeated Germans of World War I. Keynes's book drew such a wide following among peace-loving citizens that Winston Churchill exclaimed in frustration, "I think I can save the British Empire from anything—except the British."

In the Great War (known to Americans as World War I), the victors pretty much left Germany alone, permitting rabble-rousers like Adolf Hitler to gain a popular following. The borders of Germany were left intact. Trials of war criminals were conducted only by Germans. As a result, virtually all German soldiers and politicians were spared execution. Reparations were demanded by the Allies, but what made these penalties onerous was not the amount, but the deliberate policy of the German government to permit runaway inflation. Then when Europe and especially America fell into an economic depression, bringing international trade to a halt, the German government reversed course and permitted severe deflation, thus incurring further hardship on the population.

In World War II, by contrast, the victorious Allies took a tough line. There would be no armistice—i.e., a temporary cessation of hostilities—as at Versailles; to the contrary, there was a full-blown surrender to the "Tripartite Supreme Authority" of the United States, Britain, and Russia. The victors demanded severe reparations—and made sure they got paid. They divided Germany into occupation zones, with Berlin left isolated deep inside the Soviet zone. Unlike World War I, in which most of the fighting took place outside of Germany, World War II was just the opposite: by the end of the war, most of Germany's cities had been bombed into ruins. Walls were still standing, but roofs and windows were totally blown out. "Skeleton cities," they were called, such ruins being even more demoralizing than if they had been completely flattened. No matter, Germany must be taught a lesson. "We've got to be tough with Germany and I mean the German people, not just the Nazis," said FDR. Churchill and FDR imposed a harsh program of de-Nazification and deindustrialization. According to JCS-1067 instructions to General Eisenhower, Germany "will not be occupied for the purpose of liberation, but as a defeated enemy nation." All steps "designed to maintain or strengthen the German economy" were prohibited. The occupying forces seized all the banks and stopped foreign trade. When told that an onerous "Carthaginian Peace" could not be imposed on Germany, one American general replied sarcastically, "Well, now, you don't hear too much from those Carthaginians nowadays."

Eisenhower meant business. When he saw photographs of GIs giving children chewing gum, he blew up: "This must be nipped in the bud immediately." Fraternization of any kind with Germans was verboten. If hunger and suffering was their fate, so be it. Whereas a human being normally needs two thousand calories a day, what was available in Germany provided only 1,200 calories. Many Germans lived on the verge of starvation.

The U.S. Army stationed hundreds of thousands of troops in Germany, and made Germany pay the full costs of occupation. Unlike the 1930s, when Germany had substantial assets abroad that it used to finance rearmament, the U.S. now tracked down and confiscated all German assets outside of the country. It conducted the Nuremberg Trials, and put the key German militarists in prison for a long time, and in some cases put them to death. In the meantime, the Soviets took half of Germany and shipped many of its industrial assets to Russia. The major coal-producing region of Germany—the Saar—was given to France. Quotas were imposed, restricting German steelmaking capacity to 25 percent of prewar volume. More than four million German soldiers were taken and used as forced labor in the UK, France, and the Soviet Union.

No way was Germany going to rearm, in any shape or form. There were no soldiers, no weapons, even the police were disarmed. Antique hunting guns and swords from the Franco-Prussian War were col-

lected and destroyed. Any German caught violating the arms ban got eight years in jail. After conducting a massive search for bombs, mines, and other armaments, the Allies had disposed of 302,875 tons of German chemical weapons containing fourteen different kinds of toxic agents.

Nor was Germany going to buy its way out of poverty by printing hundreds of millions of deutsche marks. With the American advisors in firm control, Germany had no choice but to pursue sound economic and trade policies to prove she belonged to the world economy and would make every effort to repay the reparations. In 1947, when it became apparent that the health of Europe depended on vigorous trade among all European nations including Germany, the U.S. shifted gears and offered a carrot, the Marshall Plan. What made the Germans so cooperative was the total defeat they had suffered during the war, plus the stiff conditions they had endured during 1945 to 1947, a true "Carthaginian Peace."

❧

Japan fared no better. The United States took over the country, installed a military dictatorship under General Douglas MacArthur, and ruled the country with an iron fist. It is no accident that William Manchester titled his biography of MacArthur *American Emperor*. That MacArthur ruled wisely is a testimony to his observance of American heritage and democratic principles but should not obscure the fact that his rule was total. Imperious to the core, MacArthur ruled like a neocolonial military dictator possessing complete executive and legislative authority. "I could by fiat issue directives," he informed the U.S. Senate, and he did.

Observes historian John Dower in his Pulitzer Prize–winning book *Embracing Defeat*, "Such an audacious undertaking by victors in war had no legal or historical precedent." It was the greatest experiment in "nation building" ever taken, a thorough remake of a society from top to bottom.

Unlike Germany, the United States did not have its allies to worry about. Even though it was called a multinational coalition—"The Allied Occupation of Japan"—the rule of Japan was solely by the United States; the allies were just figureheads. When the occupation began, most Americans—including MacArthur—assumed it would last no more than three years. It ended up being six years. During U.S. control, from 1945 to 1952, Japan lost its empire, reparations were extracted, the military forces were dismantled totally, a complete land-reform bill was imposed, and the zaibatsu conglomerates and holding companies controlled by the old guard were eliminated. Some 200,000 people were enjoined from holding public offices. No Japanese citizen was permitted to travel abroad. The occupation, the United States made abundantly clear, would last for however long it took for Japan to establish "a peacefully inclined and responsible government"—with America being the sole judge, jury, and executioner. To add insult to injury, in a nation where 3.7 million families were homeless, America insisted that Japan bear all costs of maintaining the occupation army. In 1948, fully one-third of the government budget ("war termination costs") went to pay for housing the American occupying troops.

The United States sought nothing less than "remaking the entire political, social, cultural, and economic fabric of a defeated nation." Despite all efforts to bring in food, many Japanese people suffered terribly. A bag of rice that cost 2.7 yen in mid-1946 cost 62.3 yen by early 1950—assuming you could buy it. The 1946 black-market price wasn't 2.7 yen: on the streets it was almost 380 yen. The United States managed to get the black-market premium down to two times the official price by 1949, but during this time many Japanese were starving to death, trying to live on 1,000 calories a day.

Japan was a totally defeated nation, and the peace terms dictated by the victor were absolute. Only under such circumstances could a militarist society continually at war since 1931 change its ways. That the Japanese met the challenge is due largely to the fact that they had no choice.

Total defeat, properly managed, can yield long-lasting peace.

When the Depression Finally Ended

➤**1947** World War II didn't end the Depression any more than the New Deal did.

In 1932, 13.7 million Americans were out of work. Despite the morale boost provided by FDR and all the programs implemented by his administration, the New Deal of 1933–40 made only scant progress in ending the Depression. In fact, many countries had started to recover from the worldwide collapse of prices; the U.S., by comparison, was a laggard. The most successful economy was Nazi Germany. Chile, Sweden, and Australia had annual growth rates in the 20 percent range; America's was a pathetic -7 percent. England's national income in 1937 was 25 percent higher than the high-water mark of 1929; the United States's national income was 15 percent lower than in 1929. Recalled the famed newscaster David Brinkley, "By the winter of 1938–39, Roosevelt knew, but was not yet willing to say, that the New Deal, as a social and economic revolution, was dead."

The unemployment rate was 17 percent. Some 10 million Americans still had no job. Recognizing the obvious, FDR came out and admitted as much: "Dr. New Deal" had been replaced by "Dr. Win the War."

But even World War II and the booming demand for war materials and American men and women failed to end the Depression. The boom provided by wartime was only temporary, and was pretty much confined to the defense sector (while other sectors suffered). Americans were terrified of the economic consequences of peace when the soldiers would come home and the factories stopped: 15 million jobs would disappear and the U.S. would be back where it was in 1932. "It would be the Pearl Harbor of Peace," wrote one correspondent. Cassandras were everywhere. Wrote the historian Merle Curti, "The individualism and the opportunity of an earlier America seemed to have faded, and some felt that the United States had suddenly grown old." Paul Samuelson, soon to become the country's best-known economist because of his popular college textbook, predicted "the greatest period of unemployment and industrial dislocation which any economy has ever faced." "Peacetime prosperity," he thundered, "could be assured only if the slack left by business investment and expenditures could be taken up by government expenditures." Other New Deal economists cited intractable problems such as uncertainties in foreign trade, the enormous disparities in the price and wage structure, and the inability of consumption to ever catch up with the country's enormous production capacity.

For a year or two, they were right. But as price controls were lifted on consumer products and government spending fell two-thirds from $98.4 billion in 1945 to

$33 billion in 1947, genuine recovery began to occur and the American economy never looked back.

This caught many people by surprise. "Keynesian economists," says the historian Thomas DeLorenzo, "expected a two-thirds reduction in government spending to lead to another depression, but they were dead wrong." Instead, what ensued was the fastest, most startling economic boom in American history.

Probably America's Most Successful War

➤**1951** It may seem ironical to call the Korean War—"the forgotten war"—America's most successful military endeavor, but it achieved its objectives and had the most satisfactory long-term results.

The purpose of waging war is not just to win battles, but also to secure a political peace. World War I was an obvious failure in this regard. But even America's two most decisive wins left a legacy of animosities and unresolved differences. The first one, World War II, resulted in America becoming the most powerful nation on earth—only because of its sole ownership of the bomb. The Soviets, who had done most of the fighting, still had vastly superior manpower forces, thus opening the door for Soviet expansionism. The result was the Cold War.

The other military slam-dunk, the Gulf War, secured the West's oil supplies, but left Saddam Hussein in power. Free to do as he pleased, he threw out UN weapons inspectors and taunted the world that he had weapons of mass destruction (a dangerous bluff).

The Korean War, on the other hand, stands up well to the test of history. It was a military stalemate and a very unpopular war at the time (which is why Harry Truman quietly refrained from seeking re-election in 1952). But in terms of achieving a stable, long-lasting peace, the Korean War was remarkably fruitful. The country we saved, South Korea, eventually went on to become one of the world's strongest democracies. For more than a half century, both the U.S. and the Soviets/Chinese have respected the Thirty-eighth Parallel that physically separates the two countries. Even more significant, both sides refrained from using nuclear weapons or launching massive invasions of a million men, which they could easily have done. By their conduct of the war, all parties—Americans, Koreans, Chinese, and Russians—signaled "limits" to each other. In so doing they initiated the era of limited war that has characterized warfare to this day.

The Thirty-Eight Witnesses Who Weren't

➤**1964** On a cold March night, returning home from work at 3:00 a.m., Kitty Genovese was brutally murdered. At the time, nobody noticed—just another homicide in the Queens borough of New York City. Two weeks later the *New York Times* ran a front-page story, "37 Who Saw Murder Didn't Call," reporting that thirty-eight witnesses watched her being stabbed repeatedly, and never once during ninety minutes did anyone come to her rescue. (Only at the end did one witness finally call the police.)

Overnight, the Kitty Genovese case made front-page headlines across the country and became a textbook case for psychologists and social scientists. Coming at a time of national trauma, three months after the Kennedy assassination, "the thirty-eight witnesses who watched their neighbor die" touched the national consciousness like an electric jolt. "Thirty-eight!" people said over and over. "Thirty-eight!" Many citizens saw the witnesses' apathy as a sign of the moral collapse of America: "Dear God, what have we come to? . . . Are we living in a jungle?" When newspapers did follow-up stories, they didn't talk to the witnesses, they interviewed sociologists and psychologists and other third-party experts who had a field day pontificating about group social behavior. One expert suggested the murderer vicariously gratified the sadistic impulses of those who witnessed it: "They were deaf, paralyzed, hypnotized with excitation. Fascinated by the drama, by the action, and yet not entirely sure that what was taking place was actually happening."

Fair to say if the expert had been there, but of course he hadn't. Yes, there was a murder. But the story of thirty-eight witnesses who witnessed the knife stabbing and did nothing is incorrect, so much so that the prosecutor described the witnesses as virtually useless in testifying at the murderer's trial. The prosecutor said he could find only five or six people who saw or heard anything—not thirty-eight. "I don't know where that came from, the thirty-eight," he said. Even the half-dozen people couldn't give enough evidence for a conviction; the murderer was arrested on a fluke, and convicted for life only because he confessed.

What really had happened? This sensationalist story began when a newspaper editor had lunch with a frustrated city police commissioner. Now, police commissioners have a lot on their mind, ranging from accusations they aren't doing enough about crime . . . to lack of cooperation from the citizens they are trying to serve. Both concerns came to the fore during this luncheon. Out of the blue, the police commissioner suddenly blurted, "That Queens story is one for the books. Thirty-eight people had watched a woman being killed, and not one of them called the police."

In other words, it was the public's fault. The editor assigned the story to a junior reporter who came back with an article that was quickly published and subsequently won an award for excellence from the Newspaper Reporters Association of New York. Alas, the reporter—and subsequent reporters from the *Times*—never interrogated the witnesses about exactly what they saw or heard, and when. All they were interested in knowing were the witnesses' explanations for their "assumed" apathy. Certainly the comments appeared quite damning. "We thought it was a lovers' quarrel," said one witness. "I didn't want my husband to get involved," said another. "We went to the window to see what was happening, but the light from our bedroom made it difficult to see the street. I put out the light and we were able to see better." "I was tired, I went back to bed." Why not call the police? "I don't know."

But the most interesting comment, one that all outsiders failed to grasp, was: "I wish everyone would leave us alone." What exactly did this mean? Was it another expression of bland apathy, or did it signal something deeper? Was this a community of "Stepford wives," or was it a community numbed into submission by relentless accusations?

Some forty years went by, and eventually people started asking more in-depth questions about exactly what had happened. Certainly there were a lot of inconsistencies. It was a freezing cold night, with windows closed tight, so how could witnesses hear what they thought they might have heard after they had learned to their horror what had occurred? How could they see the assailant when the attack took place under the shadows of a tree? How could they see "the third stabbing" when there were only two? Why

should they become suspicious when there was a bar nearby, and people frequently got into shouting arguments at 3:00 a.m.? And last but not least, this being an era before there were 911 emergency phone lines, where were the phone calls that other witnesses claimed they had made to the police precinct? Were the police pointing at the witnesses to clear themselves?

In an example of citizen activism to correct history similar to Robert Edsel's (see Chapter 2), a local lawyer named Joseph De May started conducting exhaustive research on the Genovese killing and found many discrepancies. In 2004 the *New York Times*, which had once bragged that "seldom has the *Times* published a more horrifying story than its account of how thirty-eight respectable, law-abiding, middle-class citizens watched a killer stalk his young woman victim," ran a quite different story. Titled "Kitty, 40 Years Later," the article gave credence to De May's findings that "the great majority of the thirty-eight so-called witnesses did not see any part of the actual killing; and that what most of them did see, was fleeting and vague." Also giving credence to De May was the *Financial Times* of London, which cited De May for eviscerating the *Times*'s original story. In 2007 there appeared a lengthy article in *American Psychologist* analyzing the witnesses' alleged behavior. The article stated up front, "The story of the thirty-eight witnesses who remained inactive during the murder of

Kitty Genovese is not supported by the evidence."

For forty years it was a powerful story that sold a lot of newspapers and unleashed a frenzy of recrimination. But it didn't happen the way the *New York Times* said it did.

The Day Israel Attacked America

➤**1967** In the middle of the Six-Day War between Israel and the Arab states of Egypt, Jordan, and Syria, the U.S. Navy sent a spy ship into the eastern Mediterranean to do a little snooping. An order sent five times from Washington DC that the ship stay one hundred miles from shore was never received, so in the heat of a war the ship cavalierly patrolled international waters fifteen miles off the Egyptian coast. Nearby were several Soviet ships, presumably also monitoring the Israeli-Arab war. On board the USS *Liberty* were Russian and Arab translators, but no Hebrew translators—a most curious omission given the ship's location, and one that soon proved deadly.

On a clear, sunny day, the ship—flying the American flag—was spotted by Israeli reconnaissance planes. Because of the lack of Hebrew translators on board the ship, communication between the ship and the planes was impossible, and the planes went away. Six hours later, fighter jets suddenly arrived, attacking the *Liberty* with machine-gun fire. At the appearance of torpedo boats, the *Liberty* responded with its own machine-gun fire, prompting the torpedo boats to release several torpedoes. As the sailors lowered their rubber rafts to escape the burning ship, they were strafed. When the captain finally managed to communicate that the ship was an American one, the Israeli attackers stopped and backed off. A day later, the Israeli government issued a formal apology to the United States. Thirty-four American sailors were dead and seventy-five severely wounded.

In the uproar that followed, Israel claimed a case of mistaken identity, saying it had been assured by the United States that there were no American ships in the area and so it had confused the *Liberty* with an Egyptian ship known to be in the area, the *El Quseir*. How an air force as highly trained as Israel's could make such a blunder struck many people as inconceivable. The *Liberty* was twice as big as the *El Quseir*, with a superstructure of satellite dishes and antennae that made it "look like a lobster." The ship had a prominent identifying number on its hull that read "5-GTR" (GTR stands for General Technical Research, the designation for American spy ships). "I never believed that the attack on the USS *Liberty* was a case of mistaken identity," said naval commander Thomas Moorer, chairman of the Joint Chiefs of Staff. Added the secretary of state, Dean Rusk: "I was never satisfied with the Israeli explanation. . . . I didn't believe their explanations then, and I don't believe them to this day." "Unbelievable," said presidential advisor Clark Clifford. Even more blunt was CIA director Richard Helms: "The Israelis knew exactly what they were doing."

The Israeli government, giddy over its trouncing of Egypt in the Six-Day War, took a hard line. It refused to conduct a full-scale investigation like the United States demanded; instead it produced a report by a low-level officer with no experience in espionage or flying. No interviews of the Israeli pilots who attacked the *Liberty* in broad daylight were conducted. Nor were there any interviews of government officials who might have ordered the attack. When the United States complained about the lack of serious investigation, the Israelis took the offensive and said the United States was partly to blame because it had failed to alert Israel of the *Liberty*'s presence. Israel claimed the novel theory that any boat traveling at more than twenty knots—even in international waters—must be "hostile." It claimed the *Liberty* had been traveling at twenty-eight knots (nearly twice the *Liberty*'s maximum), had failed to identify herself, was engulfed in black smoke, and "behaved suspiciously."

Such gall outraged leading members of the American military. But the United States was caught in an awkward position: how to explain the presence of a U.S. spy ship in a war zone? Certainly the Arabs and Egyptians would not be happy knowing a U.S. intelligence ship was in the area, presumably feeding information to the Israelis. The U.S. also had a dilemma explaining to the American public how a staunch ally could dare attack one of its ships. What kind of an ally was this? Finally, the timing was most inauspicious: President Lyndon Johnson and Defense Secretary Robert McNamara had their hands full, coping with mounting problems in Vietnam. The last thing they wanted was a mini-war in the Middle East, especially with a presidential election coming up.

Clark Clifford, the staunchest supporter of Israel in the entire administration, smelled a rat: "Something had gone terribly wrong—and was covered up." He urged a tough line: "Handle [the incident] as if Arabs or USSR had done it." But political considerations reigned. Led by Defense Secretary Robert McNamara and executed by Admiral John McCain (father of the 2008 presidential candidate), a gag order was imposed on all the sailors of the ship. When the National Security Agency director concluded that the attack "couldn't be anything else but deliberate," Assistant Secretary of State Cyrus Vance told him to keep his mouth shut. The *Liberty*, which was held up in Malta being repaired and painted, was off-limits to the media: they would never get a chance to photograph it riddled with torpedo explosions and 821 shell holes, "shot up as a tin can on a firing range." Even the conservative columnist William F. Buckley was appalled at the gag order: "Is the *Liberty* episode being erased from history? So it would seem . . . What has happened to our prying journalistic corps and our editors, normally so indignant of attempted suppression of the news?"

In the meantime, the commander of the *Liberty*, William McGonagle, was put up for the Medal of Honor. Almost always, this award, the nation's highest award for heroism, is presented by the president at the White House. Not in this case. Due to the sensitivity of the *Liberty* incident, the award was given to McGonagle at the Washington Navy Yard by Admiral Moorer, while the president stayed at the White House and handed out diplomas to high-school students. A "back-handed slap," said Moorer. No White House press release announcing McGonagle's award was ever issued.

Had the attack on the *Liberty* been a "tragic accident" as the Israelis claimed, one would expect Israel to pay full reparations and issue a heartfelt apology, not a bland statement of regret. Such was not the case. The Israelis stonewalled every step of the way and steadfastly refused to pay reparations to the families of the seventy-four sailors and officers who died. Then when it did, it offered only a paltry $1.54 million . . . then reduced it to $1.25 million (all from a nation that received hundreds of millions every year in U.S. aid). U.S. State Department officials were extremely annoyed. Finally, after a year of nitpicking and haggling, Israel issued a check for $3.3 million. Lest anyone get the wrong message, Israel issued a statement denying it had any legal liability

for "death and material damage resulting from the attack," and that it had paid the $3.3 million only because it was "motivated by humanitarian considerations relating to the economic hardship suffered by the families of the deceased." Secretary of State Dean Rusk went ballistic, calling Israel's posture "totally unacceptable." Still unresolved was the issue of compensation for the injured sailors. It took another year of haggling before Israel issued a second check, for $3.6 million. The United States also wanted compensation for the massive damage to the *Liberty*; Israel refused and made a counteroffer of $100,000, which the United States took as an insult. The issue remained unresolved for years and might have been forgotten had it not been for the miracle of compound interest. Because of interest, the $7.6 million repair bill had grown to double digits and was noted on the annual claims report of money owed by foreign governments submitted to Congress. Congressmen started asking lots of questions. In 1980 Israel settled its $17.1 million bill for $6 million, payable in three annual installments of $2 million.

This 1967 tragedy is now a mere footnote in American history. However, it deserves to be remembered in the context of when Israel launched a massive attack on Beirut in 2006 in retaliation for the kidnapping of two soldiers. Compared to the 2006 provocation to Israel, the 1967 provocation to the United States yielded restraint, not war. One of the landmark traits of the Cold War was that the United States and the Soviets, with plenty of battleships and nuclear submarines in the Mediterranean eyeing every move like cornered cats ready to pounce, remembered the lessons of World War II and declined to bite at the provocations of a minor player. Said Richard Nixon in one of his televised addresses to the nation in 1973, "When the action gets hot, keep the rhetoric cool."

There is an old slogan, "It isn't my enemies I fear, it's my friends." Big nations eyeing each other warily think twice, three times, four or five times before engaging in hostilities. Small nations are much more prone to act recklessly.

Irresponsible Investigation, Lapdog Media

►**1979**   One doesn't think of a rock drummer, living quietly in Ohio and reading an adult magazine on a hot summer day, as the man who cracked open America's most notorious crime case. But stranger things have been known to happen.

First, some background. In 1975, in an effort to resolve the lingering question of who killed JFK, Congress authorized a new investigation. Already the assassination had been subject to extensive investigations by five different groups, each acting independently—the Secret Service, the Dallas Police Department, the FBI, the CIA, and the Warren Commission—

all of which had reached the same conclusion: Lee Harvey Oswald had acted alone. But with government credibility at an all-time low after the Watergate cover-up, and many people expressing doubts about the Warren Report, Congress decided another investigation was in order. Enter the House of Representatives Select Committee on Assassinations (HSCA).

For three years the twelve-member HSCA labored over thousands of pages of evidence and sworn testimony, and was on the verge of unanimously arriving at the same conclusion as before. Then suddenly, out of the blue, two weeks before the findings were to be released, a new piece of evidence cropped up that had everyone confused. It was a police Dictabelt recording on which it sounded as if four shots had been fired. If true, that meant there had to be more than one assassin.

Now, the cardinal rule in any investigation is *verify*. Virtually everyone present at the assassination in Dealey Plaza had stated they heard only three shots. So when a police motorcycle tape recording appeared that might suggest four shots, the logical next step would be to have the policeman listen to the tape and verify that it came from his motorcycle's radio. For reasons that are inexplicable, this was never done. The committee declined to hear his eyewitness testimony, stating it was more interested in the technical analysis by acoustics "experts." After reviewing the tapes and acoustics experts' interpretation claiming that four shots was "a 95 percent probability," the committee at the last minute amended its report. It stated it had no hard evidence of any conspiracy, but that given the possibility of four shots, there "probably" had been a conspiracy, though it was "unable to identify the other gunmen or the extent of the conspiracy." The committee specifically excluded the obvious suspects such as Russia, Cuba, and the Mafia. The best it could do was attribute the conspiracy to several individuals, identities unknown.

The media immediately went into a frenzy. Conspiracy buffs had a field day. Countless books and videos claiming conspiracy made their authors rich.

❧

Enter the drummer. It was July 1979, several months after the HSCA report had been released. When Steve Barber came home and opened his monthly issue of the adult magazine *Gallery* and something fell out, he had a surprise: not a stunning pinup, but a plastic flexi-disc recording of the Dictabelt evidence. Being a "sound junkie," he plugged the tape into his tape recorder and became mesmerized. "I played this thing to death," he said, "just trying to hear the gunshots and hear for myself what they really said was 95 percent evidence of conspiracy."

Steve Barber, being a trained musician, had better ears than the acoustics experts. During the six-second period where the experts said there were four shots, Barber picked up the barely audible words "Hold everything secure . . ." and figured out that these must be the same words spoken by a second police officer on a different channel, one minute later: "Hold everything secure until the homicide and other investigators can get there. . . ." In other words, what he was hearing was the recording not of one motorcycle but of two motorcycles! What sounded like four shots in Dealey Plaza might possibly be a crossover of sounds, from two different sources.

For the HSCA, the discovery of *two* motorcycles on the recording was most embarrassing. The committee's chief legal counsel had already gone on record as saying that if the Dictabelt evidence turned out to be flawed, he would change his mind about the existence of a conspiracy. Fair enough, but nobody likes being made a fool. Furthermore, it is common among smart people that they don't change their minds easily; instead they use their keen intellect to rationalize new reasons why they were always right. The chief counsel dug in his heels and clung to his confidence in his technical experts.

In 1982, at the request of Congress, the National Academy of Sciences conducted a thorough review of the Dictabelt recordings. Known as the Ramsey Report, after its chairman, the Harvard professor and Nobel Prize–winning physicist Norman Ramsey, the NAS investigation began with the analysis offered by Steve Barber and had the policeman listen to the tape. The policeman denied that all the sounds came from his Dictabelt. Utilizing more-sophisticated technology, Ramsey found several acoustic errors in the HSCA experts' report and blasted the HSCA for its lack of professionalism: the HSCA had been totally wrong in its interpretation of the evidence. There was no fourth shot from "the grassy knoll." Only three shots were on the recording (the alleged "fourth shot" was a different sound recorded a mile away and one minute later—and wasn't even a gunshot).

Alas, what should have been a media bombshell turned out to be a dud. The press paid no attention. Technical scientific reports do not make for exciting media copy, especially coming three years after a much more interesting story.

In 1991, a movie came out by Oliver Stone, *JFK*, based on—there is no kinder word for it—a pack of lies.* Observed Brent Staples of the *New York Times*, "Historical lies are nearly impossible to correct once movies and television have given them credibility. The children of the video will swallow *JFK* whole." Said one historian, "The assassination has become part of the entertainment industry." Added another, "It wasn't a handful of cranks that drew the country into the conspiracy camp. It was the mainstream media." Certainly the media never reported the background and details fully—"the story behind the story" of the HSCA delibera-

tions and how it flip-flopped at the last minute. Such laziness, in a story as important as a conspiracy to assassinate a president, carried a high price. Said Warren Commission counsel David Belin in a scathing denunciation of the media: "If priority to misrepresentations and deceit goes so far as to infiltrate our school system with the virus of lies, the present course of the electronic media poses a clear and present danger for the future of democracy in America."

Nonetheless, the media juggernaut carried on. Observed the historian Gerald Posner:

In 1991 the Today *show showed a version of the Zapruder home movie of the assassination, supposedly with sounds from the police Dictabelt superimposed over it. Four loud shots were clearly audible.* Today *never informed its audience that the four bullets were re-created in a studio and dubbed onto the recording. They do not exist in the original.*

In other words, the American public was being duped by a sensationalist-hungry press. In most countries, England for example, misrepresenting evidence is considered perjury and the *Today* show producers could find themselves in jail. But not in America, where a "free" press is sacrosanct.

---

* The movie glorified New Orleans prosecutor Jim Garrison for identifying Clay Shaw as part of a conspiracy to assassinate the president. In fact, in a 1969 trial of Clay Shaw, the jury—after a six-week trial—had reached a verdict of not guilty in less than an hour. In 1971, Shaw countersued Garrison and won, causing Garrison to spend the last years of his life in shame and ignominy. So much for Hollywood's treatment of "history."

Alarmed about the *JFK* movie and other media fabrications, Congress took an unprecedented step in order to clear the record. It created the Assassination Records Review Board to examine all the government records related to the assassination, declassify them as fully as possible, and release them to the public. Little publicity attended this honorable effort, but millions of pages of documentation released in 1994 gave all conspiracy advocates the information they needed to embellish their cases. None were forthcoming. To the contrary, in these files, available for all to see and put the case to rest, is the Ramsey Report, confirmed by an extensive study in 2003 by independent researcher Michael O'Dell. Also in 2003, there finally appeared a quality piece of journalism when ABC News aired its own investigation. Titled *Peter Jennings Reporting: The Kennedy Assassination—Beyond Conspiracy*, it concluded that the sound recordings on the police Dictabelt could not have come from Dealey Plaza and that the police officer was correct in his claim that he was nowhere near the scene when his microphone picked up the mysterious sounds.

The HSCA's last-minute change had been an error, a classic case of a professional investigation suddenly gone awry at the eleventh hour (or, as one historian put it, not "the eleventh hour—no, make it one minute to midnight!"). Admitted one congressman ruefully, "We rushed to our conclusions . . . We did a great job up to the last minute." Had the HSCA checked

out the Dictabelt issue more thoroughly and stuck to its original conclusion, many conspiracy theories never would have seen the light of day.

Such national trauma is unlikely to happen again. Nowadays, should an assassination occur, investigators have access to sophisticated technologies such as computer and laser-assisted simulations, digital enhancement of photographs, spectrographic analysis of acoustic impulses, and neutron-activated analysis of bullet fragments. All these tools have been used in recent years, and have confirmed the findings of the Warren Report. Yet to this day, 70 percent of Americans still believe there was a conspiracy.

Myths do not die easily. After Kennedy's death, a plaque was placed on the building from which Oswald fired his shots: "On November 22, 1963, the building gained national notoriety when Lee Harvey Oswald shot and killed President Kennedy."

Later it was replaced by a new plaque that said, ". . . when Lee Harvey Oswald allegedly shot and killed President John F. Kennedy."

Why "allegedly"?

Four Presidential Elections Decided by a Single Vote

► **2000** "A single vote?" you say. "Impossible!" Yes, indeed. Only in this case, the 2000 election, there are several people who qualify for this dubious honor. At the top of anyone's list would be Katherine Harris, Florida secretary of state responsible for certifying all the ballots, who had a clear conflict of interest in doing everything possible to ensure victory for her political party, the Republicans. But then, she was the occupant of the state job in accordance with all proper procedures, and who is to say a Democratic equivalent might not have done the same? If anything is to blame for Katherine Harris's conflict of interest, it is the system, not the occupant. "If men were angels," goes the old saying, "government would not be necessary."

Many unhappy Democrats blamed the Republican-dominated* Supreme Court for giving Bush the election by a one-vote margin, 5–4. This is incorrect. The critical vote was the one where the court ruled 7–2 that selective recounts violated the equal protection clause of the Constitution. The subsequent 5–4 vote confirmed the remedy, not the violation of the law.

Anyway, the whole imbroglio was started by the confusing "butterfly ballot," which had been approved by Theresa LePore, a Democrat. The incredible sloppiness of this one person threw a presidential election into chaos, an election that subsequent independent newspaper surveys of a statewide recount indicated that George W. Bush had won anyway. Even more interesting, as the journalist Jeff Greenfield pointed out, Gore lost the election not be-

cause he lost Florida but because he also—most important of all—lost his home state, Tennessee (the first time in American history this has happened). And not only did Gore lose his home state, he also lost Bill Clinton's home state next door. Now, that takes a real effort.

The election of 2000 *was* decided by a single person. But it wasn't Katherine Harris or Theresa LePore, or any of the five Supreme Court justices—though they all played a role in the mess as they tried to sort out proper voting procedures.

The real culprit was Ralph Nader. By making himself a candidate, though he had to know he was hurting Democrats more than Republicans, he garnered 2.8 million votes that prevented Al Gore from becoming president. Never before in American history had a third-party candidate managed to subvert a presidential election.

But wait! What matters is not the total number of votes, but how those votes affect the electoral votes. In this election, there were several candidates, as in 1860 when Lincoln was so lucky as to have many candidates dividing up the opposition vote. Same for 2000: not only was there a third-party candidate—Nader—who got 2.7 percent of the vote, there was a fourth candidate—Pat Buchanan of the Reform Party—who got 0.4 percent of the vote. Now here is where it gets inter-

* Republican-dominated? Not necessarily: of the nine justices, five of them (Scalia, Kennedy, Souter, Ginsberg, and Breyer) had been approved by Al Gore as senator and vice president.

esting: in Florida—Palm Beach County, to be more specific—Buchanan got an unusually large number of votes: more than two thousand. And it wasn't because Buchanan was a potential dark horse, it was because of the butterfly ballot. Even Buchanan saw it that way. Appearing on the *Today* show, he said, "When I took one look at that ballot on election night . . . it's very easy for me to see how someone could have voted for me in the belief that they voted for Al Gore."

So maybe it was Pat Buchanan, not Ralph Nader, who cost Gore the election. Take your pick.

The 2000 election, wild though it was, was hardly an aberration. Three other elections also have been decided by a kingmaker. In 2000, everyone was looking at the other ultra-tight election, 1876, but was ignoring two other disputed elections where a single person called the shots: 1800 and 1824. For all of us Americans who take pride in our country founded on "the will of the people," the following does not make for happy reading.

➤ **1800** Thomas Jefferson had a problem, a big problem: his future career as president was about to be blown away.

As vice president of the United States, he had the duty—one of the very few duties assigned by the Constitution to this otherwise unremarkable job—to count the electoral votes of a presidential election.

Problem was, Jefferson himself was one of the candidates. When he looked at the ballot coming from Georgia (a state he had counted on to win), he saw irregularities that possibly called for rejecting the ballot, thereby jeopardizing his candidacy. The procedure for a ballot was very specific in accordance with a 1792 congressional statute, and had been followed by every other state: the ballot was to be in a sealed envelope accompanied by a "certificate of ascertainment" signed by the state's governor, confirming the validity of the state's electors. But in this case there was no separate certificate. Georgia's envelope "contained only a single sheet of paper; the defective 'ballot' was written on the back of the certificate of ascertainment."

Where was the original ballot?

Unlike in Florida in the year 2000, there was no way to conduct a fact-finding mission to the disputed state to examine all the paperwork and try to determine "original intent." It was the middle of a snowy winter: a trip from Washington to Georgia would take at least a week, and there were only three weeks left before the inauguration.

On that fateful day, February 4, 1800, Thomas Jefferson and the members of Congress were in session to tally the states' ballots. When the tellers opened the Georgia envelope and handed Jefferson the ballot, they told him in front of all the congressmen that "there was a problem with it." Jefferson, performing his constitutional duties, examined the ballot, pretended nothing had happened, and handed it back to the tellers to be included in the total.

Had he not done so, the man inaugurated as president on March 4 probably would have been Charles C. Pinckney.

➤**1824** Like 1876, this anomaly of a national election being decided by a single vote occurred when the democratic election failed to produce a clear-cut winner, the solution devised for the House of Representatives to vote also failed to produce a winner, and so the choice was made by a single wavering vote at the last minute as both sides pressured this voter to go their way.

In 1824 the House of Representatives vote between Andrew Jackson—the front-runner—and John Quincy Adams (only tied with Jackson because of the last-minute support of Henry Clay) came down to the vote of a single congressman, Stephen Van Rensselaer of New York. Van Rensselaer was not a happy man. Cast in the role of kingmaker in this electoral tie, he tried to shirk the responsibility by voting for a third candidate, William Crawford. The two leading sides would have none of it, and arm-twisted the poor fellow nearly to tears. Burying his head in his arms, he prayed to the Lord for a providential sign. When he opened his eyes, the first thing he saw was a banner with the word "Adams" written on it, and so

he cast his vote for Adams and made John Quincy Adams president of the United States. Anyone think banners don't count?

➤**1876** He won the popular vote, but today few people know his name. To see his name, go to New York City, to the magnificent New York Public Library on Fifth Avenue and 42nd Street, and look up at the portico: the Samuel J. Tilden Trust. This is the legacy of a man who was one of the top lawyers in the country and the first self-made millionaire since Washington to run for president.

As governor of New York, Tilden enjoyed national prominence, so much so that his Republican opponent, Rutherford B. Hayes, recruited as his vice presidential running mate Tilden's lieutenant governor from New York, William A. Wheeler. But even stranger things were to happen in this election, ranging from bribes to gunfire. In the meantime, as Election Day drew near, newspaper surveys had Tilden winning by odds of 5 to 2.

Tilden was not a man who smiled much. It was said of him that he looked like a man "who smelled something bad." In the election of 1876, he smelled something very bad.

On the morning after Election Day, he woke up the winner. He had 4,300,590 popular votes and 196 electoral votes compared with Hayes's tally of 4,036,298 and 173. But as the baseball player Yogi

Berra was to say many decades later, "It's not over till it's over." While Tilden and the Democrats savored their victory, the losers noted that not all states had sent in their formal tallies. The victor needed 185 votes. Tilden had 184 votes for sure; Hayes had 163. Still to be confirmed for Tilden were the 22 votes from South Carolina, Florida, Louisiana, and Oregon where he already had the lead. For Tilden to win, he needed just one of these votes. For Hayes to win, he needed them all.

That looked like an impossibility. Tilden had 51.5 percent of the popular vote; Hayes, 48.5 percent. The major political leaders of both parties—including President Grant and the two candidates—presumed Tilden had won and would be inaugurated on March 4, 1877. "Tilden Elected President" was the common newspaper headline of the day, and Tilden started work on his inaugural speech.

The *New York Times*, however, had other ideas. In a nefarious scheme hatched in the newspaper's offices, editor John Reid and his assistants mounted a campaign announcing that the election was not a foregone conclusion and that a Republican victory could still be attained. Working closely with the Republican National Committee, the *Times*'s editor sent telegrams to trusted Republican leaders instructing them how to claim the votes in their states. Not mentioned in the telegram were time-tested means of winning elections: bribes and forged votes. The Republican stalwarts went to work.

Shortly thereafter, two sets of ballots—one Republican, the other Democrat—were presented by each of the four states. To the dismay of his campaign managers, who knew he had the popular vote, and to the astonishment of his legal advisers, who knew his love for the U.S. Constitution, Tilden agreed to the creation of an arbitration body (the Electoral Commission) not provided for in the Constitution. In bypassing the Constitution, Tilden was jeopardizing his sure advantage, for the Constitution states that in case of deadlock the House shall elect the president and the Senate the vice president, and in 1876 the House was controlled by the Democrats. But Tilden was confident of victory even under the arbitration setup, because the commission had one more Democrat than Republicans.

Then a most bizarre thing happened. The local Democrats in Illinois—acting independently of the national Democrats—chose one of their fellow Democrats on the Electoral Commission to run for U.S. senator, thereby compelling him to resign from the commission. The person chosen to replace him, Judge Joseph Bradley, was a Republican. In his sudden new role of kingmaker, Bradley cast the critical fifteenth vote in favor of Hayes in each of the four states, 8–7. "It is done," said the *Cincinnati Enquirer*, "and done fitly in the dark. . . . R. B. Hayes is 'Commissioned' as President, and the monster fraud of the century is consummated."

The supreme irony of it all was that

Hayes originally had opposed the creation of the Electoral Commission, thinking he could not win, whereas Tilden had supported it, thinking he could not lose. A major miscalculation.

❧

Could such a scenario happen again, whereby the leader of the popular vote and electoral vote fails to become president? Yes indeed, it almost happened in 1992.

If a candidate were to win just eleven states (California, New York, Texas, Florida, Pennsylvania, Illinois, Ohio, Michigan, New Jersey, North Carolina, and either Georgia or Virginia), he would have enough electoral votes to become president with only 28 percent of the popular vote. If, however, there were a three-way race and no candidate were to have a majority of the electoral votes, the election would be thrown into the House of Representatives, where the ruling congressional party would dictate who was the winner—even if he had come in last in the popular election or in the electoral count.

In 1992, there actually was a moment when it looked as though Ross Perot's candidacy would prevent George H. W. Bush from winning outright, thereby allowing the Democratic House of Representatives to put in Bill Clinton. As it turned out, though, Clinton won anyway.

TEN

Lightning Strikes Twice: It Happened Again

Who says history doesn't repeat itself?

Every time there is a change in political administrations, a portrait in the Roosevelt Room in the White House comes down and a new one is put up. When a Democrat occupies the White House, a portrait of FDR hangs above the mantel. When a Republican is president, a portrait of Theodore Roosevelt occupies the spot.

"We use historical precedents and analogies all the time," says Walter Bock. "Most of the time we use them as if history repeats itself. It doesn't." A more accurate description of what really happens, he says, is Mark Twain's aphorism, "History does not repeat, but it does rhyme."

Karl Marx said that when history repeats itself, the original tragedy returns as farce. He might well have described a modern-day American who typified "all motion, not a moment for reflection." Many years before he became famous, this college professor was asked what he thought of John Foster Dulles, Eisenhower's secretary of state. He thought for a moment and responded, "He travels too much."

The man was Henry Kissinger. Years later, as secretary of state himself, he became a perpetual-motion machine, always on a plane, rushing from one negotiation to the next. "It was not," observed historian Barbara Tuchman, "the most creative use of his time."

On a lighter note, perhaps Karl Marx was talking about evil spirits—you know, the kind that recur frequently. Anybody privileged to get a private tour of the White House may want to spend time scrutinizing the gardens in the back, wondering where the voodoo doll is. A voodoo doll? Indeed, a voodoo doll is buried in the White House garden, planted in 1919 by the outgoing president's daughter, Alice Roosevelt Longworth, to haunt her father's successor, William Howard Taft—who proceeded, of course, to have a disastrous one-term presidency. Silly, yes, but it does stimulate one's imagination about later presidents like Wilson and Nixon and Clinton, who claimed they were being jinxed and hounded by their enemies—or like Gerald Ford, who lost his marbles in the Carter presidential debate about how Poland was not a prisoner of the Soviet empire—or like George W. Bush, who rambled on and on in the Kerry debate about how "it's a hard job . . . it's a . . . *hard* . . . job." Now we know.

Back to serious matters: certainly many people would have performed better had they studied their history and allowed time for reflection. Writes H. D. S. Greenway in a recent column in the *International Herald Tribune*:

Americans are notorious for ignoring historical precedents because they believe in American exceptionalism to such a degree that what befell other countries in the past can have no relevance to the present or the future. I once asked an American general in Vietnam if he had read anything about the French experience in Indochina, and he said there was no point because the French had lost and, therefore, had nothing to teach Americans.

Greenway goes on to quote several leaders about the situation in Iraq:

• "Our armies do not come into your cities and lands as conquerors or enemies, but as liberators."

• "Iraq could be a model for development and democracy for the entire region."

• Our policy is actually working, and if "prematurely curtailed, the result would be disastrous. . . . Withdrawal would lead inevitably to anarchy."

• "The only way to leave with honor would be to redefine the standards of success and overstate Iraq's achievements."

These quotes do not come from George Bush or Donald Rumsfeld, but from British diplomats and generals describing Mesopotamia in the 1920s, when the British policy "ultimately changed from nation-building to doing anything to get out."

To dramatize an argument about historical interpretation, it helps sometimes to use prolepsis, or flash-forward. Representing a future action as imminently accomplished, or a present action as already completed, provides historical perspective: so what else is new?

Take 9/11. This sudden attack on an American landmark unified the nation overnight. In the space of an hour, Americans concerned about a potential enemy were ready to go to war. "The whole population, men, women, children, seem to be in the streets with (———) favors and flags . . . (———) war is freely accepted everywhere." People "switched from pacifism to militarism overnight." It was, wrote one historian in 2001, "as though all the floors had given way at once, and everyone found themselves sitting on the ground together. Overnight, the one solution no one had advocated became the one solution everyone agreed on . . . go to war." The nation's leading advocate of nonviolence now sang a different tune: "Sometimes gunpowder smells good."

Substitute "Union" in the first blank and "civil" in the second, and you describe the aftermath of the April 12, 1861, Confederate attack on Fort Sumter, which unified the North overnight as 9/11 did for America (the one exception being that there were no deaths at Fort Sumter). The pacifist who liked the smell of gunpowder was Ralph Waldo Emerson. Abraham Lincoln, elected president by the narrowest of margins in a four-way race, now had his mandate for war. Within three days, he issued

a call for volunteers, and thousands of Northerners responded. In one state, Vermont, 34,000 out of 37,000 men eligible for military service volunteered. The all-out war was on.

Take another war. Flouting the rights of neutrality on the high seas, the British navy exerted control over seaports on the Atlantic and prevented American ships from trading with European countries. Trade plummeted. American vessels languished in their home ports, and more and more Americans urged their president to declare war on Great Britain. The president, knowing his country was ill-prepared to take on a European power, stalled as best he could. He sent a delegation to London to work things out, but to no avail. Britain, seeing the weak state of the American fleet in 1914, tightened the blockade. Americans seethed with fury. According to adviser Colonel Edward House, Woodrow Wilson:

> . . . read a page from his history of the American people telling how during Madison's administration the War of 1812 was started in exactly the same way as this controversy is opening up . . . the President said: "Madison and I are the only two Princeton men that have been President. The circumstances of the War of 1812 now run parallel. I sincerely hope they will go no further."

"We cannot escape history," said Lincoln.

"No, don't!" says one proverb. "Don't dig up the past! Dwell on the past and you'll lose an eye." Fair enough, but listen to what the rest of the proverb says: "Forget the past and you'll lose both eyes." Anything in the past can happen again. What has happened twice may happen thrice. The late legendary investor Sir John Templeton used to say that the most dangerous words in investing were "This time it's different." Almost always it's not different, it's another variation of the same.

Forty Percent of the Nation's Banks Go Belly-Up

►**1837** The first major depression was not in 1930–33, but in 1837–43. Like Herbert Hoover, this president-elect came into office with a sterling résumé: secretary of state, ambassador to the Court of St. James, and vice president. Like Hoover, he was a firm believer in states' rights and individual responsibility. When Hoover said that federal aid would cause "degeneration of that independence and initiative which are the very foundation of democracy," he was emulating Martin Van Buren, the only president who came into office with no national debt. "All communities are apt to look to government for too much," said Van Buren. "It is not the objective of government to make men rich—nor repair their losses." In a message to Congress that predated Herbert Hoover, he pronounced, "The less Gov-

ernment interferes with private pursuits, the better for the general prosperity."

"In both cases," observed the Nobel Prize–winning economist Milton Friedman about 1837 and 1930, "erratic or unwise government policy with respect to money played an important part."

In 1835 the federal government had finally repaid all its war debts, and was now running a budget surplus. But in reality the U.S. economy was only sputtering along, supported by credit from abroad. From 1830 to 1836, American imports had tripled from $62 million to $181 million, causing the nation's trade balance to go from $8 million positive to $62 million negative. All Americans relished the gravy train of easy credit. They'd never had it so good. Said the senator from New York, "The credit system is the distinguishing feature between despotism and liberty. It is the offspring of free institutions."

Foreigners, however, thought differently: they became alarmed and wanted their money back. When the Bank of England raised the discount rate from 3 to 6 percent and cut the volume of commercial credits available to finance the import trade in the United States, hard currency began to flow out of the United States, and American banks found themselves unable to grant any more credit. In increasing numbers, they found themselves unable to repay their own debts, and started to go under.

This all began only two weeks after Martin Van Buren had taken office. Probably no other incoming president faced such a crisis except Abraham Lincoln in 1860 and Franklin Roosevelt in 1932. Van Buren chose a very cautious conservative course, making nobody happy. "Your friends," he was told bluntly, "think you a little exalted in the head on the subject," though of course nobody had any positive suggestions how to pull off a miracle. From 1839 to 1843, cotton prices fell from thirteen cents a pound to 7.85 cents in New York, and from 12.4 to 5.7 cents in New Orleans. Average commodity prices fell from $125 to $67. Annual imports fell from $159 million to $43 million. When the flow of English capital to finance internal improvements dwindled to virtually zero, nine states went into default on their loans. Out of 850 banks in the United States, 343 banks (a whopping 40 percent) went out of business, and another sixty-two failed partially and had to suspend operations.

To make matters worse, there was a real estate bubble going on. Just as the wild buying of stocks on margin helped cause the Crash of 1929, so speculation in real estate helped trigger the monetary collapse of 1837. In the city of Mobile, Alabama, the real estate valuation skyrocketed from $1.3 million in 1831 to $27 million in 1837; by 1846 it had sunk back to a more realistic $8.6 million. The real estate value of New York City in 1836 was higher than it would be in 1851, when it was a much larger and more prosperous city. But the most interesting market dysfunctionality occurred in the West, where the price of public land was fixed by law at $1.25 an acre. Speculators moved in, leveraging themselves to the hilt. Annual public land sales averaged $1.3 million during 1820–29, then started going up, reaching $2.6 million in 1832 and $4.8 million in 1834. Then the roof blew off: sales jumped to almost $15 million in 1835, and $25 million in 1836. Any contraction of ever-ready credit—which of course was inevitable—would cause the market to collapse.

Had Alan Greenspan been around then, undoubtedly he would have uttered his infamous phrase, "irrational exuberance."

On to Baghdad!

➤ **1861** This new president, aided by his vice president and secretary of war, was confident of a quick victory and of being able to bring home the troops in less than a year. Once the U.S. had captured the enemy's capital city, the war would be over. The president got congressional approval to launch the war in retaliation for an attack made by the enemy, along with his requested supply of 75,000 troops.

An experienced military man—the top general in the army—cautioned the president and his war hawks that they were going into hostile territory with too few troops. To keep the peace after capturing the enemy's capital, some 500,000 troops would be needed, plus a lot more planning for the occupation.

His warnings went ignored. The president's team of armchair experts and political strategists told the president they had the situation well in hand, and the boys would be home soon. "On to Baghdad!"

In 1861, "On to Richmond!" was the battle cry. The Cassandra nobody wanted to hear was not General Eric Shinseki, Army chief of staff, who urged President Bush to add another 125,000 troops to his invading force of 175,000. It was General Winfield Scott, the most experienced general in the United States, who urged Lincoln to add 500,000 troops to his force of 75,000. Scott had fought in the War of 1812, had won numerous engagements with the Indians, and had served as commander of the Mexican War, where he had supervised promising young officers like Lee, Grant, McClellan, and Jefferson Davis. He was now seventy-five and retired. Scott's warnings were resented by the younger men as the rantings of a curmudgeon. Nobody wanted to believe his warning that the South would be a tough adversary.

Viewed today, Scott looks like a genius. He argued that the defense of a homeland against an invading occupier gave the defender a powerful advantage. The North, while rich, was not prepared for an arduous, long-drawn-out struggle. Simply capturing Richmond was myopia; the fight would last a lot longer than that. Scott thereupon developed a strategic plan, called the Anaconda Plan, whereby the North would set up a naval blockade all along the eastern seaboard from the Chesapeake down to the Gulf of Mexico, coupled with an army of sixty thousand men to blockade the Mississippi from Illinois to New Orleans. It would surround the enemy like a snake and choke it. Only by sealing the borders and cutting off supplies, he argued, could the North force the South into submission.

Had the U.S. implemented an Anaconda Plan for Iraq modeled after the ideas of General Winfield Scott, rather than the "army lite" concept of Donald Rumsfeld, there would have been no looting after the "capture" of Baghdad, no loose borders, and certainly no multiple insurrections plunging the country into chaos.

A Prima Donna General

➤**1862** This war-weary president was getting fed up with the nation's most charismatic general, a prima donna and presidential candidate who was acting unctuously. When this general took the nation—and his boss—by surprise by issuing his own political orders for areas under his command, the president was deluged with mail urging him to take a stand one way or the other. It was the most controversial moment of his presidency. Finally, on October 24, the outraged president "decided to fire the troublesome general."

Many years before Harry Truman fired General Douglas MacArthur, there was another prima donna general, the re-

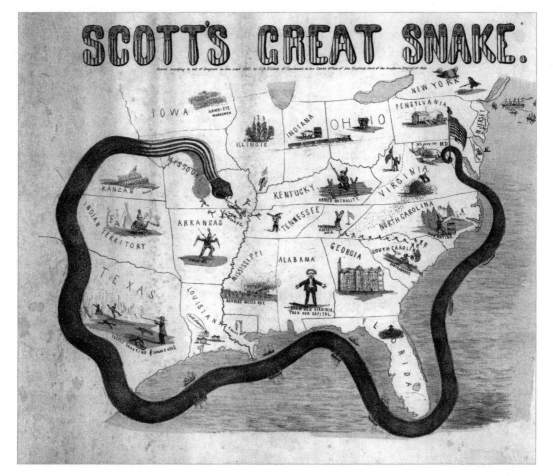

nowned John C. Frémont. For issuing orders authorizing the emancipation of slaves in Missouri without presidential permission, Lincoln fired him on the spot.

As for MacArthur, he should have known better: the same thing had also happened to his own father. Back in the early 1900s, General Arthur MacArthur, military governor of the Philippines, made the stupid mistake of not recognizing the superior authority of the civilian governor, William Howard Taft, who later became

president. Years later, when MacArthur's turn came to be promoted to army chief of staff, Taft blackballed him.

Raising Taxes and Plunging into Deficit Spending to Finance a War

➤ **1864** After four years, this president had run up the greatest government deficits ever. He was the first president of the United States to go on public record as believing that neither deficits nor the national debt constituted a serious problem.

When war came and the government needed money desperately, he sought to reassure the American public that although the government's finances were in terrible shape, the government could spend its way out of it:

> *Held, as it is, for the most part by our own people, the debt has become a substantial branch of national, though private, property. For obvious reasons the more nearly this property can be distributed along all the people the better. . . . The greater advantage of citizens being creditors as well as debtors with relation to the public debt is obvious. Men readily perceive that they can not be much oppressed by a debt which they owe to themselves.*

As president, he revolutionized the financial methods of the United States. During his tenure he established a national banking system, increased taxes and tariffs, and made U.S. dollar bills a monopoly medium of exchange vis-à-vis state bank notes. Every year his administration incurred relatively large deficits and accumulated a large national debt.

He died just as the war ended, and did not like to see his Keynesian economics applied in peacetime conditions. His successor presidents renounced his philosophy and made fiscal prudence and elimi-

nation of the budget deficit a high priority of their administrations.

It wasn't until FDR was elected that Keynesian economics became accepted policy. The president who first espoused it was Abraham Lincoln.

Jinxed Building

➤**1865** When Alice Roosevelt Longworth planted a voodoo doll in the White House garden, she had good history to go on: Ford's Theatre. After Lincoln's assassination in 1865, the federal government took over the building and turned it into a records facility for the War Department. In 1893 the building collapsed and killed twenty-two federal clerks.

In the presidential box with Lincoln were his wife, Mary, and a young couple, Colonel Henry Rathbone and his fiancée, Clara Harris. Mary Lincoln became insane in 1875 and had to be institutionalized for several months, and ended up spending the rest of her life in seclusion, much of it in Europe. But she wasn't the only member of the presidential party to go off the deep end; there were also Henry Rathbone and Clara. As a result of that awful night, Clara's dress was totally bloodstained, putting her in a quandary. What to do with the dress? She thought all the blood was Lincoln's, but actually it was Rathbone's; he had been knifed by John Wilkes Booth. She didn't want to throw the dress away, but she obviously didn't want it lying around, either. So she put it away in a closet. Finding this procedure a bit creepy, she called in the bricklayers and had the closet entombed behind a brick wall, the dress still inside.

In the meantime she married Henry Rathbone and had three children. But Rathbone had demons of his own, and in 1883, on Christmas Eve no less, he entered the bedroom with a gun and a knife just as Booth had, and proceeded to murder his wife with a gunshot, then turned the knife on himself and stabbed himself six times, trying to kill himself. He failed and spent the rest of his life in a home for the criminally insane.

In 1910 the Rathbones' son had the brick wall torn down and found the bloodstained dress still there. Believing it to be a curse on his family, he had the dress burned.

Not part of the 1865 presidential party were three people who had been invited but chose not to come: Robert Todd Lincoln and General and Mrs. Ulysses Grant. How lucky they were.

Worse than Katrina

▶**1900** In 2006, Hurricane Katrina caused a political uproar when 1,600 people died as the levees failed and the Gulf of Mexico waters poured into New Orleans. The devastation of the city was nothing to be astonished about. Had federal officials and the city mayor paid more attention to the history of hurricanes, they would have been ready for Katrina. Such lack of appreciation of history borders on legal negligence.

More prosperous than Houston or Dallas in its day, Galveston in 1900 was the major trading port of Texas, "the New York of the Gulf," served by forty-five steamship lines and twenty-six foreign consulates. Ornate classical houses adorned its major streets, and the city boasted more millionaires than the Robber Baron retreat of Newport, Rhode Island. Galveston, wrote the historian Eric Larson,

> *was too pretty, too progressive, too prosperous—entirely too hopeful—to be true. Travelers arriving by ship saw the city as a silvery fairy kingdom that might just as suddenly disappear from sight, a very different portrait from that which would present itself in the last few weeks of September 1900, when inbound passengers smelled the pyres of burning corpses a hundred miles out to sea.*

Galveston had been a disaster waiting to happen. Almost as vulnerable as New Orleans situated below sea level, Galveston was an island of sand, whose average elevation was five feet above sea level. And as with Katrina, there was plenty of warning ahead of time, but owing to civic "it can't happen here" pride, people did not heed warnings to flee until it was too late. To the city officials of Galveston, the prospect of a hur-

Galveston, Texas, after the hurricane

ricane flooding the city was an "absurd delusion." The city didn't even have a seawall, figuring such expensive precautions were unnecessary.

Everyone in Galveston knew in advance that a hurricane was rapidly approaching; it was even reported in the newspapers. Telegraph reports four days old told of havoc in the Caribbean, and ships arriving at the Galveston port reported stormy seas in the Gulf of Mexico. The day before the hurricane arrived, official warning flags were posted through-out the city. But less than half of the population bothered to evacuate. To the contrary, many hundreds of people came over from Houston to enjoy the thrill of a storm—a thrill most of them failed to live to tell about. The hurricane, with 200 mph winds, came in and blanketed the city with seawater ten feet high; by the time it receded the next day, twelve city blocks—nearly three-quarters of the island city—had been destroyed and 20 percent of the population killed.* It was the worst natural disaster ever to occur

---

* A 200 mph wind "can generate pressure of 152 tons per square foot, or more than 60,000 pounds against a house wall." That's thirty tons.

in America. Six thousand people died—more than in the legendary Johnstown Flood, the San Francisco Earthquake, the Great Chicago Fire, and Katrina combined.

Determined that such a catastrophe never happen again, Galveston embarked on one of the most remarkable engineering wonders of the world: it not only built an eighteen-foot seawall, but lifted itself up to the seawall level. It did this by jacking up various buildings one by one, then filling in the empty space with earth. An entire cathedral was raised with hand jacks and filled in with earth underneath. "So today," observes CNN, "a visitor to Galveston gets a very different sense of the island's relationship to the sea than a visitor would have had in 1900."

Galveston learned its lesson from this tragedy. Other cities, like New Orleans, did not.

Dumping Foreign-Made Cars in the United States

➤**1904**   America's auto industry faced stiff competition from across the ocean, where the world's largest auto producer threatened to dump more and more cars in the United States. Responding to pleas for help from the auto industry, Congress passed legislation that succeeded in stemming the flow of auto imports.

The year was 1904: France, the world's largest auto producer, got socked with a 45-percent tariff. This congressional measure saved the U.S. auto industry, as France turned its attention to the UK, where it quickly captured substantial market share. The U.S. tariff stood until 1913, when it was finally reduced to 30 percent. (As for Japan in the 1980s, there was no formal U.S. government legislation, just friendly pressure on the Japanese urging "voluntary" restrictions; furthermore, these restrictions failed to stem the tide. Japan's annual quota of cars increased from 1.68 million in 1981 to 2.3 million in 1985, and Japanese auto companies moved upscale and generated record revenues and profits, while Detroit's "Big Three" auto companies struggled and two of them eventually went belly-up.)

The Automobile: The Bigger, the Better

➤**1911**   Nothing characterizes America's "unique way of life" more than the automobile. On page 320, see what people back in 1911 thought the car would look like in fifty years.

Note that this car is riding "off road." Such a car has extra wheels to provide the necessary traction, and a powerful engine to enable the vehicle to roar up the hill. Obviously, for such a behemoth, gasoline was no problem: America was awash in cheap oil.

Today this car—utilizing modern technology and electronics—is the SUV, ac-

"*Things the Motorist Wants to Know*"—*1911 vision of 1961 car*

counting for 55 percent of new car sales. Unfortunately the energy component essential to sustain this love affair has changed. If U.S. vehicles that average 24 mpg as in Europe and Japan, the United States wouldn't need to import a drop of oil from the Persian Gulf, and we would never have heard of Osama bin Laden.

Reappearance of the Laffer Curve

►**1917** President Reagan introduced the Laffer Curve in 1981 as an instrument of government policy. According to the economist Arthur Laffer, a reduction in the tax rate would increase revenues because people would be rewarded for

producing more and declaring all of their income instead of trying to shelter it.

What Laffer and Reagan never mentioned was that the Laffer Curve idea had been tried before, sixty-five years earlier. In 1917 the United States had experimented with a dramatic change in the tax rates, with equally dramatic changes in taxpayer behavior and realized tax revenues.

	1916	1921
Tax Rate	7%	77%
$300,000-$1M	1,090	225
$1M+	206	21
Tax Revenues	$ 81.4M	$ 84.8M

In 1916 the minimum income tax was 7 percent. It was increased to 15 percent that year, then up to 67 percent the following year, then up to 77 percent in 1918. As the previous page shows, confiscatory taxes drove wealth underground. The number of people declaring high incomes ($300,000–$1 million) dropped from 1,090 to 225, and the number of people declaring millionaire incomes dropped from 206 to 21. The government's tax revenues increased hardly at all.

Defying World Opinion

➤**1923** This small but powerful 20th-century nation, after taking over nearby territory, was becoming increasingly belligerent, to the point of installing the most powerful weapons of the day (subsequently called weapons of mass destruction). The prospect of the rogue country having such weaponry terrified the world's major powers, especially the United States. The international body representing all the world's nations sought to get its inspectors in, but was rebuffed. Because this international arbiter had no military force of its own, and because no member nation was strong or daring enough to challenge this aggressive small country, the country continued to defy world opinion. Finally war came and the country was attacked and defeated by the United States, sending its troops halfway around the world.

We are talking not about Iraq and its refusal to let in the UN weapons inspectors, but about Japan and the League of Nations. Shortly after World War I, Japan had laid claim to the Caroline, Marianas, and Marshall Islands, generally known as Micronesia. The League of Nations refused to recognize Japan's claim. The Japanese navy, however, had other ideas. It launched a massive military buildup on the islands and refused to allow any visitors. The situation got so bad that by as early as 1923, the U.S. Navy concluded that these military installations posed a threat to U.S. security, and General Billy Mitchell was warning his superiors that the next war would be a surprise Japanese attack on Pearl Harbor on a Sunday morning—a warning viewed as being so provocative that it got Mitchell court-martialed.

In the early 1930s, in response to the League of Nations' demand to let in the inspectors, Japan told the world to "shove it" by withdrawing from the League. And, of course, Japan did attack Pearl Harbor on a Sunday morning.

Not Vietnam

➤**1925** At the famous Scopes trial concerning whether evolution should be taught in schools, Clarence Darrow stated, "History repeats itself, and that's one of the things that's wrong with history."

Our Vietnam experience might not have fared so badly had our government strategists and military personnel paid more attention to previous experience.

Here are some stories that we later repeated in the mid-1960s:

No End in Sight

"Intervention will begin on a small scale, but with each step forward in its demand for ships, men, money, and materials. . . . If we intervene, going further as we succeed, we shall be swallowed up." So wrote the number-two man to his boss, the American ambassador to Moscow, about a guerrilla war ten thousand miles away. The president of the United States, who had entered office saying, "It would be an irony of fate if my administration had to deal with foreign policy," agreed. "In my opinion, to try to stop a revolutionary movement with ordinary armies is like using a broom to sweep back a great sea." Later during his term, he lamented how much easier it was to get into a war than to get out of it.

Unpopular War

It was the most unpopular war America had ever fought. In this mismatch between a world industrial superpower and a small agricultural country, the U.S. embarked on a venture "for reasons that were inadequate and ill-advised, if not confused." Many American soldiers, feeling that their own patriotic obligation was self-defense of American shores, refused to go off to a foreign country and resisted the draft. Utilizing dated weaponry from a previous war, the army forces failed to mount a sustained campaign capable of knocking out the enemy from the north. To finance the war effort, the president had to go to great extremes to persuade Congress to enact a tax measure. Still, less than one third of the cost of the war was financed by taxation; the rest was financed by government borrowing.

Public opposition to the war grew bitter and widespread, especially among the well-to-do. There was loose management of American military supplies, much of which ended up in the hands of the enemy. The war was going badly, and despondency gripped the nation.

Drug Problems

To relieve the boredom of the long campaign and especially to alleviate the excruciating pain of severe battlefield wounds, many American soldiers resorted to drugs. Soldiers returning home from this war faced daunting prospects. Many employers viewed them as unstable and unmanageable. A military newsletter advised men not to disclose their military service. With America beginning to encounter a serious drug-abuse problem for the first time, many people accused soldiers of having brought home a social ill that threatened to undermine the nation. More than 45,000 drug addicts did not improve the reputation of veterans, especially as the numbers continued to grow. A government study completed twenty years later found that the number of veteran drug addicts had increased fivefold, to more than 250,000.

Fighting for What?

Sent off to fight in a blistering warm country, many soldiers fought bravely without any sense of purpose. "I am not afraid and I am always ready to do duty," wrote one, "but I would like someone to tell me what we are fighting for." The U.S. had stepped in after the departure of a defeated European colonial power, and soon found itself in an even deeper quagmire, fighting the local revolutionary leader it had previously supported and provided aid to. After years of frustrating fighting, topped by an ambush by a team of twelve-year-olds posing as women, a U.S. commanding officer went bonkers and ordered his troops to kill anyone in sight: "I want no prisoners. I want you to kill and burn—the more the better."

After the massacre of innocent civilians, the U.S. was gripped by a dramatic trial that captured national attention. The commanding officer was court-martialed and sentenced to prison (though he was eventually set free because of "mental attitude"). Wrote America's most famous novelist, "We have debauched America's honor and blackened her face before the world."

Liberal President

This liberal president, who had just won reelection in the biggest landslide in history, expected gratitude for the many social programs he had inaugurated. But the moment he suggested college students might have to go overseas to fight, the honeymoon ended. Antiwar movements started up on university campuses throughout the country. An angry protest letter signed by two hundred college presidents arrived at the White House. A third of college students said they would not fight in any war unless America was invaded; more than another third said they would not fight even then. This exuberant president was dismayed.

Intellectual Elite

The intellectual elite of this superpower formed a chorus urging that this war in a faraway land was morally wrong. The country's most renowned politician spoke out in public: the war was "unjust in its principles, impracticable in its means, and ruinous in its consequences . . . conquest is an impossibility." The country's most influential writer urged "the thinking friends of government" to take action and seek peace.

Even the nation's top general came to believe the war was unwinnable. Seeing no signs of an uprising by any of the local population, for whom the nation was fighting, he became discouraged by the lack of sufficient troops to stage a quick military rout, and frustrated by constant civilian interference from above. "Without money, provisions, ships or troops adequate to any beneficial purpose," he wrote his superior back home, he could not win. In another memo he complained of not being given free rein to do his job: "If you want me to do anything, leave me to myself and let me adapt my efforts to the hourly change of circumstances." Several months later he wrote another report arguing "the utter impossibility of carrying on the war without reinforcement." If he could not get more troops, he would like permission to resign.

Knowing that time was on their side, the small faraway country waged a war of attrition, led by a brilliant field commander in the south. An international military expert opined that in a war of numbers, the defenders were following the proper strategy, one based on the Chinese model: "to lose a battle to you every week until you are reduced to nothing."

Dissent

Leading politicians pleaded with the nation's leader to be more flexible in negotiating a peace settlement, but the leader said no, the enemy must be taught a lesson and national pride was at stake. Protesters declared the war a violation of "those eternal principles of political justice which should be most dear" and that a military victory would be "an ill omen."

A key figure in the administration denounced the war as "most accursed, wicked, barbarous, cruel, unjust and diabolical." When news came that the American military had suffered a horrendous defeat, a liberal congressman who later became secretary of state leaped from his chair and clapped his hands.

⁂

No End in Sight. The quote about "intervention" comes from the American consul in Moscow, concerned about America's ill-fated venture in Siberia during 1918–19. The president, of course, was Woodrow Wilson.

Unpopular War. Substitute Great Britain for the United States as the industrial superpower, and Canada for North Vietnam as the foreign country American draft resisters refused to invade, and you have the War of 1812.

Drug Problems. There is a little-known dark side to the Civil War that has pervaded all our subsequent wars: the use of addictive drugs as painkillers. Hypodermic syringes were introduced into the United States in 1856, where they quickly became handy during the Civil War. Two thousand doctors equipped with syringes used the best available painkiller, morphine, on their wounded soldiers. When they didn't have syringes, they used 10 million opium pills and 2.8 million ounces of powdered opium and other opiates such as laudanum and paregoric. By the turn of the century, when scientists had figured out how to turn morphine into heroin, the Civil War soldier—like his Vietnam counterpart one hundred years later—became associated with drug abuse.

Fighting for What? In 1898 the United States took over the Philippines from Spain, only to find that the local leader it had brought in from Hong Kong, Emilio Aguinaldo, had different ideas about freedom and independence: he wanted freedom from the Americans as well as from the Spanish. The commanding officer was Brigadier General "Hell Roaring Jake" Smith, precursor to Lieutenant William Calley of Vietnam fame. Further atrocities were committed after the completion of the Smith trial. The U.S. Senate launched an extensive investigation and heard testimony about American use of water torture, burning of towns, and other war crimes. Among the more interesting revelations was that the U.S. military had conducted no fewer than forty-four trials for military atrocities. Secretary of State John Hay to the contrary, it was hardly "a splendid little war." The author Mark Twain had it right. Let us wave the flag, he said, "but with the white stripes painted black and the stars replaced by the skull and crossbones."

Liberal President. The president was Franklin D. Roosevelt in 1934, trying to cope with isolationists such as the Hearst newspapers, Father Charles Coughlin, the Republican Congress, and the U.S. Senate, which thereafter retaliated by conducting an extensive investigation into munitions profiteering. The Senate even passed a law effectively forbidding the president to make loans to friendly countries resisting aggression.

Intellectual Elite. Turn back the clock more than two hundred years and meet the powerful writer with "thinking friends," Edward Gibbon, authority on the decline and fall of empires. England's renowned politician who opposed the war in America was the former prime minister, William Pitt. The British field commander was General Sir Henry Clinton. His repeated pleas for more reinforcements were turned down by the war minister, Lord Germain, and his demand to be relieved of duty was rejected by King George. The American general using the Chinese model of warfare was Nathaniel Greene, and the British military expert who admired him was the governor of Quebec, a man obviously familiar with how to fight in the woods.

Dissent. King George III was not about to listen to the leading politicians of the day, William Pitt and Charles Fox, even though one of them was his prime minister and the other had served briefly as his secretary of foreign affairs. Pitt declared the war was "most diabolical," a violation of "those eternal principles which should be to all Englishmen most dear," and would result in a victory that "would be an ill omen for English liberty." Charles Fox, the man who rejoiced in Cornwallis's defeat, was Pitt's major political opponent: the two men disagreed about virtually everything, but agreed fully that the war on America was a disaster that would result in loss of empire. For his radical views, Fox was forced out of office and became a leading opposition figure in Parliament. Two years after Yorktown, he returned to his old position as secretary of foreign affairs.

Not OPEC

►**1931** When the major petroleum-exporting countries formed their OPEC organization in 1973 and jacked up the price of oil, Americans howled with rage. How dare they try to manipulate the market and subject the world to artificially high prices?

What Americans forgot was that it had been done before, and done so successfully that it lasted more than forty years. The model? The Texas Railroad Commission in 1931.

Up until the 1950s, when the Middle East began producing oil in huge quantities, the major oil producer was Texas, generating more than half of the world's oil. Regulating the Texas oil industry was the Texas Railroad Commission, originally set up to regulate railroad commerce, which also had the power to regulate other "common carriers" such as oil pipelines. As a regulatory agency, the commission was further empowered to take whatever measures it deemed necessary to prevent waste of oil and gas resources.

Because it is so big and capital-intensive, the oil business is a complex business involving a delicate balance of its major players. Contrary to the popular perception that the oil industry wants high prices, the best level of prices is a stable, midlevel one that assures oil consumers, oil producers, and oil refiners that they won't be hit with a shortage or a surplus. The history of the oil industry, unfortunately, is one of swings between too much production, which leads to low prices, and too little production, which leads to high prices. In early 1930, oil was selling for $1.30 a barrel. Then came the discovery of the Kilgore Field in Texas, the biggest oil deposit ever found. Within months it was producing more than a million barrels a day (equivalent to 50 percent of all American oil consumption). By the summer of 1931, there was so much supply that people were stealing oil from the Kilgore field and selling it on the black market for as little as ten cents a barrel.

In a business where the cost of production was eighty cents, such widespread panic selling threatened the oil industry with ruin. "The time will come," warned the Texas Railroad Commission, "when our oil and gas resources will be greatly depleted or exhausted . . . the calamity will be too serious to contemplate." Said one oilman, "There was much unrest, with talk of threats of blowing up wells and pipelines" to curb competitors' output.

Facing ruin, some 1,200 oil producers and wildcatters met with Texas governor Ross Sterling and asked him to save them from themselves. By unanimous vote, they passed a resolution requesting him to declare martial law. That 1,200 oilmen agreed on anything, let alone unanimously, was a miracle readily appreciated by the governor, himself a former oilman. Sterling wasted not a moment. In a move that violated every U.S. law prohibiting anticompetitive practices and price collusion, he declared a state emergency and imposed martial law. With his full support, the Texas Railroad Commission announced a new system of monthly production quotas (called allowances), specifying what percentage of production the Texas wells could pump each month. To enforce the Railroad Commission's edicts and to prevent desperate sellers from undercutting the market, the governor sent in state troops to shut down all wells temporarily. This show of force worked, production fell to more reasonable levels, and by 1934 the price of oil was back to more than one dollar a barrel.

Because of the volume of oil coming from Texas, this control of Texas oil pricing had the effect of dictating the world price of oil. When the Middle Eastern countries replaced Texas as the primary source of oil in the 1950s and 1960s, they appreciated the need for joint cooperation of some kind. Looking for a model, they had to look no further than the obvious one in the United States.

❧

Oil isn't the only case of outrageous trading practices having their origin in the United States. Another example is copyright infringement, especially by China.

For years artists and writers in the world's most powerful nation have seethed at the theft of their creative works by a large developing country on the other side of the ocean. No matter that the two countries were major trading partners, it was vital that copyright protection be observed. One of the powerful nation's most popular novelists visited the developing nation and was horrified to find thousands of copies of his novels being printed locally and hawked on the streets for a fraction of what they could be sold for at home (with no royalty to him, of course). After much trade negotiation spanning a half-century, an agreement was reached whereby the developing country granted copyright protection for foreign authors. But there was a condition: the books still had to be manufactured locally. No imports were allowed. The powerful nation continued to push for full copyright protection for its writers and creative artists, and finally got it—ninety-five years later.

China's policy of copyright infringement follows early American practice. The novelist appalled at the theft of copyright was Charles Dickens, visiting America in 1842. England granted copyright protection to American authors, but it wasn't until 1891 that the United States did the same for English authors—with conditions attached (the books had to be printed in America). These conditions were not removed until Congress amended U.S. copyright law in 1986. If we replace the year 1842 with the year 2010 and follow this same pace of copyright reform, then American artists can look forward to obtaining copyright protection in China in the year 2154.

The First Japanese Attack on Pearl Harbor

►**1932** This daring admiral was convinced the Americans would be sleeping on a Sunday morning, a good time to attack Pearl Harbor and get rid of the American menace once and for all. At his disposal were two aircraft carriers and four destroyers in the Pacific, but his chosen weapon of assault would be aircraft—a form of attack never attempted before. Everything depended on surprise. Launching 152 planes at dawn, he succeeded in hitting every ship in Pearl Harbor and destroying all the defending planes on the ground. The carnage on the ground was awesome. Needless to say, his stunning

victory was greeted with horror by his superiors in the country's capital.

He was Harry E. Yarnell, U.S. rear admiral and later commander of the Asiatic Fleet. Conducting a military exercise in 1932 and pretending to be a Japanese admiral, he destroyed the U.S. forces at Pearl Harbor. The exercise, known as Fleet Problem 13, involved a fleet of "Blue" attacking planes launched from the USS *Saratoga*, attacking Pearl Harbor defended by "Black" planes resting on the ground. In a classic example of "loose lips sink ships," the exercise was duly reported in the *New York Times*. Its report from Honolulu, dated February 7, began, "A vast fighting force of the air rose out of the horizon today, delivered a smashing attack on the defenders of the island of Oahu and then wheeled around and disappeared over the bend of the sea towards its floating base in the Pacific. . . . They made their attack unopposed by the defense, which was caught virtually napping and escaped to the motherships without the slightest damage being inflicted upon them."

The next day the *New York Times* followed up with another story making it abundantly clear how stunning Yarnell's victory was: "The sky-hawks circled over the land air base and rained down bombs while the defense, with its interior air force, watched and waited."

The Japanese consulate in Honolulu was so astounded by what it read that it immediately cabled full details to Tokyo.

Yarnell (third from right) conducting inspection prior to launching his surprise attack on Pearl Harbor. Notice the absence of markings on the planes—the Navy claimed he violated the rules.

Might naval air power be the next new tool of war? The U.S. Navy in Washington was so shocked and embarrassed by Yarnell's feat that it complained the rules of the war game had been skewed in his favor, and disallowed the results. Such an event could never happen in reality.

By 1941, Yarnell was gone, replaced by a more traditional admiral wedded to the primacy of destroyers and cruisers as opposed to aircraft carriers. On Thursday, December 4, a private dinner party was held at the Carlton Hotel in Washington DC to honor the vice president, Henry Wallace. Present were two dozen of the most powerful men in the nation's capital.

It was a boisterous gathering, full of jokes and camaraderie. After a round of toasts amid the cigar smoke, one man stood up and delivered a quite different message, a somber one. "I feel that I can speak very frankly, within these four walls," he said. "I want you to know that our situation tonight is very serious—more serious, probably, than most of us realize. We are very close to war. War may begin in the Pacific at any moment. Literally, at any moment. It may even be beginning tonight while we're sitting here, for all we know. We are that close to it."

He paused to let the words sink in, then he went on, his voice rising confidently lest he be a party-pooper: "But I want you to know that whatever happens, the United States Navy is ready!" he thundered. "Every man is at his post, every ship is at its station. The Navy is ready. Whatever happens, the Navy is not going to be caught napping."

The speaker was Frank Knox, secretary of the Navy. Everyone went to bed and slept soundly.

Seventy-two hours later, the Japanese bombed Pearl Harbor. The "surprise" attack of 1941 had followed the 1932 Yarnell trial run exactly.

Admiral Harry Yarnell

Precursor to Global Warming, Man-made

►**1935** Today, as we consider global warming, anybody who thinks climate change isn't catastrophic should consider the greatest environmental disaster of the twentieth century. It wasn't a natural disaster; it was caused by man and his refusal to heed the warning signs.

"Get a farm while land is cheap—where every man is a landlord!" said the land speculators in the 1920s. "Grow wheat and get rich!" said the railroads. Heeding the call were millions of American farmers and immigrants pursuing the American Dream by moving to the Great Plains to build a new life in the area covering southern Kansas and Colorado and northern Oklahoma, Texas, and New Mexico. The locals thought they were crazy. The Indians, forced off the land, had no say. But even the local cowboys scoffed: "You guys are crazy, the Panhandle is good only for growing grass."

No matter. The invading settlers tore up the ground and its 470 native species of grass that had thrived for thousands of years, and planted wheat. In less than ten years they went from subsistence living to modest wealth. Thanks to the tractor, where it had taken fifty-eight hours to plant and harvest an acre by hand, it now took only three hours.

By the summer of 1929 the U.S. had a wheat surplus and prices dropped. To maintain their income, the new farmers tore up more grass to increase their wheat output in a futile chase of the rainbow. Overleveraged just like their fellow Americans on Wall Street, farmers saw wheat prices crash to one-eighth the normal price. Unable to prevent foreclosure, many farmers abandoned their farms, leaving the upturned soil exposed naked to the wind. Others stayed, trying to eke out a subsistence living in the droughts of 1931–32, in hopes that things would get better.

Then came the dust storms, an anomaly of nature. In Oklahoma in early 1933 the temperature fell more than 70 degrees in less than twenty-four hours, to -14 degrees. Forty-mile-per-hour dust storms in subzero temperatures wreaked havoc. But worse was still to come. In May 1934 a huge dust storm from the Dakotas moved east, covering 1,800 miles, all the way to New York State, and dumping 350 million tons of dust—equivalent to three tons for every American. In just five hours an avalanche of 5,400 tons of dust landed on Chicago and 1,300 on New York City—were it so fortunate! Dust even seeped through the windows of the White House, causing minor panic.

At least for the president this was a one-time shock. But in the High Plains, now known as the Dust Bowl, the dust never stopped. A snowstorm had so much dust it was called a "snuster" (snow mixed with dust). Over the course of the year there were fifty-four snusters.

Now, dust particles can be a lot more dangerous than what you see on your desktop or counter. Extremely fine (one-fifth the size of the period at the end of this sentence), they clog the sinuses, throat, respiratory system, and even the stomach. Everywhere, farmers covered the doors and windows with sheets and blankets. All crops—whatever was left after the drought—were destroyed, and farm animals died. Many homes and fields were under ten feet of dust. A new disease emerged—dust pneumonia. People breathed through sponges. Black dust came from Kansas, red from Oklahoma, yellow-orange from Texas, and green from sources unidentified.

Then came "Black Sunday," April 14, 1935. In Kansas, a dust storm in March followed by another storm in April dumped a total of 9.4 tons per acre, crushing trees and causing house roofs to collapse. In Oklahoma the dust storm roared in at more than forty miles an hour—for a hundred hours. In Kansas, the volume of dust blowing from one side of the state to the other was equivalent to 46 million truckloads. In a single afternoon the storm carried twice the amount of dirt removed over a seven-year period to build the Panama Canal. Temperatures dropped 25 degrees in one hour in Denver as the dust storm came in and obliterated all sunlight. In Kansas, the dust wave was two thousand feet high, coming in at sixty-five miles an hour. Car drivers turned on their headlights but could not see ahead, or even see their passengers sitting next to them. "It was like three midnights in a jug," recalled one survivor. It was the mother of all dusters. Woody Guthrie, then a twenty-two-year-old struggling folk singer, was thinking what it must have been like for the Israelites as the Red Sea closed in. When one of the people in the bar said, "This is it, the end of the world," Guthrie started humming the opening of a song: "So Long, It's Been Good to Know You."

Observed the war journalist Ernie Pyle, certainly a man used to seeing the worst, "I saw not a solitary thing, but bare earth and a few lonely, empty farmhouses. . . . There was not a tree or a blade of grass, or a dog or a cow or a human being—nothing whatsoever . . . the saddest land I have ever seen."

Today the land is resettled, and nature has not misbehaved, but lost in the dust is the suffering of 221,000 people who had to flee, their lives ruined, all brought about by their defiance of nature. So ended America's greatest ecological disaster.

Could it happen again? Consider the aftermath. The response of FDR was to pour money into the distressed region by providing funds for irrigation systems to provide water. Subsequent administrations further opened the money spigot to build dams to provide water for the

Dust storm, Great Plains

Southwest desert, leading to a population boom in Las Vegas, Arizona, and southern California. Yet from an ecological view, this is risky. The next time bomb waiting to happen in the West is the fight over water. In 1900 a person used twenty gallons of water a day. By 1973 it was 175 gallons per person. Plus, there's population growth . . .

"The United States," says one engineer, "is two countries—one humid and one arid, with the boundary following the hundredth meridian, a little west of the Mississippi River." One part has water, the other doesn't.

The First Terrorist Attack on America

➤**1942** Code-named Operation Pastorius, launched with the personal endorsement of Adolf Hitler, the German *U-202* submarine crept up to the shores of Long Island near New York City and dropped off four terrorists (called "saboteurs" in those days). A month later, another U-boat delivered a second group of four to the coast of Florida. Equipped with explosives, the saboteurs were to blow up bridges and power plants and strike fear in the American heartland. Only there was a problem: chosen because they had lived in America and spoke good English, all the Germans had loyalties to America; some even had American wives. None of them had the killer instinct needed for such a

dangerous mission. Upon landing, the ringleader of the Long Island contingent panicked and turned himself in, along with his comrades, and even signed a 250-page typewritten confession giving all the details of the plot. The FBI promptly tracked down and arrested the Florida contingent, most of whom were spending their cash on fine restaurants and a shopping spree in New York. With the war going badly, FDR needed any propaganda coup he could get. For the beleaguered president, the swift capture of these incompetents was manna from heaven.

He ordered the captives to be tried immediately by a military court chosen by him, where justice would be swift, and the death sentence imposed by a two-thirds vote. "I want one thing clearly understood," he told his attorney general, "I won't give them up. . . . I won't hand them over to any United States Marshal armed with a writ of habeas corpus. Understand!"

Behind closed doors, the military court quickly pronounced all eight men guilty. Six were executed; two were given lengthy prison terms, then eventually extradited back home. The United States trumpeted the capture and execution as a rousing success, and letters and telegrams poured into the White House: "It's high time that we wake up here in this country and show the world we are not a bunch of mush hounds," wrote one.

The defense lawyers appealed to the Supreme Court about the constitutional-

German saboteurs on trial, U. S. military court

ity of a secret military trial carrying the threat of execution. Several of the German saboteurs were U.S. citizens, obviously deserving of a public jury trial. None of the Germans had committed a crime, but had only been involved in a plan to commit a crime, which they had abrogated by voluntarily turning themselves in. If anything, maybe their revelations had even helped the U.S. war effort.

They had good history to go on: the Constitution. It guarantees the right of habeas corpus ("bring the body"), meaning that citizens have the right to appear in court. But what about enemy combatants? In the American Revolution, when John André was caught as a spy for the British, he was tried by a military court and hanged. During the Civil War, Abraham Lincoln had used the same principle and suspended habeas corpus. In 1866, to restore civil liberties, there occurred a landmark case, *Ex parte Milligan*, won by James A. Garfield, who later became president, in which the Supreme Court ruled that civilians could never be brought before a military court when there were "available and functioning" civilian courts.

One of the justices, William O. Douglas, liked to say that 90 percent of Supreme Court cases were decided on emotion, and only 10 percent on the law. Such was the case here in 1942: it was wartime, and passions were high. In a stunning reversal of precedent (which Douglas opposed), the Supreme Court ruled in favor of the government and "agreed on a verdict without agreeing on the reasons for the verdict, a reversal of normal procedure." The justices also specified that their ruling applied only to this particular situation, and could not be used as a precedent in future cases.*

Thus was established the unilateral power of a president to use military tribunals, utilized by President Bush in justifying the imprisonment of captives in Guantánamo.

Kangaroo Court of Justice

➤**1953** When Congress passed the Patriot Act in 2001, denying basic civil liberties to people suspected to be terrorists or aiding terrorists, it had good precedent to go on.

This American president, described by his assistant defense secretary as "a simple man, prone to make up his mind quickly and decisively—a thorough American," reveled in America's military might and issued an "insistent note of unilateral responsibility" for the use of his superior force "as a sacred trust for the rest of the world." In a well-publicized 1946 speech at an open outdoor site in New York City, packed with hundreds of anxious people, he reassured his fellow citizens that there would be absolutely no "compromises with evil." Placing America's security on its ability to wage a "preemptive military strike," he increased the defense and espionage budget dramatically and permitted his FBI director to undertake whatever illegal wiretaps were deemed necessary to identify potential "security risks."

One man, who had graced the cover of *Time* magazine as an "authentic contemporary hero" for his contributions to American security, expressed concerns about such aggressive measures. Asked "What instrument would you use to detect an atomic bomb hidden somewhere in a city?" Robert Oppenheimer sarcastically replied that it would take a screwdriver, to open each and every suitcase or crate coming into the U.S.—a clear impossibility. "It is clear to me that wars have changed," he said, meaning that the advantage now rested with the stealthy aggressor, not the well-fortified powerful defender.

Such ideas did not go down well with Harry Truman and his military advisers, especially when Oppenheimer, "the father of the atom bomb," questioned the logic of building an even bigger bomb, the hydrogen bomb, calling it a weapon of "mass genocide." Said the president to Secretary of State Dean Acheson, "I don't want to see that son of a bitch in this office ever

---

* This was the same rare "precedent but not a precedent" caveat used by the Supreme Court in 2000 when it awarded Bush the presidency.

again!" Over the next seven years the FBI conducted a massive investigation amounting to some eight thousand pages of illegal wiretap and surveillance reports on Oppenheimer, but could find no "smoking gun." For J. Edgar Hoover, this was a major embarrassment, and Hoover was not a man who tolerated being made a fool. Surveillance of Oppenheimer continued. In the meantime, by 1953 both the U.S. and the USSR had developed the hydrogen bomb.

That year, acting on a letter that he knew offered "little new evidence," but fearful of Senator Joseph McCarthy's charges that he was being "soft" on communism, President Eisenhower ordered Oppenheimer's security clearance to be lifted—and *then* for a review to take place. Having failed several times already to get Oppenheimer declared a security risk, the director of the Atomic Energy Commission was now jubilant: "We're going to get him this time."

Oppenheimer's friend Albert Einstein caught the mood well: "The German calamity of years ago repeats itself: People acquiesce without resistance and align themselves with the forces of evil."

From the beginning it was obvious to Oppenheimer that he faced a kangaroo court. He was permitted to read the charges against him, but not to take the document out of the room or call a lawyer. He was given twenty-four hours to resign or face the wrath of the government. When he finally did meet with his lawyers, their deliberations were recorded by hidden FBI microphones. The court of review was not a civil court or a trial by jury, but an administrative hearing closed to the press or the public. By calling it an "inquiry" rather than a court, the government avoided having to comply with rules of due process—though everyone knew full well a trial was taking place. The three judges were hand-picked by the government prosecutor, and had access to all the prosecutor's evidence before the hearing began. Oppenheimer's lawyers were denied access to the government's depositions and list of witnesses, whereas the government had full access to Oppenheimer's, thanks to the FBI. No accusation of a specific crime was brought against Oppenheimer, just the vague possibility that he was "a threat to national security" for failing to advocate "the strongest offensive military posture for the United States." (Ignored by the court was the fact that the United States had just completed the successful test of a new, second hydrogen bomb seven hundred times more powerful than the Hiroshima atom bomb—putting the U.S. far ahead of Russia. In the dark days of McCarthyism, however, this was not enough military "security.")

Secretly kept informed of the progress of the hearing was President Eisenhower, who promptly burned the interim report lest he expose himself to possible impeachment for improper meddling in a judicial matter.

Despite such overwhelming government power, Oppenheimer almost pulled it out, losing by one vote, 2–1. Stripped of his security clearance, he never served his government again and lived out his days as director of the Institute of Advanced Study in Princeton. In 1962, recognizing the injustice that had been done, President Kennedy invited Oppenheimer to a White House reception, and in 1963, following Kennedy's initiative, President Lyndon Johnson awarded Oppenheimer the prestigious Enrico Fermi Prize for public service.

Actually, more than injustice was done. This was a betrayal of American security. In its zeal to convict Oppenheimer, the government applied two sets of standards for admitting evidence: witnesses for the defense were denied security clearance, whereas witnesses for the prosecution were granted full security clearance and could now say whatever they knew, even if it formerly had been secret. Observes the historian Priscilla McMillan, "Scientists all over the world pored over the transcript after it was published, and the official British historian Lorna Arnold wrote that the transcript of the Oppenheimer hearing helped British weaponeers invent an H-bomb of their own." There is no written record of the Russian reaction, but obviously the Russians must have been astounded at their good luck. How could the Americans be so dumb? Not a shred of evidence was produced to show that Oppenheimer had given away any se-crets to the Russians. But in an American court, the U.S. government was perfectly willing to do so if it would help secure a conviction against a political adversary.

When the English jurist Edmund Burke called patriotism "the last refuge of a scoundrel," he meant that patriotism often was misused by ruthless men to mask their own personal agendas. If a luminary like Robert Oppenheimer couldn't stand up to it, who can?

Missing: Weapons of Mass Destruction

➤**1957** When George W. Bush was eleven years old, the U.S. embarked on a massive two-year search for weapons of mass destruction. Every intelligence tool was employed, with no luck. Nonetheless, the issue became a critical issue in the forthcoming presidential election, until afterward the Pentagon sheepishly admitted the whole episode had been much ado about nothing: the weapons were nonexistent. The new president of the United States, John F. Kennedy, ordered a study done to make sure such a foul-up would never occur again. In 1963 the completed study arrived on the desk of the assistant secretary of defense, Paul Nitze. Its title: "But Where Did the Missile Gap Go?"

It would seem, judging from events when GW did become president, that no one in his administration had ever heard of it, much less read it. Had they done so, they might have empathized with the pressure of an unknown threat and how easy it is to overreact and see only the facts that support one's beliefs and assumptions. It is like the district attorney who twists the facts to convict a man he absolutely and unequivocally knows is guilty—or does he? Even the brilliant Dean Acheson, Harry Truman's secretary of state, admitted in his memoirs that in pushing for a massive U.S. arms buildup against what he saw as a grave Soviet threat, he had sometimes erred in trying to make his points "clearer than truth."

The Soviets' launch of the *Sputnik* satellite in October 1957 came as a stunning shock to America: how could this possibly happen? Any notion of U.S. technological superiority vanished overnight. Adding to Americans' shock and loss of pride was the taunting of the Russian premier. Unable to restrain himself, Khrushchev gloated that the USSR was building missiles "like sausages."

All over Washington, fingers pointed at each other, placing blame. For more than a year the U.S. had U-2 spy-plane flights flying over Russia trying to assess Russian missile capabilities, but the flights were top-secret, and anyway, the information coming in from the flights was slow and cumbersome, and did not cover the wide expanse of Siberia. In the absence of hard and complete information, and in a climate of fear, a turf war erupted between the CIA and the Air Force, with the Air Force taking the pessimistic view. The Air

Force claimed there could be hundreds of Soviet ICBMs, whereas the CIA argued there were no more than a dozen.

Eventually the dispute was leaked to the press, where John F. Kennedy made it a major campaign issue, charging the Eisenhower administration with failing to protect the nation's security. After JFK took office, Secretary of Defense Robert McNamara undertook further study and concluded the CIA had been right after all: there had never been any missile gap, and whatever missile gap existed had always been in favor of the United States. Instead of two hundred missiles, it turned out that Russia had only four. (The U.S. had 1,000.) To admit that a major issue that helped make JFK president had all been a mirage was most embarrassing. Reminisced McNamara many years later, "It led, the next day, to Senator Dirksen, the Republican minority leader of the Senate, charging the election had been a fraud and asking it be re-run! It was a terrible situation!"

At the end of 1962, after the resolution of the Cuban Missile Crisis, JFK, meeting with several of his advisers, started reflecting on the infamous missile gap that had made him president. It must have been an awkward moment, to say the least, but he plunged ahead. "There was created a myth in this country that did great harm," he said. "It was created by, I would say, emotionally guided but nonetheless patriotic individuals in the Pentagon." Admitting himself as "one of those who put that myth around—a patriotic and misguided man," he ordered: "I want some research . . . dig up the record. . . . Otherwise what it looks like is we, some of us, distorted the facts and created a myth of the gap that didn't exist."

Talking about the officials who had created the missile-gap myth, Kennedy said, "There are still people of that kind in the Pentagon. I wouldn't give them any foundation for creating another myth."

Forty years later, of course, it happened.

Potential Impeachment of a Republican President

►**1959**   This Republican president had ordered a top-secret raid on the opposition to glean valuable information. The raid was highly illegal, but the potential rewards outweighed the risks—or so he thought.

When the raiding force got arrested, the president, "seeing the darkening clouds of an enormous election-year scandal forming," went into high-octane denial. Petrified of the growing press inquiries, he ordered his staffers to cover up and issue a new statement replacing the cover story, and to stick with it, no matter what.

"Once set in motion, however, the lie would soon gain a life of its own and no one would be able to control it," wrote espionage expert James Bamford. The president's employees stood up in front of the television cameras and told "lie after lie for the better part of an hour."

When a tape recording of the actual events turned up, flatly proving the president of the United States had lied, the president faced the worrisome prospect of impeachment. He was so depressed he told his loyal secretary, "I would like to resign." But he did not. After a good night's sleep, he instructed his staff that they must continue to hide his personal involvement in the ill-fated project. Cabinet officers, he instructed further, should hide their knowledge of his involvement even while under oath. "No information should be divulged," he said. In front of a Senate investigating committee, the president's closest adviser stonewalled and told the senators right off, "I don't discuss what the president says to me or I say to the president."

Eisenhower survived. The raid was not the raid on the Democratic Party headquarters in 1972, but the U-2 spy flights over Russia, exposed by Khrushchev.

Vice President Richard Nixon, lurking in the shadows, drew the obvious lesson: stonewall, and you just might get away with it. A dangerous lesson.

Beware of Ice—Especially on a Maiden Voyage

►**1963**   It is a fact of maritime and aeronautical physics that ice is a phenomenon to be avoided wherever possible. Ice causes metal and rubber to become brittle, and prevents the easy flow of air and water. This is hardly rocket science, just plain common sense—especially when it's happened before. But unfortunately some people never learn, even if the first time it happened it was the greatest maritime disaster of all time.

Fifty-one years after the *Titanic*, she was the finest, largest ship of its kind ever built—a marvel of nautical engineering. The ship had so many redundant technologies and backup systems she was deemed unsinkable: "There were backup systems that even backed up the backup systems." She was also the most luxurious, far more spacious and roomy than sister ships. The man chosen as captain was one of the top captains available, and crewmen eagerly signed up to serve on this prestigious new boat. After passing its sea trials, the ship left port and headed out into the Atlantic.

The first of the U.S. Navy's modern class of submarines, the USS *Thresher* could dive deeper, run quieter, and run longer than any other submarine. She was America's ultimate weapon in the Cold War.

On her maiden voyage into the Atlantic, she sprang a leak (a commonplace occurrence on submarines). But before the crewmen could fix it with their wrenches, the water shorted out the *Thresher*'s electrical system and the backup system. That, in turn, shut down the ship's nuclear reactor. Hovering a thousand feet beneath the surface, working in pitch blackness and with no power, the crewmen resorted to manually blowing the electric-powered

ballast tanks. Here they encountered a design flaw: on the blow valve were strainers to protect it from sand particles. The process of blowing caused moisture to form on the strainers. Now, this was not a problem per se—any more than the *Titanic* encountering ice conditions in the North Atlantic was a problem—but under certain circumstances it could be fatal. In the *Thresher*'s case, where the calamity happened at a depth of one thousand feet, the cold water and increased pressure turned the moisture into ice, thereby clogging the drain valves.

Unable to force the water out while new water was coming in, the ship sank to 1,500 feet where it imploded like an eggshell and crumbled to the sea bottom, all 129 lives lost. So much for the most advanced ship in the world, the safest vessel in the United States Navy.

❧

Just because an accident happens twice—first the *Titanic*, then the *Thresher*—doesn't mean it can't happen a third time. In 1981, disaster struck again. The space shuttle *Challenger* had trouble from the beginning, when its maiden voyage was postponed four times because of fuel leaks. Unlike previous spacecraft that could only be used once, then discarded, the *Challenger* was allowed to perform multiple missions. On its tenth trip, disaster stuck. Just seventy-six seconds into its flight, it exploded and all lives were lost. The cause: ice-cold conditions had caused rubber O-rings on the booster rockets to become brittle, allowing red-hot exhaust gases to escape and burn through the wall of the shuttle's liquid-fuel tank.

But this had come as no surprise: everyone knew the O-rings were a potential problem: "Guidelines prohibited launch if the temperature on the nose cone of the external fuel tank fell below 45°F." The night before launch, the temperature was 18 degrees. NASA assembled a three-way telephone conference involving thirty-six people representing NASA and its contractors, to discuss the problem. There was bitter dissent from the primary contractor's engineers, but they lost out. When one of the engineers went home and his wife asked what was wrong, he told her, "Oh, nothing, honey, I had a great day. We're going to launch tomorrow and kill the astronauts. That's all."

The following morning found much of the shuttle shrouded in ice. No matter, the flight proceeded.

So ended the maiden voyages of the most advanced ocean liner and submarine, and the tenth voyage of the spacecraft. Maybe the next time someone will pay closer attention to temperature conditions. Sure enough, the United States government in 2006 announced that it will soon launch its most ambitious extraterrestrial mission to date: sending an unmanned probe to Europa, one of the moons of the planet Jupiter, to explore Europa's subsurface water ocean.

Water? Perhaps it should try "ice." Jupiter is a very, very cold place.

Poor Planning for Emergency

➤ **2001** Any huge man-made edifice, no matter how well engineered, is a potential disaster waiting to happen. It behooves designers, therefore, to prepare for the worst-case scenario.

The collapse of the World Trade Center raised parallels with an equally dramatic disaster a century before, the sinking of the *Titanic*. Both were regarded as indestructible, and in both cases the majority of deaths came not from the actual calamity, but from lack of safety measures enabling people to escape.

The *Titanic*, you will recall, stayed afloat for almost three hours—plenty of time for everyone to get off. The reason so many died was that there were not enough lifeboats. Yet at the U.S. Senate investigation and the British Board of Inquiry hearing, it was pointed out that the *Titanic* actually had four times the number of lifeboats required by safety regulations at the time. Obviously the safety regulations were woefully out of date. Same for the World Trade Center: in conformance with local building codes, the 110-story towers had only three stairwells, the same number as a building with six stories.

Future history books will not remember

because it came to such a dramatic end, but the World Trade Center ranked among mankind's greatest engineering marvels, a modern-day equivalent to the ancient Seven Wonders of the World. Completed in 1972, the towers were designed to withstand the impact of a Boeing 707 aircraft. They were so well built that they survived the 1993 basement bombing with no problem. Every day, for decades, they withstood wind loads thirty times the force of an airplane crashing into them. In fact, the buildings were so solid and soundproof that when the South Tower fell, most of the people in the North Tower had no idea what was happening two hundred feet away (though the rest of the world knew).

How could two buildings staying up for so long—the North Tower (hit first) for

This painting, by Venetian artist Ludovico de Luigi in 1986, is meant to portray centuries of aspirations, hopes, and dreams. Coming from a city slowly sinking into the sea and fearful of "seeing Venice for the last time," he pinned his hopes on New York. Little did he know that he was seeing the Twin Towers for the last time.

102 minutes, and the South Tower for fifty-seven minutes—result in so many deaths? The answer is hubris. It never occurred to anyone that a 747 airliner is quite different from a 707, especially one full of tons of jet fuel. It never occurred to anyone that more than one floor might be totally incapacitated at once. Certainly the building management never bothered to have regular bimonthly fire drills so everyone knew exactly what to do in case of emergency. Each floor, it was assumed, could make do with its own survival communications system, fire extinguisher system, and communications system (just as an ocean liner's hull is divided into several watertight compartments to contain overflow).

As in the *Titanic*, there was no immediate sense of urgency. Don't go to the lifeboats, don't go down the stairwell, just stay where you are and wait until help arrives. The New York City Fire Department told tenants of the World Trade Center to stay put, and sent firemen up to rescue them. The firemen, each weighed down by 80–150 pounds of equipment, took precious time struggling up the stairs in a race against time. Most of them barely made it up to the fortieth floor when everything came to an end. Like the *Titanic*, which could not get out enough SOS signals, the rescue teams at the World Trade Center did not have proper radios to communicate with each other. Police radios worked on one frequency, fire department radios on a different frequency, and neither could penetrate the thick walls of the mighty World Trade Center. When the fire department realized the cause was hopeless and tried to contact the firemen to order for them to evacuate immediately, it could not reach them.

On the *Titanic*, 1,506 died in 1912; 2,749 died in the World Trade Center in 2001. Most of these deaths could easily have been avoided.

AFTERWORD

In 2005 I visited Gore Vidal at his magnificent cliffside home in Ravello, Italy, and told him I was writing a book on America's forgotten past. He remarked dryly, as if I didn't already know, "American history is a big subject."

Indeed. This book covers a big subject. Yet the fact remains that a book is only as valuable as what you can learn from it and act upon. A book like this, with its hundreds of snapshots that have a message, runs the risk of leaving the reader at the end with the feeling, "Well, so what?"

This is a book not with two hundred messages, however. It has three.

First, read more and keep learning. If a story particularly intrigues you, go to the footnotes and source material and plunge into them. I endeavored to identify the key themes, but all events are complicated and complex. Whatever you read more of, read it thoroughly so you can remember it and share it with friends—as Abraham Lincoln did. In-depth learning of one or two subjects is more valuable than scatter-shot familiarity. True excellence requires concentration.

Second, don't take what you read for granted. The gift of all good historians is an ability to use their imagination and make sense of the past. Most people get bogged down in the details, and eschew the effort of making connections and seeing the larger picture. Ask questions, think big. Think like William Lear.

Third, relate the past to the present. What we are experiencing today when we read the newspapers is the history of the future. History does not repeat itself, but it does rhyme. No two situations are identical, but they are often pretty close. History is an important part of a liberal education because of what we in business call experience, or what psychologists call pattern recognition: "the ability to see the relevance of other non-identical situations." Pattern recognition is a key component of sound decision-making.

It may surprise you to know that the inspiration for this book was not a history book, but a public policy book by an investment banker. It was Peter Peterson's *Running on Empty: How the Democratic and Republican Parties Are Bankrupting Our Future and What Americans Can Do About It*, published in 2004. Peterson, secretary of commerce under Nixon and founder of America's largest private equity firm, the Blackstone Group, is no historian per se. But his book had so many insightful historical references that I realized that being concise and getting straight to the point is a skill more natural to a businessman than to many professional historians. As a businessman myself, might I not be a historian, too?

Peterson's book is about how America is sliding downhill because its politicians are making irresponsible promises they know they can't deliver. He concludes, "I propose that a simple curriculum be developed and taught in the schools that would instruct young people on the full range of rights and duties that belong to all Americans as citizens." America needs more civics education. The value of such education has to do with more than just patriotism, but with enhancing genuine self-awareness. "If we forget what we did," said Ronald Reagan in his farewell address, "we won't know who we are." Many years ago, when she was twelve years old, Oprah Winfrey was asked what she hoped to do with her life. "I want to be a leader of people," she said. "And where do you want to lead them to?" she was asked.

"To themselves," she said.

NOTES

PREFACE: HISTORY THROUGH THE SKYLIGHT

"history . . . academics": Gore Vidal, *United States: Essays 1952–1992*, p. 726.; Greek concept of *istoria*: Angel Gurria-Quintana, "Telling Details Amid the History Lessons," London *Financial Times*, April 8–9, 2006, p. W4; Barbara Tuchman from *American Heritage*, Winter 2008, p. 15; John Adams's desk: the Harvard professor was Frank Friedel; Thomas Watson: Cerf & Navasky, *The Experts Speak*, p. 208; William Lear: C. P. Gilmore, "William Lear: Two Hundred Million Dollars," in Max Gunther, *The Very, Very Rich and How They Got That Way*, p. 148; British empire and Sir Cecil Rhodes: Sir Ranulph Fiennes, *Race to the Pole*, p. 2–3; Alice Paul: Elyce J. Rotella, "The Equal Rights Amendment— Yes, But *Whose*?" in Donald N. McClosky, ed., *Second Thoughts*, pp. 72–75; Washington and his frustration with the number of congressional committees: Thomas Fleming, *Washington's Secret War*, p. 13; Confederation of American States $3 million bill: Stanley Lebergott, *The Americans: An Economic Record*, pp. 48–49; "The past is a foreign country": David Lowenthal, *The Past Is a Foreign Country*; Attempt to impeach Washington by Andrew Jackson: Sidney Hyman, *The American President*, p. 82; Andrew Jackson and the Treasury Building from James Humes, *Which President Killed a Man?* p. 154; Lincoln and his son Willy: Katherine Ramsland, *Cemetery Stories*, p. 7; Lincoln and his wife: Jim Bishop, *The Day Lincoln Was Shot*, pp. 3–25; Thomas Jefferson's "Life, Liberty and Property": Stephen Jay Gould, *Bully for Brontosaurus*, p. 29; "liberty for property" from Lewis H. Lapham, "Holy Dread," *Lapham's Quarterly* 1, no. 2 (Spring 2008): 14; Eleanor Roosevelt/FDR: Dorothy Height, "The Civil Rights Movement," in Brian Lamb, *Booknotes on American Character*, p. 139; Chernobyl radiation statistic: "Ecological Concerns," *Motion: The Magazine of Olympic Airways*, Spring–Summer 2000, p. 99; Nevada radiation statistic: James W. Loewen, *Lies Across America*, p. 87; Oliver Wendell Holmes, "through the skylight": compiled by M. Shawn Cole, #26510, *Cole's Quotables*, www.quotationspage.com; John Maynard Keynes: Joshua S. Goldstein, *The Real Price of War*, p 15; "a surprise that was expected": John Lukacs, *Outgrowing Democracy*, p. 15; JFK grassy knoll: John Kaplan, "The Case of the Grassy Knoll: the Romance of Conspiracy," in Robin Winks, *The Historian as Detective*, p. 387; $6.50 boat fare: Herman D. Hover, *Fourteen Presidents before Washington*, pp. 90–91; Henry Ford: Harold Evans, *They Made America*, p. 244; American Bar Association from Scott's Turow's review of *America's Constitution: A Biography* by Akhil Reed Amar, in www.amazon.com; 83 percent of Americans from James W. Loewen, *Lies Across America*, p. 25; Martin Luther King Jr. from Valerie Strauss, "Despite Lessons on King, Some Unaware of His Dream," *Washington Post*, Jan. 15, 2007, p. B-1; students rating Clinton higher than Washington from Peter A. Lillbeck, "Rehabilitating George Washington, Man of Character," *Washington Times*, July 10, 2006, p. 32; *Common Sense* statistics (600,000 sales; 500,000 voters out of population of 3 million) from Howard Fineman, *The Thirteen American Arguments*, pp. 9, 80; Stephen A. Douglas from William H. Rehnquist, *Centennial Crisis*, p. 10; for a lively essay on why history matters, see Stephen Fry, "The Future's in the Past," http://observer.guardian.co.uk/review/story/0,,1815961,00.html; Benjamin Franklin: James C. Humes, *The Ben Franklin Factor*, p. 47; "thrill of learning singular things": Marc Bloch, *The Historian's Craft*, p. 8;

Quotations

Arthur M. Schlesinger Jr., quoted in Joanna L. Stratton, *Pioneer Women*, p. 11; Dana Lindaman and Kyle Ward, *History Lessons*, The New Press, 2004, p. xx; Larry McMurtry, *Oh What a Slaughter*, p. 40.

ONE: A Razor's Edge: It Almost Never Happened

Gore Vidal from Alan Taylor, "Casa del Gore," *Edinburgh Sunday Herald*, 29 July 2001, http://www.sundayherald.com/17204; Hugh Trevor-Roper quoted in John Costello, *Days of Infamy*, p. 331; Marshall Plan 16 percent of 1948 federal budget from Peter G. Peterson, *Facing Up*, p. 56; Senator Vandenberg's vacations from Joseph C. Goulden, *The Best Years: 1945–1950*, p. 275; George Washington escape from David McCullough, "What the Fog Wrought," in Robert Cowley, ed., *What If?: The World's Foremost Military Historians Imagine What Might Have Been*, p. 191; servant arrested by German patrol from A. J. Langguth, *Patriots*, p. 414; Louisiana Purchase offered to England from David Louis, *2001 Fascinating Facts*, p. 175; Jefferson and U.S. bonds from Kenneth C. Davis, *Don't Know Much About History*, p. 103; Mexico treaty one day after gold discovery from *Reader's Digest Strange Stories*, p. 372; Melvyn Bragg, *The Adventure of English*, pp. 39–40; Alfred North Whitehead from Marcus Cunliffe, "What If?" *American Heritage*, Dec. 1982, p. 18.

A Statement of Allegiance . . .

Prewar negotiations from Barbara W. Tuchman, *The March of Folly*, pp. 193–95; Grand Union flag from Thomas Fleming, *1776*, p. 35; "English colors but more striped" from Thomas Parrish, *The American Flag*, pp. 56–57; "Olive Branch Petition" from David McCullough, *1776*, p. 10; wartime negotiations from Barbara W. Tuchman, *The First Salute*, pp. 198–201; Howe response and 1876 Centennial from Kevin Keim, *A Grand Old Flag*, p. 11.

Crucial Messages . . .

Washington from Thomas Fleming, *1776*, p. 430; Rall from A. J. Langguth, *Patriots*, p. 414; Grant from James M. McPherson, "If the Lost Order Hadn't Been Lost," in Robert Cowley, ed., *What If?* pp. 225–38; Lt. Joseph McDonald testimony from Proceedings of Army Pearl Harbor Board, http://www.ibiblio.org/pha/myths/radar/mcdonald_1.html; military historian Harry A. Butowsky, "Early Warnings: the Mystery of Radar in Hawaii," http://crm.cr.rips.gov./archive/15-8/15-8-2.pdf; Corp. George Mooney testimony from http://deceitatpearlharbor.com/; FDR cover-up of MacArthur from John Costello, *Days of Infamy*, pp. 3–4, 42, and from Ronald H. Spector, *Eagle Against the Sun*, pp. 98, 117–18.

Watching the Whales

Barbara Tuchman, *The First Salute*, pp. 289–92; Robert Harvey, *A Few Bloody Noses*, p. 7; Don Cook, *The Long Fuse*, pp. 340, 346–48; Robert Leckie, *The Wars of America*, p. 213.

Three Financiers . . .

King George and Haym Salomon quotes from Shirley Milgrim, *Haym Salomon*, pp. 83, 59; Howard Fast, *Haym Salomon*, pp. 233–51; see Charles E. Russell, *Haym Salomon and the Revolution*; U.S. postage stamp commemoration from www.absoluteastronomy.com/ref/haym_salomon; George Wilson, *Stephen Girard*, pp. 263, 269, 278–81; Morgan quote from James Brown Scott, *Robert Bacon*, pp. 73–79; Ron Chernow, *House of Morgan*, pp. 71–75; see Jean Strouse, *Morgan: American Financier*.

Arriving on Time

Gary Wills, "The Words That Remade America: Lincoln at Gettysburg," *Atlantic Monthly*, June 1992, p. 58.

The Day that Saved the North . . .

Charles B. Flood, *1864: Lincoln at the Gates of History*, pp. 189–91; U. S. Grant, *Personal Memoirs of U. S. Grant*, vol. 2, p. 306; casualty statistics from David J. Eicher, *The Longest Night: A Military History of the Civil War*, p. 717, and from Gary W. Gallagher, "Monocacy," in Frances H. Kennedy, ed., *The Civil War Battlefield*, pp. 235–38.

House in a Shambles

Sarah Booth Conroy, "Salute to Navy Reformer," *International Herald Tribune*, Sept. 25, 1998, p. 26; William Howard Adams, *Jefferson's Monticello*, pp. 254–62; Marc Leepson, "The Levys at Monticello," *Preservation Magazine*, March/April 1998; see Mark Leepson, *Saving Monticello*.

President Because of Two Deaths . . .

Paul Grondahl, *I Rose Like a Rocket: The Political Education of Theodore Roosevelt*, pp. 242, 319, 359; Butler from Clarence Macartney, *Lincoln and His Generals*, pp. 64–65.

Barely Got Off the Ground

Gone with the Wind from Christopher Cerf and Victor Navasky, *The Experts Speak*, pp. 172–73; *Reader's Digest* from Charles Panati, *Extraordinary Origins of Everyday Things*, pp. 362–63; Audubon from Richard Rhodes, "The Genius of John James Audubon," *Smithsonian*, December 2004, pp. 76–80; Dickinson, Melville, and Thoreau from Don Gifford, *The Farther Shore*, p. 160; Webster's *Dictionary* from J. North Conway, *American Literacy*, p. 48; F. Scott Fitzgerald from David Heenan, *Double Lives*, p. 215; Gertrude Stein, Anaïs Nin, Mae West, Margaret Mitchell, and Ayn Rand from Claudia Roth Pierpont, *Passionate Minds*, pp. 40, 52, 90, 100, 201, 206–7, 210; *The Fountainhead* from Nora Ephron, *Wallflower at the Orgy*, pp. 49–51, and Richard E. Ralston, "Publishing *The Fountainhead*," in Robert Mayhew, *Essays on Ayn Rand's* The Fountainhead, pp. 65–75.

A Race to the Death

Leslie Groves, *Now It Can Be Told*, pp. 33, 37, 51, 178, 184; Sengier quote from www.answers.com/topic/edgar-sengier.

Worse Things Happen at Sea

Samuel Eliot Morison, *History of the United States Naval Operations in World War II*, vol. 4, *Victory in the Pacific 1945*, pp. 319–30 ("only a fool could have missed" and Voltaire's quip, pp. 322, 327–28); "pride of the enemy fleet" from Gordon Thomas and Max Morgan Witts, *Enola Gay*, pp. 101, 33, 106, 176, 210–12; "shorten the war" and "sustain even one torpedo" from Dan Kurzman, *Fatal Voyage*, pp. 19, 15; "Adrian Marks, 81, World War II Navy Pilot," *New York Times* obituary, March 15, 1998; Raymond Lech, *All the Drowned Sailors*, pp. 87–122; see Doug Stanton, *In Harm's Way*; www.ussindianapolis.org/pfinnstory.htm.

Might the Interim Have Been Otherwise?

Nixon and China from James C. Humes, *The Ben Franklin Factor*, p. 60; FDR and China from Barbara W. Tuchman, *Practicing History*, p. 188; Buchanan and Cuba from Shelley Ross, *Fall from Grace*, p. 86; Eisenhower and Churchill, and 1963 test ban treaty, from Arthur M. Schlesinger Jr., *The Cycles of American History*, pp. 393–94, and p. 66.

The "Tipping Point" . . .

VIETNAM: Walt Brown, *The People vs. Lee Harvey Oswald*, p. 61; JFK to Mansfield, and LBJ quote from Gary A. Donaldson, *America at War Since 1945*, pp. 94–97; "Win the war!" from Robert S. McNamara, *In Retrospect*, pp. 102, 93–94; JFK shift in priorities from John M. Newman, *JFK and Vietnam*, pp. 426–27, 442–43, 449.
POST-9/11: "through the roof" from Barton Gellman, "Fears Prompt U.S. to Beef Up Nuclear Terror Detection," *Washington Post*, March 3, 2002 (quoted in Ivo H. Daalder and James M. Lindsay, *America Unbound*, p. 119).

TWO: Forgotten by History

Amerigo Vespucci from J. North Conway, *American Literacy*, pp. 22–24, David Abulafia, *The Discovery of Mankind*, pp. 242–43; see David Boyle, *Toward the Setting Sun*; Theodore Roosevelt from

Ben Macintyre, "He's Lost It," *New York Times Magazine*, July 7, 1993, p. 11, and John M. Cooper, *The Warrior and the Priest*, p. 118.

A Signature Worth Millions . . .

H. L. Gee, *American England*, pp. 152–53.

Ten Presidents Before Washington

For Lincoln's July 4, 1861, special message to Congress, see http://www.fordham.edu/ halsall/ mod/1861lincoln-special.html; Lincoln quote on "four legs and one tail" from www.russpickett.com/ ushist/uscontif.htm, the historian is Stanley L. Klos, *President Who? Forgotten Founders*, p. 25; "minuscule amount of official correspondence" from Klos, pp. 105–6; see Forrest McDonald, *E Pluribus Unum*, Gordon S. Wood, *The Creation of the American Republic, 1776–1787*, and George Grant, *Forgotten Presidents: America's Leaders before George Washington*.

Our Nation's Capital

Hamilton from Thomas K. McCraw, "The Strategic Vision of Alexander Hamilton," *The American Scholar*, Winter 1994, p. 31; radial streets from Jay Winik, *April 1865*, p. 24; Banneker from Louis Haber, *Black Pioneers of Science and Invention*, pp. 4, 12, 16; see Fergus M. Bordewich, *Washington*.

Facing Down the Mob

Richard J. Barnet, *The Rockets' Red Glare*, pp. 48–51.

The Next George Washington?

Carl J. Vipperman, *William Lowndes and the Transition of Southern Politics, 1782–1822*, pp. xi, 154, 174, 257, 265; Harriott H. Ravenel, *Life and Times of William Lowndes of South Carolina, 1782–1822*, pp. 236, 239; Leslie H. Southwick, *Presidential Also-Rans and Running Mates, 1788–1980*, p. 75; Mark Hanna from Steve Tally, *Bland Ambition*, p. 34.

"The Eighth Wonder of the World" . . .

Peter L. Bernstein, *Wedding of the Waters*, pp. 63, 68, 178, 259–60, 294; John Steele Gordon, *An Empire of Wealth*, p. 105.

The Crime of the Century . . .

"not only scalped . . ." from Sally Denton, *American Massacre*, p. 150; "thanks to God" from Jon Krakauer, *Under the Banner of Heaven*, p. 225; "woe, woe . . ." from Ronald W. Walker et al., *Massacre at Mountain Meadows*, p. 43; "it was a righteous thing," "die a dog's death," and "he took the massacre in stride" from Larry McMurtry, *Oh What a Slaughter*, pp. 79–80, 85, 88; "a crime that has no parallel," Mark Twain, Harriet Beecher Stowe, and "most important criminal case" from Denton, *American Massacre*, pp. 193, 211, 221; "darkest deed" from Will Bagley, *Blood of the Prophets*, p. xiii; for a vivid Hollywood movie about the massacre, see *September Dawn* (2007).

America's Greatest Invention / Innovation

Patent Office commissioner from Cerf and Navasky, *The Experts Speak*, p. 203; telephone used for listening to opera from Martyn Roetter, quoted in *Technology Review*, Aug–Sept. 1994, p. 46; American Revolution musket and interchangeable parts from Gerald Gunderson, *The Wealth Creators*, pp. 85,88.

The Number-One Bestseller

Peter Baida, *Poor Richard's Legacy*, pp. 240–41; Grolier Electronic Encyclopedia from www.pink monkey.com/dl/library1/mess.pdf; Elbert Hubbard, *A Message to Garcia*; Donald R. Morris, "Garcia Doesn't Get the Message These Days" from http://homeport.usnaweb.org/garcia.html.

A Far Cry from Enron

Percentage of households using electricity from Stanley Lebergott, *Pursuing Happiness*, p. 120. TESLA: "I will make for you some daylight" from Chauncey M. McGovern, "The New Wizard of the World," *Pearson's* magazine, May 1899; Edison's "Tesla always going to do something" and "50,000 years" from Margaret Cheney, *Tesla*, pp. 4, 30, 162, 186; ancestors stealing inventions from Henry G. Prout, *A Life of George Westinghouse*, p. 27; *Encyclopaedia Britannica* from Gray Basnight, "Reinventing Radio," New York *Daily News*, July 1, 1992, p. 30; see Marc J. Seifer, *Wizard*.
WESTINGHOUSE: Steve Massey, "Who Killed Westinghouse?" *Pittsburgh Post-Gazette*, http://post-gazette.com/westinghouse/cbsempire.asp; Jill Jonnes, *Empires of Light*, p. 12, 337; Vanderbilt quote from http://www.karenbowden.com/images/founding1.pdf; Samuel Gompers from George Westinghouse Museum website http://www.janetplan-it.com/westnghse/gw_museum.htm; "earn a dollar" from Charles Oliver, "George Westinghouse: Problem-Solver," Foundation for Economic Education, http://www.fee.org/vnews.php?nid=5195; Henry G. Prout, *A Life of George Westinghouse*, pp. 18, 245.
INSULL: Harold Evans, *They Made America*, pp. 307, 320–23, 327, 331; John F. Wasik, *The Merchant of Power*, pp. 55, 202, 232, 235.

Entangled in Another Nation's Civil War

Wilson comparison to the American Revolution from John Lukacs, "America and Russia, Americans and Russians," *American Heritage*, Feb–March 1992, p. 67; Wilson quote on European mistake from Carol Wilcox Melton, *Between War and Peace*, p. 155; Robert L. Willett, *Russian Sideshow*, pp. 127, 140, 178; Senator Hiram Johnson from Benjamin D. Rhodes, *The Anglo-American Winter War with Russia, 1918–1919*, p. 122.

The Golden Age of Sport

Statistics on Babe Ruth's lifetime batting average and pitching record from Lawrence S. Ritter and Mark Rucker, *The Babe*, pp. 276–77; statistics on complete games from Robert W. Creamer, *Babe: The Legend Comes to Life*, p. 142; Tris Speaker quote from Cerf and Navasky, *The Experts Speak*, pp. 172–73; Peter Joffre Nye et. al., *The Six-Day Bicycle Races*, p. 173, 185; Dean Cabow, "When America Loved Cycling," *Team Evergreen's Bike Beat* newsletter, April 2007, p. 6, www.teamevergreen.org/pdf/TEBB2007046.pdf; Ron Rapoport, *The Immortal Bobby*, pp. 70, 82, 119, 157, 314–16; Craig

Lambert, "Bobby Jones," *Harvard* magazine, March–April 2002; see Frank Deford, *Big Bill Tilden*, and Charles Price, *A Golf Story: Bobby Jones*.

The Towering Giant . . .

Larry Tye, *Rising from the Rails*, pp. 114, 208–9, 218; Jervis Anderson, *A. Philip Randolph*, pp. 215, 315.

Hollywood with Brains

Fleming Meeks, "I Guess They Just Take and Forget About a Person," *Forbes*, May 14, 1990, pp. 136–38; Hans-Joachim Braun, "Advanced Weaponry of the Stars," cover story, American Heritage *Invention & Technology* magazine, Spring 1997; Rob Walters, *Spread Spectrum*, pp. 135–42; p. 3 of http://electronicdesign.com/Articles/ArticleID/2851/2851.html.

Winning Hearts and Minds . . .

Robert M. Edsel, *Rescuing Da Vinci*, pp. 1, 127, 132, 136, 140, 253, Robert M. Edsel, *The Monuments Men*, pp. 290, 296, 362, 371, 400, 422; James J. Rorimer, *Survival*, p. 19; see www.monumentsmen.com and the movie *The Rape of Europa* (2007).

Bipartisanship at Its Best

Cabell Phillips, *The Truman Presidency*, pp. 34–35; Donald H. Riddle, *The Truman Committee*, pp. 26, 354, 370; Arianna Huffington, *Huffington Post*, Feb. 5, 2005; Charles Schumer from http://www.acsblog.org/separation-of-powers-key-senator-calls-for-new-iraq.

THREE: The Past Was Different Then

Ninety percent of the automobile market, horse waste, and flour milling industry from Ruth Schwartz Cowan, *A Social History of American Technology*, pp. 72, 232–34; "atomic-powered cars" and year 1900 statistics from Joel Best, *More Damned Lies and Statistics*, pp. 66, 18; Jefferson's "1,000 years" from John Steele Gordon, *An Empire of Wealth*, p. 171; Gerald Gunderson, *The Wealth Creators*, pp. 59, 72; Cuba expansionism and Western territorial limits from Arthur M. Schlesinger Jr., *The Cycles of American History*, p. 150; Upton Sinclair from *Reader's Digest Strange Stories*, p. 55; "unwarranted diversion" from Patricia Lee Holt, *George Washington Had No Middle Name*, p. 117; Pehle and McCloy from Arthur D. Morse, *While Six Million Died*, pp. 359–60; Arthur M. Schlesinger Jr., "Did FDR Betray the Jews?" *Newsweek*, April 18, 1994, p. 14; "more than all other Western countries combined" from Thomas Fleming, *The New Dealers' War*, p. 257; Hoover quote from Kenneth C. Davis, *Don't Know Much About History*, p. 272.

Our First 200 Years . . .

Gerald Gunderson, *The Wealth Creators*, pp. 11–14, 23–25.

Gory Times

Kenneth Silverman, *The Life and Times of Cotton Mather*, pp. 17–20.

Colonial Anti-Tobacco Lobby

Walter W. Jennings, *A History of Economic Progress in the United States.* pp. 30–31.

Slow Communication

Battle of Bull Run and British intervention from Jay Monaghan, *Abraham Lincoln Deals with Foreign Affairs*, p. 247; Constitutional Convention and American Revolution from Don Gifford, *The Further Shore*, pp. 115–16; Thomas Jefferson from John Train, *John Train's Most Remarkable Occurrences*, p. 13; War of 1812 from T. Harry Williams, *The History of American Wars*, pp. 96, 133, and George Wilson, *Stephen Girard*, p. 259; Edmund Burke from Paul Johnson, *A History of the American People*, p. 132; Edward Preble from Robert Leckie, *From Sea to Shining Sea*, pp. 92, 97; Edwin Drake from Harold Evans, *They Made America*, pp. 102–7.

A Superior Way to Raise Children?

Crevecoeur from Bill Adler, *500 Great Facts about America*, p. 46; Franklin from Walter Isaacson, *Benjamin Franklin*, p. 153; Franklin and Bacon from Thom Hartmann, *What Would Jefferson Do?* pp. 26, 186; Francis Jennings, *The Founders of America*, p. 69.

America in 1800

Boston–Washington from Ruth Schwarz Cowan, *A Social History of American Technology*, p. 94; cost of shipping from Carol Sheriff, *The Artificial River*, p. 15; Federalist newspapers from Peter L. Bernstein, *Wedding of the Waters*, p. 239; size of federal government from Thomas Fleming, *The Louisiana Purchase*, p. 12; description of Federal City, D.C., from Alan Pell Crawford, *Unwise Passions*, p. 149; America unknown in Constantinople from Joshua E. London, *Victory in Tripoli*, p. 87; president's salary and house, Harvard and Princeton tuition, U.S. map and population from Olivier Bernier, *The World in 1800*, pp. 127, 141–42, 174, 185–88.

High Educational Standard

Bill Adler, *500 Great Facts about America*, p. 27; *Time*, Dec. 9, 1996, p. 38; Lincoln from Doris Kearns Goodwin, *Team of Rivals*, p. 54, and William Lee Miller, *Lincoln's Virtues*, pp. 49–52; JFK from Gore Vidal, *Inventing a Nation*, pp. 187–88.

Big Distances . . .

Gerald Gunderson, *The Wealth Creators*, p. 60; Erie Canal and Great Pyramid from John Steele Gordon, *An Empire of Wealth*, p. 105; Erie Canal financing from Robert Sobel, *The Money Manias*, pp. 49–50; Thomas J. DiLorenzo, *How Capitalism Saved America*, pp. 79–84; Stanley Lebergott, *The Americans: An Economic Record*, p. 121.

Small White House Staff

"the most powerful President" from Charles Adams, *For Good and Evil*, p. 328; Harold Holzer, *Dear Mr. Lincoln: Letters to the President*, pp. 5–18; FDR and Lincoln receptions from Arthur M. Schlesinger Jr., *The Cycles of American History*, pp. 333–35.

A Speech Where Every Word Counted

Gettysburg Address from Don Gifford, *The Further Shore*, p. 38; Abraham Lincoln from Harold Holzer, *Dear Mr. Lincoln*, pp. 278–79, and Walter Berns, "The Prattling Presidency," *Wall Street Journal*, Oct. 31, 1995; 1876 election from Lloyd Robinson, *The Stolen Election*, p. 16; Gore Vidal, *United States: Essays 1952–2002*, p. 1014.

A Near-Fatal Misstep

Louisiana vote from Gore Vidal, *United States: Essays 1952–1992*, pp. 679, 690; Emancipation vote from Jay Winik, *April 1865*, p. 249.

Not as Originally Intended

Franklin stove from Phil Patton, *Made in U.S.A.*, p. 243; Levi's blue jeans from *Earth Island Journal*, Fall 1990, p. 19; Coca-Cola from David Bodanis, *The Secret House*, pp. 72–73; typewriter from Phil Patton, *Made in U.S.A.*, pp. 77–79.

The Twitter of Its Day

Mark Twain, *1601, and Is Shakespeare Dead?*, p. 7; Lawrence Levine, "William Shakespeare in America," *Highbrow/Lowbrow*, p. 17–20, 25, 28, 32; Nigel Cliff, *The Shakespeare Riots*, p. 13–18; www.shakespeareinamericanlife.org.

Transforming the Shopping Experience

"best known man" from Thomas Kessner, *Capital City*, p. 37; retailing innovation from Bellamy Partridge and Otto Bettman, *As We Were: Family Life in America, 1850–1900*, p. 108; Wolfgang Schivelbusch, *The Railway Journey*, pp. 188–90; Ulysses Grant story from William S. McFeely, *Grant*, p. 10; see Stephen N. Elias, *Alexander T. Stewart*.

A Country of 300 Local Times

Railroad compared to the church from Thomas Kessner, *Capital City*, p. 96; 4.8 mph from L. J. K. Setright, *Drive On! A Social History of the Motor Car*, p. 7; Vanderbilt time from John Steele Gordon, *An Empire of Wealth*, p. 236; see Jack Beatty, "The Track to Modernity," *Atlantic Monthly*, January 2003.

Answering the Phone

Telegraph from Henry David Thoreau, *Walden*, p. 52; Rutherford Hayes quote from Cerf and Navasky, *The Experts Speak*, p. 206; Cleveland answering his own phone from Thomas A. Bailey, *Presidential Greatness*, p. 37.

America in 1900

William Randolph Hearst from Judy Crichton, *America 1900*, p. 2; "electric changing stations" from James Surowieki, *The Wisdom of Crowds*, p. 25; automobile imports from James J. Flink, *The Automobile Age*, pp. 13, 19.

Belief in Infallibility . . .

Carpathia captain quote from Marshall Everett, *Wreck and Sinking of the* Titanic, p. 255; British Inquiry judgment of Captain Smith, *Carpathia* extra precautions, Lightoller quote, Captain Smith quote, photo and *Carpathia* captain quote from Mark Chirnside, *The Olympic-Class Ships*, pp. 212–13, 187, 205, 70, 186, and 79; essential rule of good seamanship from Captain L. M. Collins, *The Sinking of the* Titanic, pp. 137, 34, 99; survivor lookout quote from Tom Kuntz, ed., *The Titanic Disaster Hearings*, p. 178; Daniel Allen Butler quote from letter to the author, July 15, 2009; see Butler, *The Other Side of the Night*.

The Might of General Motors

David Halberstam, *The Fifties*, p. 118; Harlow Curtice from Richard Beales, "GM Swings a Cautionary Tale on Deficit," London *Financial Times*, April 29–30, 2006, p. 11; Douglas Brinkley, *Wheels for the World*, pp. 525–28; Peter F. Drucker, *Adventures of a Bystander*, p. 292; Toyota from John Dower, *Embracing Defeat*, p. 512.

Recycling Coca-Cola Bottles

Phil Patton, *Made in U.S.A.*, p. 24.

FOUR: American Self-Identity and Ideals

David Brooks, *New York Times*, May 24, 2009, book review section, p. 6; Tocqueville from Howard Fineman, *The Thirteen American Arguments*, p. 19; "log cabin built with his own hands" from Stephen B. Adams, *Mr. Kaiser Goes to Washington*, p. 5; Emerson from David Walker Howe, *What Hath God Wrought*, p. 853; Adams, Wilson, and TR from Arthur M. Schlesinger Jr., *The Disuniting of America*, pp. 25, 35, 118; Washington from Andrew Roberts, *A History of the English-Speaking Peoples Since 1900*, p. 23; Baron von Steuben from Robert Harvey, *A Few Bloody Noses*, p. 291, and A. J. Langguth, *Patriots*, p. 470; Thoreau, Agar, Macaulay, and Henry Ford from John Lukacs, *Outgrowing Democracy*, pp. 157, 161, 37–38; Emerson from Christophe Canto and Odile Faliu, *The History of the Future*, p. 85; Benjamin Franklin quoted by Gerald J. Gruman in http:///www.cyronics.org/prefacela.html; David Halberstam and Earl Warren "no dissents" from David Halberstam, ed., *Defining a Nation*, pp. 20, 80; Gladstone from Maxim E. Armbruster, *The Presidents of the United States*, p. 85; American abundance from David M. Potter, *People of Plenty*, pp. 134–41; Earl Warren sports pages from LeRoy Ashby, *With Amusement for All*, p. 284.

Did Slavery Generate Racism . . .

Henry N. Drewry, "Slavery and the Plantation," in Rhoda L. Goldstein, ed., *Black Life and Culture in the United States*, pp. 116, 118, 127–29; Thomas Jefferson from *Notes on the State of Virginia*, Query XVIII, 1787, www.yale.edu/lawweb/avalon/jevifram.htm; Frederick Law Olmsted, *The Cotton Kingdom*, vol. 2, pp. 275, 280, 281; Colin Powell from *Newsweek*, Oct. 10, 1994, p. 32.

The Plaque with No Name

Geoffrey C. Ward, "The Great Traitor," *American Heritage*, May–June 1994, pp. 14, 16; see Clare Brandt, *The Man in the Mirror*.

Twenty-Four Hours that Changed the World

Dennis Brindell Fradin, *The Signers*, introduction p. viii–ix, p. 32, illustration p. 38; A. J. Langguth, *Patriots*, pp. 342, 359–63; smallpox scare from Charles C. Mann, *1491*, p. 107.

A Nation Legally, But Not Emotionally

English requirement from Don Cook, *The Long Fuse*, p. 368; New Jersey secession threat from Walter LaFeber, *The American Age*, pp. 47–48; only one British envoy, three New England governors, and new constitution from Richard J. Barnet, *The Rockets' Red Glare*, pp. 24, 67–68; Garry Wills, "The Words That Remade America: Lincoln at Gettysburg," *The Atlantic Monthly*, June 1992, p. 79; Marcus Cunliffe, *George Washington*, p. 155; Scott proposal from Clarence Macartney, *Lincoln and His Generals*, p. 17.

Religion, the Bane of Freedom

Alexis de Tocqueville, *Democracy in America*, p. 303; twelve colonial religions from Robert Leckie, *From Sea to Shining Sea*, p. 133; Quaker hangings from Kenneth C. Davis, *Don't Know Much About History*, p. 29.

"We Think in English"

Alexander Hamilton from Richard J. Barnet, *The Rockets' Red Glare*, p. 25; Nancy Astor from Andrew Roberts, *A History of the English-Speaking Peoples Since 1900*, p. 285; John Lukacs, *Outgrowing Democracy*, pp. 148–49; Nathan Rosenberg and L. E. Birdzell Jr., *How the West Grew Rich*, pp. 116–17; John Adams from Paul Johnson, *A History of the American People*, p. 212; Benjamin Franklin from Gordon Wood, *The Americanization of Benjamin Franklin*, p. 197; John Locke, Horace Greeley, and the Homestead Act from John C. Weaver, *The Great Land Rush and the Making of the Modern World 1650–1900*, pp. 48, 62, 66; Butler, Bismarck, and Hay from Roberts, *A History*, pp. 39, 5, 32; British Army Bureau of Current Affairs from Juliet Gardiner, *Wartime*, p. 470; Winston Churchill's parents from Henry G. Prout, *George Westinghouse*, p. 8; British philologist from Roberts, *A History*, p. 572.

Generosity and Unselfishness

Howard Swiggett, *The Extraordinary Mr. Morris*, p. 441.

Black Affiliation with America . . .

Arthur M. Schlesinger Jr., *The Disuniting of America*, pp. 82–84; African slave trade from Herbert S. Klein, *The Atlantic Slave Trade*, pp. 57, 72, 102, 103; blacks enslaving blacks from Nathan Huggins, *Black Odyssey: The Afro-American Ordeal in Slavery*, pp. 20, 22; Thomas Sowell from Duane Lester, "Five Black Minds Obama Supporters Should Get Behind," www.allamericanblogger.com/2655/five-black-minds-obama-supporters-should-get-behind.

Ban the Book!

William Noble, *Bookbanning in America*, pp. 209–10, 221, 269, 325–27; Concord, Massachusetts, public library banning from Baumann Rare Books ad, *New York Times Book Review*, Jan. 13, 1994, p. 13; Emerson from Louis Menand, *The Metaphysical Club*, p. 18; U.S. military from Richard Severo and Lewis Milford, *The Wages of War*, p. 292; Gore Vidal from Paul McLeary book review of Vidal's *Perpetual War for Perpetual Peace*, March 10, 2002, http://www.freewilliamsburg.com/march_2002/gore _vidal.html.

Imaginative Philanthropy

James Bryce from Richard Severo and Lewis Milford, *The Wages of War*, p. 184; Carnegie quote from http://www.pbs.org/wgbh/amex/1900/peopleevents/pande2.html; Nathan Straus from John Steele Gordon, "Saint Straus," *American Heritage*, July–August 1990, p. 14, 16; Edward Harkness from Samuel Eliot Morison, *Three Centuries of Harvard: 1636–1936*, p. 476; Julius Rosenwald from James V. Carmichael Jr., "Imaginative Philanthropy," *American Heritage*, May–June 1994, Letters to the Editor, p. 12; Laszlo Tauber from Vance Packard, *The Ultra Rich*, pp. 122–23; Henry Aaron Yeomans, *Abbott Lawrence Lowell: 1856–1943*, pp. 182, 188, 189.

The Eastern View of the Wild West . . .

David McCullough, *Brave Companions*, p. 70.

Immortalized in Granite

Bruce Tindall and Mark Watson, *Did Mohawks Wear Mohawks?*, pp. 68–70.

Special Consideration . . .

David Brinkley, *Washington Goes to War*, p. 105; grandson quote about "sob stuff" from Curtis Roosevelt, "FDR: A Giant Despite His Disability," *International Herald Tribune*, August 5, 1998, newspaper editorial, "Show FDR's Disability," and grandson's quote "FDR guarded his condition closely" from David Roosevelt, "Show Him As He Wished," *USA Today*, Dec. 7, 1994; FDR's physical strength from Joseph Persico, *Roosevelt's Secret War*, p. 221, and Winston S. Churchill, *The Second World War*, vol. 4, *The Hinge of Fate*, p. 338.

The Word "Impossible" . . .

Calvin Gene Sims, "Hoover Dam Was a Test of Engineers' Theories," *New York Times*, Oct. 15, 1985; Richard Wolkomir, "Inside the Lab and Out, Concrete Is More Than It's Cracked Up to Be," *Smithsonian*, Jan. 1994, p. 28; Marc Reisner, *Cadillac Desert*, p. 134; Samuel Eliot Morison, *History of United States Naval Operations in World War II*, vol. IV, p. 81; Victor Davis Hanson, *Carnage and Culture*, pp. 373–75; Peter Elphick, *Liberty: The Ships that Won the War*, pp. 20, 80, 83, 91, 100; Samuel B. Adams, *Mr. Kaiser Goes to Washington*, p. 9; Frederic C. Lane, *Ships for Victory*, p. 258.

America's Most Notable Aristocratic Family

FDR like "an English lord" from Harold Evans, *The American Century*, p. 238; TR genealogy from Kathleen Dalton, *Theodore Roosevelt*, p. 15; Roosevelt family lifestyle and newsboy anecdote from Betty Boyd Caroli, *The Roosevelt Women*, pp. 5, 7, 53, 75; Peter Collier, "The Roosevelt Dynasty," in Brian Lamb, ed., *Booknotes: Stories from American History*, pp. 230–33; China trade fortune from Edward P. Crapol, *John Tyler*, p. 132; H. Paul Jeffers, *Theodore Roosevelt, Jr.*, pp. 1, 3, 31–35; A. J. Liebling from Edward J. Renehan Jr., *The Lion's Pride*, p. 239.

History 101 . . .

Hamilton and Jefferson from Walter Williams, "Do We Want Democracy?" http://capmag.com/article.asp?ID=1670; Carl J. Vipperman, *William Lowndes and the Transition of American Politics*, p. xv; Adams from Walter Williams, "Are We a Republic or a Democracy?" http://capmag.com/article.asp?ID=4080; number of French governments from Gore Vidal, *United States: Essays 1952–2002*, p. 670.

FIVE: A Warlike Nation, Not a Militarist One

Gen. Tommy Franks, Richard Armitage, Gen. Colin Powell, and George Washington from Andrew J. Bacevich, *The New American Militarism*, pp. 22, 24, 202, 214; Robert Leckie, *The Wars of America*, vol. II, p. 835; George Washington "Where's the money?" from David McCullough, *1776*, p. 79; Washington and Eisenhower farewell address quotes from http://www.lewrockwell.com/orig4/johnson-chalmers3.html; Gen. George Marshall from Earl Wavell, *Soldiers and Soldering*, p. 47; Congress belief in short war from Thomas Fleming, *1776: Year of Illusions*, p. 38, and Thomas K. McCraw, *The American Scholar*, Winter 1994, pp. 42, 50; 1791–97 interest payments from Lewis H. Kimmel, *Federal Budget and Fiscal Policy, 1789–1958*, p. 10; $2 billion cost to compensate slave owners, and value of the slaves, from Paul Johnson, *A History of the American People*, pp. 312, 557; post–Civil War downsizing from Robert Leckie, *The Wars of America*, vol. I, pp. 538–39; post–World War II downsizing and Soviet strength from Ronald Schaffer, *Wings of Judgment*, pp. 190–91; FDR refusing to launch a preemptive strike from Harold Evans, *The American Century*, p. 308; Truman and U.S. eagle from David McCullough, *Truman*, pp. 474, 488; John Freeman Clarke from John Lukacs, "America and Russia, Americans and Russians," *American Heritage*, Feb.–March 1992, p. 66; Oliver Wendell Holmes from Louis Menand, *The Metaphysical Club*, p. 45; Charles Eliot from Barbara Tuchman, *Practicing History*, p. 35; National Security Council from Peter G. Peterson, *Facing Up*, pp. 187–88; Abraham Lincoln as military leader from Stephen B. Oates, *Abraham Lincoln*, p. 128.

Lack of Imperial Ambition . . .

Lord Clive from Robert Harvey, *A Few Bloody Noses*, p. 127; Benjamin Franklin from Gordon Wood, *The Americanization of Benjamin Franklin*, p. 169, and West Indies and Ireland "if it wished" from Paul Johnson, *A History of the American People*, p. 150; dozen senators and Polk from Herman D. Hover, *Fourteen Presidents before Washington*, p. 83; Marx and Engels, and Henry Adams, from Arthur M. Schlesinger Jr., *The Cycles of American History*, pp. 120, 150–51; Hamilton from Walter LaFeber, *The American Age*, p. 50; Jefferson from Thomas A. Bailey, *A Diplomatic History of the American People*, p. 165; Treaty of Paris from Fred Anderson and Andrew Clayton, *The Dominion of War*, p. 334; Champ Clark from Maxim Armbruster, *The Presidents of the United States*, p. 259.

Nonsupport at Home

American Revolution from Wallace Brown, "The Loyalists and the American Revolution," in Nicholas Cords and Patrick Gerster, *Myth and the American Experience*, p. 107; Valley Forge from John Alden, *George Washington*, p. 76; War of 1812 from T. Harry Williams, *The History of American Wars*, pp. 99, 105, 221, 225; Gen. William Sherman from Michael J. Swagger, "Federal Conscription and the New York Draft Riots of 1863," http://www.suite101.com/article.cfu/381/23843; World War II from Barbara Tuchman, *The March of Folly*, p. 31.

In the Steps of Julius Caesar

Julius Caesar and U.S. Civil War from Archer Jones, "Military Means, Political Ends," in Gabor S. Boritt (ed.), *Why the Confederacy Lost*, pp. 46–47; American Revolution from Curtis P. Nettels, *The Emergence of a National Economy, 1775–1815*, pp. 8–13; Nine cartridges and Bunker Hill from Barbara W. Tuchman, *The First Salute*, p. 8; World War II production statistics from Kenneth C. Davis, *Don't Know Much About History*, p. 297; Stalin from Louis L. Snyder, *The War: 1939–1945*, p. 325; Adm. King from Byron W. King, "Hubbert's Defense Department," *Whiskey & Gunpowder* investment newsletter, Oct. 12, 2006; Eisenhower's four weapons from Robert Leckie, *The Wars of America*, vol. II, p. 785.

The Costs of War

War-cost importance from Margaret G. Myers, *A Financial History of the United States*, pp. 50, 170, 292, 360; George Washington from Don Cook, *The Long Fuse*, p. 334; American Revolution cost from Thomas K. McCraw, *The American Scholar*, Winter 1994, p. 42; War of 1812 cost from T. Harry Williams, *The History of American Wars*, p. 103; Gulf War cost from "Commitments for Gulf War," *The Wall Street Journal*, June 9, 1992, p. A-12; cost of acquiring Indian territories from Robert V. Remini, *Andrew Jackson and the Course of American Democracy*, p. 314; Gadsden Purchase (Arizona and New Mexico) and Philippines cost from Richard J. Barnet, *The Rockets' Red Glare*, pp. 108, 136; race to the moon cost from Harold Evans, *The American Century*, p. 555; Civil War pension liabilities from Richard Severo and Lewis Milford, *The Wages of War*, p. 172; American Revolution inflation from Stanley Lebergott, *The Americans: An Economic Record*, pp. 42, 49; Civil War inflation from Patricia Lee Holt, *George Washington Had No Middle Name*, p. 81; direct war costs and income taxes from Robert Higgs, "How War Mobilization Hurts the Economy," in Donald N. McCloskey, *Second Thoughts*, pp. 34–35; Thomas Jefferson from John T. Morse Jr., *American Statesmen*, pp. 82–83; James Madison from Doris A. Graber, *Public Opinion, the President, and Foreign Policy*, p. 196.

Our Greatest President . . .

Major L. Wilson, *The Presidency of Martin Van Buren*, pp. 147, 158, 161, 166–67; Jeffrey Rogers Hummel, "Martin Van Buren: The Greatest American President," *The Independent Review* 4, no. 2 (Fall 1999), p. 258–60.

Odds of Getting Killed

War death statistics from http://www.cwc.lsu.edu/other/stats/warcost.htm; concept of annual fatality ratio from Richard Severo and Lewis Milford, *The Wages of War*, p. 117; see Bruce D. Porter, *War and the Rise of the State*, pp. 249–54; Grant from Gore Vidal, *United States: Essays 1952–1992*, pp. 712, 1010; Gettysburg long-range rifles from Louis Menand, *The Metaphysical Club*, p. 49; Civil War fatality ratio from Edward P. Crapol, *John Tyler*, p. 271.

Fighting the Real Enemy

Julie L. Horan, *The Porcelain God*, pp. 169–71, 174–75; Hans Zinsser, *Rats, Lice and History*, pp. 153, 291; Mexican War statistics from Patricia Lee Holt, *George Washington Had No Middle Name*, p. 85; Spanish-American War statistic from J. Buschini, "The Spanish-American War," Small Planet Communications, 2000, pp. 4–5; World War I statistic from Douglas Brinkley, *Wheels for the World*, pp. 250; drugs from Dennis Worthen, *Pharmacy in World War II*, pp. 86, 94–98.

Missing: The Ferocity of a Lion

Napoleon's axiom about the lion and the sheep from Gene Smith, *Lee and Grant*, p. xiv; Faulkner quote from William Faulkner, *Go Down Moses*, pp. 288–89; number of soldiers and Grant statistic from Russell F. Weigley, *The American Way of War*, p. 130; Lord John Russell from Jay Monaghan, *Abraham Lincoln Deals with Foreign Affairs*, p. 42; Southern economy from Stanley Lebergott, *The Americans: An Economic Record*, p. 234, 239–43; only 25 percent of Southerners owning slaves from Thomas Sowell, *Ethnic America*, p. 190; Lee and desertions from Gary W. Gallagher and Alan T. Nolan, ed., *The Myth of the Lost Cause and Civil War History*, p. 25; squabbling among the Confederate states and Alexander Stephens from David J. Eicher, *Dixie Betrayed*, pp. 21, 121, 150–51.

The General Who Would Have Been Better . . .

3:1 and 5:1 offense/defense from Robert Leckie, *The Wars of America*, vol. II, p. 1153; rifle firepower quote from Louis Menand, *The Metaphysical Club*, p. 49; Liddell Hart from Thomas L. Connelly, *The Marble Man*, p. 208; Grant's critical judgment of Lee from J. Russell Young, *Around the World with General Grant*, vol. 2, pp. 458–59, quoted in Gary W. Gallagher and Alan T. Nolan, eds., *The Myth of the Lost Cause and Civil War History*, p. 162; Lee's mediocre career, Scott quote about "greatest mistake," and "terrible war" from Connelly, *The Marble Man*, pp. 8–9, 194, 205; for description of the Gettysburg battle, see Michael Shaara, *The Killer Angels*; for analysis of how Lee could have won, see Bevin Alexander, *How the South Could Have Won the Civil War*; Lee on slavery from Elbert B. Smith, *Francis Preston Blair*, p. 283, and Alan T. Nolan, *Lee Considered*, pp. 23, 51; Theodore Roosevelt's "the very greatest of all the great captains that the English-speaking peoples have brought forth" and Winston Churchill's "one of the noblest Americans who ever lived" from "Legacy" in http//en.wikipedia.org/wiki/Robert_E._Lee, and Gallagher and Nolan, *Myth of the Lost Cause*, p. 48; Eisenhower from http://www.eisenhowermemorial.org/speeches/19540529; Boy Scouts' removal from *New York Times*, May 15, 2003, p. A-32.

Know Thine Enemy

Hiroyuki Agawa, *The Reluctant Admiral*, pp. 70–75, 82–86; Yamamoto and poker from http://www.twoplustwo.com/farce/html; Ronald H. Spector, *Eagle Against the Sun*, 1985, pp. 65, 78–79, 81, 90.

Generals for Hire

James Madison and the Portuguese navy from Patricia Lee Holt, *George Washington Had No Middle Name*, p. 48; Garibaldi from *Reader's Digest Strange Stories*, p. 577; John Paul Jones from Samuel Eliot Morison, *John Paul Jones: A Sailor's Biography*, pp. 362–63; Winfield Scott from Timothy D. Johnson, *Winfield Scott*, p. 209; Douglas MacArthur from Carol M. Petillo, *Douglas MacArthur*, p. 205, Ronald H. Spector, *Eagle Against the Sun*, p. 116, John Costello, *Days of Infamy*, p. 52, Marshall Schaller, *Douglas MacArthur*, p. 24, and Emily S. Rosenberg, *A Date Which Will Live*, p. 129.

Japanese Treatment of Prisoners

Victor Davis Hanson, *Carnage and Culture*, pp. 336–37, 346; Japanese and German POW death rate from John Dower, *Embracing Defeat*, p. 446; Richard B. Frank, *Downfall*, p. 161.

A Battle He Never Fought In

Timothy B. Benford, *World War II Flashback*, p. 3; Robert Leckie, *Delivered from Evil*, vol. II, pp. 672–73.

The Courage of the Common Soldier

Tim Giago, "Indian's Compassion, Valor Put German on New Path," *Albuquerque Journal*, Aug. 27, 2000, p. 1.

Our Only Militarist President

Einstein quote from www.brainyhistory.com/events/july_16_1941_100014.html; 1950s military build-up statistics from John Lukacs, *Outgrowing Democracy*, p. 64; Truman restraint from Arthur M. Schlesinger Jr., *The Cycles of American History*, p. 398; Strategic Air Command from Ronald Schaffer, *Wings of Judgment*, p. 207; Eisenhower bellicosity from Schlesinger, pp. 400, 402, 404 and Robert S. McNamara, *In Retrospect*, p. 173; Khrushchev quote from James Bamford, *Body of Secrets*, p. 51; Wilson use of the military from Carol Wilcox Melton, *Between War and Peace*, p. 211.

The Beginning of World War IV

Andrew J. Bacevich, *The New American Militarism*, pp. 4, 179–81.

Forgotten Victims of War

Dalton Trumbo, "1990 Addendum to Introduction," *Johnny Got His Gun*; Iraq fatalities and wounded statistics from Martin Sieff, "Insurgents Target Iraqis Over U.S. Troops," UPI, Feb. 3, 2006, http://www.spacewar.com/reports/Insurgents_Target_Iraqis Over_US_Troops.html, and Eric Reinagel, "Wounds of War: Overcoming the Psychological Scars of War" and "Advances Help Amputees Cope," *Meadville* (Pennyslvania) *Tribune*, Oct. 20 and 25, 2006, http://www.meadvilletribune.com.

SIX: In Pursuit of Riches

FDR and Sears Roebuck catalog from David M. Potter, *People of Plenty*, p. 80; John Marshall from Peter Messer, *Stories of Independence*, p. 168; Tocqueville from Lewis Lapham, "Holy Dread," *Lapham's Quarterly*, Spring 2008, p. 16; Abraham Lincoln from *Wall Street Journal*, April 17, 2008; William Seward from Charles Flood, *1864*, p. 96; Marc Bloch, *The Historian's Craft*, p. 66; Washington from John Steele Gordon, *An Empire of Wealth*, p. 68; Jefferson from Lewis H. Kimmel, *Federal Budget and Fiscal Policy, 1789–1958*, p. 14; Coney Island from Lena Lencek and Gideon Bosker, *The Beach*, p. 168, and Ric Burns and James Sanders, *New York: An Illustrated History*, p. 260.

A Bigger Job . . .

Halsted L. Ritter, *Washington as a Businessman*, pp. 68–84, illustration p. 112.

Better than Yum-Yum

Pat Choate, *Hot Property*. pp. 27, 37, 57, 65, 67; Abraham Lincoln, "Lecture on Discoveries and Inventions," Abraham Lincoln Online: Speeches and Writings, http://showcase.netins.net/web/creative/lincoln/speeches/discoveries.htm, last two paragraphs; five marble buildings from Dorothy Meserve Kunhardt and Philip B. Kunhardt Jr., *Twenty Days*, p. 113; Coca-Cola from Tom Bethell, *The Noblest Triumph*, pp. 261–62.

The Surest Path . . .

Andro Linklater, *Measuring America*, pp. 163, 173, 193; George Washington secrecy and land acquisitions, and Thomas Paine from A. M. Sakolski, *The Great American Land Bubble*, pp. 7–12; George Washington and Henry George from John C. Weaver, *The Great Land Rush and the Making of the Modern World, 1650–1900*, pp. 88, 96, 338; European visitor quote from James H. Cassidy, *Demography in Early America*, pp. 154–55; population reproduction rate from Sam Bass Warner Jr., *The Urban Wilderness*, p. 16; Robert P. Swierenga, "Land Speculation and Its Impact on American Economic Growth and Welfare," *Western Historical Quarterly* (Utah State University) vol. 8, no. 3 (July 1977), 283–85; see Daniel M. Friedenberg, *Life, Liberty and the Pursuit of Land*.

Massive Debt Financing . . .

"burst in a tornado" from A. M. Sakolski, *The Great American Land Bubble*, p. 192; Jefferson's constitutional difficulties from John Kukla, *A Wilderness So Immense*, pp. 301–5; New Orleans closing ceremony from Wayne T. DeCesar and Susan Page, "Jefferson Buys Louisiana Territory, and the Nation Moves Westward," *Prologue* magazine (U.S. National Archives and Records Administration), Spring 2003, vol. 35, no. 1; $400 billion from Samuel H. Williamson, "Five Ways to Compute the Relative Value of a U.S. Dollar Amount, 1790–2005," www.measuringworth.com; historian quote about London banking firm from Pierce Mullen, "The Bottom Line," page 3 of 5, http://www.lewis-clark.org/content/content-article.asp? ArticleID=316; House of Baring and Federalist objections from Thomas Fleming, *The Louisiana Purchase*, pp. 127, 130; Marie Antoinette and Josephine from Dana Thomas, *Deluxe*, p. 22.

Fool's Gold

Jack London, "The Economics of the Klondike," *The Atlantic Monthly Review of Reviews*, Jan. 1900, pp. 70–72; clothes washed in Hawaii from W. E. Woodward, *The Way Our People Lived*, p. 274; John Sutter from Andro Linklater, *Measuring America*, pp. 238–40.

She Loved Money Too Much

Louis Menand, *The Metaphysical Club*, pp. 165–75; for a more technical explanation of the mathematics, see http://www.law.berkeley.edu/faculty/sklansky, "Chapter 9 Problems," and especially Paul Meier and Sandy Zabell, "Benjamin Pierce and the Howland Will," *Journal of the American Statistical Association*, vol. 75, no. 371, pp. 497–506, http://listserv.dartmouth.org/scripts/wa.exe?A2=ind0105d&L=chance&D=1&T=O&P=176.

When the Will Got Read

Vanderbilt wealth and currency circulation from Michael Kazin, "Ruthless in Manhattan," *New York Times*, May 10, 2009, p. 24; Frank Kintrea, "The Great Vanderbilt Will Battle," in Byron Dobell, ed., *A Sense of History*, pp. 361–409; "as much as anyone ought to have" and "give away the surplus" from Wayne Andrews, *The Vanderbilt Legend*, p. 173.

Living Well . . .

Wayne Andrews, *The Vanderbilt Legend*, pp. 217–23.

Fiddling with the Clock . . .

Mark Perry, *Grant and Twain*, pp. 130–33, 157–59.

Midas

"Any fool can make a fortune" from Arthur T. Vanderbilt II, *Fortune's Children*, p. 73; "No yachts for me!" and Andrew Carnegie from Wayne Andrews, *The Vanderbilt Legend*, pp. 228, 368; Frederick Vanderbilt from Jerry E. Patterson, *The Vanderbilts*, pp. 279–80; *New York Sun* quote from W. A. Croffut, *The Vanderbilts*, p. 244; 1973 family reunion from Arthur T. Vanderbilt II, *Newsweek*, July 9, 1990, Letters to the Editor, p. 10.

Cash-Flow Miracle

Previous two bankruptcies from Gerald Gunderson, *The Wealth Creators*, p. 190; startup capital and factory size from James J. Flink, *The Automobile Age*, p. 41; amount of capital needed over the next forty years from Peter Baida, *Poor Richard's Legacy*, p. 194; ninety-three-minutes-per-car production line from Wyn Craig Wade, *The Titanic: End of a Dream*, p. 20; "sixteen cars behind" from Harold Evans, *They Made America*, p. 245.

Rent, Don't Sell

Peter Harry Brown and Pat A. Broeske, *Howard Hughes*, p. 10; Warren Buffett from Cort Furniture Rental (a Berkshire Hathaway company) ad, *Forbes*, Oct. 30, 2006, p. 225.

Acres of Diamonds

Russell H. Conwell, *Acres of Diamonds*, Harper & Brothers, 1915, p. 12; Henry Comstock from Robert Sobel, *The Money Manias*, p. 105; Alexander Graham Bell from Pat Choate, *Hot Property*, pp. 62–63; Alvah Roebuck from John Steele Gordon," No Respect," *American Heritage*, Sept. 1993, p. 16; Alex Malcolmsen from Douglas Brinkley, *Wheels for the World*, p. 241; Will Durant from Stephen Birmingham, *Our Crowd*, p. 349–50; Lenin from Peter Schweizer, *Reagan's War*, p. 7; Warner and Zanuck from http:/www.tenonline.org/art/usa/008.html and 9812.html; Carlson and Eastman Kodak from Elizabeth Brayer, *George Eastman*, p. 607; Ford and Volkswagen from James J. Flink, *The Automobile Age*, pp. 308, 321, 324; Toyota and Nissan from Douglas Brinkley, *Wheels for the World*, p. 588; Ray Kroc from John F. Love, *McDonald's*, pp. 70–71; Steve Jobs and Steve Wozniak from www.tenonline.org/art/usa/9812.html; Truman from Ralph Keyes, *The Wit & Wisdom of Harry Truman*, p. 74.

A Model Businessman-Philanthropist

"most thanked man in the world" and refund of war contract profits from Carl W. Ackerman, *George Eastman*, pp. 493, 271 (the actual word in the *New York Times* quote is "bethanked," which we modernized into "thanked"); "largest single contribution," "would up a liberal," "extra pay for extra work," war contracts profit, "pie-faced mutts," and Seneca quote from Elizabeth Brayer, *George Eastman*, pp. 278, 362, 178, 401, 346, 527; Ford's 370% turnover, "a workman sticks up his head, hit it," and "war all the time . . . keep one part of one's heart a little soft," from Richard Tedlow, *Giants of Enterprise*, pp. 164, 112, 93; see Bernard Weisberger, "You Press the Button, We Do the Rest," *American Heritage*, October 1972 (vol. 23, no. 6) and www.georgeeastmanhouse.org.

The Year the Stock Market Recovered

Bernard Baruch from Christopher Cerf and Victor Navasky, *The Experts Speak*, pp. 48–49; "five 30-percent rallies" from *Fortune*, Nov. 2, 1992, p. 35; Mark Hulbert, "25 Years to Bounce Back? Try 4 (1/2)," *New York Times*, April 26, 2009, p. BU-5.

Economic Boom

Henry Wallace from Cerf and Navasky, *The Experts Speak*, p. 54; Joseph C. Goulden, *The Good Years: 1945–1950*, pp. 92–94.

America's Best-Kept Secret

Astor quote from Stephen Birmingham, *America's Secret Aristocracy*, p. 115; JFK and father's wealth from Paul B. Fay, *The Pleasure of His Company*, pp. 10–11; young Alice Roosevelt from Betty Boyd Caroli, *The Roosevelt Women*, p. 398, and Michael Teague, *Mrs. L: Conversations with Alice Roosevelt Longworth*, p. 14; Lawrence H. Summers and Laurence J. Kotlikoff, "The Role of Intergenerational Transfers in Aggregate Capital Formation," *Journal of Political Economy* 89 (1981), pp. 706–32, quoted in Carole Shammas, *Inheritance in America*, p. 3; see John A. Brittain, *Inheritance and the Inequality of Material Wealth*.

SEVEN: **Running for President**

Voter participation statistics from www.infoplease.com/ipa/A0781453.html; Grover Cleveland from Harold Evans, *The American Century*, p. 30; Theodore Roosevelt from Paul Grondahl, *I Rose Like a Rocket*, p. 182; Harry Truman from *Bits 'n' Pieces*, Jan. 1988, pp. 9–12; John Lukacs, *Outgrowing Democracy*, pp. 259–60; Senator Paul Simon from Frank J. Williams, Lincolniana in 1988, paragraph 13 of "Editorials," http://jala.press.uiuc.edm/10/williams.htm/; TR from Stephen Jay Gould, *Bully for Brontosaurus*, pp. 209–10; President Grover Cleveland to five-year-old FDR from James Humes, *Which President Killed a Man?* p. 214; FDR career goals and objectives from Wesley O. Hagood, *Presidential Sex*, p. 63; Joe Kennedy from Robert Dallek, "Lyndon Johnson and the 1960 Election," in Brian Lamb, ed., *Booknotes: Stories from American History*, p. 335; John C. Calhoun from Steve Tally, *Bland Ambition*, p. 55; Joseph Lane from William Lee Miller, *Lincoln's Virtues*, pp. 465–67.

The Electoral College ...

Kenneth C. Davis, *Don't Know Much About History*, pp. 420–21; Arthur M. Schlesinger Jr., *The Cycles of American History*, pp. 317–20.

Second-Choice Candidate

Washington from Robert Leckie, *The Wars of America*, vol. I, pp. 111–12; Lincoln from Stephen B. Oates, *Abraham Lincoln*, pp. 75–76, David Herbert Donald, *Lincoln*, p. 256, and William Lee Miller, *Lincoln's Virtues*, p. 394.

Running for First Lady

David Herbert Donald, *Lincoln*, p. 85; Stephen Hess, "Big Bill Taft," in American Heritage Press, *A Sense of History*, pp. 563, 574; Carl S. Anthony, *Nellie Taft*, p. 148.

First Steps First

William Lee Miller, *Lincoln's Virtues*, pp. 153–60, 316, 319; David Herbert Donald, *Lincoln*, p. 113.

Luck

1860 election statistics from Stephen B. Oates, *With Malice Toward None*, p. 190; discussion of election results from Emerson David Fite, *The Presidential Campaign of 1860*, p. 233; "A fluke" from Jay Winik, *April 1865*, p. 241; Lincoln quote from David Herbert Donald, *Lincoln*, p. 529; McPherson quote from "American Victory, American Defeat" in Gabor S. Boritt, ed., *Why the Confederacy Lost*, p. 39; "54 percent not voting" from David Herbert Donald in Brian Lamb, *Booknotes: Life Stories*, p. 98; valet's quote on Hughes from Herman D. Hover, *Fourteen Presidents before Washington*, p. 191; see Merlo J. Pusey, *Charles Evans Hughes*; Woodrow Wilson medical cover-up from David Fromkin, *In the Time of the Americans*, p. 247; Richard Nixon presidential debate from Frank Stanton, "The First Debate Over Presidential Debates," *Newsweek*, Oct. 2, 2000.

Doing What It Takes . . .

Richard Severo and Lewis Milford, *The Wages of War*, pp. 129, 143, 146–48; Gen. George Thomas from Tom Wheeler, *Mr. Lincoln's T-Mails*, p. 168.

Mailing a Letter to Himself

Kenneth J. Ackerman, *Dark Horse*, pp. 405, 429.

The Questionable Virtue of Youth

New York Times, July 5, 1960, p. 20; Sorenson comment from Gerald Gardner, *All the President's Wits*, p. 214; Breckenridge from Steve Tally, *Bland Ambition*, pp. 107–14; Mansfield comment from Harvey C. Mansfield, "Tocqueville's Democracy in America," in Brian Lamb, ed., *Booknotes: Stories from American History*, p. 67.

Campaign Cover-Up

Barbara Tuchman, *Practicing History*, pp. 106, 117.

From Secretary of State . . .

Merlo J. Pusey, *Charles Evans Hughes*, vol. I, pp. 361–62; Truman from Joseph C. Goulden, *The Best Years: 1945–1950*, pp. 231–32.

It Helps to Stay Alive

Theodore Roosevelt's death from David Fromkin, *In the Time of the Americans*, p. 226.

Secret Deal for the Presidency

Richard J. Barnet, *The Rockets' Red Glare*, p. 318; Hillary Clinton from Haynes Johnson and David S. Broder, *The System*, p. 19.

Sexual Time-Bomb

Wesley O. Hagood, *Presidential Sex*, pp. 139, 143.

Presidential Training Ground . . .

Steve Tally, *Bland Ambition*, pp. 341, 372–73.

The Common Touch

David Herbert Donald, *Lincoln*, p. 89; Reagan from *Forbes*, Nov. 11, 1991, pp. 201–2, 210.

What Our Presidents Say . . .

Washington watching Bush on TV cartoon by Jeff MacNelly, cover illustration, Eileen Shields-West, *The World Almanac of Presidential Campaigns*; Garfield's Pythagorean theorem from John Steele Gordon, *The Scarlet Woman of Wall Street*, p. 269; Herbert Hoover from John L. Moore, *Speaking of Washington*, p. 109; FDR from John Lukacs, *Outgrowing Democracy*, p. 41; Clinton from *People* magazine, Sept. 13, 1993, p. 51; Grant from Gene Smith, *Lee and Grant*, p. 96; Truman and Harding from Harold Evans, *The American Century*, pp. 374, 189; Lincoln's father from Stephen B. Oates, *Abraham Lincoln*, p. 36; Washington's father from Richard Norton Smith, "George Washington," in Brian Lamb, *Booknotes: Life Stories*, p. 3; FDR's night alone from Blanche Wiesen Cook, *Eleanor Roosevelt, vol I: 1884–1933*, pp. 478–80, and Doris Faber, *The Life of Lorena Hickok*, pp. 116–17, 156, 160; FDR "easy!" from Paul F. Boller Jr., *Presidential Anecdotes*, p. 266; Jefferson's modesty from Thomas K. McCraw, *The American Scholar*, Winter 1994, p. 31, and Dumas Malone, *Jefferson and His Time*, vol. VI, *The Sage of Monticello*, p. 499; John Quincy Adams from David Mc-Cullough, *Brave Companions*, p. 227; Jefferson on Washington, and TR's relinquishing control to Taft from Stephen Skowronek, *The Politics Presidents Make*, pp. 65, 253; historian quote on statesmanship by John Freeman Clarke in John Lukacs, *American Heritage*, Feb.–March 1992, p. 66; Lowndes description from Harriet H. Ravenel, *Life and Times of William Lowndes of South Carolina, 1782–1822*, p. 240; Lincoln quote on God from James C. Humes, *Instant Eloquence*, p. 220; Harry Truman quote on polls from Robert H. Ferrell, ed., *Off the Record: The Private Papers of Harry S Truman*, p. 310; Orson Welles and FDR from Richard J. Barnet, *The Rockets' Red Glare*, p. 218; John Adams on George Washington from David McCullough, *1776*, p. 146; Lincoln's cabinet ("They will eat you up") from Jay Monaghan, *Abraham Lincoln Deals with Foreign Affairs*, p. 14; Lincoln and Seward from Emerson David Fite, *The Presidential Campaign of 1860*, p. 214, and Stephen B. Oates, *With Malice Toward None*, p. 234; Lincoln and Chase from Peter Huber, "Kate Chase Tries to Help Her Father Become President," *Old News*, March 1992, pp. 10–12; Washington on hiring friend versus adversary from Alfred Steinberg, *The First Ten*, p. 23; James A. Garfield from Kenneth D. Ackerman, *Dark Horse*, pp. 236–37; Truman on Madison from Ralph Keyes, *The Wit and Wisdom of Harry Truman*, p. 14; Lincoln's "ayes" from John L. Moore, *Speaking of Washington*, p. 68; TR on Jefferson as the worst president, from Theodore Roosevelt, *The Naval War of 1812*, p. 405; Woodrow Wilson from Alan Wolfe, *Return to Greatness*, p. 22.

EIGHT: Simple Mathematics, My Dear Watson

Fermi quote from www.ecclesiastes911.net/theory_of_aces.html; Benjamin Franklin from Walter Isaacson, *Benjamin Franklin*, p. 150; "thirtyfold remarkable" 200-year growth from William J. Bernstein, *The Birth of Plenty*, p. 211; Klu Klux Klan number of deaths from Eric Foner, "Rethinking American History in a Post-9/11 World," http://hnn.us/articles,6961.html; Vietnam number of deaths from Ray Smith, http://www.rjsmith.com/war_myth.html; 641 Hiroshimas from William James Gibson, *The Perfect War*, p. 319; Britain "most powerful empire" in 1763 from Gordon S. Wood, *The Americanization of Benjamin Franklin*, p. 105.

A Venture Capital Investment

Martha J. Lamb, *History of the City of New York*, vol. 1, p. 121; Dave Barry, "A Certified Wacko Rewrites History's Greatest Hits," *Milwaukee Journal-Sentinel*, Dec. 26, 1999; "Manahactanienk" from Giles Milton, *Nathaniel's Nutmeg*, p. 186.

Mathematical Coincidences . . .

John Allen Paulos, *Innumeracy*, p. 29; Tyler and Truman from James Humes, *Which President Killed a Man?* p. 54; Tyler, Taylor, and Madison from Harold I. Gullan, *First Fathers*, pp. 54, 62; Jefferson and Marshall from Robert Leckie, *From Sea to Shining Sea*, p. 510, and Humes, *Which President*, p. 99; FDR's relatives from *Reader's Digest Strange Stories*, p. 106; Robert E. Lee relatives from David J. Eicher, *Robert E. Lee*, p. 6; Yalta relatives from Timothy B. Benford, *World War II Flashback*, p. 188, and William Manchester, *American Caesar*, p. 17; great-great-great-great-grandfather from Humes, *Which President*, p. 211; McCain and Obama from Amy Harmon, "The Candidates as Cousins Much Removed," *New York Times*, March 26, 2008, p. A-14.

George Washington's Compensation

Marvin Kitman, *George Washington's Expense Account*, p. 31; government audit from A. J. Langguth, *Patriots*, p. 561; inflation chart from Stanley Lebergott, *The Americans: An Economic Record*, p. 43; $2,500 loan from Halsted L. Ritter, *Washington as a Businessman*, p. 182; Jefferson's debts from Jay Winik, *April 1865*, p. 8.

The Mathematical Formula . . .

John R. Stilgoe, *Common Landscape of America, 1580 to 1845*, pp. 99–106; Andro Linklater, *Measuring America*, pp. 12, 256.

A "Third World" Nation

Jeffrey G. Williamson, "How Tough Are Times in the Third World?" in Donald N. McCloskey, ed., *Second Thoughts*, p. 12.

200,000 Afro-Americans . . .

Benjamin Butler from "Black Glory: The African-American Role in Union Victory," in Gabor S. Boritt, ed., *Why the Confederacy Lost*, pp. 140–41, 151–54; Jefferson Davis ordering execution of Butler from Kevin and Peter Keim, *A Grand Old Flag*, p. 119; Lincoln quote from Ann J. Lane, "The Civil War, Reconstruction, and the Afro-American," in Rhoda L. Goldstein, ed., *Black Life and Culture in the United States*, pp. 140–41; Earl of Dunmore from Robert Harvey, *A Few Bloody Noses*, pp. 183–86, and Simon Schama, *Rough Crossings*, pp. 70, 108, 120, 189.

Fake Government Surpluses

Gary M. Anderson, "The U.S. Federal Deficit and National Debt: A Political and Economic History," in Buchanan, Rowley, and Tollison, eds., *Deficits*, pp. 18–19.

What Immigration?

John L. Shover, *First Majority—Last Minority*, p. 4; ethnic return statistics from Ronald Takaki, *A Different Mirror*, pp. 162, 264, 283; thirty-seven emigrants from Harold Evans, *The American Century*, pp. xxi, 90–91.

The Ally We Chose to Forget

John Lukacs, *Outgrowing Democracy*, p. 107; "Cold War inaccessible . . ." from Helene Keyssar and Vladimir Pozner, *Remembering War*, pp. xiv, 17–19, 23, 79, 141; Peter G. Peterson, *Facing Up*, pp. 72–73; footnote (Russia's advance knowledge of Pearl Harbor) from Kurt Singer, *Spies Who Changed History*, p. 158.

Lucky to Be in Port

Timothy B. Benford, *World War II Flashback*, p. 153; Adm. Chester Nimitz from Gordon Prange, *Miracle at Midway*, p. 9, and John Costello, *Days of Infamy*, p. 241.

Saving American Convoys . . .

Patrick Blackett from Fred Kaplan, *The Wizards of Armageddon*, p. 53; U.S. ship construction from Norman Davies, *Europe at War*, pp. 26–27.

The Japanese City . . .

Leslie R. Groves, *Now It Can Be Told*, p. 265; Japanese government control of information from Ben Ami Shillony, *Politics and Culture in Wartime Japan*, pp. 91–109; leaflets from Ronald Schaffer, *Wings of Judgment*, p. 142; FDR from Andrew Roberts, *A History of the English-Speaking Peoples Since 1900*, p. 374; A. G. Gardiner, *Leaves in the Wind*, p. 143; Gen. LeMay from Richard Rhodes, *Dark Sun: The Making of the Hydrogen Bomb*, p. 21; Tokyo and Hiroshima death toll from Robert Leckie, *The Wars of America*, vol. II, p. 825, 831; Cologne bomb power from Juliet Gardiner, *Wartime: Britain 1939–1945*, p. 584; conventional bomb vs. atom bomb power from Richard B. Frank, *Downfall*, pp. 253, 264, 285; General Marshall from Max Hastings, *Retribution*, p. 476.

The Most Controversial Number . . .

Frankfurter and Stimson from Gar Alperovitz, *The Decision to Use the Atomic Bomb*, pp. 469, 486; Winston Churchill from Maj. Lee T. Wyatt III, "Tainted Decision: The Atom Bomb and America's Rush to End World War II," March 25, 1986, www.globalsecurity.org; number of American POWs from John Dower, *Embracing Defeat*, p. 54; MacArthur from Edwin Fogelman, *The Decision to Use the Bomb*, p. 92; Japanese blaming their militarist leaders (35 percent) rather than America (19 percent) from the 1946 U.S. Strategic Bombing Survey; Japanese emperor and kamikaze threat from Richard B. Frank, *Downfall*, pp. 321, 311; Oppenheimer from Tamara L. Roleff, ed., *The Atom Bomb*, p. 193.

More Important Than the Amount . . .

Mark A. Stoler, *George C. Marshall*, pp. 162–63; Forrest C. Pogue, *George C. Marshall*, p. 231; *New York Times* from Harold Evans, *The American Century*, p. 410; "critical difference" from John Williamson, "Trade and Payments after Soviet Disintegration," UNDP "Roundtable on Global Change" conference, Bucharest, Romania, September 1992, p. 7; U.S. ambassador to France from Andrew Roberts, *A History of the English-Speaking Peoples Since 1900*, p. 395; Barry Newman, "The Marshall Plan Had Different Goals in a Different Era," *The Wall Street Journal*, Feb. 23, 1994, p. A-8; current value of $13.4 billion from www.measuringworth.com.

Not the Right Asterisk

Ruth versus Maris from Alex Patton, "Babe Didn't See the Best," *USA Today Baseball Weekly*, Oct. 5–11, 1994, p. 19; "better game when blacks were given the opportunity" from David Craft, *The Negro Leagues*, p. 83; Mike Vaccaro, "Total Disasterisk," *New York Post*, Feb. 22, 2009, p. 87; Walter Payton (with Don Yaeger), *Never Die Easy*, p. 98.

The Warren Commission . . .

Timing of rifle shots from Gerald Posner, *Case Closed*, pp. 318–23; rifle scope distance and stationary limousine from Mel Ayton, *The JFK Assassination*, pp. 70, 117; CIA/FBI intelligence cover-up from Max Holland, "Paranoia Unbound," *Wilson Quarterly*, Winter 1994, pp. 88–89; see Vincent Bugliosi, *Reclaiming History*.

Vietnam: Fudging the Numbers

James Reston from *Reader's Digest Amazing Stories*, p. 111; refugee count falsification, Orwell's *1984*, and atom-bomb tonnage from James William Gibson, *The Perfect War*, p. 269, 159, 177, 319; Arthur Goldberg and Dean Acheson from Gary A. Donaldson, *America at War Since 1945*, p. 118; statistics from Ray Smith, http://www.rjsmith.com/war_myth.html, and Charles C. Moskos and John Sibley Butler, *All That We Can Be*, p. 8.

Unraveling the Archaeological Mysteries of the Titanic

Michael Davie, *Titanic*, p. 221; "giant finger" survivor quote by Lady Duff-Gordon from Marshall Everett, ed., *Wreck and Sinking of the* Titanic, p. 164; John Curtain from John F. McKeown, "Hubris, Not an Iceberg, Sank the *Titanic*," *New York Times*, August 13, 1986, Letters to the Editor, p. A-22; Robert D. Ballard, *The Discovery of the* Titanic, p. 196; gash mathematics from Walter Lord, *The Night Lives On*, pp. 74–75; *Titanic* hull photo, *Carpathia* captain quote, and Coriolis force/earthquake theory from Captain L. M. Collins, *The Sinking of the* Titanic, pp. 84–85, 158, 165–67; drifting lifeboats and *Carpathia*'s position from Robert D. Ballard (with Michael S. Sweeney), *Return to* Titanic, p. 61; mysteries of the deep and the pair of shoes from James Hamilton-Patterson, *The Great Deep*, p. 177.

The Magic Number of U.S. Troops . . .

Bruce Berkowitz, "The Number Racket," *The American Interest*, Autumn 2006, pp. 129–38; George Packer, *The Assassin's Gate*, pp. 110, 132, 138, 186, 385, 443; Donald Rumsfeld from *Newsweek*, Nov. 20, 2006, p. 38; Aparisim Ghosh, "Life in Hell: A Baghdad Diary" cover story, *Time*, August 14, 2006.

NINE: Not What You Think

The King and I from Don Hewitt, *Tell Me a Story*, p. 125; the source of the mythical Nelson story is Ed Offley, "From Landed Gentry to an Unmarked Grave," *Soldiers for the Truth* online newsletter, July 4, 2005, http://www.sftt.org/main.cfm?actionID=globalShowStaticContent&screenKey=cpm Defense&htmlCat, also in Thom Hartman, *What Would Jefferson Do?* p. 53; corrections to the story by Jim Elbrecht, "False Revolutionary History Circulating Since at Least 1956, Debunked," http://blacksheep.rootsweb.com/shame/price.ttm; see also Barbara and David P. Mikkelson, "Urban Legends Reference Pages: History (The Price They Paid)," http:www.snopes.com/history/American/pricepaid.asp; Tolstoy from Gore Vidal, *United States Essays 1952–1992*, p. 696; Boston Tea Party from John Harris, *The Boston Tea Party*, pp. 52, 56, 59–60, and Robert J. Alison, *The Boston Tea Party*, pp. 41–42, 56–60; Alex Haley from Arthur M. Schlesinger Jr., *The Disuniting of America*, p. 85; Will Rogers from Walter Mead, "Life in the Global Briar Patch," *Worth*, Dec–Jan. 1995, p. 57; New England rebellion from Robert Leckie, *From Sea to Shining Sea*, p. 332; American Revolution blacks from Richard Severo and Lewis Milford, *The Wages of War*, p. 68; FDR and Pearl Harbor from David Fromkin, *In the Time of the Americans*, p. 284; LBJ from Barbara W. Tuchman, *The March of Folly*, pp. 298–99; LBJ opinion of Diem from David Halberstam, *The Best and the Brightest*, p. 135.

Muzzling the Radical

Gore Vidal, *Inventing a Nation*, pp. 32–33.

Alternative to War . . .

Bevin Alexander, *How America Got It Right*, pp. 54–59; Adams, Crittenden, Lincoln, Greeley, and Seward from Albert D. Kirwan, *John J. Crittenden*, pp. 371, 380, 386–87, 403, 405; Lincoln's 1862 proposal to buy out the slaves of four states from www.library.rochester.edu/rbk/lincoln ("March 14, 1862"); Lincoln's plan to pay $400 million from Clarence Macartney, *Lincoln and His Generals*, p. 116; see Harold Holzer, *Lincoln President-Elect*, and David M. Potter, *Lincoln and His Party in the Secession Crisis*.

Unpopular War

James M. McPherson, "American Victory, American Defeat," in Gabor S. Boritt, ed., *Why the Confederacy Lost*, pp. 26–27; 5.5 percent white slaveholders statistic from Ronald Takaki, *A Different Mirror*, p. 119; 100,000 Confederate deserting soldiers from Jim Powell, *Great Emancipations*, p. 138.

The Two Generals . . .

Lee's army and Union army statistic from Robert Leckie, *The Wars of America*, vol. 1, p. 519; Jay Winik, *April 1865*, pp. 144, 157, 278–80, 295, 319.

The Cruel South

Louis Haber, *Black Pioneers of Science and Invention*, pp. xiii, 124.

Did He Really Say It?

Vanderbilt from Wayne Andrews, *The Vanderbilt Legend*, pp. 194–95; Charles E. Wilson from David Halberstam, *The Fifties*, p. 118.

Freemen Yet Slaves . . .

John Goff, *Robert Todd Lincoln*, pp. 70–71, 119–20, 236; Larry Tye, *Rising from the Rails*, pp. 72, 92, 100, 111; "lily white affair" from *Smithsonian*, February 2009, p. 35; "summer home" from Charles Lachman, *The Last Lincolns*, p. 342.

Dark Side of a Liberal President

Thomas F. Gosset, *Race*, pp. 277–80; Larry Tye, *Rising from the Rails*, p. 76; Harold Evans, *The American Century*, p. 192.

A Gift to the Moon

Dan van der Vat, *The Grand Scuttle*, pp. 214–15; David Bodanis, $E = mc^2$, pp. 293–94; www. worldwar1.co.uk/scuttle.html.

Fierce Opposition to the ERA

Elyce J. Rotella, "The Equal Rights Amendment—Yes, But *Whose?*" in Donald N. McCloskey, *Second Thoughts*, pp. 72–75.

A Hidden Motive . . .

Winston Churchill from Maj. Gen. J. W. C. Fuller, *MH*, vol. 3, p. 324; Cambridge, Massachusetts, ordinance from Richard J. Barnet, *The Rockets' Red Glare*, p. 293; General Sherrill from Arthur D. Morse, *While Six Million Died*, p. 182; Lord Halifax from Helene Keyssar and Vladimir Pozner, *Remembering War*, p. 3.

Tougher Peace Terms . . .

Andrew Roberts, *A History of the English-Speaking Peoples Since 1900*, pp. 380–81; Martin Lorenz-Meyer, *Safehaven*, pp. 89–92, 278; Gerhard L. Weinberg, *A World at Arms*, pp. 897, 899–900; Eisenhower and demilitarization from Edward N. Peterson, *The American Occupation of Germany*, pp. 138, 154; chemical weapons from Peter Elphick, *Liberty*, p. 408; Japan from John Dower, *Embracing Defeat*, pp. 74–78, 82–84, 115–118, 525.

When the Depression Finally Ended

Country recovery statistics from Thomas Fleming, *The New Dealers' War*, p. 63; David Brinkley, *Washington Goes to War*, p. 105; "Dr. Win the War" from Richard J. Barnet, *The Rockets' Red Glare*, p. 219; 15 million jobs lost from John Lukacs, *Outgrowing Democracy*, p. 399; Samuelson and Curti from Robert Sobel, *The Great Boom*, pp. 28–31; Thomas J. DiLorenzo, *How Capitalism Saved America*, p. 184.

Probably America's Most Successful War

Robert Leckie, *The Wars of America*, vol. 2, pp. 934–35.

The Thirty-Eight Witnesses Who Weren't

Martin Gansberg, "37 Who Saw Murder Didn't Call," *New York Times*, March 27, 1964; A. M. Rosenthal, *Thirty-Eight Witnesses*, McGraw-Hill, 1964, pp. 23–24, 44, 51–52; Joseph De May, www.kewgardenshistory.com; Jim Rasenberger, "Kitty, 40 Years Later," *New York Times*, Feb. 8, 2004; Matthew Engel, "The Error of His Wars," *Financial Times* (London), May 19, 2007; Rachel Manning, Mark Levine, and Alan Collins, "The Kitty Genovese Murder and the Social Psychology of Helping: The Parable of the 38 Witnesses," *American Psychologist* 62, no. 4 (Sept. 2007): 555–62.

The Day Israel Attacked America

James Scott, *The Attack on the Liberty*, p. 163–67, 210–14, 221, 228–29, 253, 274–80; http://en.wikipedia.org/wiki/USS_Liberty_incident; Moorer, Rusk, Helms, and Clifford quotes from http://www.ussliberty.org/; James Bamford, *Body of Secrets*, p. 202–204; Nicholas Kralev, "Israel Blamed for USS Liberty Attack," *Washington Times*, Feb. 13, 2004; William F. Buckley from *National Review*, June 27, 1967; for the "deliberate attack" view, see James M. Ennes Jr. (one of the surviving sailors), *Assault on the Liberty*; for the "mistaken identity/tragic error" view, see A. Jay Cristol, *The Liberty Incident*.

Irresponsible Investigation . . .

Ramsey report, Brent Staples, journalists, and David Belin from Mel Ayton, *The JFK Assassination*, pp. 57–58, 70, 106–107, 211, 238, 253, 256; *Today* show and Steve Barber from Gerald Posner, *Case Closed*, pp. 239–42; "one minute to midnight" from Michael Holland, "The Docudrama That Is *JFK*," http//mcadams.posc.mu.edu/1297/holl.htm; Ramsey Report (National Academy of Sciences) executive summary from http://www.jfk-online.com/nas01.html; Michael O'Dell study from http://mcadams.pose.mu.edu/odell/; addition of "allegedly" on building plaque from Henry R. May, http://home.cfl.rr/commayhr01/dallas2.html.

Four Presidential Elections . . .

Nader from Jeff Greenfield, *"Oh Waiter! One Order of Crow!"*, p. 305; Jefferson from Bruce Ackerman and David Fontana, "How Jefferson Counted Himself In," *The Atlantic Monthly*, March 2004, pp. 84–95; Van Rensselaer from Steve Tally, *Bland Ambition*, p. 56; Tilden from Dee Brown, *The Year of the Century: 1876*, pp. 288–336; see Lloyd Robinson, *The Stolen Election*; present-day electoral college calculations by the author.

TEN: Lightning Strikes Twice: It Happened Again

Walter H. Bock, "A Powerful System for Using Historical Examples," Amazon.com book review of Richard E. Neustadt, *Thinking in Time: the Uses of History for Decision Makers*; Kissinger from Barbara Tuchman, *Practicing History*, pp. 104, 108; Alice Roosevelt Longworth's voodoo doll from Kathleen Dalton, *Theodore Roosevelt*, p. 357; H. D. S. Greenway, "Heeding British Ghosts," *International Herald Tribune*, June 7, 2006, p. 9; Fort Sumter and volunteers from Louis Menand, *The Metaphysical Club*, pp. 250, 31–32; Wilson from John Dos Passos, *Mr. Wilson's War*, p. 114; Lincoln from Patrick J. Buchanan, *The Death of the West*, p. 175; "Forget the past" proverb from John S. Friedman, *The Secret Histories*, p. 94; Sir John Templeton from *Forbes*, Feb. 2, 2007, p. 19.

Forty Percent of the Nation's Banks . . .

Jeffrey Rogers Hummel, "Martin Van Buren: The American Gladstone," footnote 16, http://www .mises.org/story/2201; Milton Friedman, *A Program for Monetary Stability*, p. 10; Major L. Wilson, *The Presidency of Martin Van Buren*, pp. 44–46, 49, 133; see James C. Curtis, *The Fox at Bay*, pp. 64– 103; real estate valuations from "Panic of 1837," Wikipedia.

On to Baghdad!

Howard W. Simpson, *Invisible Armies*, pp. 195–97.

A Prima Donna General

Harold Holzer, *Dear Mr. Lincoln*, p. 44; Taft from Harold Evans, *The American Century*, p. 114.

Raising Taxes . . .

Lewis H. Kimmel, *Federal Budget and Fiscal Policy, 1789–1958*, p. 17.

Jinxed Building

Charles Lachman, *The Last Lincolns*, pp. 288–89.

Worse than Katrina

Erik Larsen, *Isaac's Storm*, pp. 13, 67, 195; "Hurricane that Wrecked Galveston Was Deadliest in U.S. History," CNN, Sept. 8, 2000.

Dumping Foreign-Made Cars . . .

James J. Flink, *The Automobile Age*, p. 19.

The Automobile . . .

1911 car picture from Ford Motor Company ad in the *New York Times*, March 1, 1993; mpg statistics from Clyde Prestowitz, *Rogue Nation*, p. 34.

Reappearance of the Laffer Curve

Charles Adams, *For Good and Evil*, pp. 380–81, 431.

Defying World Opinion

Henri Keyzer Andre (with Hy Steirman), *Age of Heroes*, pp. 120–21.

Not Vietnam

War in Siberia from Benjamin D. Rhodes, *The Anglo-American Winter War in Siberia*, p. 124; Wilson's "irony of fate" from Gary A. Donaldson, *America at War Since 1945*, pp. 96–97; Wilson's "sweep back a great sea" from Carol Wilcox Melton, *Between War and Peace*, p. 134; Wilson's "harder to get out than it was to get in" from Rhodes, *The Anglo-American Winter War*, p. 99; unpopular War of 1812 from T. Harry Williams, *The History of American Wars*, p. 93, 103, 105; Civil War drug abuse and Philippines from Richard Severo and Lewis Milford, *The Wages of War*, pp. 137–38 and 213, 215, 218, 227; Mark Twain, "To the Person Sitting in Darkness," *North American Review*, Feb. 1901; FDR from David Fromkin, *In the Time of the Americans*, pp. 345–47; British and the American Revolution from Barbara W. Tuchman, *The First Salute*, pp. 196–97, 232–34. King George III, William Pitt, and Charles Fox from Charles Mills Gayley, *Shakespeare and the Founders of Liberty in America*, pp. 198–200.

Not OPEC

http://www.rre.state.tx.us/history/h01.html; http:www.tsl.state.tx.us/exhibits/railroad/oil/page6.html; see Daniel Yergin, *The Prize*, and William R. Childs, *The Texas Railroad Commission*.

The First Japanese Attack . . .

"Blues 'Seize' Hilo in Games at Hawaii," *New York Times*, Feb. 8, 1932, p. 3; "45 Planes Down in Hawaii Battle," *New York Times*, Feb. 9, 1932, p. 3; Thomas Fleming, *The New Dealers' War*, pp. 43–44, and "February 7, 1932—A Date That Would Live in Amnesia," *American Heritage*, July/August 2001; Knox from Bruce Catton, *The War Lords of Washington*, p. 9.

Precursor to Global Warming, Man-made

Timothy Egan, *The Worst Hard Time*, pp. 8, 47, 150–53, 188, 220–21, 256; Donald Worster, *Dust Bowl*, pp. 5, 29; Georg Bergstrom, *World Food Resources*, pp. 203, 207.

The First Terrorist Attack . . .

Joseph E. Persico, *Roosevelt's Secret War*, pp. 200–5; Michael Dobbs, *Saboteurs*, pp. 146, 196, 200, 204.

Kangaroo Court of Justice

Kai Bird and Martin J. Sherwin, *American Prometheus*, pp. 334–37, 349, 429, 483, 487, 496, 501, 514; Priscilla J. McMillan, *The Ruin of Robert J. Oppenheimer*, pp. 10, 187, 193, 196–99, 208.

Missing: Weapons of Mass Destruction

Fred Kaplan, "Was Bush Lying about WMD?" *Slate*, June 27, 2003; Fred Kaplan, *The Wizards of Armageddon*, pp. 255, 289; McNamara from http://www.cnn.com/SPECIALS/cold.war/episodes/12/interviews/mcnamara; see Christopher A. Preble, *John F. Kennedy and the Missile Gap*.

Potential Impeachment . . .

James Bamford, *Body of Secrets*, pp. 51–60.

Beware of Ice . . .

Thresher submarine from Ace Collins, *Tragedies of American History*, p. 206; *Challenger* spacecraft from Christopher Burns, *Deadly Decisions*, pp. 44, 47, 55.

Poor Planning . . .

Jim Dwyer and Kevin Flynn, *102 Minutes*, pp. 40, 51, 54, 110, 223; Ludovico De Luigi, *Viaggiatore dell'Arte*, pp. 26–27.

AFTERWORD

Pattern recognition from Charles Murray, *Real Education*, p. 119; "I propose a simple curriculum" from Peter Peterson, *Running on Empty*, p. 223; Reagan from Patrick J. Buchanan, *The Death of the West*, p. 147.

BIBLIOGRAPHY

Author's note: For those of you who may be interested in reading further, let me share with you my favorites. In boldface, I have identified some thirty books that I found particularly stimulating and provocative.

Abulafia, David. *The Discovery of Mankind: Atlantic Encounters in the Age of Columbus*. Yale University Press, 2008.

Ackerman, Carl W. *George Eastman*. Houghton Mifflin, 1930.

Ackerman, Kenneth J. *Dark Horse: The Surprise Election and Political Murder of President James A. Garfield*. Carroll & Graf, 2003.

Adams, Charles. *For Good and Evil: The Impact of Taxes on the Course of Civilization*. Madison, 1993.

Adams, Samuel B. *Mr. Kaiser Goes to Washington*. University of North Carolina Press, 1997.

Adams, William Howard. *Jefferson's Monticello*. Cross River Press, 1983.

Adler, Bill. *500 Great Facts About America*. Avon Books, 1992.

Agawa, Hiroyuki. *The Reluctant Admiral: Yamamoto and the Imperial Navy*. Tokyo: Kodansha, 1980.

Alden, John R. *George Washington*. Louisiana State University Press, 1996.

Alexander, Bevin. *How America Got It Right*. Crown, 2005.

———. *How the South Could Have Won the Civil War: The Fatal Errors That Led to Confederate Defeat*. Crown, 2007.

Allison, Robert J. *The Boston Tea Party*. Commonwealth Editions, 2007.

Alperovitz, Gar. *The Decision to Use the Atomic Bomb*. HarperCollins, 1995.

Ambrose, Stephen E. *Personal Reflections of an Historian*. Simon & Schuster, 2002.

Anderson, Fred, and Andrew Cayton. *The Dominion of War*. Viking, 2004.

Anderson, Jervis. *A. Philip Randolph: A Biographical Portrait*. University of California Press, 1972.

Andrews, Wayne. *The Vanderbilt Legend: The Story of the Vanderbilt Family*. Harcourt Brace, 1941.

Anthony, Carl S. *Nellie Taft: The Unconventional First Lady of the Ragtime Era*. William Morrow, 2005.

Armbruster, Maxim E. *The Presidents of the United States*. 6th edition. Horizon Press, 1975.

Ashby, LeRoy. *With Amusement for All: A History of American Popular Culture Since 1830*. University Press of Kentucky, 2006.

Ayton, Mel. *The JFK Assassination: Dispelling the Myths*. Woodfield Publishing (UK), 2002.

Bacevich, Andrew J. *The New American Militarism*. Oxford University Press, 2005.

Bagley, Will. *Blood of the Prophets: Brigham Young and the Massacre at Mountain Meadows*. University of Oklahoma Press, 2003.

Baida, Peter. *Poor Richard's Legacy: American Business Values from Benjamin Franklin to Donald Trump*. William Morrow, 1990.

Bailey, Thomas A. *A Diplomatic History of the American People*. Appleton-Century, 1955.

———. *Presidential Greatness*. Appleton-Century, 1966.

Ballard, Robert D. *The Discovery of the Titanic*. Madison Publishing, 1987.

———. *Return to Titanic*. National Geographic Society, 2004.

Bamford, James. *Body of Secrets*. Random House/Anchor Books, 2001.

Barnet, Richard J. *The Rocket's Red Glare: When America Goes to War—The Presidents and the People*. Simon & Schuster, 1990.

Beattie, Owen, and John Geiger. *Frozen in Time: The Fate of the Franklin Expedition* (revised edition). Greystone Books (UK), 2004.

Benford, Timothy B. *World War II Flashback*. Longmeadow Press, 1991.

Bernier, Olivier. *The World in 1800*. John Wiley, 2000.

Bernstein, Peter L. *Wedding of the Waters: The Erie Canal and the Making of a Great Nation*. W. W. Norton, 2005.

Bernstein, William J. *The Birth of Plenty: How the Prosperity of the Modern World Was Created*. McGraw-Hill, 2004.

Best, Joel. *More Damned Lies and Statistics: How Numbers Confuse Public Issues*. University of California Press, 2004.

Bethell, Tom. *The Noblest Triumph: Property and Prosperity Through the Ages*. St. Martin's Griffin, 1998.

Bird, Kai, and Martin J. Sherwin. *American Prometheus: The Triumph and Tragedy of Robert Oppenheimer*. Alfred A. Knopf, 2005.

Birmingham, Stephen. *Our Crowd*. Harper & Row, 1967.

———. *America's Secret Aristocracy*. Little, Brown, 1987.

Bishop, Jim. *The Day Lincoln Was Shot*. Harper & Bros., 1955.

Bloch, Marc. *The Historian's Craft*. Random House/Vintage, 1964.

Bodanis, David. *The Secret House*. Simon & Schuster, 1986.

———. *$E = mc^2$. A Biography of the World's Most Famous Equation*. Walker & Co., 2000.

Boller, Paul F., Jr. *Presidential Anecdotes*. Penguin, 1982.

Bordewich, Fergus M. *Washington: The Making of the American Capital*. HarperCollins/Amistad, 2008.

Borgstrom, Georg. *World Food Resources*. Intext Educational Publishers, 1973.

Boritt, Gabor S., ed. *Why the Confederacy Lost*. Oxford University Press, 1992.

Boyle, David. *Toward the Setting Sun: Columbus, Cabot, Vespucci, and the Race for America*. Walker & Co., 2008.

Bragg, Melvyn. *The Adventure of English*. Hodder & Stoughton (UK), 2003.

Brandt, Clare. *The Man in the Mirror: A Life of Benedict Arnold*. Random House, 1994.

Brayer, Elizabeth. *George Eastman*. Johns Hopkins University Press, 1996.

Brinkley, David. *Washington Goes to War*. Alfred A. Knopf, 1988.

Brinkley, Douglas. *Wheels for the World*. Viking, 2003.

Brittain, John A. *Inheritance and the Inequality of Material Wealth*. Brookings Institution, 1978.

Brown, Dee. *The Year of the Century: 1876*. Scribner's, 1966.

Brown, Peter Harry, and Pat A. Broeske. *Howard Hughes: The Untold Story*. Dutton, 1996.

Brown, Walt. *The People vs. Lee Harvey Oswald*. Carroll & Graf, 1992.

Buchanan, Patrick J. *The Death of the West: How Dying Populations and Immigrant Invasions Imperil Our Country and Civilization*. St. Martin's Press, 2002.

Buchanan, Rowley, and Tollison, eds. *Deficits*. Blackwell, 1987.

Bugliosi, Vincent. *Reclaiming History: The Assassination of John F. Kennedy*. W. W. Norton, 2007.

Burns, Christopher. *Deadly Decisions: How False Knowledge Sank the* Titanic, *Blew Up the Shuttle, and Led America into War*. Prometheus Books, 2008.

Burns, Ric, and James Sanders. *New York: An Illustrated History*. Alfred A. Knopf, 1999.

Butler, Daniel Allen. *The Other Side of the Night: The Carpathia, the Californian, and the Night the Titanic Was Lost*. Casemate, 2009.

Canto, Christophe, and Odile Faliu. *The History of the Future*. Flammarion (France), 1993.

Caroli, Betty Boyd. *The Roosevelt Women*. Basic Books, 1998.

Cassidy, James H. *Demography in Early America: Beginnings of the Statistical Mind*. Harvard University Press, 1969.

Catton, Bruce. *The War Lords of Washington*. Harcourt Brace, 1948.

Cerf, Christopher, and Victor Navasky. *The Experts Speak: The Definitive Compendium of Authoritative Misinformation*. Pantheon Books, 1984.

Cheney, Margaret. *Tesla: Man Out of Time*. Dorset Press, 1981.

Chernow, Ron. *House of Morgan*. Atlantic Monthly Press, 1990.

Childs, William R. *The Texas Railroad Commission*. Texas A&M University Press, 2005.

Chirnside, Mark. *The Olympic-Class Ships:* Olympic-Titanic-Britannic. Tempus Publishing (UK), 2004.

Choate, Pat. *Hot Property: The Stealing of Ideas in an Age of Globalization*. Alfred A. Knopf, 2005.

Churchill, Winston. *The Second World War*. 5 vols. Houghton Mifflin, 1951.

Cliff, Nigel. *The Shakespeare Riots*. Random House, 2007.

Collins, Ace. *Tragedies of American History: 13 Stories of Human Error and Natural Disaster*. Plume Penguin, 2003.

Collins, L. M. *The Sinking of the Titanic: The Mystery Solved*. Souvenir Press Ltd. (UK), 2004.

Connelly, Thomas L. *The Marble Man: Robert E. Lee and His Image in American Society*. Alfred A. Knopf, 1977.

Conway, J. North. *American Literacy: Fifty Books That Define Our Culture and Ourselves*. William Morrow, 1993.

Conwell, Russell H. *Acres of Diamonds*. Harper & Bros., 1915.

Cook, Blanche Wiesen. *Eleanor Roosevelt: Vol. I: 1884–1933*. Viking Penguin, 1992.

Cook, Don. *The Long Fuse: How England Lost the American Colonies, 1760–1785*. Atlantic Monthly Press, 1995.

Cooper, John M. *The Warrior and the Priest: Woodrow Wilson and Theodore Roosevelt*. Harvard University Press, 1983.

Cords, Nicholas, and Patrick Gerster. *Myth and the American Experience*. Glencoe Press, 1973.

Costello, John. *Days of Infamy: MacArthur, Roosevelt, Churchill—The Shocking Truth Revealed*. Pocket Books, 1994.

Cowan, Ruth Schwartz. *A Social History of American Technology*. Oxford University Press, 1997.

Cowley, Robert, ed. *What If?: The World's Foremost Military Historians Imagine What Might Have Been*. Berkley Books, 2000.

Craft, David. *The Negro Leagues*. Crescent Books, 1993.

Crapol, Edward J. *John Tyler*. University of North Carolina Press, 2006.

Crawford, Alan Pell. *Unwise Passions*. Simon & Schuster, 2000.

Creamer, Robert W. *Babe: The Legend Comes to Life*. Penguin, 1974.

Crichton, Judy. *America 1900*. Henry Holt, 1998.

Cristol, A. Jay. *The Liberty Incident*. Potomac Books, 2002.

Croffut, W. A. *The Vanderbilts and the Story of Their Fortune*. Bedford, Clarke & Co., 1886.

Cunliffe, Marcus. *George Washington*. New American Library, 1982.

Curtis, James C. *The Fox at Bay: Martin Van Buren and the Presidency, 1837–1841*. University Press of Kentucky, 1970.

Daalder, Ivo H., and James M. Lindsay. *America Unbound: The Bush Revolution in Foreign Policy*. Brookings Institution Press, 2003.

Dalton, Kathleen. *Theodore Roosevelt: A Strenuous Life*. Alfred A. Knopf, 2002.

Davie, Michael. *Titanic: The Death and Life of a Legend*. Alfred A. Knopf, 1987.

Davies, Norman. *Europe at War: 1939–1945*. Macmillan (UK), 2006.

Davis, Kenneth C. *Don't Know Much About History: Everything You Need to Know About American History But Never Learned*. Avon Books, 1990.

de Luigi, Ludovico. *Viaggiatore dell'Arte*. Edizioni Galleria Ravagnan (Italy), 2002.

Deford, Frank. *Big Bill Tilden: The Triumphs and the Tragedy*. Simon & Schuster, 1975.

Denton, Sally. *American Massacre*. Alfred A. Knopf, 2003.

DiLorenzo, Thomas J. *How Capitalism Saved America*. Crown Forum, 2004.

Dobbs, Michael. *Saboteurs: The Nazi Raid on America*. Random House/Vintage Books, 2005.

Dobell, Byron, ed. *A Sense of History: The Best Writing from the Pages of American Heritage.* American Heritage, 1985.

Donald, David Herbert. *Lincoln*. Simon & Schuster, 1995.

Donaldson, Gary A. *America at War Since 1945*. Praeger, 1996.

Dos Passos, John. *Mr. Wilson's War*. Hamish Hamilton (London), 1963.

Dower, John. *Embracing Defeat: Japan in the Wake of World War II*. W. W. Norton, 1999.

Drucker, Peter F. *Adventures of a Bystander*. Harper & Row, 1979.

Dwyer, Jim, and Kevin Flynn. *102 Minutes: The Untold Story of the Fight to Survive Inside the Twin Towers*. Times Books, 2005.

Edsel, Robert M., *The Monuments Men: Allied Heroes, Nazi Thieves, and the Greatest Treasure Hunt in History*. Center Street (Hachette), 2009.

————. ***Rescuing Da Vinci,* Laurel Publishing, 2006.**

Egan, Timothy. *The Worst Hard Time: The Untold Story of Those Who Suffered the Great American Dust Bowl*. Houghton Mifflin, 2006.

Eicher, David J. *Robert E. Lee: A Life Portrait*. Taylor Publishing, 1997.

————. *The Longest Night: A Military History of the Civil War*. Simon & Schuster, 2001.

————. *Dixie Betrayed: How the South Really Lost the Civil War*. Little, Brown, 2006.

Elias, Stephen N. *Alexander T. Stewart: The Forgotten Merchant Prince*. Praeger, 1992.

Elphick, Peter. *Liberty: The Ships That Won the War*. Chatham Publishing (London), 2001.

Ennes, James M., Jr. *Assault on the Liberty*. Ballantine Books, 1987.

Ephron, Nora. *Wallflower at the Orgy*. Bantam, 1987.

Evans, Harold. *The American Century.* Alfred A. Knopf, 1998.

————. ***They Made America.* Little, Brown, 2004.**

Everett, Marshall. *Wreck and Sinking of the* Titanic. L. H. Walter (UK), 1912.

Faber, Doris. *The Life of Lorena Hickok: E.R.'s Friend*. William Morrow, 1980.

Fast, Howard. *Haym Salomon: Son of Liberty*. Julian Messner, 1941.

Faulkner, William. *Go Down Moses*. Random House Modern Library, 1955.

Fay, Paul B. *The Pleasure of His Company*. Harper & Row, 1966.

Ferrell, Robert H., ed. *Off the Record: The Private Papers of Harry S Truman*. Harper & Row, 1980.

———. *Harry S. Truman: His Life on the Family Farms*. High Plains Publishing, 1991.

———. *Harry S. Truman: A Life*. University of Missouri Press, 1994.

———. *Truman, A Centenary Remembrance*. Viking Press, 1994.

Fiennes, Ranulph. *Race to the Pole: Tragedy, Heroism, and Scott's Antarctic Quest*. Hyperion, 2004.

Fineman, Howard. *The Thirteen American Arguments: Enduring Debates That Define and Inspire Our Country*. Random House, 2008.

Fite, Emerson David. *The Presidential Campaign of 1860*. Kennikat Press, 1967 (reprint of 1911 edition).

Fleming, Thomas. *1776: Year of Illusions*. W. W. Norton, 1975.

———. *The New Dealers' War: The War Within World War II*. Basic Books, 2001.

———. *The Louisiana Purchase*. John Wiley & Sons, 2003.

———. *Washington's Secret War: The Hidden History of Valley Forge*. Smithsonian, 2005.

Flink, James J. *The Automobile Age*. MIT Press, 1988.

Flood, Charles Bracelen. *1864: Lincoln at the Gates of History*. Simon & Schuster, 2009.

Fogelman, Edwin. *The Decision to Use the Bomb*. Scribner's, 1964.

Fradin, Dennis Brindell. *The Signers: The 56 Stories Behind the Declaration of Independence*. Walker & Co., 2002.

Frank, Richard B. *Downfall: The End of the Imperial Japanese Empire*. Random House, 1999.

Friedenberg, Daniel M. *Life, Liberty and the Pursuit of Land: The Plunder of Early America*. Prometheus Books, 1992.

Friedman, John S. *The Secret Histories*. Picador, 2005.

Friedman, Milton. *A Program for Monetary Stability*. Fordham University Press, 1960.

Fromkin, David. *In the Time of the Americans*. Alfred A. Knopf, 1995.

———.*The King and the Cowboy: Theodore Roosevelt and Edward the Seventh, Secret Partners*. Penguin, 2008.

Gallagher, Gary W., and Alan T. Nolan, eds. *The Myth of the Lost Cause and Civil War History*. Indiana University Press, 2000.

Gardiner, A. G. *Leaves in the Wind*. J. M. Dent & Sons, Ltd. (UK), 1920.

Gardiner, Juliet. *Wartime: Britain 1939–1945*. Headline (UK), 2004.

Gardner, Gerald. *All the Presidents' Wits: The Power of Presidential Humor*. Beech Tree Books, 1986.

Gayley, Charles Mills. *Shakespeare and the Founders of Liberty in America*. Macmillan, 1917.

Gee, H. L.. *American England*. Methuen & Co. (London), 1943.

Gibson, James William. *The Perfect War: The War We Couldn't Lose and How We Did*. Random House Vintage, 1988.

Gifford, Don. *The Farther Shore: A Natural History of Perception 1798–1984*. Atlantic Monthly Press, 1984.

Goff, John. *Robert Todd Lincoln: A Man in His Own Right*. University of Oklahoma Press, 1969.

Goldstein, Joshua S. *The Real Price of War: How You Pay for the War on Terror*. New York University Press, 2004.

Goldstein, Rhoda L., ed. *Black Life and Culture in the United States*. Thomas Y. Crowell, 1971.

Goodwin, Doris Kearns. *Team of Rivals: The Political Genius of Abraham Lincoln*. Simon & Schuster, 2005.

Gordon, John Steele. *The Scarlet Woman of Wall Street*. Weidenfeld & Nicolson, 1988.

———. *An Empire of Wealth: The Epic Story of American Economic Power*. HarperCollins, 2004.

Gosset, Thomas F. *Race: The History of an Idea in America*. Southern Methodist University Press, 1963; Schocken, 1977.

Gould, Stephen J. *Bully for Brontosaurus*. W. W. Norton, 1992.

Goulden, Joseph C. *The Best Years: 1945–1950*. Atheneum, 1976.

Graber, Doris A. *Public Opinion, the President, and Foreign Policy*. Holt, Rinehart & Winston, 1968.

Grant, George. *Forgotten Presidents: America's Leaders Before George Washington*. Cumberland House, 2001.

Greenfield, Jeff. *"Oh Waiter! One Order of Crow!": Inside the Strangest Presidential Election Finish in American History*. G. P. Putnam's Sons, 2001.

Grondahl, Paul. *I Rose Like a Rocket: The Political Education of Theodore Roosevelt*. Free Press, 2004.

Groves, Leslie. *Now It Can Be Told*. Da Capo Press, 1982.

Gullan, Harold I. *First Fathers: The Men Who Inspired Our Presidents*. John Wiley & Sons, 2004.

Gunderson, Gerald. *The Wealth Creators: An Entrepreneurial History of the United States*. Truman Talley Books, 1989.

Gunther, Max. *The Very, Very Rich and How They Got That Way*. Playboy Press, 1973.

Haber, Louis. *Black Pioneers of Science and Invention*. Harcourt Brace Jovanovich, 1970.

Hagood, Wesley O. *Presidential Sex: From the Founding Fathers to Bill Clinton*. Birch Lane Press (Carol Publishing Group), 1993.

Halberstam, David. *The Best and the Brightest*. Random House, 1969.

———. *The Fifties*. Random House, 1993.

———, ed. *Defining a Nation: Our America and the Sources of Its Strength*. Tehabi Books (National Geographic), 2003.

Hamilton-Patterson, James. *The Great Deep*. Random House, 1992.

Hanson, Victor Davis. *Carnage and Culture: Landmark Battles in the Rise of Western Power*. Anchor Books, 2002.

Harris, John. *The Boston Tea Party*. *Boston Globe* 200th Anniversary, 1974.

Hartmann, Thom. *What Would Jefferson Do?* Random House, 2004.

Harvey, Robert. *A Few Bloody Noses: The American War of Independence*. John Murray (UK), 2001.

Hashimoto, Mochitsura. *Sunk: The Story of the Japanese Submarine Fleet, 1941–1945*. Henry Holt, 1954.

Hastings, Max. *The Korean War*. Simon & Schuster, 1987.

———. *Retribution: The Battle for Japan, 1944–45*. Alfred A. Knopf, 2008.

Heenan, David. *Double Lives*. Davies-Black Publishing, 2002.

Hewitt, Don. *Tell Me a Story: Fifty Years and 60 Minutes*. Public Affairs, 2001.

Holt, Patricia Lee. *George Washington Had No Middle Name*. Citadel Press, 1988.

Holzer, Harold. *Dear Mr. Lincoln: Letters to the President*. Addison-Wesley, 1993.

———. *Lincoln President-Elect: Abraham Lincoln and the Great Secession Winter 1860–1861*. Simon & Schuster, 2008.

Horan, Julie L. *The Porcelain God: A Social History of the Toilet*. Birch Lane Press, 1996.

Hover, Herman D. *Fourteen Presidents Before Washington*. Dodd Mead, 1985.

Howe, David Walker. *What Hath God Wrought: The Transformation of America, 1815–1848*. Oxford University Press, 2007.

Hubbard, Elbert. *A Message to Garcia*. Peter Pauper Press, 1982.

Huggins, Nathan. *Black Odyssey: The Afro-American Ordeal in Slavery*. Pantheon Books, 1977.

Humes, James C. *Instant Eloquence*. Harper & Row, 1973.

———. *The Ben Franklin Factor: Selling One to One*. William Morrow, 1992.

———. *Which President Killed a Man?* MJF Books, 2003.

Hyman, Sidney. *The American President*. Harper & Brothers, 1954.

Isaacson, Walter. *Benjamin Franklin*. Simon & Schuster, 2003.

Jeffers, H. Paul. *Theodore Roosevelt, Jr.: The Life of a Hero*. Presidio Press, 2002.

Jennings, Francis. *The Founders of America*. W. W. Norton, 1994.

Jennings, Walter. *A History of Economic Progress in the U.S.* Thomas Y. Crowell, 1926.

Johnson, Haynes, and David S. Broder. *The System*. Simon & Schuster, 1996.

Johnson, Paul. *A History of the American People*. Harper Perennial, 1999.

Johnson, Timothy D. *Winfield Scott: The Quest for Military Glory*. University Press of Kansas, 1998.

Jonnes, Jill. *Empires of Light: Edison, Tesla, Westinghouse and the Race to Electrify the World*. Random House, 2003.

Kaplan, Fred. *The Wizards of Armageddon*. Stanford University Press, 1983.

Keim, Kevin, and Peter Keim. *A Grand Old Flag: A History of the United States Through Its Flags*. DK Publishing, 2007.

Kennedy, Frances H., ed. *The Civil War Battlefield*. Houghton Mifflin, 1990.

Kessner, Thomas. *Capital City*. Simon & Schuster, 2003.

Keyes, Ralph. *The Wit and Wisdom of Harry Truman*. HarperCollins, 1995.

Keyssar, Helene, and Vladimir Pozner. *Remembering War*. Oxford University Press, 1990.

Keyzer-Andre, Henri, with Hy Steirman. *Age of Heroes*. Hastings House, 1993.

Kimmel, Lewis H. *Federal Budget and Fiscal Policy, 1789–1958*. Brookings Institution, 1958.

Kirwan, Albert D. *John J. Crittenden: The Struggle for the Union*. University of Kentucky Press, 1962.

Kitman, Marvin. *George Washington's Expense Account*. Perennial Library, 1988.

Klein, Herbert S. *The Atlantic Slave Trade*. Cambridge University Press, 1999.

Klos, Stanley L. *President Who? Forgotten Founders*. Estoric.com, 2004.

Krakauer, Jon. *Under the Banner of Heaven*. Doubleday, 2003.

Kukla, John. *A Wilderness So Immense: The Louisiana Purchase and the Destiny of America*. Alfred A. Knopf, 2003.

Kunhardt, Dorothy Meserve, and Philip B. Kunhardt Jr. *Twenty Days*. Castle Books, 1993.

Kuntz, Tom, ed. *The* Titanic *Disaster Hearings: The Official Transcript of the 1912 Senate Investigation*. Pocket Books, 1990.

Kurzman, Dan. *Fatal Voyage: The Sinking of the USS* Indianapolis. Atheneum, 1990.

Lachman, Charles. *The Last Lincolns: The Rise and Fall of a Great American Family*. Union Square Press, 2008.

LaFeber, Walter. *The American Age*. Norton, 1989.

Lamb, Brian. *Booknotes: Life Stories: Notable Biographers on the People Who Shaped America*. Three Rivers Press, 1999.

———. *Booknotes on American Character: People, Politics, and Conflict in American History*. Perseus Press, 2004.

Lamb, Brian, ed.. *Booknotes: Stories from American History*. Penguin, 2002.

Lamb, Martha J. *History of the City of New York*. A. S. Barnes & Co., 1877.

Lane, Frederic C. *Ships for Victory*. Johns Hopkins University Press, 1951 (2001 edition).

Langguth, A. J. *Patriots: The Men Who Started the American Revolution*. Simon & Schuster, 1988.

Larsen, Erik. *Isaac's Storm*. Crown, 1999.

Lebergott, Stanley. *The Americans: An Economic Record*. W. W. Norton, 1984.

———. *Pursuing Happiness: American Consumers in the Twentieth Century*. Princeton University Press, 1993.

Lech, Raymond. *All the Drowned Sailors*. Stein & Day, 1982.

Leckie, Robert. *Delivered from Evil: The Saga of World War II*. Harper & Row, 1987.

———. *The Wars of America*. 2 vol. HarperCollins, 1992, 1993.

———. *From Sea to Shining Sea*. HarperCollins, 1993.

Leepson, Marc. *Saving Monticello: The Levy Family's Epic Quest to Rescue the House That Jefferson Built*. Free Press, 2001.

Lencek, Lena, and Gideon Bosker. *The Beach: The History of Paradise on Earth*. Viking Penguin, 1998.

Levine, Lawrence. *Highbrow/Lowbrow: The Emergence of Cultural Hierarchy in America*. Harvard University Press, 1988.

Lindaman, Dana, and Kyle Ward. *History Lessons: How Textbooks from Around the World Portray U.S. History*. The New Press, 2004.

Linklater, Andro. *Measuring America*. HarperCollins, 2002.

Loewen, James W. *Lies Across America: What Our Historic Sites Got Wrong*. Touchstone, 1999.

London, Joshua E. *Victory in Tripoli*. John Wiley & Sons, 2005.

Lord, Walter. *The Night Lives On*. William Morrow, 1986.

Lorenz-Meyer, Martin. *Safehaven: The Allied Pursuit of Nazi Assets Abroad*. University of Missouri Press, 2007.

Louis, David. *2001 Fascinating Facts*. Greenwich House, 1983.

Love, John F. *McDonald's: Behind the Arches*. Bantam Books, 1986.

Lowenthal, David. *The Past Is a Foreign Country*. Cambridge University Press, 1985.

Lukacs, John. Outgrowing Democracy: A History of the United States in the Twentieth Century. Doubleday, 1984.

Macartney, Clarence Edward. *Lincoln and His Generals*. Dorrance & Co., 1925.

Malone, Dumas. *Jefferson and His Time*. vol. 6, *The Sage of Monticello*. Little, Brown, 1981.

Manchester, William. *American Caesar: Douglas MacArthur 1880–1964*. Little, Brown, 1978.

Mann, Charles C. *1491: New Revelations of the Americas before Columbus*. Alfred A. Knopf, 2005.

Mayhew, Robert. *Essays on Ayn Rand's* The Fountainhead. Lexington Books, 2006.

McCloskey, Donald N., ed. *Second Thoughts: Myths and Morals of U.S. Economy*. Oxford University Press, 1993.

McCullough, David. Brave Companions: Portraits in History. Simon & Schuster, 1992.

———. *Truman*. Touchstone Books, 2003.

———. *1776*. Simon & Schuster, 2005.

McDonald, Forrest. *E Pluribus Unum: The Formation of the American Republic, 1776–1787*. Houghton Mifflin, 1965.

McFeely, William S. *Grant*. Norton, 1982.

McMillan, Priscilla J. *The Ruin of Robert J. Oppenheimer*. Viking, 2005.

McMurtry, Larry. Oh What a Slaughter: Massacres in the American West. Simon & Schuster, 2005.

McNamara, Robert S. *In Retrospect: The Tragedy and Lessons of Vietnam*. Random House Vintage Books, 1996.

Melton, Carol Wilcox. *Between War and Peace: Woodrow Wilson and the American Expeditionary Force in Siberia, 1918–1921*. Mercer University Press, 2004.

Menand, Louis. *The Metaphysical Club*. Farrar, Straus and Giroux, 2001.

Messer, Peter C. *Stories of Independence: Identity, Ideology, and History in Eighteenth-Century America*. Northern Illinois University Press, 2005.

Milgrim, Shirley. *Haym Salomon: Liberty's Son*. Jewish Publication Society, 1979.

Miller, William Lee. *Lincoln's Virtues*. Random House Vintage Books, 2003.

Milton, Giles. *Nathaniel's Nutmeg*. Hodder & Stoughton (UK), 1999.

Monaghan, Jay. *Abraham Lincoln Deals with Foreign Affairs*. Bobbs-Merrill, 1945 (1997 University of Nebraska Press edition).

Moore, John L. *Speaking of Washington*. Congressional Quarterly Books, 1993.

Morison, Samuel Eliot. *Three Centuries of Harvard: 1636–1936*. Harvard University Press, 1936.

———. *John Paul Jones: A Sailor's Biography*. Atlantic Monthly Press, 1959.

———.*The Oxford History of the American People*. Oxford University Press, 1965.

———. *History of United States Naval Operations in World War II*. vol. 4. Atlantic Monthly Press, 1967 (reprint of 1949 edition).

Morse, Arthur D. *While Six Million Died: A Chronicle of American Apathy*. Random House, 1967.

Morse, John T., Jr. *American Statesmen*. Houghton Mifflin, 1898.

Murray, Charles. *Real Education*. Crown, 2008.

Myers, Margaret G. *A Financial History of the United States*. Columbia University Press, 1970.

Nettels, Curtis P. *The Emergence of a National Economy. 1775–1815*. Harper & Row, 1962.

Newman, John M. *JFK and Vietnam: Deception, Intrigue and the Struggle for Power*. Warner Books, 1992.

Nicholas, Lynn H. *The Rape of Europa: The Fate of Europe's Treasures in the Third Reich and the Second World War*. Alfred A. Knopf, 1994.

Noble, William. *Bookbanning in America*. Paul S. Eriksson, 1990.

Nolan, Alan T. *Lee Considered*. University of North Carolina Press, 1991.

Norman, Michael M, and Elizabeth M. Norman. *Tears in the Darkness: The Story of the Bataan Death March and Its Aftermath*. Farrar, Straus & Giroux, 2009.

Nye, Peter Joffre, with Jeff Groman and Mark Tyson. *The Six-Day Bicycle Races: America's Jazz-Age Sport*. Van Der Plas Publications/Cycle Publishing, 2006.

Oates, Stephen B. *With Malice Toward None: The Life of Abraham Lincoln*. Harper & Row, 1977.

———. *Abraham Lincoln: The Man Behind the Myths*. Harper & Row, 1984.

Ogelsby, Carl. *The JFK Assassination: The Facts and the Theories*. Signet Books, 1992.

Olmsted, Frederick Law. *The Cotton Kingdom: A Traveller's Observations on Cotton and Slavery in the American Slave Trade*. 2 vols. Mason Brothers (New York), 1861.

Packard, Vance. *The Ultra Rich: How Much Is Too Much*. Little, Brown, 1989.

Packer, George. *The Assassin's Gate*. Farrar, Straus & Giroux, 2005.

Panati, Charles. *Extraordinary Origins of Everyday Things.* Harper & Row, 1987.

Parrish, Thomas. *The American Flag*. Simon & Schuster, 1973.

Partridge, Bellamy, and Otto Bettman. *As We Were: Family Life in America, 1850–1900.* McGraw-Hill, 1946.

Patterson, Jerry E. *The Vanderbilts.* Harry N. Abrams, 1989.

Patton, Phil. *Made in U.S.A.* Grove Weidenfeld, 1992.

Paulos, John Allen. *Innumeracy: Mathematical Illiteracy and Its Consequences.* Hill & Wang, 1988.

Payton, Walter, with Don Yaeger. *Never Die Easy: the Autobiography of Walter Payton.* Villard Books, 2000.

Perry, Mark. *Grant and Twain.* Random House, 2004.

Persico, Joseph E. *Roosevelt's Secret War: FDR and World War II Espionage.* Random House, 2001.

Peterson, Edward N. *The American Occupation of Germany.* Wayne State University Press, 1977.

Peterson, Peter G. *Facing Up: How to Rescue the Economy from Crushing Debt and Restore the American Dream.* Simon & Schuster, 1993.

———. *Running on Empty: How the Democratic and Republican Parties Are Bankrupting Our Future and What We Can Do About It.* Farrar, Straus and Giroux, 2004.

Petillo, Carol M. *Douglas MacArthur: The Philippine Years.* Indiana University Press, 1981.

Phillips, Cabell. *The Truman Presidency.* Macmillan, 1966.

Pierpont, Claudia Roth. *Passionate Minds: Women Rewriting the World.* Random House/ Vintage Books, 2001.

Pogue, Forrest C. *George C. Marshall: Statesman.* Viking, 1987.

Porter, Bruce D. *War and the Rise of the State: The Military Foundations of Modern Politics.* MacMillan Free Press, 1994.

Posner, Gerald. *Case Closed: Lee Harvey Oswald and the Assassination of JFK.* Random House, 1993.

Potter, David M. *Lincoln and His Party in the Secession Crisis.* Yale University Press, 1942.

———. *People of Plenty: Economic Abundance and the American Character.* University of Chicago Press, 1954.

Powell, Jim. *Great Emancipations: How the West Abolished Slavery.* Palgrave Macmillan, 2008.

Prange, Gordon W. *Miracle at Midway.* Penguin Books, 1982.

Preble, Christopher A. *John F. Kennedy and the Missile Gap.* Northern Illinois University Press, 2004.

Prestowitz, Clyde. *Rogue Nation: American Unilateralism and the Failure of Good Intentions.* Basic Books, 2002.

Price, Charles. *A Golf Story: Bobby Jones*. Athenaeum, 1986.

Prout, Henry G. *A Life of George Westinghouse*. Beard Books, 2001 (reprint of 1921 edition).

Pusey, Merlo J. *Charles Evans Hughes*. The Macmillan Company, 1951.

Ramsland, Katherine. *Cemetery Stories*. HarperCollins, 2001.

Rapoport, Ron. *The Immortal Bobby: Bobby Jones and the Golden Age of Golf*. John Wiley & Sons, 2005.

Ravenel, Harriott H. *Life and Times of William Lowndes of South Carolina, 1782–1822*. Houghton Mifflin, 1901.

Reader's Digest Strange Stories, Amazing Facts of America's Past: Reader's Digest Association, 1990.

Rehnquist, William H. *Centennial Crisis: The Disputed Election of 1876*. Alfred A. Knopf, 2004.

Reisner, Marc. *Cadillac Desert: The American West and Its Disappearing Water*. Penguin, 1987.

Remini, Robert V. *Andrew Jackson and the Course of American Democracy, 1833–1845*. Harper & Row, 1984.

Renehan, Edward J., Jr. *The Lion's Pride: Theodore Roosevelt and His Family*. Oxford University Press, 1998.

———. *Commodore: The Life of Cornelius Vanderbilt*. Basic Books, 2007.

Rhodes, Benjamin D. *The Anglo-American Winter War with Russia, 1918–1919*. Greenwood Press, 1988.

Rhodes, Richard. *Dark Sun: The Making of the Hydrogen Bomb*. Simon & Schuster, 1995.

Riddle, Donald H. *The Truman Committee*. Rutgers University Press, 1964.

Ritter, Halsted L. *Washington as a Businessman*. Sears Publishing Co., 1931.

Ritter, Lawrence S., and Mark Rucker. *The Babe: A Life in Pictures*. Ticknor & Fields, 1988.

Roberts, Andrew. *A History of the English-Speaking Peoples Since 1900*. HarperCollins, 2006.

Robinson, Lloyd. *The Stolen Election: Hayes versus Tilden—1876*. Forge Books, 2001 (reprint of 1968 edition).

Roleff, Tamara L, ed. *The Atom Bomb*. Greenhaven Press, 2000.

Roosevelt, Theodore. *The Naval War of 1812*. Naval Institute Press, 1987 (reprint of 1882 edition).

Rorimer, James J. *Survival: The Salvage and Protection of Art in War*. Abelard Press, 1950.

Rosenberg, Emily S. *A Date Which Will Live: Pearl Harbor in American Memory*. Duke University Press, 2003.

Rosenberg, Nathan, and L. E. Birdzell Jr. *How the West Grew Rich*. Basic Books, 1986.

Rosenthal, A. M. *Thirty-Eight Witnesses*. McGraw-Hill, 1964.

Ross, Shelley. *Fall from Grace: Sex, Scandal, and Corruption in American Politics from 1702 to the Present*. Random House, 1988.

Russell, Charles E. *Haym Salomon and the Revolution*. Cosmopolitan, 1930.

Sakolski, A. M. *The Great American Land Bubble: The Amazing Story of Land-Grabbing, Speculations, and Booms from Colonial Days to the Present Time*. Harper & Bros., 1932.

Santayana, George. *Dominations and Powers: Reflections on Liberty, Society, and Government*. Scribner's, 1951.

Schaffer, Ronald. *Wings of Judgment: American Bombing in World War II*. Oxford University Press, 1985.

Schaller, Marshall. *Douglas MacArthur, The Far Eastern General*. Oxford University Press, 1989.

Schama, Simon. *Rough Crossings: Britain, the Slaves and the American Revolution*. HarperCollins, 2006.

Schivelbusch, Wolfgang. *The Railway Journey: Trains and Travel in the 19th Century*. Urizen Books, 1980.

Schlesinger, Arthur M., Jr. *The Cycles of American History*. Houghton Mifflin, 1986.

———. *The Disuniting of America: Reflections on a Multicultural Society*. W. W. Norton, 1993.

Schweizer, Peter. *Reagan's War*. Anchor, 2003.

Scott, James. *The Attack on the Liberty: The Untold Story of Israel's Deadly 1967 Assault on a U.S. Spy Ship*. Simon & Schuster, 2009.

Scott, James Brown. *Robert Bacon: Life and Letters*. Ayer Publishing, 1975.

Setright, L. J. K. *Drive On! A Social History of the Motor Car*. Granta Books (UK), 2003.

Severo, Richard, and Lewis Milford. *The Wages of War: When America's Soldiers Came Home—from Valley Forge to Vietnam*. Simon & Schuster, 1989.

Shaara, Michael. *The Killer Angels*. Ballantine Books, 1975.

Shammas, Carole. *Inheritance in America*. Rutgers University Press, 1990.

Sheriff, Carol. *The Artificial River*. Hill & Wang, 1997.

Shields-West, Eileen. *The World Almanac of Presidential Campaigns*. Pharos Books, 1992.

Shillony, Ben-Ami. *Politics and Culture in Wartime Japan*. Oxford University Press, 1981.

Shover, John L. *First Majority—Last Minority: The Transforming of Rural Life in America*. Northern Illinois University Press, 1976.

Silverman, Kenneth. *The Life and Times of Cotton Mather*. Columbia University Press, 1985.

Simpson, Howard W. *Invisible Armies: The Impact of Disease on American History*. Bobbs-Merrill, 1980.

Skowronek, Stephen. *The Politics Presidents Make*. Harvard University Press, 1993.

Slaughter, Anne-Marie. *The Idea That Is America: Keeping Faith with Our Values in a Dangerous World*. Perseus Books, 2007.

Smith, Elbert P. *Francis Preston Blair*. Macmillan Free Press, 1980.

Smith, Gene. *Lee and Grant*. New American Library, 1984.

Snyder, Louis L.. *The War: 1939–1945*. Messner, 1962.

Sobel, Robert. *The Great Boom: 1950–2000: How a Generation of Americans Created the World's Most Prosperous Society*. St. Martin's Press, 2000.

———. *The Money Manias: The Eras of Great Speculation in America 1770–1970*. Beard Books, 2000 (reprint of 1973 edition).

Southwick, Leslie H. *Presidential Also-Rans and Running Mates, 1788–1980*. McFarland, 1984.

Sowell, Thomas. *Ethnic America*. Basic Books, 1981.

Spector, Ronald H. *Eagle Against the Sun: The American War with Japan*. MacMillan/Free Press, 1985.

Stanton, Doug. *In Harm's Way*. Henry Holt, 2001.

Steinberg, Alfred. *The First Ten: The Founding Presidents and Their Administrations*. Doubleday, 1967.

Stilgoe, John R. *Common Landscape of America, 1580 to 1845*. Yale University Press, 1982.

Stoler, Mark A. *George C. Marshall: Soldier Statesman of the American Century*. Twayne, 1989.

Stratton, Joanna L. *Pioneer Women: Voices from the Kansas Frontier*. Simon & Schuster, 1981.

Strouse, Jean. *Morgan: American Financier*. Random House, 1999.

Surowieki, James. *The Wisdom of Crowds*. Doubleday, 2004.

Swiggett, Howard. *The Extraordinary Mr. Morris*. Doubleday, 1952.

Takaki, Ronald. *A Different Mirror: A History of Multicultural America*. Little, Brown, 1993.

Tally, Steve. *Bland Ambition*. Harcourt, 1992.

Teague, Michael. *Mrs. L: Conversations with Alice Roosevelt Longworth*. Doubleday, 1981.

Tedlow, Richard S. *Giants of Enterprise: Seven Business Innovators and the Empires They Built*. HarperBusiness, 2001.

Thomas, Dana. *Deluxe: How Luxury Lost Its Luster*. Penguin, 2007.

Thomas, Frank. *Last Will and Testament: Wills Ancient and Modern.* St. Martin's Press, 1972.

Thomas, Gordon, and Max Morgan Witts. *Enola Gay.* Stein & Day, 1977.

Thoreau, Henry David. *Walden.* Princeton University Press, 1973.

Thorndike, Joseph J., Jr. *The Very Rich: A History of American Wealth.* American Heritage, 1976.

Tindall, Bruce, and Mark Watson. *Did Mohawks Wear Mohawks?* Quill, 1990.

Tocqueville, Alexis de. *Democracy in America.* Alfred A. Knopf, 1945 edition.

Train, John. *John Train's Most Remarkable Occurrences.* HarperCollins, 1990.

Trumbo, Dalton. *Johnny Got His Gun.* Citadel Press, 1991.

Tuchman, Barbara W. *Practicing History.* Ballantine Books, 1982.

———. *The March of Folly: From Troy to Vietnam.* Alfred A. Knopf, 1984.

———. *The First Salute: A View of the American Revolution.* Cardinal Books (UK), 1989.

Twain, Mark. *1601, and Is Shakespeare Dead?* Oxford University Press, 1996.

Tye, Larry. *Rising from the Rails: Pullman Porters and the Making of the Black Middle Class.* Henry Holt, 2004.

van der Vat, Dan. *The Grand Scuttle: The Sinking of the German Fleet at Scapa Flow in 1919.* Hodder and Stoughton (London), 1982.

Vanderbilt, Arthur T., II. *Fortune's Children: The Fall of the House of Vanderbilt.* William Morrow, 1989.

Vidal, Gore. *United States: Essays 1952–1992.* Random House, 1992.

———. *Inventing a Nation: Washington, Adams, Jefferson.* Yale University Press, 2003.

Vipperman, Carl J. *William Lowndes and the Transition of American Politics. 1782–1822.* University of North Carolina Press, 1989.

Wade, Wyn Craig. *The* Titanic: *End of a Dream.* Rawson Wade Publishers, 1979.

Walker, Ronald W., Richard E. Turley Jr., and Glen M. Leonard. *Massacre at Mountain Meadows: An American Tragedy.* Oxford University Press, 2008.

Walters, Rob. *Spread Spectrum: Hedy Lamarr and the Mobile Phone.* BookSurge (UK), 2006.

Warner, Sam Bass, Jr. *The Urban Wilderness: A History of the American City.* Harper and Row, 1972.

Wasik, John F. *The Merchant of Power.* Palgrave Macmillan, 2006.

Wavell, Earl. *Soldiers and Soldiering.* Jonathan Cape, 1953.

Weaver, John C. *The Great Land Rush and the Making of the Modern World 1650–1900.* McGill-Queen's University Press, 2003.

Weigley, Russell F. *The American Way of War: A History of United States Military Strategy and Policy*. Indiana University Press, 1973.

Weinberg, Gerhard L. *A World at Arms: A Global History of World War II*. Cambridge University Press, 1994.

Wheeler, Tom. *Mr. Lincoln's T-Mails: How Abraham Lincoln Used the Telegraph to Win the Civil War*. HarperCollins, 2006.

Willett, Robert L. *Russian Sideshow: America's Undeclared War 1918–1920*. Brassey's, 2003.

Williams, T. Harry. *The History of American Wars*. Alfred A. Knopf, 1981.

Wilson, George. *Stephen Girard: The Life and Times of America's First Tycoon*. Combined Books, 1995.

Wilson, Major L. *The Presidency of Martin Van Buren*. University Press of Kansas, 1984.

Winik, Jay. *April 1865: The Month That Saved America*. Harper Perennial, 2006.

Winks, Robin, ed. *The Historian as Detective: Essays on Evidence*. Harper & Row, 1968.

Wolfe, Alan. *Return to Greatness: How America Lost Its Sense of Purpose and What to Do About It*. Princeton University Press, 2005.

Wood, Gordon S. *The Americanization of Benjamin Franklin*. Penguin, 2004.

———. *The Creation of the American Republic, 1776–1787*. University of North Carolina Press, 1969 (1998 edition).

Woodward, W. E. *The Way Our People Lived: An Intimate History*. E. P. Dutton, 1944.

Worster, Donald. *Dust Bowl: The Southern Plains in the 1930s*. Oxford University Press, 1979.

Worthen, Dennis B., *Pharmacy in World War II*. Haworth Press, 2004.

Yeomans, Henry Aaron. *Abbott Lawrence Lowell: 1856–1943*. Harvard University Press, 1948.

Yergin, Daniel. *The Prize*. Simon & Schuster, 1991.

Young, J. Russell. *Around the World with General Grant*. Vol. 2. American News, 1879.

Zinsser, Hans. *Rats, Lice and History*. Little, Brown, 1934.

PHOTO CREDITS

Page 57 Courtesy of Library and Archives Division, Senator John Heinz History Center

Page 64 Corbis

Page 67 Courtesy of Anthony Loder (Hedy Lamarr's son)

Page 69 Courtesy of Anthony Loder (Hedy Lamarr's son)

Page 71 Courtesy of the National Archives (Army Signal Corps)

Page 72 Courtesy of the National Archives

Page 75 Courtesy of Harry S Truman Library

Page 98 Courtesy of the Durand Union Station Inc., Durand, Michigan

Page 100 Courtesy of the Library of Congress

Page 102 Courtesy of Widener Library, Harvard College Library / Public Domain

Page 105 Courtesy of J&C McCutcheon Collection/Mark Chirnside, *The Olympic-Class Ships: Olympic, Titanic, Britannic*

Page 147 Courtesy of the National Archives

Page 153 Courtesy of the National Archives

Page 163 Courtesy of the Naval History and Heritage Command, #NH-78628

Page 177 Author's private collection

Page 187 Courtesy of Brown Brothers

Page 198 Courtesy of Harry S Truman Library

Page 199 Courtesy of the George Eastman House, International Museum of Photography and Film

Page 200 Courtesy of the George Eastman House, International Museum of Photography and Film

Page 201 Courtesy of the George Eastman House, International Museum of Photography and Film

Page 227 Courtesy of the estate of Jeff MacNelly

Page 240 Courtesy of the Michigan Society of Professional Surveyors Institute

Page 243 Courtesy of the National Archives

Page 246 Courtesy of the Georgia O'Keeffe Museum, Santa Fe/Artists Rights Society, New York

Page 251 Courtesy of the New York Public Library / Public Domain

Page 264 Courtesy of the Father Browne SJ Collection, Dublin, Ireland

Page 276 Courtesy of the Library of Congress

Page 278 [top] Courtesy of the Library of Congress

Page 278 [bottom] Courtesy of the Library of Congress

Page 280 Author's private collection

Page 283 Courtesy of Hildene, the Lincoln Family Home, Manchester, VT

Page 284 Author's private collection

Page 286 [top] Courtesy of Jan Faul / www.artfaul.com

Page 286 [bottom] Courtesy of Jan Faul / www.artfaul.com

Page 315 Courtesy of the Library of Congress

Page 318 Courtesy of Rosenberg Library, Galveston, Texas

Page 320 Author's private collection

Page 329 Courtesy of the Naval History and Heritage Command

Page 330 Courtesy of the Naval History and Heritage Command

Page 332 Courtesy of the National Archives

Page 334 Courtesy of the National Archives

Page 342 Courtesy of Ludovico de Luigi

INDEX

ABOUT THE AUTHOR

Seymour Morris Jr. is an international business entrepreneur and former head of corporate communications for the world's largest management consulting firm. Living abroad for the past twelve years, interviewing foreign students for Harvard University, forced him to see his country as an outsider and compelled him to examine American history from a fresh perspective. He holds a degree in American history from Harvard and an MBA from Harvard Business School. He lives in New York City and Connecticut with his wife.